Ethnicity and Nation-building in the Pacific

Note to the Reader from the UNU

The United Nations University carried out a series of research activities on contemporary ethnic problems under its Ethnic Minorities and Human and Social Development Project. The principal objective of the Project was to shed light on the dynamic relationships between various ethnic minorities on the one hand and state and global society on the other. The Project also aimed at enlightening the public about the complex problems of ethnicity as well as at helping policy makers in formulating cultural and educational policies relating to ethnic minorities.

Ethnicity and Nation-building in the Pacific is the outcome of an international symposium that the United Nations University organized in co-operation with the University of the South Pacific in Suva, Fiji, in August 1986. The symposium, the first of its kind ever held, gathered together experts to examine ethnic issues in Hawaii, Australia, New Zealand, Fiji, Western Samoa, Papua New Guinea, New Caledonia, Micronesia, and Indonesia, from both historical and comparative perspectives.

Ethnicity and Nation-building in the Pacific

Edited by Michael C. Howard

THE UNITED NATIONS UNIVERSITY

The views expressed in this publication are those of the authors and do not necessarily reflect the views of the United Nations University.

The United Nations University
Toho Seimei Building, 15-1 Shibuya 2-chome, Shibuya-ku, Tokyo 150, Japan
Tel.: (03) 499-2811   Telex: J25442   Cable: UNATUNIV TOKYO

Typeset by Asco Trade Typesetting Limited, Hong Kong
Printed by Permanent Typesetting and Printing Co., Ltd., Hong Kong
Cover design by Tsuneo Taniuchi

EM-1/UNUP-689
ISBN 92-808-0689-0
United Nations Sales No. E.89.III.A.6
03500 P

Contents

Foreword   vii

1 Ethnicity and the State in the Pacific
    Michael C. Howard   1

2 Discourses of Ethnicity: The Faces and the Masks
    Susana B. C. Devalle   50

3 Ho'omauke Ea O Ka Lahui Hawai'i: The Perpetuation of the Hawaiian People
    Davianna Pomaika McGregor   74

4 Myth of the Golden Men: Ethnic Elites and Dependent Development in the 50th State
    Noel J. Kent   98

5 Aboriginality in a Nation-State: The Australian Case
    Jeremy Beckett   118

6 Aboriginal Ethnicity and Nation-building within Australia
    Robert Tonkinson   136

7 Colonisation and Development of the Maori People
    Rangiuni J. Walker   152

8 From Race Aliens to an Ethnic Group – Indians in New Zealand
    Jacqueline Leckie   169

9 Banabans in Fiji: Ethnicity, Change, and Development
    Hans Dagmar   198

10 Race, Class, and Ethnicity in Western Samoa
    Paul Shankman   218

11 Ethnicity and Nation-building: The Papua New Guinea Case
    Ralph R. Premdas   244

12 Independence and Ethnicity in New Caledonia
    Donna Winslow   259

13 Pohnpei Ethnicity and Micronesian Nation-building
    Glenn Petersen   285

14 Indonesia: Nation-building, Ethnicity, and Regional Conflicts
    Ernst Utrecht   309

Contributors   332

Foreword

The processes of social development and modernization are based on the assumption that ethnic and cultural differences within nation-states will tend to disappear, and the broad literature on economic and social development has paid relatively little attention to the ethnic question. It is assumed that social cleavages and social mobilization centre around functional groups (social classes, occupational categories, urban-rural settings, political parties, and interest groups), and policies are devised for the solution of eminently "developmental" problems.

However, it is becoming increasingly recognized that many of the developmental "failures" of recent years cannot be traced merely to technical, financial, or economic shortcomings, but are due to the cultural and ethnic complexities involved in "nation-building." A number of countries have attempted to deal squarely with these problems; others have ignored or neglected them. Yet all over the world in recent years there has been a resurgence of ethnic and cultural demands by minority peoples and of social movements based on these demands. Indeed, many of the major political conflicts that the world has witnessed these past years (including violent ones) have a clear-cut ethnic dimension.

The United Nations University, to respond to this challenge, launched in 1983 a project entitled "Ethnic Minorities and Human and Social Development" which aimed at a better understanding of the relationship between ethnic minorities and their cultures on the one hand, and global society on the other within the framework of national and regional development processes. The project was co-ordinated by Professor Rodolfo Stavenhagen of El Colegio de México.

The fourteen papers included in this volume were presented and discussed at a symposium organized by the United Nations University in co-operation with the University of the South Pacific in Suva, Fiji, from 11 to 15 August 1986. Professor Michael C. Howard, then teaching at the University of the

South Pacific, assumed the organizational responsibility of the symposium and subsequently edited the papers which constitute this publication.

The symposium was, by all accounts, the first international meeting on the subject of ethnicity and nation-building in the region and attracted considerable attention. The present book will, it is hoped, contribute much to an "accurate understanding of ethnicity in the Pacific among scholars and the public," as one reviewer has put it.

The United Nations University wishes to express its deep gratitude to Professor Howard and Professor Stavenhagen, as well as to all the participants in the symposium for their scientific contributions to this important area of research. At a time when ethnic problems and conflicts are becoming increasingly serious in different parts of the world, may this publication serve for a better understanding of the problems, the first step in their solution.

Kinhide Mushakoji
Vice-Rector, United Nations University
July 1989

1

Ethnicity and the State in the Pacific

MICHAEL C. HOWARD

All the states in the Pacific today have two things in common: they are products of colonial rule and they are firmly entrenched in the capitalist political and economic bloc. Most have one other thing in common too: they have significant migrant populations. The principle question I wish to address in this chapter is the place of ethnicity within the context of the creation and maintenance of these nation-states. Linked to this are questions concerning the relationship of ethnicity to class formation and class struggle and also of the relevance and nature of their integration into the capitalist world-economy. The point is that ethnicity in the Pacific cannot be divorced from international capitalism, although the precise relationship remains to be explored.

Historically, analysis of ethnicity in the region can be divided into four phases: the precolonial, colonial, transition to political independence, and independent periods. Within each of these phases, ethnicity is conditioned by what went before and by the special nature of the period in question. Thus, ethnicity during the colonial era within a given state will be conditioned in various ways by the nature of the precolonial situation and by the act of colonial rule itself. Moreover, with the exception of the precolonial phase, the overall dynamic of ethnicity in any of these settings should be seen as an integral part of the dialectic between the evolution of the capitalist world-economy and the internal political economy. In broad outline, this is fairly apparent. What is perhaps less obvious is the manner and extent to which this is true in a particular setting.

The geographical scope of this chapter encompasses approximately 25 states or territories included within what is generally recognised as the Pacific – in contrast to the Pacific Rim. Most are extremely small states with very limited land areas and populations numbering a few thousand to a few hundred thousand. A few states or territories in the middle range include Fiji and Hawaii, which have populations of a half million to one million. And at the top is Australia, followed by New Zealand, Papua New Guinea, and other large ones. Though a few smaller states (e.g., Tokelau, Niue, Tuvalu, and Tonga) have relatively homogeneous populations, most have populations with significant ethnic distinctions. Throughout all, however, ethnicity has at one time or another been of sizable political and economic importance. Thus, Tuvalu was created through separation from a larger colonial entity, the Gilbert and Ellice Islands Colony, and large proportions of Tongans and Niueans live overseas, where they comprise ethnic minorities. For those remaining behind, external immigration policies and the status of those living abroad is of great significance in their lives.

Also relevant is that the region as a whole has had a shared identity for some time, manifested in regional organisations such as the South Pacific Commission, and that within the region are significant cultural-political blocs, exemplified in the links that exist among the Melanesian states. Significant economic links are also evident. With the exception of territories falling within the American sphere of influence, Australia and New Zealand serve as economic points of reference through trade and other forms of economic transaction for the rest of the region. The chance of this pattern expanding to include several of those territories that are now within the American sphere is strong, and as a whole, regionalism within the Pacific has remained much more meaningful than in other parts of the third world. Such larger forms of identification are also an important part of the ethnic issue in the Pacific.

THE PRECOLONIAL SETTING

Interestingly, the largest single land mass in the region, Australia, was one with the least population. Elkin (1954: 10–11) estimated the entire Aboriginal population of Australia to be around 300,000, a figure that tends to have been accepted, but Jones (1970: 3) has argued for a much lower estimate of around 200,000, and others have sought to establish a larger figure. This population was divided into 400 to 500 tribal groupings, each with populations ranging from about 100 to sometimes as high as 1,500 (see Berndt and Berndt 1977: 28–37). Though different forms of economic and ceremonial exchange existed among tribes, by and large they were self-contained. Internal political organisation tended to be fairly weak, and though a sense of pan-tribal identity was sometimes found, in practical terms, identification was at the tribal or even subtribal level.

In close proximity to Australia are the islands that compose what is known as Melanesia, which can be divided into two sections: Mainland Melanesia, consisting of Papua New Guinea and West Papua, and Island Melanesia, consisting of the eastern islands of Papua New Guinea, the Solomon Islands, Vanuatu, New Caledonia, and western Fiji. The precolonial population of Mainland Melanesia was probably relatively large – perhaps as high as 3 million – with some areas being very densely populated by the standards of reliance on horticultural production. Forms of social organisation varied throughout Melanesia, but in general, we can discern two patterns: relatively egalitarian units made up of a few hundred to perhaps a thousand or so individuals and more hierarchical societies that likewise tended to include at most a thousand or more individuals. The low level of political organisation is exemplified in the approximately 1,200 languages spoken in the region – an average of one language for every 200 to 300 people. Again, there was economic and ceremonial exchange among these diverse peoples, and larger confederacies would sometimes be assembled, but for the most part social and cultural identity was very narrowly defined.

The Polynesian islands were occupied by relative newcomers to the region, and for this and other reasons represent a much more homogeneous population. These islands include New Zealand, Hawaii, French Polynesia (Tahiti, the Marquesas, and others), Tonga, Samoa (American and Western), the Cook Islands, Tuvalu, Niue, Tokelau, Wallis and Futuna, and eastern Fiji. The total land area is much smaller than that of Melanesia or Australia, but when these islands first experienced European contact, they were much more densely populated, with a total population probably in excess of 500,000. The two largest groups were in Hawaii (with around 200,000 people) and New Zealand (between 100,000 and 150,000 people). Socially, culturally, and linguistically, the Polynesian population was much more unified than those of Melanesia or Australia. Also, the largest sociopolitical units were found among the Polynesians: the "kingdoms" of Hawaii, the Society Islands, and Tonga. Not all groups, however, were so large. The island of Futuna, with less than 2,000 inhabitants, was divided into two primary kingdoms; the Cook Islands, with about 5,000 people, was divided into several autonomous political entities. The Maoris of New Zealand had about 40 tribes, but even these small units tended to be much larger than most political entities in Melanesia and Australia. Thus, whereas tribes and even subtribes in New Zealand often warred with one another, there were also loosely formed federations of tribes that recognised descent from a common ancestor. Tongan imperialism and Tongan raiders who established themselves in areas of the South Pacific also played an important role in creating a unity of sorts within their sphere of influence.

Micronesia consists of four groups of islands: the Marianas, Caroline, Marshall, and Gilbert islands. It includes a few larger islands, such as Saipan, Guam, and Pohnepi, besides a great many atolls (among the larger ones, Tarawa and Kwajalein). At initial European contact, its total population was a little more than 150,000. The people spoke a dozen or so distinct languages. As Alkire (1972: 14) points out:

It is interesting to note that the languages with the widest geographic distribution were those associated with coral-island populations, that is, central Carolinean and Marshallese. Not only does this reflect, perhaps, a shorter period of separation, but also the intensive contact maintained between these islands of limited resources. . . . In contrast, most of the high islands of Micronesia were populated by groups speaking languages of restricted distribution and whose inhabitants rarely took their canoes beyond the sight of their own coastline.

Nearly all Micronesian societies had systems of ranking and recognised chiefs, but the degree of hierarchy sizably varied. Great variation was also obvious in centralisation. The most common pattern was one of autonomous districts, which might encompass all of a smaller island or only a portion of a larger one, that were at times formed into interdistrict alliances. Kosrae, in the Caroline Islands, with much authority vested in a paramount chief from one of its districts, had the most centralised structure. During the years immediately before and around the time of initial European contact, as in Polynesia, significant moves were apparent to establish a few larger political units by local warlords.

THE COLONIAL STATE

The creation and intensification of the capitalist world-economy was accompanied by the creation of a form of political and economic organisation known as the colonial state. Modelled on the European state, it was significantly different from such states because its primary purpose was to serve the interests of wealthier and more powerful capitalist states elsewhere. Although colonial states sizably differed, depending on earlier structures of political organisation, the imperial power to which each was linked, and other factors, as Clapham (1985: 18) comments, these differences "only became significant within the context of the common features imposed by colonialism on the colonised territories and societies as a whole." At its most elementary level, the creation of the colonial state often meant the imposition of a boundary and the establishment of a territory where neither had previously existed. Quite commonly, disparate social groups were joined on the basis of imperial convenience. Beyond this were other, perhaps more profound, changes. A new economic order was established – a colonial capitalist economy. A new political and administrative order also came into being. Along with these changes evolved a colonial culture that took precedence over what had existed before.

Whereas securing control over resources in the face of competition from other imperial powers was an important element of colonialism, this was not the only, or even, it can be argued, the most important, consideration. Immanuel Wallerstein (1983: 39) places highest priority on the "search for low-cost labour forces." He points to the extent to which colonial policies sought to facilitate capital accumulation in accordance with this concern over cheap labour. This is seen most clearly in policies seeking to create structures of domestic organisation centred around "households in which wage labour played a minority role as a source of income" (Wallerstein 1983: 76; see also Smith, Wallerstein, and Evans 1984) that also were compelled to provide some of their members for wage labour and to expend some of their energy in production of goods for the market. It was a balancing act in which a "reserve army" of producers and labourers was created that minimised costs to the imperial power.

Local conditions, however, were not always right for transforming the population into a reserve army or to employ it in the production of cash crops. Under these circumstances, appropriate labour had to be recruited elsewhere – at first mostly from Africa, then, in growing numbers, from Asia. Under colonialism, massive movements of people took place to create a match between production desires and labour requirements to meet those desires. Thus, when the indigenous population of the New World proved inadequate to meet the requirements of the new colonial economy, millions of slaves were brought from Africa. This process thoroughly transformed the social, cultural, and political nature both of Africa and the New World. Later, huge numbers of Asians were sent to western North Amercia, the Caribbean, Australia, and elsewhere to work mainly in construction and on plantations.

The period immediately before the imposition of colonial rule and during its early years was often unsettled. The creation of political order was rarely a simple matter because the imperial power sought to establish an effective monopoly of the use of physical force. Eventually, conditions generally became more stable as the colonial administration intervened "in other spheres of social life . . . in order to reduce the need to use coercive power directly" (Thomas 1984: 7). This search for hegemony was seldom pursued far, and the colonial state usually continued to be characterised by "the relatively greater development of the coercive and judicial apparatuses of the state as compared to its other aspects" (Thomas 1984: 24). In this way, it fell far short of the developed capitalist state where the need for force was submerged beneath an array of other, more subtle, hegemonic devices.

An indigenous élite, linked to the imperial power while also possessing some degree of legitimacy within the indigenous context, was an important element in establishing political order within most colonial states. Webster (1984: 77) writes:

The colonial system did not necessarily mean the complete destruction of local political and legal institutions; indeed, not only would this have been socially impossible but it would also have been regarded as foolish by many colonialists. They saw their task as being the introduction of the new capitalist rigours of production as quickly as possible without, however, encouraging the local population to become competitors to the colonial power by establishing their own enterprise. . . . It was also felt that the maintenance of local authority structures would help to check any threat from local ambition. A few indigenous structures were allowed to prevail so long as the capitalist interests of the colony (and Europe) were served.

Differing colonial strategies played a role in determining how the indigenous compradorial class evolved. The French advocated assimilation and centralisation, with "indirect rule" assuming a transitory nature. In this way, the initial structure of indirect rule gave way to one in which a Europeanised indigenous élite was incorporated within a centralised administration. British rule, in contrast, was less centralised and less assimilationist. The British were keen to create an indigenous colonial élite imbued with British values, largely to make administration easier and cheaper, but they held no illusions that an amalgamation of the colonial and British state was possible, even if it had been desirable: "For the British, the idea of assimilation was unthinkable, as a result perhaps of a view... which sees political culture in particularist rather than universalist terms, and partly of a racial exclusiveness which implicitly denied that any of the indigenous peoples of the empire could ever become really English" (Clapham 1985: 22). Too much can be made of these differences, however, and in practice one finds great similarity in terms of ethnic exclusivity and the role assigned to the indigenous compradorial élite. All European and American colonies were characterised by an ethnic hierarchy in which a white élite was at the top of the political and administrative spheres, even though things could become more ambiguous at lower levels.

Below the top horizontal line, colonial states tended to have important vertical divisions. The simple act of amalgamating formerly distinct social and cultural entities created ethnic categories from formerly autonomous indigenous peoples. But these divisions rarely proved transitional in the face of pressures toward homogenisation and the creation of a culturally and socially more unified state. In fact, just the opposite was true: they tended to become increasingly institutionalised. Moreover, the process was almost never fortuitous, but, as has been observed many times, was part of a strategy of "divide and rule." Wallerstein (1983: 76) argues, however, that it was more than a strategic device to ease colonial administration. He sees it as being firmly rooted in the colonial economic structure as a means of ensuring the maintenance or reproduction of cheap labour. In his discussion of the creation of household structures that supported and were in fact a key element of the overall colonial economy, he states (1983: 76): "One way in which such households were 'created', that is, pressured to structure themselves, was the 'ethnicisation' of community life in historical capitalism." He continues with a definition of ethnic groups specifically in terms of the labour process:

What we mean by 'ethnic groups' are sizable groups of people to whom were reserved certain occupational/economic roles in relation to other such groups living in geographical proximity. The outward symbolisation of such labour-force allocation was the distinctive 'culture' of the ethnic group – its religion, its language, its 'values', its particular set of everyday behaviour patterns.

From this perspective, ethnicity becomes linked to, an imperative of, the colonial economy and to the development of the colonial class structure.

Ethnicity then became a key hegemonic device of colonial rule and a central component of the colonial economy. Ethnicity in this regard must be seen essentially as a product and vital part of colonialism and of the colonial state.

The Settler Colonies

Europeans began to settle in the Pacific, starting in Australia, in sizable numbers from the late 18th century onwards. Though in most of the islands of the Pacific the European population never assumed major demographic proportions, there were several exceptions. This was clearest in Australia, New Zealand, and to a slightly lesser extent Hawaii, where white settlers eventually overwhelmed the indigenous population politically, economically, and even demographically. A few other territories had fairly large white settler populations. In New Caledonia, a rough balance between Europeans and Melanesians was achieved, and in Guam and Tahiti, whites came to represent a sizable minority.

When the first 1,000 European settlers arrived in Australia in 1788, they were a small minority outnumbered by the 200,000 to 300,000 Aborigines. By 1901, when Australia became independent, the situation had drastically changed. The Aboriginal population had declined to some 100,000, while the European population had increased to almost 4 million. During the first half of the 19th century, the demographic balance had changed gradually, but after the discovery of gold in 1851, the pace of change increased sharply.

Although the colony almost constantly suffered from labour shortages, Burgmann (1978: 20) argues that "it was Aboriginal land that was wanted, not Aboriginal labour." Clearly land was wanted, but a closer look at the situation indicates it was not so much that Aboriginal labour was not wanted as it was that experience proved it unsuitable. Reynolds (1981: 115) points out that "The move from the bush into white society was much more than a spatial journey. It was among other things a transition from one economic system to another, from the domestic mode of production to the burgeoning capitalist economy of Colonial Australia." And one area where adjustment proved especially difficult was in developing labour discipline within a capitalist context:

The historical record bristles with colonists' complaints about their problems in trying to get Aborigines to behave as 'voluntary labourers' for wages. . . . But it was not just the habit of labour that had to be induced but also those concomitants, the subordination of servant to master and the separation of the worker from the means of subsistence and production (Reynolds 1981: 117,118).

Having by and large given up on Aborigines as a reliable source of labour, the white settlers relegated Aborigines to the far corner of the colonial economy (and also of its political structure) and turned to other sources of labour.

European labour was sought through two means. From 1788 to 1867, about 130,000 convicts were transported to Australia from England and its neighbour-

ing possessions. During the early years of settlement, this provided a vital supplement to the colonial labour force, without which many colonial enterprises
would not have been possible. But increasingly, white migration to Australia
was voluntary, especially after 1851. The numbers were not always sufficient,
however, especially in areas of rapid economic growth. Moreover, local capitalists often felt they could do better by securing nonwhite labour.

A great many indentured workers were brought from China to work in the
gold fields or on plantations. As Cronin (1975: 240) notes, "Although the
Chinese were initially suggested only as a temporary solution for the early
labour shortages, they soon became essential workmen in jobs considered badly
paid or too menial or boring for Europeans." Their employers favoured them
for the same reasons their presence was resented by members of the white working class. Both viewed the Chinese as "cheap labour and totally incapable of
even desiring a higher standard of living, let alone fighting to obtain it" (Burgmann 1978: 25). From the 1840s, anti-Chinese sentiments grew among European
workers concerned about the labour question and more generally about the
threat posed by the great "yellow peril" of Australia being engulfed by Asians.
The Chinese population in Australia grew to 42,000 by 1859 and to 50,000 by
1881. During this period, however, anti-Chinese settlers succeeded "in preventing the Chinese from obtaining occupational advancement and, consequently,
upward social mobility" (Cronin 1975: 251). A few Chinese were able to start
small businesses and become leasehold farmers, but their position was always
insecure. It is worth mentioning that Chinese farmers sometimes employed
Melanesian and Aboriginal labourers. (They preferred Melanesians over Aborigines and tended to pay them better.) Legislation was enacted in 1888 that
prohibited further Chinese immigration, and by 1901, the Chinese population
in Australia had declined to 32,000 (Willey 1978: 5).

From 1863 to 1901, about 61,000 indentured labourers were brought to Australia from the New Hebrides and the Solomon Islands (see Parnaby 1964 and
Corris 1973). They were brought primarily to work on plantations in Queensland. The planters favoured these workers, viewed as relatively servile and
cheap, over whites who, they argued, "were culturally and physiologically incapable of sustained arduous work in the sugar fields" (Hunt 1978: 81). As with
Chinese immigrant labour, a fierce debate soon erupted. White workers argued
that Melanesian labour would deny whites a chance to work on plantations and
also serve to lessen chances of improving working conditions in agriculture. To
this was added the fear that they would "degrade community standards and
endanger even the safety of Europeans in the sugar districts" (Hunt 1978: 80).
Legislation was enacted in 1901 that prohibited the recruitment of additional
Melanesian labour and repatriated most of those still in the country (only 1,854
were exempted).

When Australia gained independence in 1901, it was viewed by most of its
citizens and, more important, by nearly all the leading political interests as a

white country and as one that should remain white. This position had a strong appeal on both nationalist and class lines. Further immigration of nonwhites was almost precluded, and the remaining Asians, Melanesians, and Aborigines were increasingly marginalised.

Europeans began settling in New Zealand in large numbers in the 1820s. During the 1830s, their number grew to 2,000, from 150. By the late 1830s, large-scale land alienation had begun, and in 1840 New Zealand became a colony under the Treaty of Waitangi. The period from 1840 until 1860 was marked by great acculturation on the part of the Maoris and by a continued rise in the European population. In 1857–58, the Maori population was 56,000 and represented 49 per cent of the total population. Maori political rights during this period were limited; the 1852 constitution had effectively disenfranchised them. The situation was different in the economic sphere. Maoris were widely engaged in commercial farming and trade. They owned flour mills and ships and were a major source of provisions for the European population. But there were problems. Land alienation continued, and there was growing pressure within the European community to exclude Maoris from commerce. Maori agriculture suffered a setback in 1856 when there was a depression in the agricultural market, and between 1860 and 1865, war broke out between Maoris and Europeans that, in the end, left the Maoris in a weakened state. Sinclair (1969: 130) comments:

The history of New Zealand was distinguished from that of previous British settlements by the fact that the country was annexed when the evangelical movement was at the height of its influence on colonial policy. New Zealand was intended to set the world an example of human colonisation. The ideal was not attained. That the British Government failed, in particular, to achieve its professed desire 'to avoid, if possible, the disasters and the guilt of a sanguinary conflict with the Native Tribes' is no occasion for surprise: rather it would be a matter of astonishment if such wars, which seem everywhere to be part of the process of colonisation, had not occurred.

After the war, the colonial government set about establishing a more distinct Maori policy. It was ostensibly an assimilationist policy, but the creation of separate Maori institutions to carry it out (such as the Department of Native Affairs and separate native schools), along with the decision to give Maoris the right to vote for four Maori seats in parliament, tended rather to reinforce Maori distinctiveness. Instead of assimilation, government policy seemed in fact to be aimed at the creation of a bi-ethnic state. Within this context, Maoris came to serve as a pool of unskilled, seasonal labour. There were a few revived attempts at commercial farming among Maoris, but a lack of capital made this difficult. The presence of this Maori labour force was perceived by elements of the European working class as a potential threat, but their views and the policies they advocated were less extreme than those of their Australian counterparts.

By the 1880s, an assertive Maori leadership had once again emerged. It consisted primarily of more traditional leaders who felt their status within Maori society increasingly under threat by trends towards acculturation. Accordingly, they sought to link a desire for improving the condition of the Maori people with traditionalism that entailed primacy of their leadership role. These leaders sent two delegates to England in the 1880s to petition for Maori self-government, and in the 1890s, a Great Council and a Maori Parliament were unilaterally established in an unsuccessful attempt to create a parallel government. The policies advocated by this group were strongly antiassimilationist. However, a younger, more acculturated Maori leadership that did not advocate separatism was beginning to make its presence felt towards the end of this period. Both groups were nonetheless committed to politics that above all else were ethnically based. This was when the Maori population had been reduced to around 40,000, or approximately 6 per cent of the total population.

Although European settlers in New Zealand might have been tolerant of the Maoris, the same could not be said of their attitude towards the Chinese. Chinese migrants began arriving in the gold fields in the late 1860s. As Grief (1974: 15) has commented:

The miners were ruthless men who knew the rugged life of competition and frustration at the sluice-box or with pan in hand, men whose only advantage over the Cantonese was the colour of their skin. Thus the prejudices of drifters, now Californian, now Australian, arrived in Otago before the Chinese even made their appearance. The Chinese would be no more welcome in New Zealand than Australia.

Feelings against the Chinese reached a peak in 1871, when anti-Chinese violence broke out. A Parliamentary Select Committee of Inquiry was established to look into charges against the Chinese: i.e., that their presence would lead to a lower standard of living for whites, that they were immoral, and that they were members of an inferior race. The committee actually found in favour of the Chinese, but this did little to stem the tide of resentment against them. Employers, however, continued to see advantages in these relatively docile workers who could be paid less and treated worse than whites.

In 1872, the recruitment of Chinese began for railway construction, since it was decided that insufficient labour was available in the colony. This led to even greater antipathy towards them by white workers. With the depression of the 1880s, anti-Chinese passions reached a high pitch. Support for these sentiments was provided by the governor, George Grey, who was strongly anti-Asian. Political leadersip for the anti-Chinese crusade came from political leader Richard Seddon (who eventually became prime minister). After two unsuccessful attempts, an act was passed in 1881 that placed severe restrictions on Chinese migration; one of these included a poll tax of £10 (increased to £100 in 1896). As a result of the depression and these restrictions, the number of Chinese in New

Zealand declined. By 1896, only 3,700 remained. Independent New Zealand was not viewed by its European residents as "for whites only"; a place was made for the indigenous population, but other nonwhites clearly were not welcomed.

The histories of Hawaii and New Caledonia differ from those of Australia and New Zealand because the European settlers failed to become such an absolute majority in these two colonies, and neither became independect states: one eventually merged into a larger political entity (the United States), and the other is currently the subject of an intense independence struggle on the part of its indigenous population. Nevertheless, the four colonies share enough in common to warrant categorising them together.

Hawaii alone of the four colonies had what could be considered a centralised precontact state. It was also able to retain independence for several decades despite the growing political and economic interest of the different colonial powers. Geschwender (1982: 195) comments:

Each of the great powers seemed to view Hawaii in a similar manner. None saw the presence of raw materials or the potential sources of wealth which were sufficiently great to justify colonizing the islands, especially against the opposition of other great powers. Yet each knew Hawaii's harbours were strategically located with respect to trade routes.

For much of the 19th century, each was satisfied to allow Hawaii to retain its independence as long as unhampered access to its harbours was assured. Economic interests focused initially on the fur trade and then sandalwood (until 1836). Whaling was the main economic activity from the 1820s until the 1850s. Profits from sandalwood and from supplying whaling vessels provided the basis for the foundation of a settler oligarchy that assumed increasing economic and political importance in Hawaii. The rise of this settler bourgeoisie was accompanied by increasasing economic marginalisation of the Hawaiian aristocracy, who became dependent allies of this bourgeoisie, and by the proletarianisation of the Hawaiian peasantry. The peasants were called on to provide a large amount of labour for the new capitalist enterprises. At the same time, subsistence production suffered, leading to famine. This took place at the same time the indigenous Hawaiian population was declining; it had reached 50,000 by the 1870s, which was equal to about a quarter of its size at the time of initial contact a century earlier.

Hawaii saw its first sugar plantation in 1835, in the wake of the decline of the sandalwood trade, but it was not until the 1850s that sugar began to assume real importance in the Hawaiian economy. During the 1850s, whaling went into decline, and the California gold rush created a demand for agricultural commodities. The basis for the expansion of plantation agriculture was provided by a restructuring of the pattern of landholding in 1848, known as the Great Mahele. The result was that 60 per cent of the land went to the crown and the government, 39 per cent was given to some 200 chiefs, and 1 per cent was left to be distributed among 11,000 commoners. Much of the land set aside for commoners eventually was lost to white commercial interests, and by 1886, foreigners were also in possession of two-thirds of all government land (see Kent 1983: 32). Profitable sugar production, however, required both cheap land and cheap labour. The declining indigenous Hawaiian population clearly would not be adequate, and debate arosē over how best to solve the problem in a way that benefited the factions within the local élite (see Daws 1968: 179–82, Kuykendall 1953: 178–95). The three primary concerns that emerged were to provide labour for the sugar industry, to provide a stable European settler population, and to find a means of "replenishing" the indigenous Hawaiian stock (Geschwender 1982: 208–9). Not surprisingly, emphasis was placed on finding cheap and docile plantation labourers – a matter made easier by a decision to treat Japanese as Pacific islanders for the purpose of recruiting people of close racial proximity to the indigenous Hawaiians.

Most plantation labourers were recruited from China and Japan. Recruitment of Chinese labourers began in 1865, and by the end of the 19th century the number recruited totaled about 50,000. Many left, however, often going to California, and the Chinese population in Hawaii was not large: 5,727 in 1888 and 2,617 in 1892. Recruitment of Japanese workers began on a limited basis in 1868, but did not become significant until 1885. From 1868 to 1898, some 30,000 labourers were recruited. Unlike the Chinese, many Japanese remained in Hawaii, totaling more than 60,000 by 1900. One thing they shared with many Chinese was their dislike of conditions on the plantations, and both tended to leave plantation work as soon as possible to go into market gardening or commerce. Recruitment of Japanese workers eventually was stopped largely because of their militancy as labourers. A few Pacific islanders were recruited during the 19th century (around 2,500), but they never became a significant labour force, and most returned home as soon as possible – ending Kamehameha V's dream of using them to replenish the Hawaiin stock. The Chinese and Japanese migrants who remained came to form distinct ethnic communities in Hawaii. In 1890, they accounted for 32 per cent of the total population; indigenous Hawaiians and part-Hawaiians accounted for 45 per cent.

The resident white population consisted of more than the small "agromercantile oligarchy." It included many immigrants from the United States, including merchants, traders, small farmers, employees of the large companies, and skilled labourers. European labourers were recruited from several countries, the largest group coming from Portugal. From 1878 to 1887, about 12,000 Portuguese workers were recruited. They often came as families, having been promised a house and a small parcel of land. They ultimately formed an intermediate class on the plantations of overseers and skilled workers. In 1890, whites accounted for 22 per cent of the population.

In 1893, a group of whites overthrew the Hawaiian monarchy and established a republic. Hawaii was then annexed by the United States in 1898. Among the the reasons given for annexation was the fear of an expansive Asian presence brought about by the growing military strength of Japan and the growing numbers of Japanese in Hawaii. As a territory of the United States, the basic ethnic-class pattern remained the same, but there were a few changes. As an American colony, Hawaii became subject to the Oriental Exclusion Act (passed in the mid-1880s), which ruled out further recruitment of labourers from such countries as Japan. On the other hand, it was now simple to recruit plantation workers from another new American colony, the Philippines. From 1909 to 1931, more than 112,000 workers were brought from there. About half either returned to the Philippines or moved on to the West Coast of the United States, but a great many remained.

Plantation owners, who were exclusively whites, sought explicitly to play ethnic groups against one another. Japanese, Chinese, Filipino, and Hawaiian labourers were housed separately and paid different rates for the same work. Under these conditions, labour organisations, when they were formed, were also ethnically based. Attempts at forming labour organisations across ethnic lines were easily crushed, and during strikes it was common practice to draw on scabs from groups not on strike. The Portuguese continued to form something of an intermediate group, and one that remained notably distinct from "white" society. Because the Asian groups remained in Hawaii longer, internal class distinctions began to develop, but who was on top of the colonial heap was never in question, Kent (1983: 83) describes the situation before World War II:

The entire system operated along the racist lines established by the plantation interests in the mid-nineteenth century, when a cultural division of labour had been imposed upon sugar production to facilitate exploitation of (and to divide) the proletariat. A somewhat different cultural division of labour was maintained throughout the pre–Pearl Harbor era: Chinese were found in small businesses, Japanese in small businesses, on small farms, and on plantations, Portuguese were plantation foremen and skilled crafts people, Filipinos were plantation labourers, and Hawaiians were low-level government workers, stevedores, and construction workers. To keep up racial 'appearances' and to maintain loyal *haole* auxiliary, whites were awarded the most prized jobs and paid more for the same labour and the same work.

The depression years of the 1930s had been severe on the Hawaiian economy. Economic recovery during and immediately after the war, however, had created opportunities for entrepreneurs among the Japanese and Chinese population. As Kent (1983: 129) notes, young Asian professionals and businessmen "were increasingly impatient with a racist system that circumscribed their social, economic and political roles." They and others began to pressure the white establishment through the International Longshoremen's and Warehousemen's Union (ILWU) (see Zalburg 1979), which had finally succeeded in forming a union movement capable of transcending ethnic differences, and the Democratic party, in which, by 1950, they had become a significant voice. At the same time, the position of the old oligarchy had changed. Military spending was becoming the prime economic force in the colony (soon to be followed by tourism), and the success of the ILWU pressured the planter oligarchy to shift its activities to poorer third world countries where labour was cheaper.

When Hawaii became a state in 1959, ethnicity was still an important political force, and the convergence between class and ethnicity was great, but the situation had changed from a few decades earlier. In the rhetoric of creating a "New Hawaii" was talk of forging a multiethnic society. This goal was also voiced by political leaders in many newly independent countries, anxious to rid themselves of an obvious and noxious legacy of colonialism. It was also a platform that promised to gain widespread support for the newly emerging national, or, with Hawaii, the Asian immigrant, bourgeoisie in its effort to gain political dominance within the new political order. Also, it was a means of using the issue of ethnicity to draw attention away from the new class divisions that were developing.

Even more than Hawaii, New Caledonia represents a settler colony where the white population failed to become an absolute majority and thus found its dominant position subject to challenge. New Caledonia has been subject to two waves of white migration. The first took place during the latter half of the 19th century, when it served as a penal colony for France. From 1864 to 1897, some 20,000 convicts were shipped to New Caledonia. Few, however, remained to settle, and initial attempts to attract other European migrants proved far from successful. As Winslow (1986: 97) notes, "After forty years of French presence, New Caledonia was a colony with very few colonists." The number of whites in New Caledonia peaked in 1901 at 23,500, then declined to a low of 16,800 in 1921. Meanwhile, the indigenous Melanesian population declined to a low of 17,000 in 1921, from around 60,000 in the early 19th century. The colonial economy initially was based on agriculture (and government subsidies), but agricultural development proved difficult, and after 1900, New Caledonia was largely reliant on mining.

Convict labour was cheap enough, since most of the cost was borne by the government, but it did not prove efficient. As for the free European settlers, they were "not particularly keen on productive work, preferring managerial or administrative employment" (Howard and Durutalo 1987: 125). Those who were given farmland tended before long to leave for the bright lights of Noumea. The indigenous Melanesians, on the whole, were not considered suitable workers, although some were employed in agriculture and a handful in government service (see Gasher 1975). Most important, they strongly resisted work in the mines. The government decided essentially to get them out of the way. From 1898 to 1900 they were resettled on reserves that comprised less than 10 per cent of the land they had occupied previously.

Nonconvict indentured labour had been recruited largely for agricultural work since the 1870s, and the New Hebrides was its major source. From 1874 to 1882, more than 5,000 workers were recruited from there. About a quarter of these died, and most of the others returned home. After 1887, competition from Australia (where wages for indentured workers were higher) made it extremely difficult to recruit New Hebridean workers for New Caledonia. A few workers were recruited from India in the early 1870s, but their number never amounted to much (see Roux 1984). In the 1890s, indentured agricultural workers were brought from Java and, in lesser numbers, from elsewhere in the Pacific.

Convict labour had never been sufficient for the mines. A few Chinese workers were recruited in the 1890s, and later a few Indonesian workers were recruited, but their number was limited. Recruitment of Japanese began in 1892, and they soon came to represent the largest body of indentured workers in the mining industry. From 1892 to 1919, almost 7,000 Japanese workers were brought to New Caledonia. To this number were added family members, who were allowed to accompany workers by a 1911 agreement that also permitted them to take up residence in the colony. A great many left mine work as soon as possible to take up farming and commerce. They were successful enough to be seen as a threat by white small-business interests, who were able to convince the administration in 1919 to halt further recruitment of Japanese. In the 1920s and 1930s, most mine labourers were recruited from Java and Vietnam: their numbers rose to 14,000 in 1929, from 3,000 in 1921. Javanese were preferred, since they were considered to be more docile than Vietnamese (Winslow 1986: 104). During this period, the indigenous Melanesians grew coffee and copra on their reserves or as share-croppers.

Although the indigenous Melanesian population had begun to recover in the 1920s, the white population had remained relatively stable. In 1936, the Melanesian population was around 29,000, the white population only 17,000. In general, the whites were on top politically and economically, but internal class differences emerged within the two main ethnic groups. In particular, a class of poorer white settlers was not entirely convinced it would share the same interests as the leading capitalists of the colony. Political activists among them, such as Florindo Paladini (who became a member of the French Communist party in the 1920s) sought, before and during World War II, to create a class alliance among Asians, Melanesians, and poor whites that transcended ethnic boundaries (see Thompson and Adloff 1971: 277–82). The attempt was not entirely successful, but it served to lay the groundwork for later political initiatives. Among the Melanesians, the colonial authorities had created a compradorial administration and a cheifly class to help control the indigenous population. Reforms in 1946 that abolished forced labour and residential restrictions severely undermined the authority of these "traditional" colonial leaders. To check Communist influence among the Melanesians, a new generation of mission-trained leaders was promoted along with policies "directed toward reviving the

Melanesians' taste for tribal life on the reservations, so that they could fulfil their manifest destiny as a peasantry" (Thompson and Adloff 1971: 289). In this and other ways, new means were devised in postwar New Caledonia for ensuring that the basic ethnic-class structure remained intact.

The demographic situation in New Caledonia began to change dramatically in the 1960s and early 1970s in the wake of France's loss of its colonies in Asia and Africa and a mining boom in New Caledonia. The loss of the colonies led to a wave of French colonial migrants from Algeria and Vietnam: what one Melanesian commentator has referred to as "all the traitors . . . the rubbish of the world" (Qunei 1985: 10). The mining boom attracted a great many migrant labourers from elsewhere in the francophone Pacific (e.g., Tahiti, and Wallis and Futuna). These developments were linked to a conscious French policy aimed at swamping the indigenous Melanesian population to undermine the growing independence movement. At present, New Caledonia's population is around 145,000: 37 per cent white, 43 per cent indigenous Melanesians, 8 per cent from Wallis and Futuna, and 12 per cent other (such as Tahitian and Vietnamese). Those who are not Melanesian are concentrated in Noumea, which has a population of 80,000, while most Melanesians live in the country-side. The Melanesians continue to form the lowest socioeconomic rung of New Caledonian society. Only 89 have received tertiary education. Only about 7,000 are in wage employment, and of these, only a handful are to be found above the lowest levels. Melanesian household income on the average is less than half the average for the population as a whole. In the middle are the nonwhite migrants and a few poorer whites. Ethnic tensions have been exacerbated by economic stagnation brought on by a drop in metal prices. Attempts to revive the economy in the late 1970s through tourism have also fallen on hard times because of the struggle for independence.

The independence movement has for the most part been a Melanesian movement. As Dornoy (1984: 259) points out in her analysis of the 1977 election: "The main issue of the 1977 election was Kanak independence. It was supported by only a third of the Caledonian electorate, but by 80 per cent of Melanesians." The Melanesians have been joined in this movement by a few whites and Tahitians. On the other hand, the anti-independence whites are supported by a conservative element within the Melanesian population and by most of those from other immigrant groups (such as Wallis Islanders, Vietnamese, and Indonesians) who see their economic future tied to continued white French dominance. Attempts by the Melanesians to convince others that the independence struggle deserves the support of members of all ethnic groups have met with little success. The extent to which employment and economic status have been linked to ethnicity in the past severely limits the appeal of an independent Kanaky under Melanesian dominance for non-Melanesians. This, combined with such a difficult demographic profile, makes prospects extremely bleak and points to continued if not enhanced ethnic hostility.

Fiji

Fiji is not a settler colony in the sense that the term is usually used – i.e., settled by a great many whites – but it was settled by a sufficiently large number of indentured Asian labourers to perhaps qualify it as a settler colony in a broader sense of the term. In the case of Fiji, the dominant group was a relatively small group of whites under which was an allied compradorial indigenous élite. Despite periodic attempts to attract white settlers in the past century, the white settler population of Fiji has remained quite small. The number of white settlers throughout the latter half of the 19th century remained at a little over 2,000. By 1921, it had reached just under 4,000 (or about 2.5 per cent of the total population). Within this small group, however, was almost the entire commercial and political élite of the colony. As Governor Arthur Richards commented of them in a letter to the Colonial Office in the mid-1930s: "A few big men have obtained a stranglehold on the place – they have won their way to the top and mean to stay there. The underdog is underpaid and powerless. A few big men control everything behind the scenes and even Government has been run with a strong bias" (quoted in Gillion 1977: 11).

Colonial rule was established on the basis of collaboration between the British and eastern Fijian chiefs. One initial problem faced by the British and their eastern allies was consolidation of colonial rule over the remainder of the archipelago. Consolidation was brought about in part through a series of brutal wars and the legacy of regional antipathy, and unequal development remains an important factor in Fiji's political economy (Durutalo 1985). Colonial policy sought to create a native Fijian peasantry with indigenous chiefs serving as intermediaries. The labour question was an important one in respect to the extent to which Fijian peasants should be allowed or encouraged to work as wage labourers. Although it was recognised that labour would be needed to develop plantation agriculture, there was fear of creating "a landless proletariat that might prove a destabilising force in the colony" (Howard and Durutalo 1987: 140). The Fijian chiefs were divided on this issue: "the leading collaborator chiefs were strongly opposed to wage labour for commoners, which they felt might undermine their positions," and "many of the minor chiefs were not opposed since it provided them with a source of income in the form of bribes and gifts for services as labour recruiters" (Howard and Durutalo 1987: 140–41). In the 1870s, labour ordinances were passed to regulate Fijian labour. It was clear, however, that more labour was needed for plantation agriculture if the supply of Fijian workers was to be limited. Fijian plantation labour initially was supplemented by recruitment of indentured workers from elsewhere in the Pacific. Most were from the Solomon Islands and to a lesser extent from the New Hebrides. From 1877 to 1911, approximately 23,000 Melanesians were recruited to work on Fijian plantations. Of these, a great many returned home, and many died of disease, but many remained and settled in Fiji. Recruitment of indentured workers from India began in the 1870s, and by the late 1880s they comprised most workers in the sugar industry (which had come to dominate Fiji's colonial economy). More than 60,000 workers were brought to Fiji from India by 1912. Of this number, about 40,000 remained to settle in Fiji.

An increasingly diverse Indian community began to develop in Fiji, with a growing number of small-holder farmers, hawkers, shopkeepers, and artisans. The government took steps to promote Indian farming settlements near sugar plantations. For the most part, the Indian migrants formed a distinct community, but many were mixing freely with native Fijian commoners. This caused concern among the chiefs, who felt it might undermine their position. The chiefs were also upset by the success of Indian businessmen, who often had dealings with native Fijians. For their part, white landowners and businessmen were making money off the Indian farmers and merchants and in general felt their presence was good for the economic development of the colony.

Recruitment of indentured workers from India came to an end during World War I, and the indenture system itself was abolished in Fiji in 1920. This presented something of a crisis for the sugar industry, but the solution was soon found in turning the indentured workers into peasant producers. The colonial government remained favourably disposed towards the Indian population in general (although it did not like the outbreaks of labour and political militancy), since it saw the Indians as making a positive contribution to the colony's development. There was also the widespread belief among whites that native Fijians were a "dying race." The native Fijian population continued to decline into the 1920s, reaching 84,000 in 1921. At the same time, the Indian population was on the increase. The demographic situation was a worry to the eastern chiefly élite. Their concern was not merely that Fiji might someday be ruled by Indians, but that Indians might rule in conjunction with the other major group of oppressed people in the colony: native Fijian commoners, who were becoming increasingly difficult to control. The leading spokesman for the eastern chiefly élite was Ratu Sir Lala Sukuna.

Sukuna was particularly aware of the threat that commoner discontent represented to the privileged position that he and other collaborator chiefs held and he devoted most of his energies to countering that threat by strengthening the chiefly elite's position within the colonial administration and by seeking to divide and thwart opposition through appeals to community loyalty, threats, and other means. He had a strongly racist view of society, and felt that each ethnic group should live in isolation from the other. He saw inter-ethnic solidarity as representing perhaps the greatest threat and promoting inter-ethnic hostility and separation became the cornerstone of his designs to maintain a society that served the interests of he and his associates above all others (Howard and Durutalo 1987: 165).

Ethnic politics came to focus on debate over a communal versus a common role for the Legislative Council. As Indo-Fijians neared achieving demographic parity with native Fijians, the eastern chiefs became increasingly agitated. In their moves to stop the threat of democratisation, they were able to gain the support of the Indo-Fijian Moslem minority (about 8 per cent of the Indo-Fijian population). Several influential Moslems sided with the colonial authorities against what they perceived to be the threat posed to them by Hindu interests. Along with the ethnic question was continued opposition by Sukuna to allow native Fijian commoners to vote.

By the end of World War II, the Indo-Fijian and native Fijian populations were roughly equal: 120,000 and 118,000 in 1946. The war years and early postwar period also witnessed the rise of a new threat to the status quo in the form of organised labour. Initially, the union movement was of no direct concern to established native Fijian interests, since essentially it was Indo-Fijian in composition. The strategy adopted by the colonial administration towards labour was one of cooptation and creation of divisions within the union movement along status and ethnic lines. Labour within industries was often organised hierarchically along ethnic lines. Thus, in the sugar industry, whites were placed at the top, and part-Europeans and Chinese tended to comprise most of the skilled workers, with most of the unskilled workers being Indo-Fijians. As part of the strategy of divide and rule and to keep their own position secure, "High ranking Native Fijian officials in the colonial government, like Sukuna, and other chiefs encouraged the formation of exclusive Native Fijian unions" (Howard 1985: 115). Militant union leaders sought to counter these moves by promoting more general unions that drew on members across ethnic boundaries. When a strike involving workers from different ethnic backgrounds led to riots in Suva in 1959, the government was quick to respond through appeals to strikers along communal lines (see Hempenstall and Rutherford 1984: 73–86; Howard 1985: 116). During the 1960s, the Fiji Industrial Workers Congress managed to reduce the number of ethnically exclusive unions and to forge a more unified, if more moderate, labour movement.

While unionists were trying to overcome ethnic divisions, political organisations were being formed almost exclusively along communal lines. Indo-Fijians belonging to the Federation of Cane Growers formed the Federation party to contest the 1963 Legislative Assembly. This party gradually became the primary "Indian party" (known as the National Federation party), with its main platform being the protection of Indo-Fijian communal interests. More conservative Indo-Fijians formed the Indian National Congress, which eventually became part of the "Fijian" Alliance party; the Alliance party emerged as the political voice of native Fijian communal interests. One other political voice to be heard was that of the western native Fijians who continued to resent the overlordship of the eastern chiefly élite. This was represented by the short-lived Western Democratic party, founded in 1962 to contest the 1963 election. Divided along such lines, Fiji moved towards an independence that, when granted, would serve to further entrench communalism.

THE OTHER COLONIAL STATES

The remaining colonial states can be divided into three groups: (1) the relatively centralised states that eventually gained independence (Western Samoa, Tonga, Cook Islands, Nauru, and to a lesser extent the Gilbert and Ellice Islands); (2) the weaker states that eventually gained independence (Papua New Guinea, the Solomon Islands, and the New Hebrides); and (3) those states that remain colonial territories (the American and French colonies and West Papua). In regard to this last group, the American territories in Micronesia are still in the process of emerging as politically independent entities and will be treated, therefore, as colonial dependencies for present purposes.

Tonga is easily the most homogeneous of the countries falling into this first group. Before contact, it was culturally unified; during the 19th century, it became a single state with no significant regional or ethnic differences. Indentured labour was almost nonexistent, and the European settler population was never very large. The 1946 census noted 550 part-Tongans, 200 Europeans, and about 500 others from a total population of 43,000. As a group, these peoples fell within the middle range of Tonga's class structure, with some being associated with the ruling class.

The situation in Western Samoa is somewhat more complicated. Under German rule (lasting until 1914), a few labourers were imported from German New Guinea until 1903, and then many more were recruited in China. The Germans were impressed with the industriousness of the Chinese, and in 1912 they were given the right to purchase land and engage in commerce in Samoa. By 1914, 3,000 Chinese were living in the colony. The mixed-blood population was also growing: 599 in 1903, 1,845 in 1926, 2,320 in 1930. German attitudes towards half-castes varied over time and in accordance with the nature of the mix (see Keesing 1934: 453–54). Reflecting the "frontier" situation, the German administration initially did little to stand in the way of Samoan-white marriages. They were less tolerant, however, of relations between Chinese labourers and Samoan women. Shortly before the First World War, growing racist sentiment in Germany led the administration to propose making mixed marriages illegal. This was met with strong protests within Samoa, where some members of the mixed Samoan-white population were prominent landowners and merchants. In 1914, a compromise law was enacted by which the child of a mixed union belonged to the ethnic group of the mother and the father was required to pay for maintenance and education: "It was hoped by such a policy to widen the gap between the two classes, and so gradually to inbreed both the Europeans and the Samoans back toward the original types" (Keesing 1934: 454).

Under the New Zealand administration, the local white and part-Samoan bourgeoisie began to lobby for greater access to land and labour and for greater political rights. Part-Samoan business interests also sought recognition by the administration to speak on behalf of the Samoan community. The colonial administration's resistance to the demands by the part-Samoan bourgeoisie soon led to conflict with the part-Samoan leadership seeking to use its ties to the Samoan community to form the anticolonial mass movement – the Samoan League, or Mau Movement. This was to form the basis of political agitation in Western Samoa until its independence in 1962. The New Zealand administration sought to divide the Samoan-white population from other Samoans, in part to weaken political opposition and to use them as a buffer.

The New Zealand authorities tried to inculcate a feeling of admiration for everything European. A special "European" status was established in the country, which could be obtained by all "Euronesians" desiring it. The New Zealand administration built a special settlement – Aleisa – for them in the west of the island of Upolu, which was granted various privileges (Puckhov 1979: 346).

In the case of the Cook Islands, the ethnic question was not so much one of indigenous versus immigrant ethnic groups as one of local versus national loyalties. Nevertheless, the population was not entirely Polynesian in ethnic origin and those of non-Polynesian origin did form distinct groups of differing status. In 1895, Rarotonga (the main island in the group) had a population of around 2,500: 1,623 Rarotongans, 687 other Polynesians (many from other parts of the Cook Islands), 98 Europeans, 38 half-castes, and 11 Chinese. Over the years, almost constant tension existed between the indigenous *petite bourgeoisie* and white merchants. Although the administration was not entirely unsympathetic to the indigenous bourgeoisie, white capitalists had decided advantages (such as their access to capital and to shipping space). Very few labourers were imported to the Cook Islands, since it was not the setting of much in the way of plantation development, but Cook Islanders did themselves go abroad as workers. During World War II, a few hundred went to New Zealand to work as domestic and unskilled workers, and several hundred were recruited for Makatea's phosphate mine. Employment opportunities on Makatea ended after World War II, but Cook Islanders continued to migrate to New Zealand, where they formed part of that country's growing Polynesian proletariat. This was part of a general pattern of New Zealand developing Polynesia as a source of cheap labour (see New Zealand Coalition for Trade and Development 1982). By 1956, there were 2,320 Cook Islanders in New Zealand. Their number reached 4,449 in 1961 and 12,913 in 1971. Thus, the percentage of Cook Islanders living in New Zealand of the total Cook Island population increased to almost 40 per cent in 1971, from 12 per cent in 1956.

The small, phosphate-rich island of Nauru developed a precise ethnic-class structure. Administration of the colonial government and the mining industry was exclusively in the hands of whites, as were all technical jobs associated with mining. The Nauruans were of relevance to the mining industry only as recipients of small royalty payments. Recruitment of Nauruan workers in 1906 had proven unsuccessful, and thereafter colonial authorities relied on imported indentured workers, largely from the Caroline Islands (which was under German control) and China. Caroline Islanders were employed mostly in shipping and Chinese in the actual mining. Relations between the Nauruans and Caroline Islanders were cordial, but much suspicion and even hostility existed between Chinese and Nauruans, with the two groups generally avoiding one another.

Under Australian rule, the overall situation on Nauru remained the same, with whites, mine workers, and Nauruans forming distinct and isolated communities. Australian treatment of the Nauruans was paternalistic, and in 1921, they were given limited self-government, in the main because their internal affairs were considered for the most part to be irrelevant to the mining industry. Most Nauruans were confined to their own districts at night, but a few who lived a European style of life were exempted from curfew regulations. Recruitment of Caroline Islanders stopped with the First World War. In 1921, an unsuccessful attempt was made to use labourers from New Guinea. Labour for the mines came to be recruited exclusively from China. The Chinese were confined to their compounds in the evening, and·they were not allowed to become permanent residents. In 1946, the population of Nauru was 2,247: 1,369 Nauruans, 778 Chinese, 79 whites, and 21 other Pacific islanders. Overall, the situation remained much the same until the time of independence.

What became the Gilbert and Ellice Islands Colony was a collection of islands with significant cultural differences. The primary cultural division was between the Micronesians of the Gilbert Islands and the Polynesians of the Ellice Islands. Within the Gilbert Islands were also differences between those in the southern and northern Gilberts and between them and the population of the more isolated island of Banaba. The Gilbert Islands were in frequent contact with visiting whalers from the 1820s until the 1850s, and about 200 Gilbertese are known to have worked as crewmen on ships. From the late 1840s, coconut oil, and later copra, dominated the commercial life of the islands. During this period, a few resident traders and missionaries were evident, but the white population remained small. Gilbertese began to be recruited as indentured workers in the 1840s, and in larger numbers in the 1860s. Their main destinations were Fiji and Samoa. From the 1860s until 1900, some 6,000 Gilbertese went abroad to work. However, most returned after their contracts expired (if they did not die of disease). Macdonald (1982: 83) comments:

The concept of wage labour was accepted and, given the poverty of the islands, henceforth seen as the path to economic advancement. Inevitably, however, those who were recruited worked as the servants, sometimes the slaves, of European masters. There was, as a consequence, a gradual evolution of stereotyped beliefs concerning the distribution of wealth and power – all were perceived in racial terms and these together with demonstrations of technological sophistication, served to establish relationships and attitudes that were to be confirmed in the colonial era.

The early history of the Ellice Islands was in some ways like that of the Gilbert Islands, with Ellice Islanders working on whaling ships and a few going away to work in plantations. Also, copra became the commercial mainstay of the economy. The most important difference was in the hegemony established over the islands by Samoan pastors from the London Missionary Society. LMS missionaries arrived in the 1860s, and before long they had become the key political and economic figures in the group. Moreover, through their brand of Christianity, they had managed to establish Samoan cultural hegemony over the Ellice Islands.

Although copra production continues to play a role in the Gilbert and Ellice Islands in the 20th century, from the early part of the century until 1979, the colonial economy was completely dominated by the phosphate mining on Banaba. The socioeconomic pattern established for the mining industry was similar to that on Nauru. The colonial administration and managerial and technical aspects of mining were exclusively the domains of whites. Like the Nauruans, the Banabans proved to be unwilling and unsatisfactory mine workers. They continued to rely on subsistence activities and, increasingly, on revenue from mine royalties. In the 1930s, a few Banabans began to work for the British Phosphate Commissioners (BPC), and they were placed in privileged positions above other Gilbertese. Before World War I, most labour for the mine was recruited from elsewhere in the Gilbert Islands. A few Ellice Islanders and Japanese also were recruited. The Gilbertese were employed for mine work, the Ellice Islanders as boatmen, and the Japanese as mechanics. After the Gilbertese went on strike in 1911, some 300 Japanese labourers were also recruited to work in the mine. After the war, recruitment of Japanese labourers stopped, and they were replaced by Chinese. The total number of workers varied from about 1,200 to 1,500, except during the depression years, when the number declined to less than 1,000. The number of Gilbertese and Chinese miners varied, but after 1932, when Gilbertese labour became more expensive as a result of an agreement between the BPC and the colonial administration, the proportion of Chinese increased. Relations between the Gilbertese and Chinese mine workers were poor, and in 1920, tensions led to a riot. Interethnic violence broke out again in 1925. The BPC did little to relieve the situation. In fact, it tended to pursue policies that served to provoke the hostility. The BPC also sought to promote Banaba, which it saw as a reserve of cheap labour, as distinct from the rest of the Gilberts. They also treated Banabans as different from other Gilbertese and tried to promote an identification of the Banabans with management rather than labour – which caused resentment on the part of the Gilbertese and Ellice Islanders. This did not stop marriages and other ties from being maintained among the islanders, but it did serve to undermine solidarity among them.

During the 1920s, under the guidance of headmaster Donald Kennedy, the Ellice Islanders began to reassert their cultural identity after more than 50 years of Samoan dominance. This and their differential treatment in relation to Gilbertese by colonial officials and the BPC weakened any sense that they might have possessed of being part of a larger state, i.e., the Gilbert and Ellice Islands Colony. This sense of distinctiveness increased after World War II. An important factor was the advantage that Ellice Islanders had over Gilbertese in education and the translation of this into a competitive edge when the British began creating posts for islanders in the colonial administration. Rivalries developed between Gilbertese and Ellice Islanders within the colonial civil service. This led the British to hold an inquiry in 1973 into the attitudes of Ellice Islanders in regard to their status within the colony. In a referendum held the following year, the Ellice Islanders voted overwhelmingly to secede (3,799 to 293), even though it meant being cut out of a share in the phosphate royalties. In 1976, administration of Tuvalu (as the Ellice Islands was then called) was moved from Tarawa to Funafuti, and in 1978, it became an independent nation with a population, according to its 1979 census, of 8,730.

The colonial administration had been opposed to BPC's desire to treat Banaba and the remainder of the Gilberts separately and had sought to maintain the integrity of the colony. The administration and the BPC came up with a partial solution to the Banaban question immediately after World War II by resettling the indigenous population of Banaba (which had been displaced by the Japanese during the war) on the island of Rabi in Fiji. Although the Banabans became citizens of Fiji, they retained ties to Banaba and continued to receive royalties. It was the question of royalties that became an increasingly sore point in the 1960s and 1970s. On the one hand was the general question of the amount paid by the BPC, which the Banabans argued was far too low; on the other hand, as the Gilbert Islands moved towards independence the question arose of how the royalties were to be shared between an independent Gilbert Islands and the Banabans living in Fiji. There was also the question of what political rights the Banabans were to retain in the Gilbert Islands after independence so that they might safeguard their interests on Banaba. Agreements not entirely satisfactory to the Banabans were eventually reached on these matters, and after the Gilbert Islands became independent in 1979, relations between Banaban and the political leaders of Kiribati (as the Gilbert Islands was now called) remained strained. There was also the legacy among I-Kiribati who had worked in the mines on Banaba of identification of the Banabans with management in labour disputes that had continued to trouble the island.

The regional divisions within the Cook Islands, Fiji, or the Gilbert and Ellice Islands Colony were minor in comparison with the situation in the the Melanesian colonies of Papua New Guinea, the Solomon Islands, and the New Hebrides. These three states were characterised by a highly segmented indigenous population. They were also notable for very weak colonial infrastructures – to the point of being almost nonexistent when World War II broke out – and for having relatively small European populations. Thus, when the Australians took over British New Guinea in the 1880s, the European population in the colony was only around 600. In the Solomon Islands, the white population reached 675 in 1914, largely because of growth in the copra industry and increased missionary activity, but then it slowly declined, falling to 497 in 1931. In the New Hebrides, several hundred whites (687 French citizens and 218 British citizens in 1939) were to be found living in the centres of Vila and Santo or scattered about on isolated plantations and missions. Relations between whites and Melanesians were not good, and until World War II, violence on both sides was still strongly in evidence, although much reduced from the 19th century, when a near state of anarchy prevailed in interethnic relations. There were still murders, massacres, shellings of villages, and punitive expeditions. In the Solomon Islands, white overseers continued to treat their Melanesian workers brutally, to the point of killing them in a few instances, and expressed amazement when colonial officials sought to punish them for such behaviour. Hilliard (1978: 238) characterised the Solomon Islands of the 1920s as "a repressive backwater of the empire."

Throughout the 19th century, these areas had served as sources of cheap labour for plantations elsewhere in the region (e.g., Queensland and Fiji). The vast majority of males in the Solomon Islands and the New Hebrides went away at some point in their lives to work on overseas plantations. Many of them died, usually from diseases, and some decided not to return, but most of those who survived returned home a little wealthier and a little wiser in the ways of the world. Plantation agriculture within these islands during the 19th century was poorly developed. It was not until the early years of the 20th century, in response to rising international copra prices, that companies such as Lever Brothers and Burns Philp began developing plantations on a large scale. In the Solomon Islands and Papua New Guinea, most plantation labour was recruited from within the colony. This recruitment served to bring people from different parts of the colony into contact, but it often served only to further people's perceptions of their having distinct identities, although in some instances it helped to promote the development of more widely shared identification among those coming from the same general area. Plantation owners and managers tended to encourage differences to keep workers from uniting, and pursued a policy of recruitment from diverse areas away from plantations with this aim in mind.

Melanesians did not always provide an adequate or satisfactory work force for the plantations, and so, as elsewhere, the planters sought to bring more reliable and pliant workers from Asia. In doing so, however, they encountered great difficulties. In the 1890s, German planter interests brought in labourers from Malaya, Java, and China. The colonial administration was not supportive of recruiting workers from the colonial territories of imperial rivals, and many of the workers died from disease. When recruitment of Solomon Island labourers proved impossible at the price desired, Lever Brothers petitioned the administration in 1909 to allow it to recruit workers from India for its plantations in the Solomon Islands. They were turned down and thus had to come to terms with the demands of the local populace. The colonial administration also blocked British planters in the New Hebrides from recruiting Asian workers.

The French administration, on the other hand, was much more liberal with its nationals (this difference in policies was one reason many British nationals in the New Hebrides supported French annexation of the islands in the 19th century rather than British). French recruitment of Asians (mostly Vietnamese and Javanese) began in 1921, and before long they were employing no Melanesians. By 1929, the number of Asians employed rose to 5,540. The number of indentured workers dropped during the depression, when the French once more employed Melanesians. As the economy improved, the recruitment of Asians resumed; 2,023 Asians and 697 Melanesians were employed by French nationals in 1938, compared with 75 Melanesians by British planters.

The Chinese came either on labour contracts or on their own and quickly moved into business, forming the bulk of the *petite bourgeoisie* throughout the area. Firth (1973: 22) lists about 200 Chinese-owned businesses in German New Guinea by 1912. In the Solomon Islands, the number of Chinese grew to 200 in 1931, from 75 in 1914. Chinese and other Asians were also employed as skilled workers. Unlike other parts of the Pacific, where the Chinese came up against competition from smaller white merchants and aspiring indigenous entrepreneurs, in Melanesia they had a clear field. They formed an intermediate group between the larger white concerns and their agents and the Melanesians.

One feature that distinguished the New Hebrides from the other two colonies was its administration by two colonial powers: the British and the French. The presence of these two administrations, along with separate settler populations and distinct missionary bodies (Protestant and Catholic), divided the Melanesian population along a further dimension: anglophone versus francophone. The effect of this was not too great before World War II, but by the 1950s it was beginning to have profound implications.

The Anglo-French government established under the Protocol created an externally imposed cleavage which came to pervade most aspects of ni-Vanuatu life. In daily interaction, the French and British administrators and their respective citizens, businesses, and churches were engaged in intense competition for the loyalty of ni-Vanuatu. . . . After decades of such rivalry, some ni-Vanuatu spoke French, attended French schools, went to French-run Catholic churches, and availed themselves of French-administered services. Other ni-Vanuatu spoke English, attended English schools, went to English (Australia)-run (mainly Presbyterian) churches and accepted English-run government services. . . . In addition, Anglophone and Francophone ni-Vanuatu had acquired the jealousies and distrust that the English and French held for one another (Premdas and Howard 1985: 178).

During the early 1970s, political parties were formed along these lines, with the anglophone party pressing for early independence and the francophone parties opposed (see Premdas 1984: 54–56). These differing views reflected the francophone Melanesians being numerically a minority and fearful they would suffer under a predominantly anglophone regime.

As talk of independence began to increase, regional tensions and questions about the status of ethnic minorities began to emerge. Between the 1950s and 1970, more than 2,000 Gilbertese had moved to the Solomon Islands under an official scheme to reduce population pressure in the Gilbert Islands (see Bobai 1979). The British had understandably not consulted with the Melanesians affected by this move, and by the 1960s a degree of resentment against the British and the Gilbertese had developed. The Melanesians tended to view non-Melanesian residents in the Solomon Islands, such as the Gilbertese, Chinese, and whites, as a privileged group (Ghai 1983: 43). Similar feelings were emerging towards the Asians and other Pacific islanders residing in Papua New Guinea and the New Hebrides – centring on the question of citizenship in a newly independent state. As independence approached in the Solomon Islands, the Chinese population declined: to 452 in 1976, from 577 in 1970. The sentiment of the Melanesians toward the Asian business community reflected peasant feelings of resentment over past injustices (real or perceived) and the aspirations of the just-emerging indigenous bourgeoisie that was quite likely to move into the slots occupied by the Asians – i.e., underneath large white-owned foreign firms. Though peasant resentment was not widespread nor probably much of a threat, the aspirations of the soon-to-be rulers of these countries and the likelihood of their mounting popular sentiment in pursuit of these goals were sufficient to make the Asian community nervous. It is worth noting that, in the end, many of these fears came to nothing.

The regional question proved to be a thornier one, reflecting the extent of unequal development and often simply the lack of development that characterised the countries. The two most striking examples of unequal development were the island of Bougainville, with the promise of copper-derived wealth, in Papua New Guinea, and the Western Province of the Solomon Islands. Azeem, Good, and Mortimer (1979: 209) argue that "Although Bougainville leaders deny it, it is hard to accept that the prospect of exclusive control over public revenues from the mine had no part in propelling the surge of secessionist activity in 1974–76." In the case of the Western Province, it was an area characterised by an unusual sense – for the Solomon Islands – of common identity and one in which the population tended to be better educated and more integrated into the cash economy than on average (Premdas, Steeves, and Larmour 1984).

Turning to the final group of colonial states, those that remain colonies or that have been colonies until recently, what almost all of them share (the sole exception being West Papua) is a high degree of economic dependency on the colonial power ruling over them. Moreover, in most cases this is the result of conscious policy on the part of the colonial power to maintain control for largely strategic reasons. This is true of all American territories in Micronesia and American Samoa and is equally true of French Polynesia. It is probably also true of Wallis and Futuna. The case of West Papua is different, but strategic concerns are not without relevance in this instance either.

French Polynesia is an amalgamation of several relatively distinct island groups: the Society Islands, Australs, Marquesas, and Tuamotus. Depopulation and migration to the centre have created a situation in which, by the 1980s, more than two-thirds of the colony's population resides on Tahiti. Puckhov (1979: 356–7) comments that:

There is also a certain friction between Tahitians, on the one hand, and other Polynesians. Among the latter there is a fear, in particular, that the Tahitians would soon absorb all the remaining Oceanian groups. These views are most typical of the Marquesas, and it is no accident that in all the elections held in the Marquesas they have invariably supported the Gaullist Party . . . against those who advocate the granting of autonomy to the country. That is due to some extent to the great influence of the Catholic Mission in the islands, which is hostile to the autonomists, considering them "pro-Communist," but the Marquesan aborigines' definite distrust of Tahitians (perhaps cultivated by the same Catholic Mission), with whom the autonomist forces are associated, also plays a big role.

The colony is also divided ethnically between whites, Polynesians, and Chinese. The white population had been relatively large from the early years of colonisation. Governor Bruat arrived in Tahiti in 1843 with some 1,000 French labourers, artisans, and soldiers, joining a small British population of traders and missionaries already there. The white population included two main factions, composed of a settler/merchant élite and an administrative corps on short-term contracts. The white population was 2,170 in 1936. It began gradually to increase after the start of the French nuclear testing programme in 1963, and whites now account for about 15 per cent of the total population.

The first Chinese indentured labourers arrived in the 1860s, and by the 1880s about 400 Chinese were residing in the colony. Further recruitment was supported by the white agricultural lobby, but opposed by white merchants, who were beginning to feel threatened by the growing number of Chinese businesses. Moves were made to curtail Chinese immigration in 1902, and these were followed by an unsuccessful attempt to enact legislation that would discriminate against Chinese businesses. The fears of the white merchants were perhaps justified. As Thompson and Adloff (1971: 97; see also Coppenrath 1967) comment, at present "There is no branch of the economy of French Polynesia in which the Chinese have not participated, and in some they have won control. Directly or indirectly, half the territory's economic activities are in the hands of the

Chinese." There was almost no further Asian migration to French Polynesia after 1928, but the number of Chinese continued to grow: 4,569 by 1936 and 5,685 by 1962. They now account for 7 per cent of the population.

Phosphate mining began on Makatea in the Tuamotus in 1911. Initially, labour was recruited from Tahiti and elsewhere in the Tuamotus. In 1920, Japanese labourers began to be recruited in small numbers. Vietnamese provided much of the labour in the 1920s and 1930s, but they proved relatively expensive. In 1938, 104 Vietnamese worked on Makatea and another 83 on Tahiti. During World War II, with Asian labour cut off, workers were brought from the Cook Islands. By and large, however, the phosphate mine did not lead to a meaningful increase in the settler population.

French Polynesia, like several other Pacific island colonies, also came to have an important half-caste population, known as *demis*. The population of the Society Islands especially was highly mixed, and during the 19th century and early 20th century, several of those of mixed parentage had taken on important intermediary roles in the administrative and economic life of the colony. During the interwar period, they began to emerge as a much more distinct group.

It is possible to distinguish a sharpening line between those Polynesians . . . who remained predominantly peasants and occasional wage earners, speaking Tahitian, and a transitional group of mixed parentage, speaking some French, which moved between rural and urban employment for regular monetary income from agriculture, business and the professions. . . . The post-war generation of *demis*, by parentage and by education, still spoke Tahitian, but they were more closely identified with the commerce and administration of the metropolitan power (Newbury 1980: 279).

A most important factor behind the creation of this group was an educational system that favoured a small segment of the population living in and around Pape'ete. At present the *demis* account for 8 per cent of the population, and they continue to form an important and distinct element in the political economy of French Polynesia.

The French colony of Wallis and Futuna, as its name indicates, combines two islands that, in fact, until the time of colonial rule, had distinct histories. Even under French rule, until after World War II, the two islands remained separate, with communication between them being limited. Economic development on the islands has been minimal, and during the 1960s and early 1970s, a great many islanders went to work in New Caledonia and in the New Hebrides. Many of those working in the New Hebrides moved to New Caledonia after the New Hebrides became independent. In the late 1970s, about 9,000 people lived on Wallis and Futuna (including less than 200 whites), and about 10,000 islanders (known collectively as Walliseans) lived in New Caledonia or the New Hebrides. Economically, Wallis and Futuna is almost entirely dependent on assistance from the French government and remittances.

Until the development of the tuna industry over the past couple of decades, American Samoa was dominated by the American naval base at Pago. In 1930, 277 whites were in the colony, 179 of whom were navy personnel, and most of the others were either government personnel or missionaries. The same census also recorded 5 Chinese, 6 Japanese, and 14 "others." Most who belonged to this residual group ran shops or engaged in other services in close proximity to the naval base. The Polynesian population in that year was 8,926. There were also 887 persons of mixed descent, in large part the product of years of residence by American sailors. Because of the lack of a permanent white population, however, those of mixed descent tended to identify with the Polynesian community. But they were distinguished by being excluded from land and title holdings within the Polynesian community. Several owned land on a freehold basis or through leases, and they were among the most vocal during the interwar period in demanding political reforms. Eventually, the most important of these reforms were granted – especially the one giving American nationality to the inhabitants of American Samoa. Since World War II, the number of American Samoans living in the United States has burgeoned. Whereas the population of American Samoa is now approximately 35,000, some 85,000 American Samoans live in Hawaii or on the West Coast. Employment opportunities remain limited in American Samoa, with the two main sources of employment being the tuna industry and the military.

The Americans assumed responsibility for colonial rule of most of Micronesia north of the equator after World War II. The 2,000 islands in the region were administered as part of the Trust Territory of the Pacific Islands. Never a thoroughly integrated colonial state, over the past 15 years the Trust Territory has gradually fragmented.

The Marianas (which includes the islands of Saipan and Guam) were under colonial rule longer than any other island territory in the Pacific. Spanish rule lasted from 1564 until 1898, followed by German, Japanese, and American administrations. During the period of Spanish rule, the indigenous population (known as Chamorros) declined to 4,000 from 50,000. Though some full-blooded Chamorros remain, many islanders today are of mixed Spanish, Filipino, American, and Japanese ancestry. Because of the large American military presence on the island of Guam, the Marianas also has a large white population. In 1982, the total population of Guam was 105,000. This included almost 20,000 military personnel and their dependents. About a quarter of Guam's population is white, and about half is composed of descendants of the indigenous Chamorros. The population of the rest of the Marianas in 1982 was 17,000. Most are Chamorros, although there is also a sizable minority from the Carolines on Saipan. As a result of the heavy American influence, in the early 1970s the people of the Marianas began lobbying to become part of the United States. The move away from the rest of the Trust Territory got under way in 1972, and in 1977 the islands were given commonwealth status, and in 1978 a separate constitution. Because of its military importance to the United States, Guam was separated from the rest of the Marianas (the latter becoming known as the Northern Marianas, which excludes Guam).

The remainder of the Trust Territory pursued a slightly more independent course and came to be divided into three separate political entities: the Republic of the Marshall Islands, the Republic of Palau, and the Federated States of Micronesia. Although Palau, with 12,000 people, and the Marshall Islands, with 30,000 people, form relatively integrated states, regionalism is an important factor for the Federated States of Micronesia, especially in the case of Pohnpei (see Petersen 1986).

THE POSTCOLONIAL STATE

As a host of commentators have noted, the optimism of the newly independent nations soon faded as they confronted the realities of the world economy and had to come to terms with internal divisions that had been patched over during the move toward independence. Colonial rule was gone, but its heritage was a powerful determinant of what was possible in the postcolonial or, as it soon became labeled, the neocolonial world. Among the legacies for most newly independent nations was a compradorial class aligned in various ways to the interests of international capital, its occasional nationalist rhetoric notwithstanding, and ethnic divisiveness. The end of colonialism put an end to the worst manifestations of white rule – to the petty discrimination of the white masters – but not to the ethnic divisions and rivalries that were so much a part of most colonial states. If anything, it made them more immediate. These divisions and rivalries resulted from the ultimate weakness of the colonial state on the one hand (i.e., its inability to create a thorough sense of national identity) and of conscious policy on the other. Such a policy (divide and rule) was itself linked to the fragility of the colonial state and of the need for such "cheap tricks" along with the ever-present threat of the use of force. Given the often precarious hold that the new ruling class itself had on the states they inherited, not surprisingly, it tended to resort to the same strategies as the former colonial masters to stay in power: force and manipulation of perceived differences. This took place behind public statements about "national unity," "freedom," "democracy," and the like.

In general terms, the postcolonial states in the Pacific can be divided into developed and underdeveloped states. The developed states of Australia, New Zealand, and Hawaii (which was part of a larger developed state) had achieved their relative economic status primarily as a result of their having been settler colonies. Moreover, continuance of this status was in many ways a reflection of international racial distinctions by which the more developed "north" continued to give preference to its racial counterparts in the "south." In Australia and, to a lesser extent, New Zealand, it was also a matter of their relative wealth in natural resources, but this too was conditioned by racial biases. It is worth noting that the status of Australia and New Zealand was part of a general trend in the late 19th century among European settler colonies. In 1895, Australia's per capita income at £51 was close to that of Britain's and ahead of that of the United States, which was £44. The development of Hawaii owed a great deal to its postwar strategic value and its appeal to white American capital.

The situation in the rest of the Pacific states was markedly different. The only state that could be considered wealthy was Nauru. However, whereas Nauru's phosphate wealth provided its extremely small population with a high per capita income, in many ways Nauru continued (and continues) to manifest characteristics of an underdeveloped country. Differences among the underdeveloped Pacific island nations by and large reflect the degree and nature of their economic dependence. The Polynesian states were already well on the way towards becoming remittance-dependent appendages of more developed states such as New Zealand and the United States. Since political independence, their position in this regard has become even more pronounced. Given their current demographic profile, these states cannot be treated as divorced from the developed states where a large proportion of their people have come to reside. The situation is different with the Melanesian states and Kiribati, which, though still highly aid-dependent, have only small overseas populations and appear to have the potential at least of becoming more independent states than their Polynesian neighbours.

A couple of other general points should be made. With the exception of Vanuatu (as a result of French colonial attitudes) and to some extent Western Samoa (with its history of the Mau Movement), all the other states went through a relatively painless transition to independence. It was a transition over which the colonial power (Britain in most cases) had a great deal of say. The result was that nominal power was simply handed over to a segment of the national bourgeoisie most acceptable to the former colonial authorities. In ethnic terms, though the worst examples of the raj mentality were removed (in some instances they were merely appropriated by the new ruling class), little else actually changed. As for the whites themselves, many in the colonial administration soon returned as experts and consultants, and since the private sector continued to be dominated by foreign capital, little change was made except at the lower levels. Tied to this smooth transition and the degree of continuity was the virtual absence of a leftist tradition in the region. The alliance of church, administration, and capital had been able to stamp out most vestiges of this perceived cancer and to brainwash the population thoroughly to instill a deep-seated fear of the left and an uncritical respect for their former colonial masters – the bringers of enlightenment and civilisation. Anticolonialism and antiwhite sentiments were minimal and took the form of little more than rhetoric among a few university graduates and others. To the extent that there was a challenge to capital, it was through a poorly developed trade union movement (see Howard 1987) that was moderate in outlook.

Former Settler Colonies

Australia's present population of some 15.5 million is overwhelmingly of European origin. Asians represent a small but growing minority (especially since the mid-1970s). A few Pacific islanders are included, taking in descendants of Melanesian labourers and many who have migrated more recently (especially from Fiji). The indigenous population, Aborigines and Torres Strait Islanders, now account for only around one per cent of the population. The Aboriginal population had declined to 90,000 by 1945, but after World War II it slowly began to increase. It is now 200,000; a third living in Queensland and about 15 to 20 per cent living in the major urban areas.

The Aborigines and Torres Strait Islanders comprise the poorest group of people in Australia. Whereas the overall per capita GDP is around US$12,000, for many Aborigines living on isolated reserves it would be less than one-tenth that figure. Even for many Aborigines living in town, a large percentage of whom are unemployed, incomes are far below the national average. A small Aboriginal bureaucratic élite exists, serving in different capacities within the general context of "Aboriginal affairs" (see Howard 1981, 1982a, 1982d), and a few have been able to "make it" as small-time entrepreneurs, but they represent only a tiny fraction of the total Aboriginal and Torres Strait Islander populations. The fate of most Aborigines has been encapsulation in a welfare environment within which they have been subject to the vagaries of white opinion concerning the best means of dealing with the "Aboriginal problem" (see Hasluck 1942 and Biskup 1973, for example, for a review of policies in Western Australia from 1829 to 1954, and Howard 1978 and 1981 for the period through the 1970s). Put quite simply:

Aborigines lack both the ideological and economic bases of power in contemporary Australian society; for the most part, they control neither things nor ideas. White Australians (and foreign-based corporations) control most resources: they control the means of production and distribution. They are influential in defining needs, and they are able, by and large, to determine how and whether or not these needs are fulfilled (Howard 1982c: 1).

This is not to say that the Aboriginal voice has been silent: far from it. But its limitations have been all too apparent.

Two main areas in which Aborigines have been employed over the years are the pastoral industry in northern Australia and the seasonal agricultural work in the south (see Castle and Hagan 1978 on the latter, and Stevens 1974, 1981, Beckett 1978, and Wilson 1980 on the former). As Hartwig (1978) and Beckett

(1982) have argued, the situation for Aborigines and Torres Strait Islanders in northern Australia is one of "internal colonialism," "based on the articulation of capitalism with noncapitalistic modes of production" in which "the rationale for this articulation is the reproduction of labour for industry through a continuing subsistence sector rather than through wages" (Beckett 1982: 152). Responsibility for maintaining the structure within which the subsistence sector persists is left to the state and its welfare machinery. However, as Howard (1982a: 85) notes, "Such welfare was not always appreciated by pastoralists and farmers, between whom and the 'do-gooders' there was antagonism despite the mutually beneficial nature of their respective activities." Another problem for employers is that although such a system may provide a cheap work-force, it does not provide one that is reliable or necessarily efficient. The problem for Aborigines in this respect is that, should their labour cost rise, they may easily find themselves out of work altogether. It is a rather common trap for labour.

An added dimension is provided by the reaction of non-Aboriginal labour to the way in which Aboriginal labour is used. As mentioned earlier, the threat that white workers saw in the presence of such a source of cheap and exploitable labour often translated itself into racist sentiments and policies in colonial Australia. This situation was carried over into postcolonial Australian society, in which organised labour was frequently outspoken in its desire to eliminate Aborigines from the work-force altogether. As Markus (1978) has demonstrated, however, the labour movement was never unified in its approach to the Aboriginal question, with significant elements on the left calling for an emphasis on class rather than ethnicity.

Closely entangled with the "Aboriginal problem" was the "half-caste problem." During the early years of the colony, when white women were in short supply, interethnic unions were not uncommon in frontier areas. But in the south-west, as in other parts of Australia:

As the country became more established during the latter part of the nineteenth century, whites became more conscious of appearances and sought to hide their relations with Aborigines . . . , it became necessary to avoid "tainted blood" in one's family. In some instances, Aborigines who had taken their surname from white kinsmen were requested or even paid to change their name to avoid embarrassing their progenitors and their families. Although sexual relations certainly continued, they became increasingly clandestine (Howard 1981: 11).

White attitudes toward those identifiable as "half-castes" varied and were subject to debate from time to time (see Rowley 1970). During the early part of the century, some sought to have them classified as Aborigines subject to the same discriminatory laws as "full-blood" Aborigines. On the other hand, some felt this group could be saved and even that progressive "whitening" of the Aboriginal population was a positive step. Some pro-Aboriginal idealists even viewed part-Aborigines as degenerate. At least until the 1950s, the first group had the upper hand. In fact, the decision to change the status of part-Aborigines to include them with full-blooded Aborigines in the early part of the century led to the first modern forms of Aboriginal protest. Later, starting in the 1940s, the tide began to swing the other way, and exemptions became available. By this time, the part-Aboriginal population was a sizable portion of the total Aboriginal population.

The question of the respective statuses of part-Aborigines and "full-blooded" or tribal Aborigines became important once again with the rise of a more assertive Aboriginal political movement starting in the late 1960s. The creation of bodies such as the National Aboriginal Consultative Committee in the early 1970s helped to promote a national or pan-Aboriginal identity. This development was clearly not welcomed by many whites in Aboriginal affairs, who saw it as a threat to existing power relations. The response was to try to divide the "tribal" and "urban" Aborigines and especially to seek to convince the more conservative tribal Aborigines that they had little in common with urban-dwelling Aborigines (see Howard 1981: 136–42). The point was also made in the moves to bar all but the more traditional Aborigines from consideration when land rights policy was being formulated.

The situation in postcolonial New Zealand bears some resemblance to that of Australia, especially in terms of white attitudes concerning Asians, but there are also significant differences. For one thing, the proportion of the population that can be classified as indigenous or immigrant Pacific islander is much larger in New Zealand than in Australia. Today, Maoris comprise approximately 9 per cent of New Zealand's 3.2 million inhabitants. The presence of Pacific islanders is also much more marked in New Zealand. In 1945, only about 2,000 Pacific islanders were in New Zealand (equal to 0.1 per cent of the total population). By 1981, their number had increased to 92,000 (equal to 2.9 per cent of the total population). Most are from Western Samoa and the Cook Islands, but large numbers are also from Tonga, Fiji, Niue, and Tokelau. The combined Indian and Chinese population is in excess of 2,000, smaller than the Asian population in Australia. From the perspective of white racism, it is perhaps of some significance that the Aboriginal and islander populations in Australia are much darker in appearance, but the Maori and islander populations in New Zealand resemble much more closely the shade of the white immigrants themselves, i.e., white racists in Australia can more easily claim that members of these ethnic minorities are "closer to the apes" than they can of members of New Zealand's minorities. These distinctions were clearly made by early European commentators such as Charles Darwin, who had a chance to observe the different groups.

During the late 19th and early 20th centuries, New Zealand erected a whites-only immigration policy, as Australia did, aimed primarily at keeping Asians out (see O'Connor 1968; Harrison 1955). Even with such barriers, and despite the small size of the Asian population within New Zealand (the 1926 census reported 3,266 Chinese and 671 Indians), hostility towards Asians persisted. One expression of this was the White New Zealand League formed during the interwar years (see Leckie 1985). Anti-Asian phobias were especially in evidence during periods of economic hardship, since many workers and small entrepreneurs saw Asians as a threat. They were in evidence, however, even during times of relative prosperity.

In the early 1950s, "the Federated Farmers of Franklin were calling for the confiscation of Asians' land and their repatriation, while other concerned locals wrote to the Minister of Immigration to draw attention to what they perceived to be the development of an 'Indian mafia'" (Leckie 1985: 124). There was also widespread fear of "Asian sexuality." In this regard, there was concern both by white and Maori racists over the threat of "contamination and a need to preserve the 'purity of the race'" (Leckie 1985: 125). Thus, the Akarana Association, a Maori organisation, was vehement in the 1920s in its opposition to marrige between Maoris and Asians. In response to this racism, the Chinese community in New Zealand before World War II was a nearly closed one that sought to maintain its cultural distinctiveness. As the more overt forms of racism lessened after the war, the Chinese community began to assimilate. An increasing number of Chinese spoke English (some to the exclusion of Cantonese), worked in nontraditional occupations, and became Christians. In terms of employment:

In 1966 . . . 57.8 percent of the male and 56.8 percent of the female work forces were engaged in only two occupations, namely agriculture and shopkeeping. The overwhelming majority of these two categories would comprise market-gardening, and fruit and vegetable shops. However, there are still over 40 percent of the total working force in "non-Chinese" endeavours, and this percentage has been constantly rising (Grief 1974: 76).

Many of those of the postwar generation were better educated than their parents and were anxious to escape from the hard work of market gardening. Over the past couple of decades, the Chinese community has lost much of its distinctiveness culturally and economically.

Many Maoris and Pacific islanders are among the poorest people in New Zealand. They are, however, on the whole much better off than Australia's Aborigines. The per capita GDP of New Zealand is approximately US$8,000. About 35 per cent of all New Zealanders earn an average of less than US$5,000. Comparable figures for Maoris would be 55 per cent and for Samoans 60 per cent. But several Maoris and Pacific islanders have joined the ranks of the professional, administrative, and entrepreneurial middle class. The number of them who have received tertiary education in comparison with Australian Aborigines is staggering and serves to highlight just how bad the Aboriginal situation is.

By the early part of the 20th century, leadership of the Maori community was largely in the hands of the "old boys" from the Anglican Church's Te Aute College for Maoris, who had formed the Young Maori party. Sinclair (1969: 194) comments that they "were better educated than most Europeans and equally at home in Maori or English society." The Maori separatist movement had largely collapsed before World War I, and the Maori leadership increasingly sought to work within the existing legal and political struture. Alienation of Maori land continued until 1929, by which time the Maori retained only a small portion of what they had possessed only a few decades earlier. The Maori too became increasingly encapsulated within the welfare milieu, but it was a much more benign one than that entrapping the Aborigines. Maori political leaders formed close relations with the Labour party and, during the early postwar period, played a central role in keeping Labour in power. As social welfare benefits increased for New Zealand as a whole, provisions were made to help the Maoris in the fields of education, health, and economic development. The Labour government had hopes of raising the Maori living standard to the level of that of whites. Although some improvements were made, the goal was not achieved.

During the decades since World War II, Maori society has gone through much change. This is reflected in the percentage of Maoris living in cities: from a small number before the war to 43.6 per cent in 1966 and 55 per cent in 1971. This has had an effect on the nature of Maori employment. Again, before the war most Maoris who worked were employed in primary production. By 1971, this accounted for only 13.3 per cent of Maori employment. Whereas more Maoris than non-Maoris are found in lower paid jobs or are umemployed, the difference is not great and their relative poverty is, to some extent, simply related to the overall class structure of New Zealand society. Nevertheless, economically they are not as well off as whites, and discrimination, poor educational opportunities, and similar difficulties continue as great problems to many. Rising Maori consciousness in recent years has perhaps helped to draw attention to remaining problems and to stimulate efforts to solve them, but this comes at a time when the entire New Zealand economy is in a state of crisis.

White Australians and New Zealanders were largely successful in limiting Asian immigration, to the point that their economic and political hegemony was fully secure and the few Asians who did settle increasingly merged into the white landscape. The situation was much different in Hawaii. The population of Hawaii in 1980 was around one million. Whites accounted for 33 per cent, Japanese 25 per cent, Filipino 14 per cent, Hawaiians 12 per cent, and Chinese 5 per cent. These percentages have changed only slightly since statehood (the Japanese percentage has dropped from 32 per cent and the white percentage has remained the same), with differences being accounted for largely by new groups of immigrants (many from other parts of Asia).

The so-called Democratic revolution of the mid-1950s essentially was a

Japanese revolution. As Cooper and Daws (1985: 42) point out, the Japanese consistently have been overrepresented in the Democratic-controlled state legislature: 67 per cent of the seats in 1960 and 60 per cent of the seats in 1980. The same can be said of the Chinese, who have held about 10 per cent of the seats. In contrast, whites, even in 1960, held only 10 per cent. As for native Hawaiians and part-Hawaiians, they have held from 3 per cent to 4 per cent of the seats, and the Filipino political presence has been almost non-existent. Among the characteristics of the "typical" successful state legislator, according to Cooper and Daws (1985: 43), is that he is not only Japanese but, more specifically, he "is likely to have been born on an outer island, meaning essentially in a plantation community," and that he tends to be an attorney. Linked to the rise in Japanese (and Chinese) political fortunes is a rise in their economic position. The generation largely of Japanese-American war veterans who came to run the Democratic state political machine and a goodly share of the economic action in the state, as Kent (1983: 130–31) notes, was infused

with an individually oriented world view exalting middle-class materialistic goals and equating success with wealth, status, and power. . . . The postwar Asian political elite, despite its working-class background and the sufferings of the prewar years, never questioned the morality or viability of capitalism, especially a capitalism that had sufficient resiliency to provide them with the kind of wealth and position they could not have even imagined achieved during their younger, leaner days.

Fortunes were made in real estate in particular during a boom in tourist development and military expenditure that lasted through the early 1970s. At the same time, the old white settler élite found its position assumed by mainland United States and Japanese-based transnational enterprises. The class perspective of the International Longshore Workers Union was largely destroyed by the anti-Communist hysteria of the 1950s. The Democratic party machine that provided support for foreign investors and the newly rich Americans built its base on Asian ethnic loyalty, a well-healed union movement, and an appeal to middle-class aspirations.

As with Australia and New Zealand, Hawaii has been the scene of an assertive native rights movement in recent years. To some extent, Hawaii's movement is a reflection of the development of an indigenous consciousness among more educated native Hawaiians. It is also a response to the almost complete hegemony that has been achieved by non-native peoples and the continuing social and economic problems faced by many native Hawaiians. Among the more radical advocates of native Hawaiian rights are those of the Sovereignty for Hawaii Committee. Besides their criticism of the manner in which Hawaii has developed under American rule, and especially of its dependence on tourism and the military, and their specific opposition to such things as the military bombardment of the island of Kaho'olawe, all common themes throughout the

movement, members of the Sovereignty Committee call for re-establishment of
Hawaiian independence. Their argument is based in part on a narrow, dis-
claimers to the contrary, and essentially genetic, concept of nationhood.

"Hawaiian" refers to our national identity rather than our cultural or racial or geographic identity. In the same way that the term "American" identifies a person whose
national identity is tied to America, then "Hawaiian" identifies a person whose national
identity is tied to the Nation of Hawaii. Significantly, because we are Hawaiians we are
not, and cannot be Americans (Laenui 1985: 117).

Others, however, have taken a more reformist approach within the context of
American citizenship and laws, seeking to establish a Hawaiian identity without challenging American sovereignty over Hawaii.

   It is apparent that ethnicity still has an important role in the political economies of these three former colonies. Its role in the postcolonial state, however,
can be argued as being far less central. Under the relatively weak colonial state,
maintenance of control by the colonial élite was seen to require such crude
methods as appeals to racism and divisions along ethnic lines. As postcolonial
states have developed and the establishment of the hegemony of the ruling class
has become increasingly thorough and secure, racism and ethnicity have lost
their perceived necessity. Ethnicity for those in power is a useful part of seeking
to garner electoral support or, in the case of Hawaii, of accumulating wealth,
but it is not a defining characteristic of these postcolonial states: it is a vestige of
the colonial state that continues to serve some utilitarain purposes. For indigenous minorities – Aborigines, Torres Strait Islanders, Maoris, and native
Hawaiians – assertion of ethnic identity and calls for political and economic
reforms along ethnic lines emerged in a postwar liberal environment in which
such notions were given encouragement by elements within the dominant culture. Their origins were also in an era of relative economic prosperity, and in
this sense it was an indulgence of those in power. Since the onset of the recession, support among those in power for native rights has weakened (especially
in Australia) when the position of the indigenous peoples themselves has taken
a turn for the worse. An important question arises concerning what is likely to
happen should the recession turn to depression. Given the structural weaknesses of these three economies, it is quite likely they will suffer greatly in a
depression, and with ethnic hostilities still in evidence, if muted by postwar
prosperity and the rise of new means of assuring class dominance, it is not so
unlikely that interethnic antagonism will increase.

Dependent Postcolonial States

Although all postcolonial states in the region are still highly dependent, there
are several that now appear locked into a permanent state of dependency in

economic and, to some extent, political terms: Western Samoa, Tonga, the Cook Islands, Niue, and Tuvalu – the Polynesian states. Their having achieved national independence assures them of some degree of national-cultural identity and a limited degree of political autonomy. Their overwhelming economic dependence, however, severely constrains any real chance of political or even cultural autonomy. In regard to their cultural identity, it should be seen as highly conditioned by the economic position that these states occupy in relation to their more developed neighbours as suppliers of cheap manufactured goods and cheap migrant labour.

Pacific islander migration to New Zealand "took off" in the 1960s when New Zealand's economy was buoyant and in need of additional workers. Many skilled workers migrated to New Zealand from other developed countries. Pacific islanders came primarily as unskilled workers. As a New Zealand Coalition for Trade and Development report (1982: 51) remarks, "The Polynesian worker is typically in an unskilled or semi-skilled factory job," and "other common occupations are bus drivers, laundry workers, cleaners, and domestics." As noted above, Western Samoa and the Cook Islands provided the largest number of migrants. The total number of Pacific islanders in New Zealand now exceeds 100,000. In terms of the smallest Polynesian nations, more than half their people live in New Zealand. The Tokelau Resettlement Programme, which lasted until 1976, contributed to there being more than 1,800 Tokelauans in New Zealand, while the population of Tokelau itself fell to around 1,600. The situation in Niue was similar: in 1971, there were 5,000 people on Niue. Significant migration to New Zealand began in the 1960s, and Niue now has less than 3,000 people, and more than 6,000 Niueans are in New Zealand.

Western Samoans have migrated to the United States, usually via American Samoa, and to New Zealand in large numbers. The Samoan economy from the early 1960s became increasingly dependent on remittances. A study by Shankman (1976) of one village found that 84 per cent of the residents relied heavily on them. Tongans also have migrated to New Zealand and the United States in large numbers, and to Australia, and remittances play a large part in the Tongan economy. In the mid-1970s, when the New Zealand economy began to weaken, a reduction in migration and a downturn in remittances occurred. Shankman (1979) found that remittances to Western Samoa declined 40 per cent from 1974 to 1978.

By the time the New Zealand policy of emptying the smaller states was halted in the mid-1970s in response to the recession, their populations had reached levels that brought into question their chances of survival. Although Tokelau appears to have come to terms with the situation, the probability of Niue's eventual disappearance would seem fairly great, despite New Zealand's financial support and such ploys to keep people on Niue as the introduction of television. Niueans would thus remain only as a small ethnic minority in New Zealand.

The larger states are not very likely to disappear, at least soon. However, an important question for them concerns the relationship between the states and their nationals living abroad as the recession continues or worsens and as the migrant community becomes more permanent and establishes an identity that is more distinct. On the one hand is the matter of continuing the flow of remittances. On the other is the question of the cultural dialectic between Tongans and Samoans residing in Samoa and Tonga and those living abroad.

Not only are changes occurring in the migrant population; significant changes are also under way within the Polynesian states associated with the evolving political economy of these states. Cultural assertiveness and praise of a special brand of tradition (i.e., one that supports the interests of those in power) was very much the hallmark of the reign of Queen Salote of Tonga and of the Samoan and part-Samoan élite that took over in Samoa at independence. Within their countries, a conscious effort was made to establish an unquestioned national Polynesian culture. This was aimed at securing their own class position and in the process served to bring the half-caste populations into the Polynesian ambit. More recently, the interests of this ruling class have begun to change as the capitalist economies of their countries have evolved, along with the aims of the ruling élite. Essentially, the colonial-feudal order is beginning to give way to a more advanced form of capitalism. As the ruling élites of these countries become increasingly concerned with industrial and small business development and with putting greater amounts of land to work under capitalist modes of exploitation, the place of tradition and culture is also undergoing change. Already it has lost much of its organic quality and has become increasingly alien to its leading proponents, for whom it is simply more and more fodder for the masses. How far this process will continue is debatable, but a course already seems set in which "typical" Samoans or Tongans before long will be found only among those relegated to the ranks of the reserve army of peasant producers.

One other issue of relevance is that of separatism within these postcolonial states. This is not an issue for Tonga or Western Samoa (or for Niue or Tokelau), but it has cropped up in the Cook Islands and Tuvalu. In the Cook Islands, separatist sentiments arose in the 1970s along with opposition to the government of Albert Henry and especially to perceptions of favouritism shown to his home island of Aututaki and to other centres of his political support. In the 1978 election, a movement evolved on Penrhyn (population 531 at that time) calling for its representative to approach the United States with the intent to become totally self-governing, or at least to separate from the rest of the Cook Islands, in free association with the United States or New Zealand (Vini 1979: 198). Since the fall of the Henry government, little more has been heard of this, and further separatist initiatives now seem very unlikely. The prospect of separatism arose in Tuvalu in 1980, shortly after independence. Ethnically, Tuvaluans are homogeneous, and at their independence in 1979, the non-Tuvaluan population was 184 of a total population of 8,364 (105 of whom were I-Kiribati). However, there is a degree of identification with one's home atoll, and in 1980 in Nanumea, the northernmost atoll in Tuvalu (with a population in mid-1983 of 906), discussion about secession arose.

Tuvalu will surely not be able to develop the eight islands in the group, and the three nearest islands to the capital have already received favourable treatment from Tuvalu whereas we, the most populated island, the furthest and the second biggest in the group, have received unfavourable treatment. It is hard to blame anybody for this. The only answer is for us to do our utmost for the good of our island home, expecting someone to assist us financially for a start . . . . I appeal to Commonwealth countries, especially Australia and New Zealand, and to the United States of America, for a loan of $8–10 million in the first five days to run and develop the government and country. Failing this, we will have to apply to Asian countries, etc. (Fati 1980: 11).

Support for secession has not entirely disappeared, but greater efforts have been made by the central government to develop the outer islands, and it is doubtful that any atoll will in fact secede.

The Other Postcolonial States

Into this category fall the Melanesian states of Vanuatu, the Solomon Islands, and Papua New Guinea, along with Fiji, Kiribati, and Nauru. As noted before, although these states are (with the exception of Nauru) poor and still dependent on aid, they exhibit a degree of autonomy not found and not likely to develop in the case of the Polynesian states.

One important question to arise in constitutional negotiations about the time of independence was the legal status of different ethnic groups. With a colonial heritage of differential treatment was a precedent for maintaining this pattern after independence. Though some states choose to reject this as an undesirable part of the colonial heritage and to treat all citizens equally, two especially opted for continuity: Fiji and Nauru. In both instances, this reflected the advantaged position that the indigenous élite had obtained under colonial rule and its desire to maintain this postion.

At independence, about half the population of Nauru consisted of indigenous Nauruans. Most of the remainder was made up of labourers from Kiribati, Tuvalu, and China. Continued Nauruan dominance was assured by a refusal to recognise non-Nauruans as even potential citizens, "considering them only temporary inhabitants of Nauru" (Puckhov 1979: 347). In 1983, the foreign workforce consisted of 785 I-Kiribati and Tuvaluans, 145 Chinese, 48 Filipinos, and 128 others (mostly whites from Australia and New Zealand in higher-level positions). The government also hired a few professionals from Sri Lanka and India (in part because they were considered cheaper than whites). Relations between Nauruans and mine workers are no better than before independence. Wages are kept low (A$3.20 a day plus accommodation and food for unskilled mine workers), and any move toward unionisation is treated with hostility. Just as before independence, efforts are made to maintain ethnic loyalties among workers (as expressed through workers' committees), and evidence exists of a conscious policy of divide and rule to weaken the position of labour.

The native Fijian élite succeeded in blocking Indo-Fijian initiatives to have a common electoral role, and divisions separating native Fijians, Indo-Fijians, and others (including white and Chinese) were institutionalised electorally and in other ways. This pushed the opposition party into the role of "defender of the Indian community" and ensured that it had little chance of developing along noncommunal lines. Meanwhile, the ruling Alliance party sought to strengthen its position further by continuing the practice of playing on divisions within the Indo-Fijian community: through appeals to the conservative Moslem minority in particular. It was also able to gain the support of wealthier Indo-Fijian businessmen with whom the native Fijian élite found common cause in their search for riches. The "others," or General Electors, having been given political representation far in excess of what was their due based on population, were thereby encouraged to support the ethnic status quo to which they perceived themselves beholden. Appeals to communal loyalty also were still used to divide organised labour; as was the practice of appealing to "tradition" among native Fijian workers as a means of keeping them under the thumbs of the chiefs. Added to these strategies was political patronage (a cornerstone of Alliance party rule) for compliant union leaders. It is now perhaps best to discontinue discussing Fiji (among recent relevant works are Durutalo 1985, 1986; Lal 1986; Taylor 1987), except to mention the recent challenge to ethnically-based politics offered by the Fijian Labour party and its policy of nonracialism.

The other main question confronting these states was that of territorial integrity. As mentioned earlier, the Melanesian states especially inherited a weak state structure, and around the time of independence, all were faced with secessionist movements. The Solomon Islands sought to reduce secessionist sympathies and regional hostilities through a policy of decentralisation in general (see Premdas and Steeves 1984, 1985) and, concerning the Western Province, through regional development initiatives (such as promotion of a growth centre in the area). Decentralisation may have lessened the threat of secession, but at the price of promoting corruption and indebtedness at the local level and also of undermining national planning and economic development. A similar approach was adopted in Papua New Guinea (see Premdas and Pokawin 1980) with perhaps even more disastrous results. Besides sizable debts provincial governments have been able to amass, as Joyce (1985: 90) argues,

the real problems centre around the use and control of power by the elites at both the central and regional level and the even more urgent problem which arises ultimately from the issue of control: lack of participation by the people in the decision-making process and the decline in the level of services, particularly in the rural areas – the very things that the process of decentralisation was meant to promote [*sic*]. The problem has become so acute that it can easily be argued that the situation of the rural population on the whole has declined rather than improved in the period since independence under decentralisation.

Decentralisation has proven in essence to be a compromise that has allowed both national and regional élites to line their pockets.

Before independence, Vanuatu's francophone minority had great fears that rule by the anglophone Vanuaaku Pati would be to their detriment (Premdas 1984: 61). Such fears were manipulated by the white French community until francophone elements rebelled and sought to secede (see Shears 1980). The rebellion served only to make matters worse for the francophone community in an independent Vanuatu.

The government of Walter Lini suppressed the secessionists, jailed or deported their leaders and enforced a regime that bore the unmistakable imprint of an English-speaking Protestant government. . . . The governing Vanuaaku Pati made few concessions to its adherents. The cabinet was composed of only its own confessional and linguistic adherents (Premdas and Howard 1985: 178).

Although the threat of secession no longer exists, the position of Vanuatu's francophone minority had improved only marginally since 1980, and Vanuatu seems to be on a course towards becoming an anglophone state. The main opposition party, the "moderates," essentially is a francophone party, and in 1983 its leader accused the Vanuaaku Pati of turning Vanuatu into a client state of Australia (Premdas and Howard 1985: 179).

With Fiji, though regional antagonism persists, the only actual secessionist threat since independence has come from the island of Rotuma. In negotiations for Fijian independence, an attempt was made by some Rotumans to regain their autonomy from Fiji (Pacific Islands Monthly 1970). They were persuaded to remain with Fiji and provided with certain privileges and guarantees, but secessionist sentiment did not die out entirely. It resurfaced in mid-1986 in debate concerning cruise ship visits to Rotuma, following discussions in late-1985 about creation of a separate Rotuman seat in the House of Representatives. As for Kiribati, the major cultural division took place before independence, when the Ellice Islands opted for separate nationhood. The Banaban question remained after independence, but it became little more than a matter of trying to score political points in negotiations over mining and later fishing royalties than of an actual threat of secession.

Thus, for the most part the prospect of a new state being formed in the region through secession now appears remote. Regional dissatisfaction, however, remains a very real problem for most of the states, although national identification in general seems to have progressed.

CONCLUSION

The promotion of ethnic divisions is at the very heart of colonial rule. On the one hand is the distinction between ruler and ruled, and on the other are the distinctions made among those who are ruled. Throughout the Pacific, even where provision was made for assimilation of a limited number of indigenous élites, the ethnic identity of the rulers was never ambiguous. Ethnic divisions among the subject peoples also were present in almost every state. These were in part a matter of colonialism having combined the territories of formerly distinct peoples into a single unit and of the practice of importing migrant labour. But it went deeper than that. Thus, as Puckhov (1979: 345) asserts, "The only thing that was quite plain in the colonial powers' policy on the national question was their endeavour to exploit the complex ethnic structures of certain Oceanic countries for their own selfish ends." But the use of a strategy of "divide and rule" was applied not only along ethnic lines. It is important also to point to the class dimension whereby the emphasis on certain aspects of culture and "tradition" were employed not simply to divide peoples along ethnic lines but also to promote internal class divisions to create intermediate classes among subject peoples that would assist in colonial rule – e.g., a compradorial élite. In this respect, it was common not only to find singular ethnic groups supportive of colonial rule because of their privileged position in relation to other subject peoples, but also to find a loyal class that identified nearly, if not more, with the colonial rulers instead of with other subject peoples.

The relevance of ethnicity in postcolonial states is much more problematic. It varies according to the hegemonic strategies of the ruling class and to the extent of which this hegemony no longer requires the use of communal loyalty. It is apparent that at the outset, largely as a result of the colonial heritage of these states, ethnicity will be important. But over time, its significance tends to weaken – not, however, to disappear. Ethnicity retains its potential as a divisive tool within postcolonial states and one that tends to come to the fore in general during times of economic hardship, more specifically, in countries such as Fiji, and during national election campaigns. It thus remains a useful supplement to other forms of class domination. For the most marginalised ethnic groups, such as the indigenous peoples in the more developed postcolonial states in the Pacific, an important inversion takes place by which ethnicity as a means of domination comes to some extent to be replaced by its use by these marginal peoples to negotiate for improvements in their status. Its role as a bargaining chip, however, must also be seen as having developed within the global context of the postwar economic upturn. Its persistence into the subsequent recession reflects several institutional, economic, and other factors, and changing economic conditions have served to lessen the receptivity of the ruling class to such appeals while also perhaps further entrenching the strategy among its adherents.

For the underdeveloped postcolonial states of the region, diverse strategies have been adopted to deal with ethnic divisions. Significantly, only in the case of Fiji has the use of ethnicity persisted as a conscious policy of the ruling élite. To a very large extent, this reflects the very close relationship the indigenous ruling élite enjoyed with the colonial administration and the communal nature of opposition to colonial rule. Although Nauru now also employs a policy of ethnic exclusivity, once the phosphate runs out, this policy will end. The other states have pursued policies aimed at reducing ethnic divisiveness with varying degrees of success. Such a goal has been much easier to achieve for the more homogeneous Polynesian states; the Melanesian states have found it far more difficult. The compromise strategy of decentralisation has not exactly been a great success, but it should probably be seen as a transitory stage and a willingness to recognise some regional differences, but not as abandonment of the goal of creation of a more unified nation. Central to these strategies also are the competing interests of different élites, and much of the future of decentralisation, for example, no doubt will depend on the positions and perspectives of these élites.

REFERENCES

Alkire, W. H. 1972. *An introduction to the peoples and cultures of Micronesia*. Menlo Park, California: Cummings.

Azeem, A., K. Good, and R. Mortimer. 1979. *Development and dependency: The political economy of Papua New Guinea*. Melbourne: Oxford University Press.

Beckett, J. 1978. George Dutton's country: Portrait of an Aboriginal drover. *Aboriginal History* 2(2-1): 2–31.

———. 1982. The Torres Strait Islanders and the pearling industry: A case of internal colonialism. In *Aboriginal power in Australian society*, edited by M. C. Howard, 131–58. St. Lucia: University of Queensland Press/Honolulu: University of Hawaii Press, 1982.

Berndt, R. M., and C. H. Berndt. 1977. *The world of the first Australians*. Sydney: the Smith.

Biskup, P. 1973. *Not slaves not citizens: The Aboriginal problem in Western Australia 1898–1954*. St. Lucia: University of Queensland Press.

Bobai, T. 1979. Gilbertese resettlement. In *Land in Solomon Islands*, edited by P. Larmour, 131–41. Suva: University of the South Pacific, Institute of Pacific Studies.

Burgmann, V. 1978. Capital and labour: Responses to immigration in the nineteenth century. In *Who are our enemies?*, edited by A. Curthoy and A. Markus, 20–34. Sydney: Hale and Iremonger.

Castle, R. G., and J. S. Hagen. 1978. Dependence and independence: Aboriginal workers on the far south coast of NSW 1920–75. In *Who are our enemies?*, edited by A. Curthoy and A. Markus, 158–71. Sydney: Hale and Iremonger.

Clapham, C. 1985. *Third World politics*. London: Croom Helm.

Cooper, G., and G. Daws. 1985. *Land and power in Hawaii*. Honolulu: Benchmark Books.

Coppenrath, G. 1967. *Les Chinois de Tahiti*. Paris: Société des Océanists.

Corris, P. 1973. *Passage, port and plantation*. Melbourne: Melbourne University Press.

Cronin, K. 1975. From plodding 'paddy' to 'the ching-chong Chinaman': The Chinese rural labourer. In *Exclusion, exploitation and extermination*, edited by R. Evans, K. Saunders, and K. Cronin, 237–53. Sydney: Australia and New Zealand Book Company.

Daws, G. 1968. *Shoal of time: A history of the Hawaiian islands*. New York: Macmillan.

Dornoy, M. 1984. *Politics in New Caledonia*. Sydney: Sydney University Press.

Durutalo, S. 1985. *Internal colonialism and unequal regional development: The case of western Viti Levu*. M. A. thesis (sociology), University of the South Pacific.

———. 1986. *The paramouncy of Fijian interest and the politicisation of ethnicity*. Suva: USP Sociological Society, South Pacific Forum Working Paper No. 6.

Elkin, A. P. 1954. *The Australian Aborigines*. Sydney: Angus and Robertson.

Fati, T. 1980. A Tuvalu secession? *Pacific Islands Monthly* 51(10): 11.

Firth, S. 1973. German firms in the western Pacific islands, 1857–1914. *Journal of Pacific History* 8: 10–29.

Gasher, P. E. 1975. Les problèms de main-d'œuvres en Nouvelle-Caledonie. *Cahiers d'Histoire du Pacifique* 1: 6–27.

Geschwender, J. A. 1982. The Hawaiian transformation: Class, submerged nation, and national minorities. In *Ascent and decline in the world-system*, edited by E. Friedman, 189–28. Beverly Hills, California: Sage.

Ghai, Y. 1983. The making of the independence constitution. In *Solomon Islands politics*, edited by P. Larmour and S. Taura, 9–52. Suva: University of the South Pacific, Institute of Pacific Studies.

Gillion, K. L. 1977. *The Fiji Indians: Challenge to European dominance 1920–1946*. Canberra: Australian National University Press.

Grief, S. W. 1974. *The overseas Chinese in New Zealand*. Singapore: Asia Pacific Press.

Harrison, N. 1955. *The formation of the white New Zealand immigration policy between 1890–1907*. M. A. thesis (history), University of Auckland.

Hartwig, M. C. 1978. Capitalism and Aborigines: The theory of internal colonialism and its rivals. In *Essays in the political economy of Australian capitalism*, edited by E. G. Wheelwright and K. Buckley, vol. 3: 119–41. Sydney: ANZ Book Company.

Hasluck, P. 1942. *Black Australians: A survey of native policy in Western Australia 1829–1897*. Melbourne: Melbourne University Press.

Hempenstall, P., and N. Rutherford. 1984. *Protest and dissent in the colonial Pacific*. Suva: University of the South Pacific.

Hilliard, D. 1978. *God's gentlemen: A history of the Melanesian Mission 1849–1942*. St. Lucia: University of Queensland Press.

Howard, M. C., ed. 1978. *"Whitefella business": Aborigines in Australian politics*. Philadelphia: Institute for the Study of Human Issues.

Howard, M. C. 1981. *Aboriginal politics in southwestern Australia*. Nedlands: University of Western Australia Press.

———. 1982a. Australian Aboriginal politics and the perpetuation of inequality. *Oceania* 53(1): 82–101.

———, ed. 1982b. *Aboriginal power in Australian society*. St. Lucia: University of Queensland Press/Honolulu: University of Hawaii Press.

———. 1982c. Introduction. In Howard 1982b, 1–13.

———. 1982d. Aboriginal brokerage and political development in south-western Australia. In Howard 1982b, 159–83.

———. 1985. The evolution of industrial relations in Fiji and the reaction of public employees' unions to the current economic crisis. *South Pacific Forum* 2(2): 106–63.

———. 1987. The trade union movement in Fiji. In *Fiji: Future imperfect?*, edited by M. Taylor, 108–21. Sydney: George Allen & Unwin.

Howard, M. C., and S. Durutalo. 1987. *The political economy of the South Pacific to 1945.* Townsville: James Cook University, South East Asian Monograph Series.

Hunt, D. 1978. Exclusivism and unionism: Europeans in the Queensland sugar industry 1900–10. In *Who are our enemies?*, edited by A. Curthoy and A. Markus, 80–95. Sydney: Hale and Iremonger.

Jones, F. L. 1970. *The structure and growth of Australia's Aboriginal population.* Canberra: Australian National University Press.

Joyce, L. 1985. Review of *Decentralisation and political change in Melanesia*, by R. Premdas and J. Steeves. *South Pacific Forum* 2(1): 90–92.

Keesing, F. 1934. *Modern Samoa.* London: George Allen & Unwin.

Kent, N. 1983. *Hawaii: Islands under the influence.* New York: Monthly Review Press.

Kuykendall, R. S. 1953. *The Hawaiian kingdom, 1854–1874.* Honolulu: University of Hawaii Press.

Laenui, P. 1985. Hawaii: The cause of Hawaiian sovereignty. *IWGIA Newsletter* 43/44: 115–56.

Lal, B., ed. 1986. *Politics in Fiji.* Sydney: George Allen & Unwin.

Leckie, J. 1985. In defence of race and empire: The White New Zealand League at Pukekohe. *New Zealand Journal of History* 19(2): 103–29.

Macdonald, B. 1982. *Cinderellas of the empire: Towards a history of Kiribati and Tuvalu.* Canberra: Australian National University Press.

Markus, A. 1978. Talka longa mouth: Aborigines and the labour movement 1890–1970. In *Who are our enemies?*, edited by A. Cuthoy and A. Markus, 138–57. Sydney: Hale and Iremonger.

Newbury, C. 1980. *Tahiti nui: Change and survival in French Polynesia 1767–1945.* Honolulu: University of Hawaii Press.

New Zealand Coalition for Trade and Development. 1982. *The ebbing tide: The impact of migration on Pacific Island societies.* Wellington: New Zealand Coalition for Trade and Development.

O'Connor, P. S. 1968. Keeping New Zealand white, 1908–1920. *New Zealand Journal of History* 2(1): 41–65.

Qunei, S. 1985. *For Kanak independence.* Auckland: Labour Publishing Co-operative Society/Corso.

Pacific Islands Monthly. 1970. The Rotumans aren't happy. *Pacific Islands Monthly* 41(7): 24.

Parnaby, W. 1964. *Britain and the labour trade in the southwest Pacific.* Durham, North Carolina: University of North Carolina Press.

Petersen, G. 1986. *Decentralisation and Micronesian federalism: Pohnpei's 1983 vote against free association.* Suva: USP Sociological Society, South Pacific Forum Working Paper 5.

Premdas, R. 1984. Secession and decentralisation in political change: The case of Vanuatu. *South Pacific Forum* 1(1): 41–75.

Premdas, R., and M. C. Howard. 1985. Vanuatu's foreign policy: Contradictions and constraints. *Australian Outlook* 39(3): 177–86.

Premdas, R., and S. Pokawin, eds. 1980. *Decentralisation: The Papua New Guinea experiment*. Waigani: University of Papua New Guinea Press.

Premdas, R., and J. Steeves. 1984. *Decentralisation and political change in Melanesia*. Suva: USP Sociological Society, South Pacific Forum Working Paper 3.

———. 1985. *The Solomon Islands: An experiment in decentralisation*. Honolulu: University of Hawaii, Pacific Islands Studies Program Working Paper Series.

Premdas, R., J. Steeves, and P. Larmour. 1984. The western breakaway movement in the Solomons. *Pacific Studies* 7(2): 34–67.

Puckhov, P. I. 1979. Policy on the national question and interethnic relations in Oceania. In *Ethnocultural processes and national problems in the modern world*, edited by I. R. Grigulevich and S. Ya. Kozlov. Moscow: Progress Publishers.

Reynolds, H. 1981. *The other side of the frontier*. Townsville: James Cook University, History Department.

Roux, J. C. 1984. Les Indiens de la Nouvelle-Caledonie. *Bull. de le Société d'Etudes Historiques de la Nouvelle-Caledonie* 58: 3–11.

Rowley, C. D. 1970. *Outcasts in white Australia*. Canberra: Australian National University Press.

Shankman, P. 1976. *Migration and underdevelopment: The case of Western Samoa*. Boulder, Colorado: Westview Press.

———. 1979. The economic impact of out-migration on Pacific communities. In *New neighbours*, edited by C. McPherson, B. Shore, and R. Franco, 5–11. Santa Cruz, California: University of California at Santa Cruz, Center for Pacific Studies.

Shears, R. 1980. *The coconut war: The crisis on Espiritu Santo*. Melbourne: Cassell.

Sinclair, K. 1969. *A history of New Zealand*. Harmondsworth: Penguin Books.

Smith, J., I. Wallerstein, and H. Evans, eds. 1984. *Households and the world economy*. Beverly Hills, California: Sage.

Stevens, F. 1974. *Aborigines in the Northern Territory cattle industry*. Canberra: Australian National University Press.

———. 1981. *Black Australians*. Sydney: APCOL.

Taylor, M., ed. 1987. *Fiji: Future imperfect?* Sydney: George Allen & Unwin.

Thomas, C. Y. 1984. *The rise of the authoritarian state in peripheral societies*. New York: Monthly Review Press.

Thompson, V., and R. Adloff. 1971. *The French Pacific islands*. Berkeley: University of California Press.

Vini, N. 1979. Penrhyn: The people's choice. In *Cook Islands politics*, edited by R. Crocombe, 192–99. Auckland: Polynesian Press.

Wallerstein, I. 1983. *Historical capitalism*. London: Verso.

Webster, A. 1984. *Introduction to the sociology of development*. London: Macmillan.

Willey, K. 1978. Australia's population: A demographic summary. In *Who are our enemies?*, edited by A. Curthoy and A. Markus, 1–9. Sydney: Hale and Iremonger.

Wilson, J. 1980. The Pilbara Aboriginal social movement: An outline of its background. In *Aborigines of the west*, edited by R. M. Berndt and C. H. Berndt, 151–68. Nedlands: University of Western Australia Press.

Winslow, D. 1986. Labour relations in New Caledonia to 1945. *South Pacific Forum* 3(1): 97–112.

Zalburg, S. 1979. *A spark is struck!: Jack Hall and the ILWU in Hawaii*. Honolulu: University of Hawaii Press.

2

Discourses of Ethnicity: The Faces and the Masks

SUSANA B. C. DEVALLE

The role that ethnicity plays in the political praxis of the indigenous peoples of the third world constitutes the focus of the discussion that follows. I have attempted in this way to approach the situation in the Pacific area.

It has long been evident that cultural, ethnic, linguistic, and religious factors have readily given some political movements a stimulus for solidarity and provided one of the bases for mobilization *at one moment* of their development. I contend that in this context, ethnicity plays as a dependent variable in the social formations of the third world and not as a product of vaguely defined primordial sentiments. Thus it appears as a historical and not a contingent phenomenon, subordinated to existing class and centre-periphery contradictions, and as an element operating in cultural dialectics.

I wish to argue that never has there been but one discourse of ethnicity, instead a plurality. By considering the ways ethnicity has been articulated in the ideological discourses of antagonistic classes and of the state and also the realities of uneven development, we can differentiate two salient faces of the phenomenon: (1) as an element to serve the hegemony of the dominant classes and of the state, in which case ethnic strategies confirm the state, its policies, and the status quo of class domination, and (2) as a counter-hegemonic force in instances in which ethnic ascription and economic subordination correlate. Especially here, ethnicity can contribute to developing an awareness of the contradictions existing in the society at large as they are experienced by the concerned social sectors. Thus the most visible part of the iceberg, ethnicity as a metaphor for opposition, becomes subversive in the eyes of the state and of the ruling classes, especially when it is articulated into ideological formulations and a social practice that stimulates the conception of an often radically different future. Diversity becomes especially subversive in the realm of culture, where the resilience and strength of indigenous styles demonstrate the limits of the hegemonic forces (see Williams 1978).

In recent decades, some Marxist social scientists in the third world have

50

begun to draw attention to the revolutionary potential of ethnicity as a political phenomenon (for instance, Varese 1978). Already in 1966, Abdel-Malek indicated the need for a shift in emphasis in the approach to the problem from economism and economic reductionism to the political, to social dialectics and the civilisational dimension, to understand the realities and the dynamics of the non-Western world, its struggles for national liberation, its socioeconomic transformations, and its search for or defence of national-cultural identity. The need for this shift in focus is seen as a response to the "inversion of the global process of historical initiative," initiative taken up by the non-Western world after the withdrawal of the colonial powers from Asia and Africa and the breakdown of Western hegemony. This change translated into the wave of national liberation movements and into the continuing efforts at decolonisation (Abdel-Malek 1966; 1981: 191–201).

The dissatisfaction with economism has not remained at the abstract level of theoretical discussion. The potentialities of factors such as ethnicity and culture in popular struggle have been played down or discarded by formal politics as possible dimensions for the organisation of political action and the development of social consciousness. This is not surprising. The different uses of ethnicity have created no little confusion at the practical level of politics. Political movements with ethnic contents are often seen by the traditional left as divisive, ethnicity considered a mark of false consciousness (see, for instance, Guerrero 1983: 31–51). Also, the right usually sees them as leftist, given their oppositional contents, and as undesirable developments to be curbed or repressed. These contradictory perceptions stem, on the one hand, from an uncritical evaluation of ethnic-based movements of various contents and social bases. On the other, they arise from the inability of formal politics to understand the different modes in which popular protest can be expressed (Gramsci's "bizarre combinations"). The indigenous movements in their turn coincide in their distrust of political parties and established ideologies. Often feeling that these do not represent them fully, indigenous peoples tend to develop their own political organisations (see, for instance, Documentos de la Segunda Reunión de Barbados 1979). In the field of formal politics, we have thus come to witness an unconfrontable correlation, pointed out by Varese (1978: 2–3):

The other side of the coin of the neocolonial bourgeois State's assimilationism or integrationism is a "revolutionary integrationism" – called by some indigenous organisations "vulgar classism" . . . [maintained by some] left positions.

While addressing these problems, I will refer first to the question of the legitimation of ethnic differences in the Pacific for the maintenance of unequal social relationships and to the implications of the projects for national integration, then briefly review the ways in which ethnicity has been approached in the area by the social sciences before offering some concluding remarks.

THE LEGITIMATION OF ETHNIC DIFFERENCES
IN THE PACIFIC AREA

At the core of the modes in which ethnic differences were structured in the Pacific in modern times, we find specific historical circumstances: the colonial expansion; the persistence of residual colonial forms of control; the development of neocolonial structures for the exploitation of people, land, strategic geographical positions, and natural resources; and the nature of the process of state formation. In this context, legitimating ideologies phrased in racial or ethnic terms have been formulated to maintain political domination and unequal socioeconomic relationships.

Also, science contributed with justifying arguments to the entrenchment of the hegemonic forces in the region. The sociological constructs of race relations and ethnicity were applied to the specific situations in the Pacific from perspectives that subsumed the nature of the existing socioeconomic structures and class relations to the primacy of racial or ethnic factors. Inequality was paraphrased as difference (racial or cultural, or both).

Scientific texts – ideas, perceptions and construction of the object – have not only resulted in a mode of knowing reality, but often in the acquisition of credentials as *the* actual realities they attempted to describe. Pacific societies were not exempted by a scientistic imagination from this process of reconstruction. The constructs of tribe and/or race as a social category, for instance, appeared with colonialism and became elements through which Europe reconstructed – both intellectually and in administrative practice – part of the reality of the societies that came under its dominance. Tribalist and racialist perspectives have either ignored or obscured the realities they sought to describe by concealing the existing and the new socioeconomic and power relationships operating in these societies. Racial, ethnic, and tribal stereotypes were forged to denote diverse modes of production, forms of social organisation, and cultures, ignoring the complexities, the dynamism, the history, and the civilisational patterns of the societies thus catalogued. In the end, taxonomies acquired the power of truth, and, in sum, these societies were rendered ahistorical.

Although the constructed categories were ideal models, the ideology derived from this perception was and is very concrete and functional, which Mafeje (1971) and Wolpe (1975: 454) already pointed out, in supporting and reproducing capitalist relations of production and patterns of power relationships and in justifying the expansion of cultural hegemony. As with the Orientalists' Orient (Said 1978, Abdel-Malek 1966), I believe we also have a comparable text-discourse on the Pacific societies, including the indigenous societies in the local central societies.

Parallel to the evolution of this discourse, other developments have been taking place at the concrete level. Indigenous movements against domination in its old and new modes, efforts at ethno-national identity assertion, and the emergence of movements called micronationalisms have arisen grounded on an identity consciousness that often has tended to cut across linguistic and cultural differences. This cirumstance may favour the emergence of regional or panregional solidarity links to contest the forces operating in the present economic-political order in the Pacific. These developments will undoubtedly encounter serious obstacles because of the correlation of forces and the international alliances dominating the area, where the reality of neocolonialism has laid bare the illusion of formal independence in the excolonial societies.

Economic and political domination has been asymmetrically established between the world or regional powers and the Pacific societies.[1] The mode this process of domination has adopted in the area makes ample use of racial, ethnic, and cultural differences as part of colonial and neocolonial policies and practices. These policies and practices aim to restructure and control entire societies to subordinate them to the Western model of capitalist development – creating a tier of dependent economies – and to carve out permanent enclaves for strategic purposes.

The panorama the Pacific societies present is one of enormous diversity and richness in terms of languages, social and economic organisation, and cultural expressions. These differences, cultural dynamism, and social patterns acquired a different meaning when structured in the frame of the colonial situation. Existing differences were enhanced to preclude any unified action of the colonized people, and a new opposition expressed in racial and/or cultural terms came into being, one between the Europeans as a superordinated group and the people under their domination. Beyond their diversity, therefore, the Pacific societies share the common experience of colonialism and the present efforts at decolonization in a context in which neocolonial structures and relationships are firmly entrenched.

In the colonial and neocolonial settings, these societies played a role that, with some modifications, has persisted until today. They were and are the sources of valuable raw materials and cheap labour, of land and mineral resources; they were made captive markets for products from the more industrialized countries and were found to be a suitable ground for multinational corporations interested in their mineral wealth. In the postwar period, they were set up as part of an international system of defence for the United States and its allies. Besides, they were made a dumping ground for nuclear waste and a zone for nuclear experiments.

It is in this context that anticolonial and nationalist movements have been developing in the Pacific, processes that have accelerated since the late '60s.

Economic and political domination benefits from the control, manipulation, or debasement of the original collective identities of the subordinated peoples. Their history and cultures have been usually denied or devalued. This task of dehistorization and deculturation and the imposition of exogenously constructed identities have been opposed by efforts of the subordinated sectors to maintain and reaffirm their threatened historical and cultural specificity, with the aim of combating social realities and forging independent historical projects.[2] In this context, the efforts at self-assertion and the emergence of ethno-national movements in the social formations of the Pacific and among the subordinated indigenous societies in the metropolitan centres of the area may serve as one strategic axis for solidarity and for the development of political actions. However, a further step is necessary: the acknowledgement of the internal contradictions present in the society at large and in the ethnic group/community itself, beyond the constructed racial and ethnic demarcations and oppositions. An awareness of this need already exists among concerned intellectuals in the non-Western world.[3]

The task of decolonization in the Pacific faces a reality in which structures of exploitation and links of economic, political, and cultural dependence with metropolitan and regional powers persist and where decolonization is threatened to be externally controlled and contained. Ethnic identity and alliances are being used in the containment of the process of decolonization in the Pacific by the indigenous élites allied to the metropolitan centre (Wolfers 1975; Fitzpatrick 1980: 198–99). Also, the consciousness of historical permanence, the maintenance of cultural and semantic fields, of forms of social and economic organisations, of mechanisms for the production and reproduction of the indigenous collective identities, imply the possibility of the development of counter-hegemonic practices to fight the conditions created by colonialism, by neocolonialism, or by the attempted all-pervading control of the modern state.[4]

ETHNICITY: A MYTHOLOGICAL HYDRA?

Ethnicity may prove not to be a many-headed monster if one is careful to distinguish its different faces. On the one hand is the construct created by social theories to catalogue phenomena and social groups and the elements it provides to the ideological discourse of the ruling classes for directing and justifying specific policies and practices. On the other hand ethnicity is encountered as it is actually lived, as a dynamic process with a specific present, entailing a singular mode of social experience. Thus ethnicity may be understood as a dependent variable whose dynamics are subordinated to the diverse ideological and practical needs and interests of the hegemonic and the subordinated sectors.

Ethnicity is not an autonomous subject suspended in an ahistorical void – as it is usually portrayed in the liberal sociological writings – and should be conceived as a process whereby evolving styles are maintained (recreated) and collective identities formulated. The time dimension (not linear, but social time) gives them either substance – as with collective identity practised in everyday life – or legitimation, as with imagined communities and invented traditions (Anderson 1983; Hobsbawn and Ranger 1983). The long and slow processes developing in the historical duration are not even, but subject to the variability of social rhythms and contradictions, finally resulting in a constantly reinterpreted synthesis: the historical specificity of a society, its historical self, and a global ethnic or national style. This process is marked by a tension between socioeconomic and political transformation and cultural maintenance (see Abdel-Malek 1981: 151–59). The evolution of the historical self of a society is not removed from the objective reality of social contradictions, class formation, and class conflicts. Although a constant point of reference, this self, this style, will be differently lived and expressed by the different classes or social sectors.

Being firmly grounded in the concrete history of singular social reality, an ethnic style cannot be understood as the immutable and intangible essence of a given people or as a fixed sociological ideal type (seen by Said [1978: ch. 1] as deriving from the West's "hegemonism of possessing minorities"). Consequently, the processes of renaissance and collective self-assertion are not accidental happenings of an idealist "existential communitas" guided by a spontaneous urge at an immediate brotherhood (cf. Turner 1969: 119 ff.).

Ethnic styles evolving in the long-term duration are expressed in daily life through the ways, forms, and codes of communication, culture, modes of social reproduction and consumption, a past, and usually a territory; these are differently shared and used by the different social sectors identified with the specific ethnic style. Also, formulations emerge of what the community is or should be, making use of traditions, modes of thought, and acting ascribed to a certain ethnic style. We thus observe the invention and legitimation of communities, resulting in constructs.

Anderson (1983: 15–16), when examining the phenomena of nation and nationalism, defines nation as "an imagined community . . . [that], regardless of the actual inequality and exploitation that may prevail [in it] . . . is always conceived as a deep horizontal comradeship." This imagining well applies to statist conceptions of the nation, where the nation-state is portrayed as an all-embracing interclass collectivity, a supercommunity with no internal contradictions. Often, it is this major construct that regional and ethnic-based movements are challenging with their alternative projects, especially in the excolonial countries of the third world.

The colonial creation of administrative units on the basis of the arbitrary delimitation of territories and the spatial reorganisation of peoples was bequested to the new ruling sectors after independence. These in turn rephrased it as the abode of the nation. Thus, the independent state, although the project of a few and born without the participation of the diverse components of the society, has come to act as the true and sole interpreter of the nation(s). Ultimately, in the statist conception of the nation, state and nation become one. In this effort to impose the constructed national unity, two apparently contradictory strategies have been followed. Either cultural plurality has been negated in the name of national integration, or differences on racial, ethnic, or cultural grounds were reinforced to cover the contradictions arising out of domination, class relations, and class conflicts, the real nature of social struggles, and to maintain specific modes of exploitation.

An instance of an imagined community in the Pacific area is the one variously translated in the formulation of the Pacific Way and the invented traditions that serve to legitimize it. Through them the indigenous élites attempt to attain a monopoly over the formation of the social project and over the drawing of the path of development to be followed by their societies. They have taken for themselves the role of *guides*, of *educators*, of the masses (Gramsci 1973: 5–23). Furthermore, their interests and superordinate positions could be safeguarded by diverting the attention from confrontations on a class basis to the racial and the ethnic. The reluctancy of these populist nationalist ideologies to acknowledge internal contradictions makes for the preservation of forces operating in the neocolonial situation and for the maintenance of the new class-ethnic alliances, with the state mediating to contain the subaltern classes (see, for instance, Fitzpatrick 1980 for Papua New Guinea; Howard 1983a for Vanuatu).

The anticolonial rhetoric that permeates these formulations is not always an indication of a deep commitment to decolonization. On the contrary, it has resulted in an attempt to bend indigenous cultures, modes of thought, organizations, and actions to suit the requirements for capitalist development (see Vusoniwailala 1978) and to control them so they will not endanger the traditional basis of power. Hardly effective in proposing solutions for the current socioeconomic problems the new independent Pacific societies face, the Pacific Way may be called reformist (see Samy 1978: 244). In the end, the stress on "traditional" social organisation and values – seen as unchanging from an ahistorical perspective – sounds similar to the one defended by past colonial policies aimed at maintaining specific structures of power and socioeconomic relations.[5]

Cultural revivalism provides legitimating support to these populist ideologies in the shape of invented traditions. Part of the history and elements of the indigenous cultures is selected and restructured in the political discourse of the élites to call for a broad ethnonational solidarity. The entire culture and history of the societies composing the new nation-state have been censored, purified; ethnicity restored, codified, made immutable, answering to the needs of the codifiers as self-styled "true" spokesmen of their societies. These invented traditions are concerned with establishing a legitimating continuity with the past, not with the understanding of historical discontinuities and the evolution of social contradictions. These new versions of identities and traditions may not – and, one assumes, do not – necessarily coincide with the perceptions, aims, and realities at a grass-roots level.

The Pacific Way constructs the models of ideal brotherhoods that are also imperfect: imagined communities. Eventually, these constructs are prone to be challenged by the alternatives posed by the masses at the objective level of experienced reality translated into the political field.

SCIENTIFIC "TEXTS" ON THE PACIFIC REALITY

Movements for ethnic self-assertion and those of a nationalist character have been evident in the Pacific for many years. This reality in itself is reason enough for a critical reappraisal of the perspectives from which the societies of the area have been studied, usually through the racial or ethnic optics.

The past two decades have witnessed an alost world-wide deluge of writings on a wide range of social phenomena that, because ethnicity is or was thought to be present in them in one way or another, have been clustered together under the same category (for instance, Cohen 1974: ix, xix–xxi). Ethnicity emerged from this feverish activity as an expanding industry and came to permeate the political discourses of modern states (such as the state ideology of multicultural-ism in Australia: see de Lepervanche 1980).

The approaches to race and ethnic relations with origins in the American and British liberal socio-anthropological traditions have been widely used to study the phenomena in central and in peripheral social formations. These approaches have been widely applied to the study of Pacific societies. This is especially true of the culturalist-assimilationist approach, the culture of poverty theory, the reconstructive ethnographical perspective, the psychological approach, and the theory of the plural society and other pluralist models. Of late, the problem has been approached from the Marxist perspective. Elsewhere we also observe the development of a civilizational approach. My feeling is that it is in these last two (related) approaches to ethnicity where new insights are more likely to arise and where theoretical discussions prove to be more fruitful.

More recently, the modes in which ethnicity was studied in the Pacific area became a matter of serious concern among some social scientists. As a follow-up, a critical reappraisal of current approaches began, leading to the undertak-ing of case-studies beyond the limitations of the established anthropological, psychological, and historical perspectives.

The studies on ethnicity in the Anglo-Saxon tradition, prevalent in the Pacific area, usually do not take into account theoretical developments outside this tradition or the discussions on the subject in which third world scholars have engaged for the past 20 years (see Denoon 1985: 119). In this way, the last word on ethnicity for many has been pronounced by Barth (1970). Considered the last watershed, it has originated the informal expression "B.B. and A.B." (before and after Barth), in which the A.B. seems to be final. To Barth, the self-called "New Ethnicists" have been lately added (from Australia; see the critique by Hinton 1981: 14–19).

It is to be noted that, with a few exceptions (for instance, de Lepervanche 1980; Howard 1983b), a critique of the bourgeois social sciences' approach to the subject is absent in the Pacific area, even though more than 20 years have passed since Maquet's (1964) liberal re-evaluation and the denunciation wave of anthropology as a "child of Imperialism" (Gough 1968) that swept the concerned academic world at the end of the '60s. One question this situation raises, and to which there is certainly an answer, is why the critique started so late. Furthermore, the critical reappraisal had already moved by the mid-'70s from the critique of an isolated discipline – anthropology and its colonial nature – to the evaluation of positivist theories in general, including economics and political science, these last the inheritors of anthropology's objects, now in the form of the new states (see Mafeje 1976).

Two important aspects of ethnicity have been largely absent from scholars' concern in the bourgeois tradition. One is that of the *historical conditions* under which ethnicity emerges as a major element for social organisation, solidarity, and conflict. The other, that of ethnicity *as lived by* the people themselves, as an expression of civilizational alternatives, its potential role and strategic value in the process of decolonisation and in the development of a socio-political consciousness among the subordinate sectors of society. Furthermore, maintaining the position of advantage of the observer and his or her illusion of objectivity, studies on ethnic identity and consciousness have been usually done on the basis of the outsider's point of view. Intellectual conceptions of socio-cultural identities have been thus put forward as the actual identities of the societies studied, when in fact they have been externally constructed, mostly on the basis of visible cultural or behavioural elements, or both. This construct of identity and its uses are what some indigenous intellectuals nowadays are denouncing (see Langton 1981: 16).

Traditionally, the Pacific area has been one of the favourite paradises for field-work for Western anthropologists and sometimes the place to test anthropological knowledge at the service of the colonial governments (for instance, Mair 1970: 1; Elkin 1953: x–xi, 141, 153–156). More recently, a new element can be added to the relations between sociological and anthropological knowledge and government administration and policies, that of the funding of research projects by multinationals, such as with Bougainville Copper (see the controversy in *Arena*: Sharp 1975; Mamak 1976). Access to the Pacific field-work paradise has become uncertain because of an increasing awareness and a critical stand of the countries of the area (Keesing 1979: 276; Strathern 1983: 9).

Important aspects of the emergent critique to the approaches for the study of the Pacific societies are beginning to be explored. Attention is being paid, for instance, to the analysis of the nature of colonialism and neocolonialism, to the social and political role of intellectuals as creators or reinforcers of ideology, and to the position of the indigenous élites. In this context, ultimately it is the meaning and scope of decolonization that should be clarified in situations currently defined according to neocolonial relations. Despite the emerging critique and the extent to which decolonization is really taking place and reaching the realm of the social sciences, it is noticeable that some Western academics are finding it hard to stop fulfilling what Owusu, with regards to Africa, calls "the role of unchallenged interpreters and translators...of cultures" (Owusu 1978; see also Onoge 1979: 54). This critique and the process of self-examination in the Pacific is for the moment in the hands of the Western-educated indigenous élite.

The study of the relations into which the Pacific peoples were drawn by the West, marked from their inception by the colonial experience, traditionally has taken as a starting point the concepts of "racial difference" and "culture contact." Ethnicity, of later use, came generally to be restricted to the perception and uses of cultural differences, either among the indigenous peoples themselves or in the relations between the descendants of earlier European immigrants and more recent newcomers (as in the Australian case).

Race and *ethnicity* emerged as conceptual tools divorced from the social totalities of which they were integral parts, masking the realities of colonialism and neocolonialism that profoundly marked the nature of social relationships. Constituted as autonomous subjects, they provided the basis for studies that were fundamentally ahistorical. Race and ethnic relations were seen as developing in situations of hypothetical social balance and controlled equilibrium, favourable to the development of gradual and non-conflictive processes of change, often called "modernisation" or "Westernisation." Thus, conflicts inherent to relations established by force and resistance to domination were rarely considered in their political dimensions. The peoples of the Pacific were usually depicted as passive recipients of externally induced changes. The studies centred their attention on the behavioural and visible cultural aspects of race and ethnicity, on issues of competition for power and resources in an ideal situation of equality. In short, theories of race relations and of ethnicity generally have ignored the colonial and class foundations of conflicts manifested in racial or ethnic terms. This aspect, however, has been treated by the Marxist tradition.

For the general state of the studies in this field of inquiry, Wolpe (1975: 238) already has suggested a corrective: "What is needed is, on the one hand, a description of the ideology and the political practices of the ethnic, racial, and national groups and, on the other, an analysis of how they relate to the mode of production and social formation in which they are located." This line of analysis has been taken up in the last decade by some scholars looking into the Pacific area.

The anthropological traditions developed in the metropolis devoted sizable efforts to the systematic study of the cultural aspects of the subordinated societies. This interest often became enmeshed in the ideological network of scientistic justifications to legitimize domination and the implementation of state policies aimed at consensus or collaboration. Besides, knowledge of the cultural field provided the foundations for the consolidation of assimilation and what was often called cultural transformation (in fact, a process of decultura-tion). Assimilation and deculturation aimed ultimately to neutralise both the actual and possible resistance to domination from indigenous culture, and at the establishment of an all-embracing hegemony. Political, economic, and cultural confrontations were thus deformed under the "culture contact" dis-guise.

The cultural-assimilationist approach totally disregarded the issues of ex-ploitation, the structuring of unequal socioeconomic relationships, and the subordinating role of racist ideologies that underlie the theories of race and ethnic relations (see changes in emphasis in Glazer and Moynihan 1963 and 1976). Usually, in the assimilationist view, the failure of the assimilation theories and corresponding policies have been blamed on the victim (for in-stance, Berndt 1962: 88; Rowley 1971: 17). The focus on assimilation is par-ticularly noticeable in the case of social scientists engaged in "welfare-relevant research" (Elkin 1951; Berndt 1977: 402–11) and those that fulfil the role of government advisors.

The notion of cultural deprivation as derived from Lewis's work and his "cul-ture of poverty" theory have also been used to equate race or ethnic differences to negative social, cultural, and psychological traits. Special racial or ethnic characteristics are detected as prime causes for the problems the subordinate minorities suffer. This perspective has been especially applied to explain the conditions of urban Australian Aborigines (see the uses of "cultural void" and "culture of poverty" in Coombs 1972: 16, 22). A spurious notion of "Aboriginal poverty" is constructed, conceived as a condition inherent to the Aborigines and as a product of their own creation (for instance, in Nurcombe and Moffitt 1973: 130–31). The historical-economic basis for this poverty, Australian socio-economic structure, and, basically, an understanding of the modes of resistance and survival of the Aborigines under extreme conditions of socio-economic oppression are absent from this approach (see Langton's 1981 critique).[6]

Even more dangerous than the negative equations proposed by the culture of poverty theory are the extreme racist analyses on the "race-civilization" correlation (for the Aborigines, see Tatz 1982: 15–16 on E. Perez).

A substantial amount of research on the peoples of the Pacific has been con-ducted on the model of "salvage anthropology," or reconstructive ethnography. The indigenous cultures are seen from this perspective as the broken remnants of past traditions that must be rescued, practically, as museum specimens. From this point of view, a perception of culture as eminently social, created and recreated in everyday life and conditioned by historical circumstances, is bla-tantly absent. The indigenous cultures are supposed to have succumbed under the influence of civilisation and to have been reduced to the category of "tradi-tional remains." Thus, during the first decade and a half of its existence until the mid-'70s, the Australian Institute of Aboriginal Studies devoted itself to a task of "recovery" and "reconstruction" of Aboriginal cultures. The living creators of these cultures did not enter the picture. These cultures were seen as static and the living contemporary Aborigines as being without culture because this was considered to belong to the past (see Rowley 1972: 17; Stanner 1969: 14; AIAS 1965–66: 6–7).

These attempts at the preservation and reconstruction of cultures as dead and unlived remains, isolated from past and present social life, recently have been opposed by indigenous intellectuals (for instance, Simet 1976; see also Current Issues Collective (UPNG) 1979: 565–66).[7]

Ethnocentrism and veiled racism mark the analyses of indigenous societies based on psychological assumptions. Here the equation is race/culture-psychopathology. This approach is exemplified by the views of J. E. Cawte, a psychiatrist interested in the study of Aborigines. He applies to them the term "sick society," defined as "a society that has a high amount of psychiatric disabilities" (Cawte 1973: 365). Not only does this approach fall into the "blame the victim" explanation, but it also follows the trend developed by some political scientists and sociologists of labelling and treating social dissent as a pathological, therefore dangerous, condition. The psychiatric explanation is so coarse and biased that one wonders how it could ever attain the level of scientific knowledge.[8]

In the theory of the plural society, race and ethnicity are given the key roles (Kuper and Smith 1969; Kuper 1974). Although the possible correlation between economic differences and ethnic ascription is acknowledged in this perspective, the pluralist theorists fall back into models based on the assumption of social equilibrium; for instance, the one followed by the modernization school. The theory of the plural society avoids the problem of the structuring of society into classes, of class relations, and minimizes the importance of the economic factor. There is a tendency to reduce racial or ethnic stratification to psychological, institutional, or cultural factors and to neglect the historical dimension of the phenomena.

The central idea of a society divided vertically into ethnic or racial blocs, complementary and interdependent of one another, is one of the characteristics of the still very influential model proposed by Barth. Devoid of any link with the dynamics of the social processes that encompass the ethnic phenomena, this approach stresses adaptation to an established social order and not the possibility of structural changes. In the Pacific area, pluralist approaches based on the assumptions of competition between equals, political incorporation, and parallel interdependence have given rise to the "multicultural approach" and policies, widely favoured in the region.[9]

Until recently, historical studies of the indigenous peoples of the Pacific were scanty. Rowley's works and the publications of academic journals such as *Aboriginal History* initiated a task that a group of young historians have since earnestly pursued. Formerly, the general trend was the production of historical writings as extensions of European history, addressed to Europeans who were also portrayed as the main actors in the accounts of the Pacific's colonial history.

The violence of conquest, the nature of colonialism, and indigenous resistance were carefully downplayed or ignored. Reynolds (1978, 1981) has noted the tendency for a self-imposed censorship among early Australian historians and the more recent conscious decision on the scholar's part to omit the violent nature of conquest and settlement of Australia.

In some cases, the counterpart to the historical amnesia regarding the situation of indigenous peoples of the Pacific was the acknowledgement of their existence in a negative light. They were presented as passive or as conservative elements (by blaming the continuity of "tradition"), and their political movements were misunderstood. Examples of caricature versions of the Pacific peoples are what Nelson (1970: 10) calls "tourist histories" for Papua New Guinea. Ignoring colonialism and the relationships established under it, indigenous resistance has been seen as part of a precolonial pattern of alliances and hostilities, as another manifestation of group oppositions.[10] In this way, anticolonial resistance would be presented as a natural activity of a war-prone people. This view has not totally disappeared and is now applied to current situations.

Efforts to expand the horizons of history encompassing the indigenous peoples and early non-European immigrants have been undertaken by a group of young Australian social scientists (Reynolds 1978, 1981; Loos 1982; Evans, Saunders, and Cronin 1975) who stress the social and political dimensions of Australian history from the times of the colonial invasion. The value of this approach to history lies in its purpose to rescue what has been hidden by colonial historiography. The amnesia of colonial historiography as an ideological weapon for the establishment of hegemony in Australia and the nature of ethnic relations, however, are not discussed at the theoretical level by these historians; their studies remain mostly empirical and area-specific, hindering to a certain extent the opening of a more far-reaching dialogue.

A new path has been opened with the study of oral history in the Melanesian context, showing the modes in which people understand their own history (Denoon and Lacey 1981). All these efforts may contribute to decolonising history, whose urgency had been lately stressed in the Pacific area.

In the Marxist analyses of race relations and ethnicity, class is placed at the centre stage. From this perspective, ethnicity is considered fundamentally a political phenomenon, grounded in the system and relations of production. The reinforcement of racial and ethnic differences is seen as a mechanism for the recreation of hegemony and for the reproduction of socio-economic inequality. Issues such as ethnic struggles reflecting class conflicts, the emergence of ethnicity as a result of colonial policies and practices or related to situations of internal colonialism have been raised within this perspective. Nevertheless, the crucial issue on the whole, namely, the way racial/ethnic differences are structured with class differences, is still the subject of much discussion and further elaboration. In many Marxist studies, a focus on the role of the ethnic/national factor in national liberation movements, on ethnic-based movements for self-determination, or on the strategic role of ethnicity for a development of consciousness and collective action among subaltern sectors is usually marginal.

Although ethnic solidarity is seen in its ideological dimension and not as a natural outcome of socio-cultural differences, ethnicity tends to be seen as an instance of "false consciousness," and its possible revolutionary potential in concrete situations of exploitation and domination is not considered. In this line, for the Pacific area and mainly from the academic centres in Australia, the reaction to the bourgeois sociological approaches has been to produce highly economistic analyses that leave ethnicity unexplained. This has led to very superficial and mechanical equations as, for example, interests of the Aborigines with those of the Australian working class (Middleton 1977, cf. Jennett 1983).

While accounting for aspects of class structure and class relations, ethnic identity and conflict in the Marxist approach sometimes remain unsatisfactorily explained as a vague superstructural phenomenon, as a creation of the ruling classes to exert domination that is thought to be readily accepted by the subaltern sectors (for instance, de Lepervanche 1980; Jakubowicz 1981). What is to be accounted for is the way in which class experiences are expressed in cultural terms in specific historical circumstances (Thompson 1968: 10) and how economic and cultural struggles are linked in a combined effort to attain socioeconomic and cultural integrity.

Exploring class and ethnic relations that resulted from the imperialist expansion, some recent studies have focused on the ideologies of ethnicity or nationalism as representing the interests of the indigenous bourgeoisie, as ideologies to mobilize mass support for the sake of the capitalist class. Fitzpatrick's (1980) study on the emergence of capitalist relations and the preservation of traditional modes in Papua New Guinea identifies race as a fundamental ideological category in the colonial context. He subordinates racial and ethnic divisions to class, very much in Wolpe's line. By examining the contents of Papua New Guinea's populist ideology, he shows the distortions in the project for decolonization as sponsored by the national bourgeoisie in its efforts to redraw its links with the metropolitan bourgeoisie. This perspective, by centring on the role of the state and the nature of the indigenous bourgeoisie, tends to highlight ethnicity as an ideological instrument of control and manipulation. We come to know less about the mass of the people that somehow appear only as objectives of these manipulations.

Out of the conceptualisation of underdevelopment by A. Gunder Frank and the writings of P. Gonzalez Casanova (1965) and R. Stavenhagen (1965) emerged the notion of internal colonialism in its application to the situation of subordinate ethnic groups. The internal colonialism thesis has been used lately to explain the structural position of the Aborigines in Australia and to disclose the roots of underdevelopment (for instance, Hartwig 1978; Jennett 1983;

Beckett 1982). While the internal colonialism thesis acknowledges the class nature of the oppression of subordinate ethnic groups, it emphasises the colonial nature of this oppression. Wolpe (1975) has criticized it on the grounds that it treats class relations as residual. In a way, the internal colonialism thesis tends to stress again, although from a different theoretical perspective, the primacy of racial or ethnic categories.

New important developments for the analysis of the situation in the Pacific have been taking place in the field of political economy (for instance, Howard, et al. 1983), e.g., looking into aspects of unequal development.

The civilisational approach remains to be considered; it was mostly developed in Latin America and Africa and specifically addressed to the realities of the present non-Western societies. Ethnicity is seen from this perspective as an expression of civilisational alternatives, based on a people's awareness of the historical depth of their collective socio-cultural style. In this light, the existence of a collective consciousness phrased in ethnic, cultural, or national terms implies the possibility of exercising a political will to develop a true process of decolonisation. Decolonisation is thus understood as a civilisational process (Abdel-Malek 1981: 20–21). This approach emphasises the political dimension, the liberationist aspect, of ethnicity, not only as a strategy for political mobilization, but also as a means to enhance social consciousness and to forge new alternative historical projects. It views conflicts expressed in ethnic terms in their full meaning, as confrontations against economic and socio-cultural domination.

This perspective developed from the dissatisfaction felt with both extremes in the spectrum of ways of comprehending ethnicity: the culturalist perspective that maintains the autonomy of ethnicity and the mechanical economistic reductionism in some variants of Marxism.

Central to this approach is the emphasis on the colonial and neocolonial contradictions between non-Western ethnonational formations and the West (see Bonfil Batalla 1981: 36). At the base of this mode of approaching ethnicity one finds the idea of scholars such as Abdel-Malek (1981) and Darcy Ribeiro (1968, 1984) with echoes of Cabral's thought.

The definition of "civilisation" is one of the axes in this perspective. Abdel-Malek places the driving forces behind the political transformations in the present world in the non-Western social formations where combined processes of renaissance and national liberation movements have taken the shape of "an explicitly civilizational process." Focusing on Latin America, Darcy Ribeiro considers combined ethnic and class demands as a possible channel to develop wars of liberation, as it happens, for instance, in Guatemala (Ribeiro 1984: 28–29). For Ribeiro, ethnic formations are "operative units of the civilizational process" (Ribeiro 1968). He gives a central role to what he calls the Emerging Peoples (*Pueblos Emergentes*) in the forging of a new society. The Emerging Peoples correspond to the historico-cultural configurations of the oppressed national ethnic groups who are presently "stressing their ethnic and cultural profiles as national minorities . . . aiming at self-determination" (1984: 28). However, as Stavenhagen points out, in the case of Latin America there is not a single unified indigenous movement, but instead "an emerging social movement and an incipient ideology based on ethnic criteria" (Stavenhagen 1984: 201).

The civilisational approach has been criticized from the economistic perspective. These criticisms have come from social scientists who share a basic Marxist perspective with the exponents of the civilisational approach, but who obviously phrase the problem differently. The criticisms tend to refer to a weak treatment of the insertion of the new indigenous movements in the class structure specific to each nation-state (Medina 1983: 6), to the idealisation of the "ethnic essence" and the drive to a "return to the sources" (Ortega Hegg, Velez, Boege 1983: 59–60), and to the emphasis on the confrontation of ethnonational groups with the West as a basic contradiction (ibid. and Guerrero 1983: 46). However, in this approach, the forms of class articulation of the indigenous populations with other sectors of the society, the articulation of different modes of production with the capitalist mode in contexts where the ethnic factor is present, and the role of the state have been neglected. It is possibly in Varese's works that one finds the more promising theoretical insights in this approach, especially on the crucial issue of class and ethnic consciousness (for instance, in Varese 1979).

This approach is not present in the Pacific area, although some similar incipient elements may be found, mostly among the indigenous intellectuals.

With a critique of the theories of assimilation, modernisation and development and their corresponding policies, some indigenous intellectuals have centred their attention on the indigenous cultures as operating in the specific social, economic, and political contexts. Art, oral tradition, new literary forms, indigenous social organisation, and modes of thought are some of the axes around which the problematic of identity and socio-political consciousness revolves (for instance, Waiko 1981). This interest in culture should not be mistaken for the classical ethnographical pursuits that centred on the material expressions and external marks of collective identification. The aspect of the historical depth of the indigenous societies is also beginning to be taken up as a major issue. Thus, Jojoga (1978: 91) has concentrated on oral history and on the role of the Papua New Guineans' awareness of their own past as a basis for their society's strength and continuity.

An evaluation of the civilisational dimension may be emerging among the Australian Aboriginal intelligentsia. It is precisely the continuity and stability of civilisational patterns that are seen as giving sense to Aboriginality as a collective identity. Continuity of Aboriginality also means dynamism because this identity is maintained and recreated in daily life (Langton 1981: 21). Nevertheless, Aboriginality in the hands of the Aboriginal élite may result in the construct of another imagined community based on an idealist horizontal brotherhood. Class issues, for instance – and importantly – are not integrated into these analyses because the category of class is rejected as a "European notion." The abstraction of Aboriginal reality in this way leads to its being conceived as restricted to the symbolic-cultural world and divorced from the global economic and political context. Another distortion of the civilisational perspective is provided by C. Tatz (1982), who ends up stressing social accommodation without questioning the basic conditions in which Aborigines live in Australia and offering proposals for the state's policy planners.

A last point should be made in relation to the current discussion in the Pacific area on the role of the indigenous intellectuals. A strong emphasis now exists on the need of the local social scientists to study their own societies, villages, and communities of origin. This attitude varies greatly in its content.[11]

A strong defence of the "insider research" has emerged as a way to counterbalance the viewpoints of Western scholars and as an inroad into their monopoly over research in the area. Taken to its extreme, such "insider research" at the microlevel of one's own community may preclude the development of macrosociological analysis and reproduce the errors of the ethnographic tradition. But it may also favour the development of social science as social practice when the intellectuals work in direct contact with their communities as a process for their – the researchers' – conscientisation.

This position had stretched to a stand that defends the indigenous intellectuals' monopoly of research by using misleading euphemisms such as "foreign" or "white social scientists" vs. "local " researchers. Though the indigenous intellectuals should engage in the rewriting of their history and in decolonising social science, the questions asked by the Current Issues Collective of the University of Papua New Guinea still hang in the air: "Is it indigenous anthropology or elite indigenous anthropology [that we are talking about]?... Who benefits from the results...?" (Current Issues Collective [UPNG] 1979: 567–68; see also Howard 1982: 159–83 on the co-optation of the Aboriginal intelligentsia.) The labels of "foreign" or "white" social science do not help to advance the critique, to look at the real nature of the relations between social science and ideology, and to criticize the theoretical assumptions and the ideological distortions that the bourgeois approaches in social science have produced. This extreme view shows the extent to which the visualization of confrontations in ethnic or racial terms permeates even the evaluation of theories and ideologies.

CONCLUSION

It is only at certain points in the history of a society and in different forms that ethnicity is asserted explicitly, though in practice it has been "lived" and "used" all the time. The conditions under which ethnicity emerges as a major element for political mobilisation should be studied by looking at specific cases. Broadly, we may argue that when class conflicts are diverted to confrontations at other levels (for instance, "locals" vs. "outsiders"), or where the development of large class-based movements encounter great obstacles, ethnicity may act as a factor of unity *at one moment* of the political struggle. However, there is *no absolute practice of ethnicity*. Ethnicity is neither revolutionary nor conservative in itself. The role played by the ethnic factor in politics will closely depend on the class situation and the interests of those sectors resorting to it to reinforce their ideological discourses and practical actions. The political formulation of ethnicity is not developed by the entire ethnic community as a bloc because this is not a homogenous entity in class terms. Thus, the actions of the different sectors of the community would be guided by different interests, based on the existence of structural class links as they are present in the society as a whole.

Looking at the problem in this way, the role that ethnic identity and consciousness play in everyday life in general and in the political realm in particular leads to a series of propositions:

1. At the level of the historical processes, it is important to clarify under what historical conditions cultural differences are stressed and become one of the bases of political action.
2. At the level of the global social system, the specific patterns of domination as translated in interethnic relations and the way in which ethnic and class differences are structured should be disclosed.
3. At the political level, the process of formation of an ethnic consciousness needs to be decoded and its role in impairing or favouring the formation of a class consciousness considered.

For oppositional grass-roots politics, ethnicity can provide a strategic axis for mobilisation against inequality and domination, engineered towards aims not limited to the economic *alone*. They will instead attempt to embrace realms of the social reality that have been subordinated by the mechanisms of formal politics to economic imperatives and to the "higher" goals of a sectorial "national interest." When appealing to their collective historico-cultural identity, the subaltern sectors are forging a new political language, expressing their concerns and views on the issues of culture and deculturation, self-respect, self-determination, the right to cultural and linguistic specificity, their views on the unequal nature of existing socioeconomic relationships; they are also stressing their will to participate actively in politics. This participation is often sought outside the existing structures through a process of redefinition of the contents of politics, standing against the inequalities present in the society at large and as specifically lived, the authoritarianism of the state, and the hegemonic attempts of the ruling sectors. These experiences and struggles provide a first and more immediate level of awareness.

Class consciousness thus develops out of the collectively experienced everyday reality and in the course of action. For those involved, class more often than not is not subject to a process of translation into abstract discourses. Class is lived as a process and "handled in cultural terms" in many different ways (see Thompson 1968: 10–12, 149–150). Oppression also is not perceived in the abstract. What flesh-and-bone people experience are concrete realities such as land alienation, rural indebtedness, inadequate wages, or the inhuman time-work discipline for the sake of increased production. Their demands will globally express a defence of basic human rights and needs.

In this context, the coalescence of class exploitation and ethnic/national subordination has usually resulted in an explosive combination. In the era of national liberation movements and decolonisation, nonclass identities – ethnicity among them – have played an important role in popular political mobilisation given the added strength they provide to mass solidarity. In these struggles, existing contradictions expressed in ethnic, regional, linguistic, and class antagonisms are being acknowledged with a holistic perspective that embraces the social, the economic, and the cultural.

Those extra non-class elements in the crucible that express class in cultural terms may make the subaltern sectors more successfully impervious to the social and moral hegemony of the dominant classes, thus enabling them to develop alternative views about the society at large and the future. These alternative views can come together into a potentially radical culture of resistance.

My hyphotheses are that, in specific situations of subordination, ethnicity may provide the foundations for the emergence of a consciousness of opposition, expressed in counterhegemonic practices; that this consciousness entails an acknowledgement of the real nature of interethnic relationships, often accompanied by an acute perception of class differences and antagonisms; and that, at the practical level, ethnicity may provide the subaltern sectors with a strategy to combat inequality and to negate forms of domination.

NOTES

1. For instance, between Australia and Papua New Guinea; the United States and Micronesia; France and Tahiti and New Caledonia.
2. "Deculturation" refers to processes usually concealed under the labels of "modernisation," "Westernisation," and "acculturation," entailing the obliteration or distortion of a society's culture and promoting its replacement by the culture of the dominator (see Ribeiro 1968).
3. With reference to Melanesia, for instance, Bugotu remarks: "The psychology of neo-colonialism is disguised and often silent. . . . In a period of decolonisation in a country, a new spirit of colonisation is usually born disguised, to excuse the existence of colonial and paternalistic attitudes" (1975: 77).
4. The idea of a consciousness of historical permanence is used here following Abdel-Malek's notion of depth of the historical field when he discusses the time dimension as a "component part of the patterns of social maintenance" through historical

evolution as "culture and though revolving around the relation of man with the time dimension . . . express the sum total of social maintenance, the *global depth reality*, the achievements, the balance sheet as well as the prospective potentials of a given society" (1981: 171. Italics in the original).

5. Hobsbawn and Ranger (1983: 266) point out in this respect:

The traditionalism of peasants . . . was constantly praised by nineteenth century conservatives as the ideal model of the subject's political comportment. . . . A "modernisation" that maintained the old ordering of social subordination . . . was not theoretically inconceivable, but . . . it is difficult to think of an example of practical success. And it may be suggested that such attempts to update the social bonds of a traditional order implied a demotion of social hierarchy, a strengthening of the subject's direct bonds to the central ruler who . . . increasingly came to represent a new kind of state.

6. In her critique of the application of this theory to urban Aborigines, Langton (1981: 18–19) remarks: "Poverty in its Western meaning is not a traditional Aboriginal condition. . . . Aboriginal poverty is inevitably regarded by Aborigines as a condition enforced upon them by the European system. . . . The maintenance of Aboriginality in these socioeconomic conditions provides not only a security against a hostile world, but as well, a 'sane' way of negotiating the demands of an 'insane' society."

7. For Papua New Guinea, Jacob Simet stresses that Tolai art is "a *living thing* responding to each new situation" and opposes "preservation by whatever means . . . [which] may produce a Tolai art that will have lost its profundity" (1976: 1. Italics added).

8. See also studies on the relations between cultural identity and mental health such as Bianchi, Cawte, and Kiloh (1973: 309–19).

9. For example, the perspective of Naidu (1975: 132–38) for the South Pacific islands and Zubrzycki (1976) and Martin (1978) on migrants in Australia. An instance of the use of Barth's model for the Australian Aborigines is Jones and Hill-Burnett's (1982: 214–46) study. Brookfield (1972: 146–58) has applied the concept of "cultural pluralism" to Melanesia.

10. Some of these studies were produced at the same time anthropological approaches using similar arguments were being thoroughly criticized, mostly in their application to Africa (for instance, see Onoge 1977: 35).

11. Hau'ofa visualises in the ideal position that the local scientist enjoys in practical terms the possibility of "extricating the discipline [anthropology] from the taint of imperialism and exploitation," and calls for the development of local anthropologists' "intuitive knowledge and built-in 'feel' for the subtleties of their cultures and of their human relationships" (1975: 288).

REFERENCES

Abdel-Malek, A. 1966. L'Orientalisme en crise. *Diogene* 44: 109–42

———. 1981. *Social dialectics*. London: Macmillan.

AIAS. 1965–66. *Annual report*. Canberra: Australian Institute of Aboriginal Studies.

Anderson, B. 1983. *Imagined communities: Reflections on the origin and spread of nationalism*. London: Verso.

Barth, F., ed. 1970. *Ethnic groups and boundaries*. Boston: Little, Brown.

Beckett, J. 1982. The Torres Strait Islanders and the pearling industry: A case of internal colonialism. In *Aboriginal power in Australian society*, edited by M. C. Howard, 131–58. St. Lucia: University of Queensland Press/Honolulu: University of Hawaii Press.

Berndt, C. 1962. Mateship or success: An assimilation dilemma. *Oceania* 33(2): 71–89.

———. 1977. Out of the frying-pan . . . ? or, back to square one? In *Aborigines and change. Australia in the 70's*, edited by R. M. Berndt, 402–12. Canberra: Australian Institute of Aboriginal Studies.

Bianchi, G. S., J. E. Cawte, and L. G. Kiloh. 1973. Cultural identity and mental health. In *The psychology of Aboriginal Australians*, edited by G. E. Kearney et al., 309–19. Sydney: J. Wiley and Sons.

Bonfil Batalla, G. 1981. *Utopia y revolución: El pensamiento político contemporáneo de los Indios en America Latina*. Mexico: Nueva Imagen.

Brookfield, H. C. 1972. *Colonialism, development and independence: The case of the Melanesian Islands in the South Pacific*. Cambridge: Cambridge University Press.

Bugotu, F. 1975. Decolonising and recolonising: The case of the Solomons. In *The Pacific Way*, edited by S. Tupouniua, R. Crocombe, and C. Slatter, 77–80. Suva: South Pacific Social Sciences Association.

Cawte, J. E. 1973. A sick society. In *The psychology of Aboriginal Australians*, edited by G. E. Kearney et al., 365–79. Sydney: John Wiley and Sons.

Cohen, A. 1974. The lesson of ethnicity. In *Urban ethnicity*, edited by A. Cohen, ix–xxv. London: Tavistock.

Coombs, H. C. 1972. *The future of the Australian Aboriginal*. Sydney: Sydney University Press.

Current Issues Collective (UPNG). 1979. Comments (to L. Morauta). *Current Anthropology* 20(3): 561–76.

de Lepervanche, M. 1980. From race to ethnicity. *The Australian and New Zealand Journal of Sociology* 16(1): 24–37.

Denoon, D. 1985. Capitalism in Papua New Guinea. *The Journal of Pacific History* 20(3): 119–34.

Denoon. D., and R. Lacey, eds. 1981. *Oral tradition in Melanesia*. Port Moresby: University of Papua New Guinea and Institute of PNG Studies.

Documentos de la Segunda Reunión de Barbados. 1979. *Indianidad y descolonización en America Latina*. Mexico: Nueva Imagen.

Elkin, A. P. 1951. Reaction and interaction: A food gathering people and European settlement in Australia. *American Anthropologist* 53: 164–86.

———. 1953. *Social anthropology in Melanesia: A review of research*. London: Oxford University Press.

Evans, R., K. Saunders, and K. Cronin. 1975. *Exclusion, exploitation and extermination: Race relations in colonial Queensland*. Sydney: ANZ Book Co.

Fitzpatrick, P. 1980. *Law and state in Papua New Guinea*. London: Academic Press.

Glazer, N., and D. Moynihan. 1963. *Beyond the melting pot*. Cambridge: MIT Press.

———., eds. 1976. *Ethnicity: Theory and experience*. Cambridge: Harvard University Press.

Gonzalez Casanova, P. 1965. Internal colonialism and national development. *Studies in Comparative International Development* 1: 27–37.

Gough, K. 1968. New proposals for anthropologists. *Current Anthropology* 9: 403–7.

Gramsci, A. 1973. *Selections from the prison notebooks of Antonio Gramsci*, edited and translated by Q. Hoare and G. N. Smith. London: Lawrence and Wishart.

Guerrero, F. J. 1983. El anticapitalismo reaccionario en antropología. *Nueva Antropología* 5(2): 31–35.

Hartwig, M. 1978. Capitalism and Aborigines: The theory of internal colonialism and its rivals. In *Essays in the political economy of Australian capitalism*, edited by E. Wheelright and K. Buckley, vol. 3: 119–41. Sydney: ANZ Book Co.

Hau'ofa, E. 1975. Anthropology and the Pacific Islanders. *Oceania* 45(4): 283–89.

Hinton, P. 1981. Where have the New Ethnicists gone wrong? *Australian and New Zealand Journal of Sociology* 17(3): 14–19.

Hobsbawn, E., and T. Ranger, eds. 1983. *The invention of traditions*. St. Albans: Paladin.

Howard, M. C. 1982. Aboriginal brokerage and political development in south-western Australia. In *Aboriginal power in Australian society*, edited by M. C. Howard, 159–83. St. Lucia: University of Queensland Press/Honolulu: University of Hawaii Press.

———. 1983a. Vanuatu: The myth of Melanesian Socialism. *Labour, Capital and Society* 16(2): 176–203.

———. 1983b. A preliminary survey of anthropology and sociology in the South Pacific. *The Journal of Pacific Studies* 9: 70–132.

Howard, M. C., et al. 1983. *The political economy of the South Pacific*. Townsville: James Cook University.

Jakubowicz, A. 1981. State and ethnicity: Multiculturalism as ideology. *Australia and New Zealand Journal of Sociology* 17(3): 4–13.

Jennett, C. 1983. Aborigines, land rights and mining. In *Essays in the political economy of Australian capitalism*, edited by E. Wheelright and K. Buckely, vol. 5: 119–44. Sydney: ANZ Book Co.

Jojoga, O. 1978. Some suggestions for promoting equilibrium in South Pacific research. In *Paradise postponed*, edited by A. Mamak and G. McCall, 90–94. Rushcutters Bay: Pergamon.

Jones, D., and J. Hill-Burnett. 1982. The Political context of ethnogenesis: An Australian example. In *Aboriginal power in Australian society*, edited by M. C. Howard, 214–46. St. Lucia: University of Queensland Press/Honolulu: University of Hawaii Press.

Keesing, R. 1979. Anthropology in Melanesia: Retrospect and prospect. In *The politics of anthropology*, edited by G. Huizer and B. Manheim, 276–80. Paris/The Hague: Mouton.

Kuper, L. 1974. *Race, class and power*. London: Duckworth.

Kuper, L., and M. G. Smith, eds. 1969. *Pluralism in Africa*. Berkeley: University of California Press.

Langton, M. 1981. Urbanising Aborigines: The social scientists' great deception. *Social Alternatives* 2(2): 16–22.

Loos, N. 1982. *Invasion and resistance: Aboriginal European relations on the North Queensland frontier 1861–1897*. Canberra: Australian National University Press.

Mafeje, A. 1971. The ideology of tribalism. *The Journal of Modern African Studies* 9(2): 253–61.

———. 1976. The problem of anthropology in historical perspective: An inquiry into the growth of the social sciences. *Canadian Journal of African Studies* 10(2): 307–33.

Mair, L. 1970. *Australia in New Guinea*. Melbourne: Melbourne University Press.

Mamak, A. 1976. Bougainville researchers: Hired but independent. *Arena* 41: 92–94.

Maquet, J. J. 1964. Objectivity in anthropology. *Current Anthropology* 5: 47–55.

Martin, J. I. 1978. *The migrant presence.* Sydney: Allen & Unwin.

Medina, A. 1983. Los grupos étnicos y los sistemas tradicionales de poder en México. *Nueva Antropología* 5(20): 5–29.

Middleton, H. 1977. *But now we want the land back: A history of the Australian Aboriginal people.* Sydney: New Age.

Naidu, V. 1975. Tribes or nations? How to build effective bridges between different ethnic groups. In *The Pacific Way,* edited by M. Tupouniua et al. 132–38. Suva: South Pacific Social Science Association.

Nelson, H. N. 1970. New Guinea nationalism and the writing of history. *Journal of the Papua and New Guinea Society* 4(2): 7–26.

Nurcombe, B., and P. Moffitt. 1973. Cultural deprivation and language deficit. In *The psychology of Aboriginal Australians,* edited by G. Kearney et al., 127–36. Sydney: John Wiley and Sons.

Onoge, O. 1977. Revolutionary imperatives in African sociology. In *African social studies,* edited by P. C. Gutkind and P. Waterman, 32–43. London: Heinemann.

———. 1979. The counterrevolutionary tradition in African studies: The case of applied anthropology. In *The politics of anthropology,* edited by G. Huizer and B. Manheim, 45–66. Paris/The Hague: Mouton.

Ortega Hegg, M., J. Velez, and E. Boege. 1983. El conflicto étnica-nación en Nicaragua. *Nueva Antropología* 5(20): 53–66.

Owusu, M. 1978. Ethnography of Africa: The usefulness of the useless. *American Anthropologist* 80: 310–34.

Reynolds, H. 1978. *Race relations in North Queensland.* Townsville: James Cook University.

———. 1981. *The other side of the frontier.* Townsville: James Cook University.

Ribeiro, D. 1968. *The civilisational process.* Washington, D.C.: Smithsonian Institution Press.

———. 1984. La civilización emergente. *Nueva Sociedad* 73: 36–37.

Rowley, C. D. 1971. *Outcasts in White Australia: Aboriginal policy and practice.* Canberra: Australian National University Press.

———. 1972. *The remote Aborigines.* Canberra: Australian National University Press.

Said, E. 1978. *Orientalism.* New York: Vintage Books.

Samy, J. 1978. Session on theory and methods. In *Paradise postponed,* edited by A. Mamak and G. McCall, 241–44. Rushcutters Bay: Pergamon.

Sharp, N. 1975. Bougainville Copper. *Arena* 38: 3–6.

Simet, J. 1976. From a letter by Jacob Simet. *Gigibor* 3(1): 1–2.

Stanner, W. E. 1969. *After the dreaming.* Sydney: ABC.

Stavenhagen, R. 1965. Classes, colonialism, and acculturation. *Studies in Comparative International Development* 1: 53–77.

1984. Los movimientos étnicos indígenas y el estado nacional en America Latina. *Civilización* 2: 181–204.

Strathern A. 1983. Research in Papua New Guinea: Cross-currents of conflict. *RAIN* 58: 4–10.

Tatz, C. 1982. *Aborigines and uranium and other essays.* Richmond: Heinemann Educational Australia.

Thompson, E. P. 1968. *The making of the English working class.* Middlesex: Penguin.

Turner, V. 1969. *The ritual process: Structure and anti-structure*. Middlesex: Penguin.

Varese, S. 1978. *El falso estado: Hipótesis sobre la multiethnicidad en Peru y México*. Oaxaca: INAH (mimeo).

————. 1979. Estrategia etnica o estrategia de clase? In Documentos de la Segunda Reunión de Barbados, *Indianidad y descolonización en America Latina*, 357–72. México: Nueva Imagen.

Vusoniwailala, L. 1978. Communicating a Pacific model for human development. In *Paradise postponed*, edited by A. Mamak and G. McCall, 115–25. Rushcutters Bay: Pergamon.

Waiko, J. 1981. Binandere oral tradition: Sources and problems. In *Oral tradition in Melanesia*, edited by D. Denoon and H. Lacey, 11–30. Boroko: University of Papua New Guinea and the Insitute of PNG Studies.

Williams, R. 1978. *Marxism and literature*. Oxford: Oxford University Press.

Wolfers, E. P. 1975. *Race relations and colonial rule in Papua New Guinea*. Sydney: ANZ Book Co.

Wolpe, H. 1975. The theory of internal colonialism: The South African case. In *Beyond the sociology of development*, edited by I. Oxaal et al., 229–52. London: Routledge and Kegan Paul.

Zubrzycki, J. 1976. Cultural pluralism and discrimination in Australia with special reference to white minority groups. In *Case studies on human rights and fundamental freedoms*, edited by W. A. Veehoven, vol. 3: 397–434. The Hague: M. Nijhoff.

3

Ho'omauke Ea O Ka Lahui Hawai'i: The Perpetuation of the Hawaiian People

DAVIANNA POMAIKA MCGREGOR

Ka Lahui Ka Po'e Hawai'i, the indigenous Hawaiian people of Hawaii, comprised 19 per cent of Hawaii's population in 1980. Of the 175,000 Hawaiians in Hawaii, only 9,366 are pure Hawaiian (Kanahele 1981: 1–2).

Despite being the original inhabitants of Hawaii, Hawaiians earn low incomes that are comparable to the most recently arrived immigrant groups, hold low-status jobs, and have the highest rate of unemployment of all the ethnic groups in the islands. In contrast, many of the descendants of Caucasian, Japanese, Chinese, and Korean immigrants earn high incomes and hold a greater portion of the managerial and professional jobs in Hawaii. A significant portion of the native Hawaiians (35 per cent) earn incomes insufficient to provide for their large families and so receive public assistance to supplement their incomes or depend entirely on welfare to meet their day-to-day needs. Thus, though comprising only 19 per cent of the population, Hawaiians make up 40 per cent of all the welfare recipients in Hawaii (Kanahele 1982: 31–36).

Hawaiians have the lowest life expectancy among the ethnic groups in Hawaii, 67.6 years, compared with 73 years for Caucasians, 77 for Japanese, 72 for Filipinos, and 76 for Chinese. Hawaiians suffer the highest incidence of hypertension and diabetes and the second highest incidence of heart disease, arthritis, and visual impairment.

Twelve per cent of Hawaiian youth from 18 to 24 have not completed high school and about half of the Hawaiian adults over 25 have not completed high school. Only 10 per cent of the Hawaiian students that are expected to apply for admission to the four-year baccalaureate state colleges actually apply. Most post-high-school education is pursued in vocational fields of training, where 12.4 per cent of the Hawaiians expected to apply at the two-year vocational colleges actually apply (Bishop Estate 1983: 37–38; Kanahele 1982:15).

About 39 per cent of the adult inmate population and 60 per cent of the youth in correctional facilities have Hawaiian ancestry.

A survey of the needs of the Hawaiian community conducted in 1976 by the non-profit Hawaiian corporation Alu Like (1976) concluded the following:

Different categories of the population have different problems. The urban higher-income group, both men and women, lack adequate educational preparation for the better jobs that they want. One-third report a desire for housing that they cannot afford. The lower-income urban group suffers from joblessness and insufficient supply of low-cost housing in the urban areas and consequent doubling-up of families. The rural group suffers from lack of job opportunities, limited range of job choices, and, particularly on Oahu, a steady loss of access to natural resources.

Hawaiians in all groups frequently report loss of pride and bitterness resulting from the historic loss of their family lands and their homeland.

Clearly, Hawaiians in Hawaii today are alienated from the social system and the political power structure that rules Hawaii. Hawaiians fall into the lowest levels of Hawaii's ethnically stratified political economy.

EXPERIENCES COMMON TO INDIGENOUS MINORITY PEOPLES

Hawaiians comprise an indigenous minority people of the United States, an indigenous minority being a people who lived in a self-sufficient sovereign prefeudal community, such as a tribe or clan system, that comprised a stable grouping of people that evolved over a historical period sharing common ancestry, economic life, culture, religion, language, and territory (see Institute of Marxism-Leninism 1977; Grigulevich and Kazlov 1981). Their process of development and cohesion into a modern nation was distorted and terminated by the encroachment and envelopment by a surrounding settler community that, through colonization and conquest, absorbed the indigenous minority people into the settler nation.

Indigenous minorities who have maintained their cohesion as a people as reflected in an identifiable land base and the perpetuation of culture, language, religion, and distinct economic activities still retain specific sovereign rights and privileges as the original inhabitants and protectors of the land.

These rights include, but are not limited to, the right to have sovereign control over their land base; the right to practise and perpetuate the speaking and transmission of their language, cultural practices, and values, including their religion; and the right to exist side-by-side with the broader society on the basis of equality. An indigenous minority people should also be provided equal access to opportunities available in the broader society – e.g., to acquire education, health care, justice, jobs, transportation, food, clothing, and shelter – upon their sovereign land base, such as reservations and reserves, or when they assimilate into the broader society. In most cases, however, because of the

historic injustices perpetrated on indigenous peoples by the broader society
through colonization and conquest, special access to these basic human needs
for survival, over and above what is equally available to members of the
dominant society, needs to be provided. This is necessary to make up for
centuries of exclusion and abuse of indigenous minorities, ranging from policies
of genocide and extermination of Aboriginal Australians and American Indians
to policies of concentration and isolation from the broader society on reserves
and reservations and of gradual assimilation and systematic suppression of the
indigenous language and culture through Christianity and the educational
system.

Indigenous people do not compose homogeneous groupings. Over the years,
large portions of these peoples have been forced to assimilate into the broader
society while a core group has remained behind on the ancestral land base and
maintained a continuous link in their traditional land customs, practices, and
language.

Those who have been forced to assimilate are usually tracked into the lowest
strata of the society's working class. In this context, the indigenous peoples cut
off from their traditional land base exist and reproduce as ethnic minority
sectors of the working class. They live in urban ghettos or in economically
depressed outskirts of metropolitan centres and serve as a reserve pool of labour
swelling the ranks of the unemployed that are last hired and first fired on an
intermittent basis. As such, the class oppression of the lowest strata of the
working class influences the working class members of that indigenous
community. They also bump up against institutional policies in the school
system, health care delivery, criminal justice, and employment that
discriminate against racial and ethnic minorities.

The existence of a core of the indigenous people on the ancestral rural lands
up through the 20th century has provided the basis for the culture to survive. It
is there that the indigenous minority group has been able to reproduce itself
from one generation to the next in a unique and distinct cultural context and to
provide for the group's perpetuation as a distinct people. This ancestral land
base provides a refuge and a retreat for the alienated urban group and serves as
an important cultural and ancestral point of reference for them.

What is of utmost significance is that, despite decades of colonisation
and abuse by large settler states and societies, indigenous minorities have
persevered and continue to exist as distinct and unique peoples. They have
survived the so-called fatal impact despite projections of total extinction and in
many cases are reproducing in ever-increasing numbers. Moreover, their
cultures have survived, although in somewhat battered form, through the
contemporary generation, which usually is taking positive steps to maintain and
perpetuate it.

Their existence demands a recognition from the governments of the settler
societies of the special sovereignty rights of indigenous peoples. These demands

are based on historical treaties, agreements, and recognised claims between the ancestors of the indigenous peoples and the founders of the settler states. They are also based on the rights of the indigenous peoples to their land established through centuries of time. As the settler states attempt to encroach further, through mining, ranching, hotels, and resorts or other developments, on indigenous peoples' land rights and extinguish their sovereignty rights over land and natural resources, indigenous rights and claims are being more militantly asserted and defined.

Without doubt, the survival and perpetuation of indigenous minority peoples and their cultures is integrally linked to the question of political sovereignty. To the degree that an indigenous people exercises sovereignty over its land base and the resources of that land base, that group can mobilise those resources to provide for the welfare of its people. Moreover, to the degree that these sovereignty rights are acknowledged, the basis is created for negotiations and transactions to be conducted between the indigenous people and the broader society on a basis of equality. Survival and perpetuation also requires the internal political organisation of the indigenous people, whereby each member of the group is empowered to take part in decisions affecting the group's future.

HAWAIIANS AS AN INDIGENOUS PEOPLE

Hawaiians in Hawaii were transformed from an independent, sovereign people into an indigenous minority people of the United States over a century of contact and settlement by Americans and Europeans.

Before European and American contact, more than a quarter-million Hawaiians lived in Hawaii, and a class of chiefs controlled all the land and resources there. Their claim to the land was based on their ancestral ties to the Hawaiian gods, who represented different life forces of nature. There was no one paramount chief. The chiefs granted parcels of land to commoners to live on and work collectively as 'ohana, or an extended family (Handy, Handy, and Pukui 1972).

Within the 'ohana, the primary unit of production work was collectively and co-operatively organised and the fruits of this labour were also shared. Fishing and cultivation of taro made up the centre-piece of the material culture. The system of irrigation, fishing, and aquaculture was highly developed and produced a surplus that sustained a sophisticated and unified social structure embracing the whole archipelago by the 12th century (Kirch 1985). Nevertheless, Hawaiian society was based on a subsistence agricultural economy. There is no evidence of a money system or commodity production, although a system of barter in essential goods between fishermen, mountain dwellers, and taro cultivators existed within the framework of the 'ohana. In the main, this exchange within the 'ohana functioned more as a sharing of what had been produced on the *ili*, or extensive land grant, that the *'ohana* held and worked on in common. Mary Kawena Pukui and E. S. Graighill Handy describe this in *The Polynesian Family System in Ka'u, Hawaii* as follows.

Between households within the "ohana" there was constant sharing and exchange of foods and of utilitarian articles and also of services not in barter but as voluntary (though decidedly obligatory) giving. Ohana living inland (ko kila uka) raising taro, bananas, wauke (for tape, or barkcloth making) and olona (for its fibre), and needing gourds, coconuts and marine foods would take a gift to some ohana living near the shore (ko kila kai) and in return would receive fish or whatever was needed. The fisherman needing poi or awa would take fish, squid or lobster upland to a household known to have taro and would return with his kao (tao) or pa'i'ai (hard poi, the steamed and pounded taro corn). In other words, it was the ohana that constituted the community within which the economic life moved (Handy, Handy, and Pukui 1976: 5–6).

The common *'ohana* not only produced all the necessities of life for their extended families. The surplus they generated sustained the class of chiefs who allotted the lands to the *'ohana* to cultivate. In return for the plots of land allotted to them, the *'ohana* had to make an annual tribute to the chiefs, cultivate the chiefs' plots of land, and provide labour service and products of the land when required to by the chiefs. The chiefs ultimately enjoyed full appropriation rights over all that was produced upon their lands. However, it was the labour of the commoners within the context of their *'ohana* that supported the entire society. Although the tenure of the commoner *'ohana* on their land grants was stable, they were not tied to the land and did have the option to move away if they chose to, although little evidence exists to indicate that this practice was ever common.

Relations between the chiefs and the people and among the people were regulated by a religious system of *kapu* restrictions, rituals, and guide-lines for behaviour. Religious *kapu* were also invoked for regulating the use of scarce resources. The foundation of the *kapu* was the Hawaiians' deep spiritual relationship to the land and nature and the belief that humans, nature, and the *akua* (gods) are harmoniously united and living together as one with respect and *aloha* for one another.

The European discovery of Hawaii by Captain James Cook in 1778 drew Hawaii into a world-wide system of trade and commerce. First the fur, then the sandalwood trades dominated Hawaii's relations with Europe and America.

The fur trade, which flourished from 1786 through 1804, introduced guns, alcohol, cloth, and other manufactured goods into Hawaii, and diseases that devastated the Hawaiian people. For the first time, the military technology was available for one chief to conquer other chiefs and to unite the islands under one central government. King Kamehameha I united all the islands except Kauai through military battles from 1782 through 1795 (Kuykendall 1968). In

1810, the islands came completely under one central government when the chief of Kauai surrendered to the superior authority of King Kamehameha I. Diseases such as measles, pneumonia, venereal diseases, and smallpox took a large toll on the Hawaiian population. In 1804 alone, half of the population is believed to have died from either cholera or bubonic plague (Malo 1839).

The sandalwood trade was dominant from 1805 to 1820. Through this trade, more foreign goods and diseases were introduced. The trade required most of the Hawaiian men to work for weeks and months at a time, cutting sandalwood in the mountains and hauling it to the beach. In their avarice for foreign trade, the chiefs ordered the people on their lands to devote most of their time to cutting sandalwood. The cultivation of the land was abandoned and the planting cycle disrupted, and as a result famine spread across the islands from Kauai to Hawaii.

The social and political upheavals caused by the fur and sandalwood trades culminated in 1819, after the death of Kamehameha I, with the abolition of the *kapu* system of religious ritual restrictions and customs and of the Hawaiian religion. The *heiau*, or religious temples, were dismantled, and the *ki'i*, or images of the gods, were destroyed (Davenport 1969; Sahlins 1981).

The whaling trade was most active from 1820 to 1860 and laid the foundation for more changes to the social and political system of Hawaii. It attracted permanent settlers to Hawaii from the whaling companies and from American and European merchant houses eager to service the needs of the whalers. It was during this period, beginning in 1820, one year after the Hawaiian religion was abolished, that the American missionaries began to arrive and settle in Hawaii. They hastened the process of social and political change among the declining numbers of the Hawaiian people, whose number had fallen to only 135,000 in 1823, one-third their number at the time of European contact (Kuykendall 1968).

The growing population of foreigners made demands on the Hawaiian monarchy for rights of private ownership of property in Hawaii and for civil rights of participation in the government. Their demands were supported by foreign gunboats.

To protect the independence of his tiny, vulnerable kingdom, King Kamehameha III reorganised the government in 1840 under a constitution patterned after that of Great Britain and the United States. In 1845, he allowed foreigners to become naturalised citizens and began to appoint them to key positions in the government, especially his cabinet. Essentially, the constitutional monarchy was a coalition government between the Kamehameha dynasty chiefs and the American and European settlers. Caving in to settler demands, King Kamehameha III abolished the traditional system of land use and control and instituted private ownership of the land under the Great Mahele of 1848, the Kuleana Act, and an Act to Abolish the Disabilities of Aliens to Acquire and Convey Land in Fee Simple. A total of 99.2 per cent of Hawaii's lands were concentrated among 245 chiefs, the Crown, and the government: 8 per cent of the land was given to 28 per cent of the commoners, and 72 per cent of the commoners were left landless – cut off from their traditional means of survival (Lind 1968: 46–47). Tranference of land from the chiefs and commoners to the foreigners was rapid. By 1862, less than 15 years after the system of private property was established, 75 per cent of all the land on Oahu was owned or controlled by foreigners, except in Waialua, where half the land was owned by foreigners (Blackman 1977: 161).

In 1843, King Kamehameha III was petitioned by 5,690 persons not to allow foreigners to become naturalised citizens, hold political office, or purchase land, but the king ignored their warnings. One petition from Kona appealed to the King as follows:

Do not sell the land to new foreigners from foreign countries. We have heard of this sale of land to foreigners. There is aroused within us love and reluctance to lose the land with love for the chiefs and the children and everything upon in our petition to you, this is to encourage you and explain to you with the painful thought and the strong thought and the thought to cut off those who assist the foreigners of other lands. We think that the land is not for the foreigner, only for us, the true Hawaiians. Do not give laws covenanting to give away our Hawaii. There is the entry (puka) where the foreigners get into the body (opu) of our own Hawaii. Perhaps they will say "We are naturalised Hawaiians therefore the land is ours, not yours, because you are brown skinned and we are white!" The result of this will be only blood – not life (Hawaii State Archives 1845).

The displacement of Hawaiians from their lands separated them from access to their traditional means of subsistence and steered them to seek jobs on a wage basis, thus contributing to the development of wage labour in Hawaii. By 1852, with only 80,500 Hawaiians in Hawaii, of whom only 29,200 were adult males, business interests began to import immigrant labourers from China to build up the work force (Schmitt 1977: 21).

With an increase in the price of sugar because of the Civil War, sugar grew to be the dominant industry in Hawaii beginning in 1860 and extending up through World War II. The sugar industry increased Hawaii's economic dependence on the US mainland, which was the primary market for Hawaiian sugar. To fulfil its labour needs, 381,800 contract labourers were imported between 1852 and 1945 to work on plantations (Coman 1903: 437–46, 503–16; 1904: 38–49).

The widespread production of sugar-cane, Hawaii's principal commodity beginning in the 1860s, caused sweeping and devastating changes to the day-to-day lives of *ka po'e kahiko*, the Hawaiian people of old, who had been accustomed to meeting their survival needs through collective cultivation of lands granted to their *'ohana* by the chiefs. The private property system changed this, and many

Hawaiians were displaced from the land to make way for sugar plantations and forced to hire themselves out to work for a wage on these same plantations.

Samuel Kamakau, a Hawaiian historian of the period, provided a poignant reflection on the effect of these changes on the Hawaiian people. In his book *Ruling Chiefs of Hawaii*, he wrote:

In the old days people who lived in out-of-the-way places were heavily burdened by the labour performed for chiefs, landlords and land agents. But although the work was hard, that today is even more so when families are broken up and one must even leave his bones among strangers.

Whether he (the working man) lives or dies it is all alike. He gets a bit of money for his toil in the house where he labours; there are not blood kin, no parents, no relatives-in-law, just a little corner for himself.

Today the working man labours like a carthauling ox that gets a kick in the buttocks. He shivers in the cold and dew laden wind or broils in the sun with no rest from his toil (Kamakau 1961: 372).

In his book, *Works of the People of Old: Na Hana A Ka Po'e Kahiko*, he wrote:

Ke po e kahiko were rich in possessions, they found their riches and provisions in the natural resources of the land. Their skill and knowledge are proven by their works. The people of today are destitute, their clothing and provisions come from foreign lands, and they do not work as their ancestors did. Some women sell their bodies for coverings and fine clothing to buy food and fish to relieve hunger and poverty. The men too have deserted the works of their ancestors – farming, fishing, painting kua ula tapas, building canoes, scraping olona, carving wooden bowls, making nets, twisting two- three- or four-ply cords making feather capes and round leis and preparing gum for snaring birds (Kamakau 1976: 123).

Hawaiian society came to be organised around sugar production. Ground and ocean transportation, utilities, housing, imports of food and retail items: all revolved around the development of the sugar industry. It was the sugar industry, whose lifeline was the US market, that bound Hawaii to the US and ultimately led to its incorporation into the United States.

The turning point in Hawaii's political and economic history was the signing of a reciprocity trade treaty in 1876 that allowed Hawaii-grown sugar into the US without having to pay a tariff.

From 1876 to 1882, 35 new plantations, representing a capital investment of $10 million, were started on 20,000 acres of newly cleared land. To cultivate, harvest, and grind sugar on these plantations 39,926 labourers were imported to Hawaii from Asia, Europe, and the South Pacific from 1876 to 1887. As a result, Hawaiians comprised only 54.9 per cent of the population by 1884. Hawaii became an economic colony of the United States selling nine-tenths of its exports to the United States and buying eight-tenths of all its imports from the United States. By 1883, Americans controlled 65 per cent of the plantation interests, the British controlled 21 per cent, the Germans 6 per cent, Hawaiians 4 per cent, and Chinese slightly less than 4 per cent (Tate 1968: 119; Thrum 1883: 14; US Department of State: 1893: 5).

When a Hawaiian nationalist movement finally emerged in the 1870s, advancing the slogan "Hawaii for the Hawaiians," and the king at that time, King David Kalakaua, aligned himself with it in 1882, the planter-missionary-factor élite in Hawaii felt threatened. In their eyes, the king and the Hawaiian nationalists became obstacles to the economic development of Hawaii, an economic system they controlled. The king had increased the national debt to $1.9 million in 1887, from $269,200 in 1882, with several extravagant projects, such as the construction of a French-style palace, the purchase of European-style crowns and crown jewels, and the minting of silver coins with the king's image on them (Stevens 1968: 117; Kuykendall 1967; McGregor-Alegado 1979). However, what was absolutely intolerable was the nationalist opposition to ceding Pu'uloa (Pearl Harbor) to the United States so that the Reciprocity Trade Treaty that expired in 1886 could be renewed.

In 1887, the planter-missionary-factor élite organised a *coup d'etat* against King Kalakaua. He was forced to sign a new constitution that severely limited the powers of the monarchy by requiring that any decision made by the monarch have the advice and consent of the cabinet. With the king under control through the constitution, the planter interests proceeded to cede Pu'uloa (Pearl Harbor) to the United States to renew the Reciprocity Trade Treaty.

The "Bayonet" Constitution of 1887 kept the monarchy under strict constraints for five-and-a-half tumultuous years, during which the Hawaiian people utilised various means to get rid of that hated instrument of rule. In January 1891, King Kalakaua died and his sister, Liliuokalani, became queen. By January 1892, the American planter-missionary-factor élite were convinced that the queen would be antagonistic, obstinate, and uncooperative with them. Moreover, they were faced with a new crisis when the US Congress passed the McKinley Tariff Act in 1891. Although the United States abided by the terms of the Reciprocity Treaty and did not impose a tax on Hawaii-grown sugar, it paid Mainland sugar growers a subsidy of two cents a pound and thus placed Hawaii sugar growers at a severe disadvantage. Hawaii sugar planters lost $4 million in the first seven months of the McKinley Tariff Act (Thurston 1893: 278).

The planter-missionary-factor élite organised an Annexation League in January 1892 and put out feelers to Washington, D.C., about American willingness to annex Hawaii. When the response from President Benjamin Harrison through the US secretary of the navy was supportive of annexation, the league began to make preparations and to await the ideal moment to overthrow the monarchy, establish a provisional government, and annex Hawaii to the United States (Thurston 1936; Kuykendall 1967: 523–34).

That moment came in January 1893. The queen was deposed by the planter-missionary-factor élite, which was supported by American marines, and a provisional government was proclaimed on 17 January 1893. In 1894, the provisional government declared itself a republic under a new constitution. Hawaiian royalists attempted to restore the queen to the throne in 1895, but their "uprising" was crushed before it could be launched.

In 1898, after the United States had acquired Cuba, Puerto Rico, Guam, the Philippines, and the Virgin Islands from Spain as the spoils of the Spanish-American War, the US Congress and newly elected President William McKinley passed a treaty for the annexation of Hawaii. The final transfer of power took place on 12 August 1898 at Iolani Palace (Liliuokalani 1964; Alexander 1891; Kuykendall 1967; Daws 1968).

Hawaii thus became an incorporated territory of the United States and the Hawaiian people became an indigenous minority people within the now-expanded borders of the United States. The *haole* ruling élite of Hawaii betrayed and abandoned the constitutional monarchy they had created and sustained with the Kamehameha and Kalakaua dynasties to attain economic security under the umbrella of the United States.

During the Territorial Period, from 1898 until Hawaii became a full-fledged state in 1959, five major corporations dominated Hawaii's economy; they were called The Big Five: C. Brewer; Theo H. Davies; Castle & Cooke; AmFac; and Alexander and Baldwin. Although they owned all the sugar plantations and other related businesses in Hawaii, they did not have a free reign over the political structure because Hawaiians held the plurality of votes and controlled the legislature and the delegate to the US Congress. Immigrant plantation workers actually comprised the bulk of the population; however, US law banned first generation Asians from becoming naturalised citizens, and the second generation descendants had not yet matured to voting age.

This gave rise to a curious alliance between a large portion of the Hawaiian community, led by the native landed élite, and the Big Five within the Republican party. Hawaiian leaders, including the man who had been designated the heir to the Hawaiian monarchy, Prince Jonah Kalanianaole Piikoi, ran for office on the Big Five's platform and programme for Hawaii and implemented it when they got elected. The alliance was held together through a government patronage, secure jobs on ranches and plantations, and anti-immigrant prejudices. Thus, part-Hawaiians held more than 50 per cent of all elected positions and judgeships in 1927, 55 per cent of all government jobs, and they made up the bulk of the fire department and all the police force. Through 1935, Hawaiians held almost a third of the public service jobs, although they comprised only 15 per cent of the population (Fuchs 1961: 161–62). Hawaiians who chose to

accommodate American rule and collaborate with the Big Five enjoyed relatively privileged positions in the economy, gaining stable jobs as government workers on ranches and in utility companies or in the construction, long-shore, and
stevedore industries.

However, despite these obvious advantages, nearly half of the Hawaiian
population did not assimilate into the developing economy. Instead, they remained in remote valleys and isolated rural pockets, providing for their large
families through subsistence farming and fishing on agricultural lands too marginal to be coveted by the plantations or the ranches. There they continued to
farm and fish according to traditional methods and to honour their ancestral
gods. They maintained and perpetuated the cultural base of the Hawaiian people living and practising Hawaiian culture, spiritual beliefs, and values and
speaking the Hawaiian language.

Although the level at which they were living was at subsistence, their living
conditions were relatively better than that of the immigrants who worked 12
hours a day in the fields or 10 hours in the mill for wages that barely allowed
them to provide for themselves. Moreover, the Hawaiians did not live under the
whip of the plantation *luna* (foreman) or the directives of the plantation man-
ager.

Thus, during the territorial period a main distinction internal to the
Hawaiian people developed between the urban Hawaiians who assimilated and
accommodated the socioeconomic system dominated by the *haole* American élite
and the rural Hawaiians who remained in the back-country areas maintaining a
more traditional Hawaiian way of life (Lind 1968: 101–3).

The first specific claim made to the United States by native Hawaiians on
behalf of the Hawaiians as a distinct people was one to set aside the former
crown lands, which had been ceded to the US government by the *haole* oligarchy
during annexation for homesteading by native Hawaiians. In response to the
squalid living conditions of native Hawaiians in tenement buildings and
makeshift squatter shelters in urban Honolulu, a movement began in 1917 to
make it possible for native Hawaiians to move away from Honolulu to rural
areas to farm and fish directly from the land. Of great concern was the high
death rate of native Hawaiians from diseases such as tuberculosis and alcoholism and the high infant mortality rate: 300 deaths per thousand compared with
33 deaths per thousand for the general population. In 1920, pure Hawaiians
numbered only 22,000 (Vause 1962: 11–12). By 1920, the movement succeeded
in having 200,000 acres set aside for homesteading by native Hawaiians of half-
Hawaiian ancestry or more on plots of land to be leased for 99 years at a dollar a
year rent. However, only third- and fourth-class agricultural lands were reserved for this purpose. The first- and second-class public lands were to continue being leased to plantations and ranches. The revenue generated from
these leases was to be used to fund the Hawaiian Home Lands Program. Since
its outset, however, the programme has been plagued with problems in its

mission to return the native Hawaiian to the land (Vause 1962; US Senate 1920).

The particular and special rights of native Hawaiians as a distinct people were again recognised at the time of statehood in 1959. At that time, the US federal government turned over to the jurisdiction of the State of Hawaii lands that had been ceded to it at the time of annexation to be held as a public lands trust. The section of the Hawaii Admission Act determining the use of this public lands trust specifies that the land be used for

the support of the public schools and other public educational institutions for the better-ment of the conditions of native Hawaiians as defined by the Hawaiian Homes Commis-sion Act, 1920, as amended, for the development of farm and home ownership on as widespread a basis as possible for the making of public improvements and for the provi-sion of lands for public use (The Admission Act 1959: Sect. 5f).

However, more coherent and aggressive demands for the recognition of native Hawaiian rights began with the organisation of the Native Hawaiian Movement in the 1970s.

BACKGROUND OF THE NATIVE HAWAIIAN MOVEMENT

The principal factor giving rise to the development of the Native Hawaiian Movement in the 1970s was the impoverished living conditions of Hawaiians at the time in comparison with the other ethnic groups in Hawaii. The depressed conditions of a significant portion of native Hawaiians were exaggerated in the 1970s following a decade of unprecedented growth and so-called progress dur-ing the first 10 years after statehood. Most sectors of Hawaiian society experi-enced a dramatic improvement in their standard of living as the economy boomed with the Vietnam War era military expenditures and tourist resort development. Most immigrants and their descendants were integrated into the work force, and they benefited directly from this rising standard of living, espe-cially in industries with organised labour unions.

During World War II, many Hawaiians left their rural enclaves to work in high-paying military jobs or to fight in the war. The war experience broadened their social horizons and raised their expectations and aspirations for a higher standard of living. Compulsory education laws also forced Hawaiian families out of the most remote areas and compelled them to send their children to school. Overall, there was a shifting of the Hawaiian population from rural areas to urban areas, primarily from the neighbouring islands to Honolulu on Oahu. At that point, a great many Hawaiians entered the work force and main-stream of society. There was also a large exodus of Hawaiians with others from Hawaii to the Mainland in search of better job opportunities.

Where Hawaiians became integrated into the work force, they participated in union organising drives and shared in the rising standard of living in Hawaii. However, a significant proportion of the Hawaiian community still remained in rural areas, especially on the neighbouring islands, and this group continued to be marginal to the work force because of the lack of jobs there; thus their standard of living stagnated. When the statehood boom occurred, they were not in a position to benefit from it. On the contrary, this boom, during which the number of hotel rooms more than tripled and the number of tourists increased fivefold, exacerbated the impoverished conditions of Hawaiians and other local people in rural areas (Coffman 1973).

Hawaiians sometimes were evicted to make way for hotels, condominiums, resorts, and high-priced subdivisions. Fishing grounds were destroyed by pollution from sewerage or increased soil run-off from inadequate drainage systems. On most islands, farmers – especially those planting taro – were deprived of their traditional water rights from streams as water resources were diverted to hotels and subdivisions. Traditional access to mountain areas or the ocean for hunting, gathering, and fishing were cut off altogether by hotels, resorts, and subdivisions. These access rights had been guaranteed by the Hawaiian government since 1850, when private property was established. Property taxes for small plots of land abutting large-scale developments soared, forcing many small landowners of Hawaiian ancestry to sell. Endangered Hawaiian plants and the habitats of endangered animals were destroyed by development.

Of special concern to native Hawaiians was the destruction by these developments of irreplaceable sites of historical, cultural, and religious signifiance: *heiau*, or traditional temples; *ko'a*, or fishing shrines; fish ponds; house sites; burial grounds and caves; and cultivation complexes. Many were destroyed before they had been thoroughly excavated, thereby destroying important links to the historical past of the Hawaiian people. Archaeology in the Pacific began to be seriously undertaken only in the 1950s, and much remains to be explored and researched among these sites.

In summary, development in the 1960s began to destroy the last remnants of the indigenous Hawaiian people. It assaulted the rural enclaves where Hawaiian people lived and perpetuated the Hawaiian way of life, spiritual beliefs, cultural practices, and language through two centuries of Western contact. It cut off access to the forests and oceans on which rural Hawaiians depended as a source of food to supplement their meagre incomes from seasonal minimum-wage jobs or welfare. It destroyed the physical artifacts and remains of the *ka po'e kahiko*, Hawaiian ancestors. Moreover, a bastardised Hawaiian culture was being made a commodity for sale to the tourists who visited Hawaii and stayed in the hotels that were destroying the established communities.

The Hawaiians displaced from the rural areas and forced to assimilate found they were poorly prepared to compete for jobs in an urban setting. They usually lacked the educational and social skills necessary to get good jobs and to keep them. Usually speaking a pidginised English and having poor writing skills, they found themselves competing with the most recent immigrants from the Philippines, South-east Asia, Samoa, and Tonga for jobs in the tourist industry that offered only manual labour, minimum wages, and instability. Many ended up joining the military for steady employment. Otherwise, they went on welfare and applied for other forms of public assistance.

As Hawaiians began to organise to protect themselves from the assault of tourist developments, to stop the breakup of their traditional rural communities, and to stop the development of native Hawaiian resources for non-Hawaiian use, they did so from a position of weakness. Just after World War II, the labour movement and the Japanese community, which by then controlled the plurality of votes, formed an alliance within the Democratic party. In 1954, this alliance won a majority in the territorial legislature and ousted the Republican alliance of the Big Five and the Hawaiians. Subsequently, Hawaiians also lost positions in government that had been acquired through political patronage. Japanese gradually began to fill appointive and administrative positions and to swell the ranks of government service that the Hawaiians had once dominated. Hawaiians thereby lost their political influence and were cut off from an important channel through which they had previously raised issues. As Hawaiians found it necessary to voice their concerns and to organise for their rights, grass-roots political pressure groups formed outside the established electoral process.

At the same time, the inspiration and direction in regard to organising for native Hawaiian rights also came from the great social movements of the 1960s in the mainland United States – the Civil Rights, Native American, and Anti-Vietnam War movements. The Civil Rights movement showed it was possible to challenge White Anglo-Saxon Protestant social values and the racism that was institutionalised in American laws, education, health care, social services, churches, and industry. The anti-war movement showed that it was not only possible, but that it was a moral obligation to challenge the US military and to work for peace even if the military did provide a chief source of income and revenue for the state and was a leading employer. The Native American movement directly and concretely focused in on what were the distinct and specific rights that indigenous people have in the United States.

Also, the Civil Rights and Native American movements succeeded in having legislation passed and programmes implemented to provide direct assistance to native Hawaiians in organising around their rights. The Civil Rights Act of 1964 and the Voting Rights Act of 1965 provided for affirmative action in employment and set up programmes such as the Office of Economic Opportunity, Model Cities, and Community Action that employed Hawaiians and trained them in how to advocate for the needs of the native Hawaiian people. Special admissions and financial aid programmes for colleges and professional schools were also set up under civil rights legislation, providing access to a broader spectrum of Hawaiians to colleges, training in the health, legal, educational, and social work professions, and to leading roles in advocating for changes in discriminatory policies toward native Hawaiians. Free legal programmes were also established under civil rights projects to assist communities in protecting their rights.

The Native American Civil Rights Act of 1968, the Native American Programmes Act of 1974, the Indian Self-Determination Act, the Native American Religious Freedom Act, and the Alaska Native Claims Settlement Act all contributed to setting up training and employment programmes, legal services, and to recognition of special rights of indigenous peoples native to the United States, including Hawaiians.

LAND: THE FUNDAMENTAL ISSUE

The one central issue that unites all the organisations that make up the Native Hawaiian Movement is land rights. Some organisations focus on land as a means of perpetuating the culture and spiritual beliefs and practices of the Hawaiian people; others as a means to generate revenues for native Hawaiian programmes; still others as a means of political sovereignty; and some as a way to place the Hawaiian on the land and allow Hawaiian families to become economically self-sufficient.

Land is central to the Native Hawaiian Movement because the Hawaiians, like all Pacific island and indigenous peoples, have a spiritual and material relationship to the land. The *'aina* (earth), including the ocean, is important to Hawaiians primarily because it provides them with the basic necessities of life: food, shelter, economic livelihood, and recreation. However, it is also important as the source of *mana*, the spiritual strength that is experienced from working in harmony with the life forces of nature. *Ka po'e kahiko*, the Hawaiian ancestors, were put to rest in the *'aina* and their spirit lives on in the remnants of their house sites, *ko'a heiau*, taro terraces, and burial sites – places of *'ohana* life, work, worship, and recreation. Control over the *'aina* is a critical measure of political sovereignty and the degree to which the Hawaiian people would be able to harness the resources necessary to provide for their welfare and to determine their future as a distinct people. To protect the *'aina* is not only to protect a basic resource for survival, it is also to protect a way of life unique to the Hawaiian islands and to protect the dignity and sovereignty of the Hawaiian people.

One major theme that has emerged to unify the various organisations working for native Hawaiian rights is "*Aloha 'Aina*." The Protect Kaho'olawe 'Ohana, which popularised this theme, describes its meaning as follows:

Aloha 'Aina is a traditional concept that lays the foundations for Hawaiian religion culture and lifestyle. *Aloha* means love and *'aina* means land. The two words together express several levels of meaning. At the deepest level the presence of our ancestors and gods of the land are acknowledged, respected and cherished through ceremonies both public and private. This intimacy with the *'aina* is also expressed in the interdependent subsistence relationship between man and his island. Man is nurtured with taro from the land and fish from the sea, and in turn cultivates and nourishes the island. This relationship is finally symbolised by pride in our homeland – patriotism for this land Hawaii (Protect Kaho'olawe 'Ohana 1986).

Aloha 'aina, with all its different levels of spiritual, cultural, and political meanings, has become a rallying point for the Native Hawaiian Movement, although different sectors emphasise and promote different aspects of the concept.

Three main native Hawaiian land bases are of critical significance because they are recognised to be for the sole benefit of the native Hawaiians. These are: (1) the Hawaiian Home Lands, which, as discussed above, was set up in 1920 to return the Hawaiians of half ancestry or more to the land; (2) at least one-fifth of the ceded lands the Public Lands Trust set aside under the Hawaii Admission Act for Hawaiians of half ancestry or more, as discussed above; and (3) the Bishop estate, which was established in 1885 by the last recognised heir to the Kamehameha lands, Princess Bernice Pauahi Bishop, and her American banker husband. The estate owns 8.5 per cent of all the land in Hawaii. The sole stated purpose of the private nonprofit estate is to educate native Hawaiians.

Each of these land-based institutions has different problems in how it serves the needs of the Hawaiian people. However, the fundamental problem common to all is that they are not under the sovereign control of the native Hawaiian people they were set up to serve.

The Hawaiian Home Lands is administered as a regular department of the State of Hawaii, having to conform to state budget policies and broader state economic planning priorities. Thus, the department still has thousands of Hawaiians on the waiting lists for lands on each island. Many have been on the waiting list for 20 to 30 years. A significant portion of the Hawaiian Home Lands is leased to non-Hawaiian ranches and commercial enterprises, supposedly to generate revenues for the department. The State of Hawaii has periodically confiscated Hawaiian Home Lands for airports, schools, parks, and highways without any compensation to the department. Only when Hawaiians demonstrated on the runways of one of these airports did the State of Hawaii begin to turn over revenues generated from the airports situated on Hawaiian Home Lands to the department. The military also confiscated Hawaiian Home Lands without any compensation. At Lualualei in Wai'anae, I'ahu, the US Navy has a communications station on Hawaiian Home Lands. At Bellows Field on Oahu, the US Air Force has part of its Giant Talk command and control communications satellite systems on uncompensated Hawaiian Home Lands. At Pohakuloa on the island of Hawaii, the combined US military services uses hundreds of acres for combat training. At Mana (Barking Sands) on Kauai, the Pacific Missile Range tracking system sits on uncompensated Hawaiian Home Lands.

The Hawaiian interest in the Public Lands Trust was decisively acknowledged and clearly designated only in the 1978 Constitutional Convention. At that time, the Committee on Hawaiian Affairs developed an amendment to the constitution to set up an Office of Hawaiian Affairs (OHA) to be funded by one-fifth of the revenues from the Public Lands Trust. The office is directed by nine trustees elected in a special election in which only Hawaiians (of any amount of ancestry) can register to vote. However, the office comes under the governor of the State of Hawaii and is subject to its policies and priorities. OHA opened in 1980 and got off to a shaky start. It suffers from a lack of direction and factional problems among the elected trustees. After six years, it has no overall assessment of the needs of the Hawaiian community or arrangement to use the existing information that has already been compiled by Alu Like or the Bishop estate. Nor does it have a master plan for a systematic and comprehensive approach to its programmes to serve the native Hawaiian community. Although the office has a great deal of potential, it has yet to be realised, and it is already apparent that the OHA will be constrained by its status as a department of the State of Hawaii. Already, OHA has had to file a lawsuit against the State of Hawaii for not including the revenues from the airports and harbours located on ceded lands in the total amount from which OHA's one-fifth share is calculated.

Meanwhile, the State of Hawaii, which is supposed to manage and protect the ceded lands as a public trust, is allowing the ceded-land base to be eroded and undermined by private enterprise and the military.

For example, the State of Hawaii recently exchanged 27,785 acres of ceded lands on the island of Hawaii for 25,807 acres of land on the same island owned by a private estate to enable it to develop geothermal energy wells. Not only did the state lose 2,000 acres of ceded lands in the exchange, but the land it got in return for the pristine natural forests it gave away included 1,000 acres that had been already logged for wood chips and about 12,000 acres of land covered over by recent lava flows. Moreover, geothermal energy development will tap into the body and life force of the Hawaiian deity of the volcano, Pele, and may deplete her energy altogether. This is of great concern to the many hundreds of native Hawaiians who honour Pele and respect her as a living *akua* (Aluili 1986).

Ceded lands are also being used by the military for shelling and training practice in the Makua Valley on the island of Kaho'olawe, and at Mokapu on Oahu.

The Bishop estate is a very important Hawaiian land-based institution because of its vast resources and its sole purpose to educate native Hawaiians. It is administered as a private nonprofit trust with five trustees appointed by the state supreme court. Until the 1970s, only 3 of the 23 trustees since 1885 had been Hawaiian (Hawaii Observer 1976). The Big Five Republican supreme courts appointed representatives of the *haole* oligarchy to manage the lucrative estate. Under the Democratic supreme court, a Chinese businessman and a Japanese land lawyer were the first two appointed to fill openings on the board of trustees. After the Hawaiian community strongly protested the appointment of a Japanese lawyer to the trusteeship, the next three appointees were native Hawaiians.

One of the main problems with the estate is that it was actually set up to serve Hawaii's business interests and only secondarily to educate native Hawaiians. The educational mission was mainly to exempt the vast landholdings from property taxes.

Since the founding of the estate's Kamehameha School in 1887, it has educated only one per cent of the Hawaiian youth at any one time. In its early years, the school advocated White Anglo-Saxon Protestant values and culture and even punished students who spoke Hawaiian in school. Until the '60s, the school provided the men with vocational and military training, and the women were prepared for becoming homemakers. Only after pressure from the Hawaiian community was a college preparatory programme introduced and Hawaiian language and studies included in the curriculum.

The estate now generates $46.5 million annually, but this represents only two per cent of the value of the estate's assets. Often, the estate trustees allowed developers to keep lease rentals and to sell development rights at huge profits while the estate earned not a penny from these transactions. Millions of dollars in revenue were lost to the estate under these agreements.

In summary, the amount of land designated for the sole benefit of native Hawaiians through the Hawaiian Home Lands, the Public Lands Trust, and the Bishop estate is substantial and more than adequate to provide for the welfare of the native Hawaiian people. In practice, however, only a small percentage of the lands actually benefits native Hawaiians. The primary problem is political in nature – Hawaiians do not have sovereign political control over these land bases.

NATIVE HAWAIIANS ORGANISE

Beginning in 1970, a dynamic and sometimes militant grass-roots movement for native Hawaiian rights emerged. Simultaneous with this political movement was a vibrant and creative renaissance of Hawaiian music, dance, language, and culture. A new level of political and cultural consciousness about the history of Hawaiians as a people was popularised in this period. Every strata of the Hawaiian people identified with the political and cultural revival of the Hawaiians as a people.

Among the first political organisations to form were those seeking to reform the Hawaiian Home Lands Program and the Bishop estate to make them better serve the native Hawaiian community. The Hawaiians that organised in 1970 played a leading role in pressuring the State of Hawaii to devote more resources to the Department of Hawaiian Home Lands and to prioritise the settlement of native Hawaiian applicants on the land. More recently, a private nonprofit Hawaiian corporation called Kahea Inc. has also pursued the issue of settling all the applicants on Hawaiian Home lands and phasing out leases to non-Hawaiians.

The Congress of Hawaiian People formed in 1971 to advocate the appointment of native Hawaiians to serve as trustees for the Bishop estate and to improve the curriculum of the Kamehameha School toward including college preparation and Hawaiian studies.

In 1972, the organisation ALOHA (Aboriginal Lands of Hawaiian Ancestry) formed to seek reparations in the form of money or land from the US Congress in compensation for the role the United States had played in the illegal overthrow of the Hawaiian monarchy.

In 1973, the Homerule Movement formed to try to steer Hawaiians into the electoral arena as a means of political empowerment.

By 1974, these organisations combined with a few other existing groups to form the Council of Hawaiian Organisations. In that year, members of the council also founded a private nonprofit corporation called Alu Like to serve as a conduit for federal monies flowing into the Hawaiian community from the Native American Programs Act administered by the Office of Native American Programs. Alu Like has branch offices statewide and administers millions of dollars in federal funds for native Hawaiians.

Also in 1974, the Native Hawaiian Legal Corporation was established to provide legal representation to native Hawaiian landowners faced with adverse possession by large estates and/or corporations and to assist native Hawaiian communities threatened with destruction of their resources.

Again in 1974, a group called 'Ohana O Hawaii was organised. This was the first native Hawaiian organisation to call for the independence of Hawaii from the United States. The organisation has filed claims at the United Nations and in the World Court for Hawaii to be granted independence from the United States. Other organisations seeking to establish an independent nation of Hawaii are the Sovereignty for Hawaii Committee and Na Oiwi O Hawaii. Native Hawaiian Task Force is looking at strategies for establishing the sovereignty of the native Hawaiian people, including the holding of a constitutional convention for a native Hawaiian nation. Also, homeless Hawaiians on Oahu who built shelters on beaches at Sand Island and along the rural coastlines of Wai'anae and Waimanalo linked their inability to have enough resources to afford a home to the loss of Hawaiian sovereignty and independence.

They registered claims to settle on these coastal areas, which are part of the ceded lands.

Several organisations have merely organised around land issues as they arise – with no strategic political programme. They are primarily grass-roots organisations of Hawaiians and supporters of the Hawaiian demands that formed to protect Hawaiian communities from destruction by poorly planned developments aimed at building high-priced condominiums and subdivisions for people from outside Hawaii while local communities are broken up and dispersed. They aim to protect and expand the capacity of the people in rural areas to continue making a livelihood by farming and fishing not only on a subsistence level, but also on a commercial basis so that the community can become economically self-sufficient without tourism. This includes efforts to maintain and expand access rights to hunt and gather from mountain areas and to fish from the ocean. These organisations are usually multigenerational and are based on the islands neighbouring Oahu. They function as 'ohana, not as Western-style political organisations. What has gradually evolved as a unifying philosophy among these groups is the practice of aloha 'aina. As an alternative to tourism, they advocate the cultivation of the land with cultural appreciation, appropriate technology, and guidance from kupuna (elders). In their view, native Hawaiian sovereignty begins with the rural native Hawaiian being able to remain on the land, fishing and farming (Protect Kaho'olawe 'Ohana 1983).

One organisation to form along these lines was Hui Ala Loa on the island of Molokai in 1975. Still an active group, it has succeeded in protecting the east end of Molokai from development, protected several historic sites from destruction, and opened access rights to beaches. Their members are involved in developing self-sufficiency agricultural and fishing projects.

In 1976, the Protect Kaho'olawe 'Ohana was formed to stop the military abuse of the island from shelling practice and war games and to advocate 'aloha 'aina on Kahoolawe. They want the island returned to the people of Hawaii for cultural, educational, religious, and scientific uses. In 1980, the 'ohana signed a consent decree with the US Navy under which military use is banned from two-thirds of the island and is stopped entirely for 10 days each month. During that time, the 'ohana takes groups to the island to help in work projects to rejuvenate natural vegetation and cultural resources. The 'ohana has managed to maintain a statewide network that also supports aloha 'aina struggles that its members are involved with on each island.

Another aloha 'aina group that formed was the Kukailimoku Village, which attempted to maintain a traditional fishing settlement where Hawaiian youth from Kailua, Kona, could be trained in traditional fishing techniques.

In Ka'u on the Big Island, a group formed to stop the projected use of Hawaiian Home lands at South Point, Ka'u, for a private missile-launching site. They are also working as a curator in conjunction with the Bishop Museum to protect Ka Lae (South Point) and its many important cultural sites and burial grounds from development. Also, they want the surrounding 11,000 acres of Hawaiian Home lands under lease to non-Hawaiian ranchers to be parcelled out to applicants from the area, many of whom have been on the list for more than 20 years.

Hui Alanui O Makena is attempting to stop the closure of a traditional shoreline trail and roadway by Seibu Corporation of Japan. If the road is closed, access to fishing, swimming, and launching of boats along that coast will be closed off to the local people whose ancestors lived and fished there for generations.

Several self-sufficiency undertakings, such as farm co-operatives and fishing projects on Oahu, Molokai, and Maui, are aimed at providing a culturally appropriate economic alternative to tourist development. Some of these projects are associated with alternative educational programmes for alienated Hawaiian and local youth in rural areas. The youth learn their basic skills in maths, science, and writing through their farming activities.

In the cultural field, Hawaiian *hula halau* (traditional Hawaiian dance schools) have proliferated, providing for the flourishing of traditional and modern Hawaiian music, chant, and hula. Several Hawaiian language teachers and students have taken up the challenge of perpetuating the use of Hawaiian. Besides language instruction at the university and high school levels, Hawaiian is also being taught in a preschool programme that uses the total immersion method of language instruction. These schools are called Punana Leo and are patterned after the Kohanga Reo schools of the Maori people. The voyages of the Hokule'a organised by the Polynesian Voyaging Society have contributed to a new interest and respect for Hawaiian scientific knowledge of astronomy and navigation.

All these efforts are contributing to the perpetuation of the Hawaiian people, their land, their cultural base, their language, and their spiritual beliefs. The present generation of Hawaiians realise that, unless positive and immediate steps are taken to perpetuate the language and culture of Hawaii, they may be lost altogether for future generations. A sense of urgency exists in these efforts and a conviction to persevere despite opposition and obstacles.

CONCLUSION

The Hawaiian people are presenting a challenge to the multiethnic society of Hawaii to recognise their distinct and particular rights and to translate that recognition into support for governmental legislation, politics, and budgets. The people of Hawaii will be called on to support bilingual and bicultural education for native Hawaiians and other interested youth from the preschool to the university levels. They will be asked to support special preventive health care programmes aimed at lowering the high susceptibility of Hawaiians to certain diseases. Native Hawaiian rural communities want support for self-sufficiency agricultural and fishing projects instead of tourist resort development. Support is needed to stop the military abuse of Kahoolawe so that the island can be used as a learning centre for native Hawaiian religion, science, and cultivation. Geothermal energy development must be stopped out of recognition and support for the Hawaiian volcano deity, Pele, and for the spiritual beliefs of the native Hawaiians generally. More important, the people of Hawaii will be asked to recognise and support Hawaiian sovereignty over their public land bases – the Hawaiian Home lands and the ceded lands – even though this may mean exclusion of non-Hawaiians from these lands and its natural resources.

The demands are real and the challenge serious and formidable. The continued development of Hawaii as a multiethnic society with tolerable race and ethnic relations demands the recognition by its people and government of the special rights of the native Hawaiian people as indigenous to Hawaii. It is only in Hawaii that the Hawaiian people can perpetuate the Hawaiian language, culture, spiritual beliefs, and values. The Japanese, Filipinos, and Chinese can go to their homelands to find their heritage. The Hawaiians have only Hawaii.

More important, essential to the perpetuation of the Hawaiian people and their culture is their perpetuation on the land, especially in rural areas, and maintenance of their livelihoods through farming and fishing. To ensure the perpetuation of the people on the land, the sovereign rights of the Hawaiian people over their land base must be established so that the Hawaiians can bring these resources to bear in providing for the welfare of their people now and in the future.

The motto of the State of Hawaii is "Ua mau ke ea o ka 'aina ka pono," which means, "The life of the land is perpetuated in righteousness." It was proclaimed by King Kamehameha III in July 1843 when Britain restored Hawaii's independence after it had been seized as a British protectorate. Given the current status of the Hawaiian people, it is also fitting to say today, "Ua mau ke ea o ka po e i ka 'aina," or, "The life of the people is perpetuated in the land."

REFERENCES

Alexander, W. D. 1891. *A brief history of the Hawaiian people.* New York: American Book Co.

Aluili, N. E. 1986. *Testimony to Hawaii's State Senate Economic Development Committee opposing the exchange of Campbell Estate's Kahauale'a lands for the State Hawaii Puna Forest Reserve and Wao Kele O Puna Natural Area Reserve.* Honolulu (manuscript).

Alu Like. 1976. *Summary of the analysis of the needs assessment survey and related data.* Honolulu (manuscript).

Bishop Estate. 1983. *Native Hawaiian educational assessment project.* Honolulu (manuscript).

Blackman, W. F. 1977. *The making of Hawaii: A study in social evolution.* New York: AMS Press.

Coffman, T. 1973. *Catch a wave: Hawaii's new politics.* Honolulu: University Press of Hawaii.

Coman, K. 1903. Contract labour in the Hawaiian Islands. *Hawaii Planters Monthly* 22: 437–46, 503–16.

———. 1904. Contract labour in the Hawaiian Islands. *Hawaii Planters Monthly* 23: 38–49.

Davenport, W. 1969. The Hawaiian cultural revolution: Some political and economic considerations. *American Anthropologist* 71: 1–20.

Daws, A. G. 1968. *Shoal of time: A history of the Hawaiian Islands.* New York: Macmillan.

Fuchs, L. H. 1961. *Hawaii Pono: A social history.* New York: Harcourt Brace Jovanovich.

Grigulevich, I. R., and S. Ya. Kozlov. 1981. *Ethnocultural processes and national problems in the modern world.* Moscow: Progress Publishers.

Handy, E. S. C., E. G. Handy, and M. K. Pukui. 1972. *Native planters in old Hawaii: Their life, lore, and environment.* Honolulu: Bishop Museum Press.

———. 1976. *The Polynesian family system in Kae'u, Hawaii.* Rutland: Charles E. Tuttle.

Hawaii Admission Act. 1959. Section 5f., March 18, 1959; see *Hawaii Revised Statutes,* Honolulu, 1976.

Hawaii Observer. 1976. *Special report, Bishop Estate: The misused trust.* Honolulu.

Hawaii State Archives. 1845. *Petition to King Kamehameha III from commoners living in Kailua, Kona Islands of Hawaii.* Honolulu (manuscript).

Institute of Marxism-Leninism. 1977. *Leninism and the national question.* Moscow: Progress Publishers.

Johannessen, E. 1961. *The Hawaiian labour movement: A brief history.* Boston: Bruce Humphries.

Kamakau, S. M. 1961. *Ruling chiefs of Hawaii.* Honolulu: The Kamehameha Schools Press.

———. 1976. *Works of the people of old: Na Hana A Ka Po'e Kahiko.* Honolulu: Bishop Museum Press.

Kanahele, G. S. 1982. *Current facts and figures about Hawaiians.* Honolulu: Project Waiaha.

Kirch, P. 1985. *Feathered gods and fishhooks: An introduction to Hawaiian archaeology and prehistory.* Honolulu: University of Hawaii Press.

Kuykendall, R. S. 1967. *The Hawaiian kingdom: 1874–1893: The Kalakaua dynasty.* Vol. 3, Honolulu: University of Hawaii Press.

———. 1968. *The Hawaiian kingdom: 1778–1854: Foundation and transformation.* Vol. 1, Honolulu: University of Hawaii Press.

Liliuokalani, Queen. 1964. *Hawaii's story by Hawaii's Queen.* Tokyo and Rutland: Charles E. Tuttle.

Lind, A. 1968. *An island community: Ecological succession in Hawaii.* New York: Greenwood Press.

McGregor-Alegado, D. 1979. *Hawaiian resistance 1887–1889.* M. A. thesis, University of Hawaii.

Malo, D. 1839. Causes for the decrease of the population in the islands (trans. with comments by Lorrin Andres). *The Hawaiian Spectator* 2(2).

Protect Kaho'olawe 'Ohana. 1983. Kaho'olawe, Aloha 'Aina and self-determination: A Native Hawaiian Alternative. *Proceedings of the 1983 Nuclear Free and Independent Pacific Conference.* Port Vila, Vanuatu.

———. 1986. *Kaho'olawe and the Protect Kaho'olawe 'Ohana* (brochure).

Sahlins, M. 1981. *Historical metaphors and mythical realities.* Ann Arbor: University of Michigan Press.

chmitt, R. C. 1977. *Historical statistics of Hawaii.* Honolulu: The University Press of Hawaii.

Stevens, S. 1968. *American expansion in Hawaii 1842–1898.* New York: Russell and Russell.

Tate, M. 1968. *Hawaii: Reciprocity or annexation.* East Lansing: Michigan State University Press.

Thrum, T. G. 1883. *Hawaiian almanac and annual for 1884.* Honolulu.

Thurston, L. A. 1893. The Sandwich Islands, I: The advantages of annexation. *North American Review* 156: 278.

———. 1936. *Memoirs of the Hawaiian revolution.* Honolulu: Advertiser Pulishing Co.

US Department of State. 1893. *Papers relating to the mission of James H. Blount, Unites States Commissioner to the Hawaiian Islands,* Part 2. Washington, D.C.: Govt. Printing Office.

US Senate. 1920. *Hawaiian Homes Commission Act 1920. Hearings on HR 13500 to Amend Act to Provide Government for Hawaii, as Amended to Establish Hawaiian Homes Commission and for Other Purposes.* 66th Cong., 3rd sess., Committee on Territories.

Vause, M. 1962. *The Hawaiian Homes Commission Act, 1920: History and analysis.* M. A. thesis, University of Hawaii.

4

Myth of the Golden Men:
Ethnic Elites and Dependent Development in the 50th State

NOEL J. KENT

Hawaii's ethnic mosaic is justly celebrated. As a social phenomenon, it has drawn attention from writers and scholars alike. Writing a generation ago, amidst the euphoria surrounding Hawaii's statehood, author James Michener broached the idea in his novel, *Hawaii*, that a culturally unique, biologically mixed people was emerging in the islands: "the Golden Men," carrying a dynamic synthesis of Asian, Polynesian, and Western traditions. Several years later, the social historian Lawrence Fuchs went further. In saluting the transformation of Hawaii from a plantation backwater to vigorous American state, he held it out as a model to the underdeveloped world: "Hawaii illustrates the nation's revolutionary message of equality of opportunity for all regardless of background or religion" (Fuchs 1968: 449).

This view became the popular wisdom of the day and was accepted almost without criticism until the 1970s. Hawaii was touted as proof positive that the liberal capitalist model of modernisation could both achieve genuine development and solve ethnic conflicts through "peaceful revolution" (Wright 1972: 2).

This chapter takes issue with this interpretation. It argues that Hawaii's recent development has merely been *a different kind of dependent development* from the earlier plantation period. Under the joint auspices of the older and new ethnic élites, the model has actually consolidated and intensified pre-existing ethnic divisions. The point of departure is the centrality of ethnicity, class, and the impress of the global system in comprehending the mysteries of modern Hawaii's transformation and status. The specific focus is on one group, the AJAs (Americans of Japanese ancestry), in their changing relationship to political and economic power and to other ethnic groups.

Because of Hawaii's geographical remoteness from any major population centre, the abundant ethnicity there is all the more remarkable. If a logic exists here, it is that of the world capitalist system that first affected the islands with the appearance of Captain James Cook in 1778 and proceeded over the next 120 years to absorb the archipelago most relentlessly. By the mid-19th century, a nascent Western commercial élite, sensing the potential of an export trade in sugar, was busily expropriating the traditional lands of the Hawaiian people along with their freed-up labour. Profitable sugar cultivation for an American market demanded, however, assemblage of large conglomerations of tightly disciplined, low-wage workers in the field and in mills – precisely the sort of labour force the decimated Hawaiians could (and would) not deliver.

So the *haole* ruling class came to display the same fondness for the importation of overseas workers as its counterparts in the Caribbean, the western Pacific, and South-East Asia. Labour recruiters began scouring the provinces of southern China in 1852, transferred their attention to Japan three decades later, and by the time of Hawaii's incorporation into the United States at the turn of the century, at least a dozen distinctive ethnic groups were on hand. Ethnic experimentation on such a grand scale was conceived in high cynicism; it was a well-formulated ploy to limit the mobilisation capacity of any one immigrant group. An exercise in what might be termed good old-fashioned divide and rule.

In pursuance of this (quite successful) strategy, the plantation environment was kept strictly communal; the different ethnic groups were separated in segregated housing camps and work gangs. Differential wages reinforced animosities and mistrust. Certain groups received privileged housing and occupational roles. So a colonial plural society in miniature was created on the plantation, highlighting stereotypes and differences and reinforcing the most narrow ethnic nationalism. Like the Caribbean sugar societies, Hawaii's social stratification was sharply pyramidal and counterpoised a small segment of Caucasians (powerful by dint of their relationship to the apparatus around sugar) to a large agro-industrial proletariat of colour. Even Caucasians of modest means profited in income and job chances from the "white skin privileges." Both the racial hierarchy and narrow economic base circumscribed non-white economic mobility.

Hawaii was not, it should be noted, "naturally" favoured as a sugar-raising area. Rather than economic, its comparative advantage was grounded in political-military linkages between the islands' plantation élite and their counterparts in Washington, who coveted Hawaii as a military base to provide security for the American Pacific Coast and a launching pad for the coming penetration of the Asia-Pacific region. Both in 1875, when the *haole* élite negotiated the Reciprocity Treaty (which effectively transformed Hawaii into an American economic satellite), and in 1898, when this same group delivered the archipelago turkey style to the United States as an indirect spoil of the Spanish-American war, their price – continuing overlordship and economic monopoly – was explicit.

In practice, after 1900 this translated into control over parameters of decision-making by the (well-empowered) territorial governors and delegates to Congress. Moreover, it meant the legal untouchability of the huge acreages of land annexed by the Big Five sugar agencies and estates during the 19th century. Cooper and Daws (1985) rightly insist, "there was never a ruling group in the history of Hawaii that did not base its power on land." During this era, the control of land was buttressed by corporate-financial-familial interlocks of Byzantine complexity – sanctioned by the American military and legal presence.

The same oligarchy found it opportune to form alliances with ethnic Hawaiian leaders to dominate local politics. The use of lucrative political sinecures lured Hawaiian leaders into co-operation, and an assortment of patronage jobs were provided to the rank-and-file voters. Access to public employment was an important income source for a people dispossessed. Meanwhile, this assured that the Republican party, the political vehicle of the planter class, would monopolise local political office.

Limited dependency is an apt characterisation of the 1900–1955 period. If the local élite was beholden to the annual American sugar quota and the mainland market for pineapple, it still retained ownership and control of the productive-financial-transportation apparatus and exercised tremendous authority on the ground in Hawaii. No mere comprador class existing as a conduit for the schemes of outsiders, it in fact quite forcefully prohibited entry of outside capital into the islands. Instead, any profitable new industries and technologies (electricity, telephones, and streetcars, for example) were immediately snapped up by oligarchy interests.

Right up to the war, the holding together of this balancing act was dependent on the maintenance of a fragile equilibrium. Through a judicious use of paternalism and coercion, the vast multiethnic underclass was managed well enough to prevent the unionisation of Hawaii's basic industries. Indeed, as symbolised by the ritualistic attendance of Big Five executives in cool tropical suits at downtown Honolulu's whites-only Pacific Club, their class and racial prerogatives remained inviolate. One might have mistaken the scene for Bombay or Kuala Lumpur of the raj. Hawaii remained during this era a classic example of the global distribution of power and prestige along colour lines brought about by the hegemony of European-American based capitalism.

Yet the basic production unit, the plantation, was always contested terrain. Its brutal racial hierarchy and wretched rewards for hard labour provoked acute resentments. The Chinese, deemed at first to be a model labour force, soon engaged in strikes, slow-downs, and occasional violence directed at oppressive foremen. Within a generation of entering Hawaii, they had decamped en masse to take up petty trade in the towns. Their successors, the Japanese, rapidly grasped the nature of American labour dynamics and showed the capacity to organise and take actions for better conditions. They were the principals in the 1909 and 1920 mass strikes that threw the islands into turmoil and brought down on them the full wrath of a legal-extralegal state power intent on strike-breaking. The Filipino immigrants, imported early in the 20th century as a corrective to Japanese "radicalism," supported the Japanese fitfully in 1920 and then launched a major strike of their own four years later which was crushed by a strong display of official violence that left 16 workers dead and many jailed. After defeating each strike in turn, the planters felt obliged to raise wages and improve housing and other conditions (see Beechert 1985; Takaki 1984).

Ethnic unionism was the Achilles' heel of the early labour movement. It proved highly difficult to draw workers out of their segregated, insular communities to combine openly with other ethnics on labour issues. Reinecke, dean of plantation historians, has noted how, even after interethnic strikes, the workers "responded by retreating into their nationalistic-linguistic camps for the protection and security to be found there." More than the fear of retribution was raising its head here. At the core were primordial loyalties, accentuated by the close, continuing ties of first-generation immigrants to the old homeland. The finely tuned art of plantation divide-and-rule also played a part. So did the ethnic estrangements caused by the political crisis in East Asia (Imperial Japan's military projects against China, Korea, and the Philippines) (Reinecke 1972: 25–90).

Hawaii's diverse ethnic groups first encountered each other in the plantation setting. This did nothing to create mutual respect and tolerance. It is revealing that when interracial unionism finally triumphed on the plantations, docks, and mills in the mid-'40s, it was under the banner of the International Longshoremen's and Warehousemen's Union (ILWU), a San Francisco-based union with Marxist proclivities headed by mainland *haoles*. Yet, even the profoundly anti-communal ILWU could not free itself of the ethnic animosities generated by plantation life. In the early postwar years, a number of key local ILWU leaders, citing "communist influence," bolted the union over what were really resentments against the *haole* leadership. In ethnic relations, the "dead hand" of the plantation will be felt long after the last one in Hawaii closes down.

The ethnic group most closely associated with Hawaii's modernisation has been the AJAs. The linchpin role they played here is a consequence not only of their size – the largest labour immigrant group – but also their unique dynamics during the plantation period itself.

Within a decade of the AJAs' arrival in the isles, because of their number, organisational skills, and the fierce pride they displayed in traditional culture (how the Issei, for example, maintained a complex of language schools, newspapers, and churches), the *haole* élite understood that they constituted the ultimate threat to continued hegemony. Here was an ethnocentricity as fully developed as the *haoles'* own; a natural adversary. During the 1898 debate in Washington over US annexation of Hawaii, the oligarchs used the Japanese presence demagogically, pointing to them as a fifth column ready to reclaim the islands for a resurgent Japan. A few years later, the Hawaiian Sugar Planters Association head, Royal Mead, told Congress, "I believe the great majority of plantation owners would rather see their fields dried up and turned into abso-lutely arid areas than to have that country turned over to the Japanese" (see Kotani 1985).

This thread was fondly picked up, in turn, by top US military officers in Hawaii, who never bothered to hide their sentiments that the local Japanese were a subversive element biding their time until the opportune moment to show their allegiance. In fact, the "Orange People" scenario developed by a still obscure Colonel George Patton in the '30s for deportation and incarceration of the Hawaiian Japanese provided a model for the 1942 mass incarceration on the Pacific Coast.

What the prewar plantation élite feared, however, was not the fanciful spectre of a local Japanese uprising against American power to deliver the islands to Tokyo, but rather the legitimate, constitutional competition of the Japanese for future political-economic hegemony. This is clear in the work of Stanley Por-teus, the University of Hawaii psychologist (linked to the oligarchy by marriage and philosophy) who provided the 1920s ideological underpinning for the cul-tural division of labour and the existing racist hierarchy. Using his "racial efficiency indexes," Proteus found the Filipinos to exist in "an adolescent stage of development," wholly unsuited for self-governance or citizenship. The Japanese, however, were clearly of a different mettle – "intensely race con-scious, ready to combine for any purposes of group advancement, aggressive and rather untrustworthy when self-interest is in question." In short, dangerous competitors. Porteus warned that the "Nordic strongholds" such as Hawaii had to be maintained because of the risk of "race suicide" (Porteus and Babcock 1976: 52).

Despite the myth being perpetuated of a monolithic AJA conspiracy to con-trol Hawaii, actually, the prewar Japanese community, given its rapid move-ment out of the plantation orbit and into small business, farming, and urban employment and the generational strains caused by assimilation, was rife with divisions. Sharp debates arose around political, religious, and assimilationist issues (see Kotani 1985; Odo 1985a,b).

As among other ethnic groups, a primary internal conflict concerned the pace and depth of assimilation. The immigrant Issei continued to look back to the old country for cultural reference points and held fast to traditions already archaic in Japan itself. The second(Nisei) generation, however, was in the much more difficult position of having to work out demands for conformity made by conflicting cultures. Its Japanese self-consciousness was strong; the Niseis attended after-school language classes and some even went to college in Japan. Moreover, urban AJAs tended to live in ethnic ghettos such as Honolulu's Kalihi, served by community-owned gas stations, bakeries, groceries, and restaurants. By 1940, the AJAs constituted 40 per cent of the territory's popula-tion and two-thirds of its retail-store owners, half the craftsmen, and three-quarters of the small farmers. The growth of such an enclave economy had strong implications for the future. It meant the Japanese had an economic base from which to branch out into the larger non-AJA society (see Portes 1981: 179–298). It meant the young Nisei grew up in a community where there was a *real, objective basis* for Japanese loyalties, where being Japanese gave one access to certain economic rights and favours (Kotani 1985: 74).

Educational policy was the prime ruling-class vehicle to maintain the Hawaiian Japanese in a subordinate position. Following World War I, the Japanese language schools – the major transmitters of Japanese culture – came under severe attack from the territorial government. Meanwhile, a ruthless Americanisation was enforced in the public schools: English language and American culture had sole legitimacy, and Asian cultural practices were pointedly disparaged. (Nisei writers would later argue they had been victims of cultural genocide.) English standard language tests channelled non-white youth into non-academic tracts in second-class high schools.

Although never precisely enunciated as such, the desired outcome seems to have been a Japanese youth both semi-Americanised and alienated from his or her heritage. Ideally, this youth would be sufficiently literate to occupy a subordinate role in the service economy but would lack the skills and sophistication to challenge the class-race hierarchy.

These policies and goals proved both incoherent and contradictory. Attacks on AJA cultural institutions reinforced community solidarity and fed the always-latent hostility towards *haole* domination, as did the enforced segregation in the schools. Americanisation did not entail only instilling loyalty to the Stars and Stripes or preaching the virtues of American efficiency, but under the purview of educators more liberal than the class that employed them, it encouraged Asians to claim their rightful place in the territory. There was, for instance, McKinley High School principal Miles Carey telling future US Senator Daniel Inouye in 1941: "In a few years, by the time this war is over, your people will have as much opportunity as any white man in the islands" (Wright 1972: 96).

The mid-late 1930s and war years were the formative period in the evolution of the Nisei élite. Assimilation has always presented second-generation Americans with dilemmas; for the Nisei, with their singular heritage as a proud, ethnocentric people subjected to degrading contract labour, forced exclusion, powerlessness, and limited options, these were accentuated. Their response has helped shape modern Hawaii. As a transitional, "convert" generation to Americanism, they chose to devote themselves single-mindedly to full assimilation. This did not, however, require a complete severance with parental values. Individualistic effort and competition for material goals and power were esteemed in both cultures.

When they did break with the Issei's old loyalties, it was to write off the nationalistic old-country rituals and cults as archaic. In their place, they hoisted the banner of a strong Hawaiian-Japanese consciousness as expressed in individual mobility and group predominance. New cultural allegiances arose directed at their cohort group within Hawaii (siblings, cousins, classmates) in the process of getting ahead. Ethnic consciousness could thus be expressed in economic-political-status terms. This demanded, of course, entry into the political arena to contest the oligarchy on its own turf.

By the time of the 1941 attack on Pearl Harbor, Nisei aspirations were plainly outgrowing whatever options a stagnant plantation culture had to offer. What they lacked was some dramatic confirmation of their right to participate in (and even lead) the society of the future. Ironically, the December 1941 attack by Admiral Yamamoto's carrier group provided it. Initially, it was a disaster-threatening event. Japanese aliens were interred on Sand Island, AJA labour organisers jailed, community and political leaders forced to adopt a very low profile. Oligarchy spokesmen denied that the Japanese could ever become "Americanised."

The contradiction to this was given by the 2,500 young Hawaiian-born AJAs who served as the core of the 442nd Regimental Combat Team, the most highly decorated unit in the US Army, and thousands of others who served their country in the war. By war's end, the Japanese community could claim a fund of legitimacy as citizens and a cadre of young, aggressive, chip-on-the-shoulder leaders boasting the strongest of patriotic credentials. Curiously, the war against Japan and the Axis had given the Hawaiian Japanese the high ground to demand inclusion in some sort of "New Hawaii" – widely felt to be on the postwar agenda. For the AJAs, it was the time to wage Offensive Ethnicity.

So ethnic consciousness was to be played out in the political-economic arena. From 1945 on, the demand that room be allotted at the top, in compensation for historic deprivations and service to the nation, was the touchstone of the Nisei political class. There was a revealing conversation between the two wounded Nisei veterans, Dan Inouye and Sakae Takahashi – future Democratic party luminaries – lying in a Jersey City, New Jersey, hospital: "Most of all, I want to know why there has to be a limit to our hopes" was how Inouye posed it. "Suppose you wanted to join the Pacific Club. Suppose you wanted to be governor of Hawaii" (Wright 1972: 114–15). Years later, when he was a Democratic party power broker, Dan Aoki reflected what he and his 442nd veterans had feared on their homecoming.

Would they have to go back to the plantations and work for a dollar a day? Would they have to go back and work for the big corporations and be paid on a dual scale – large salaries for the haoles from the mainland and only a fraction as much for them because they were Orientals from Hawaii. . . . Is this what would be in store for them – nothing better? (Speech to 442nd Regiment Meeting, October 1974).

Their perspective was filtered through a double prism: the fierce determination to reach upward into middle-class American respectability and the sense of themselves as loyal players within a larger ethnic cohort. Despite the poverty and humiliations of the prewar years, they (unlike their contemporaries in the class-conscious ILWU leadership) never criticised the morality or viability of capitalism as a system.

The quarrel they had was with the underdevelopment fostered by a *plantation* capitalism that purposely limited economic diversification and thus *their* possibilities. If the *haole* oligarchy had historically monopolised access to economic goods and social status, now the Nisei would use the political apparatus to redefine things. "The time had come for us to step forward . . ." thought Dan Inouye, "the old patterns were breaking down." During the late '40s to early '50s, the young Nisei entered the Democratic party en masse and gave it the vigour and ethnic base it had always lacked. To stay in power, the Republicans had always mobilised their own ethnic base of affluent *haoles* and working-class Hawaiians, but this paled in comparison with the 40 per cent of the voting population who were AJAs.

They were a *petite bourgeoisie* in formation, but as yet a *petite bourgeoisie* bereft of financial resources and carrying around a list of historic grievances. So there was an initial period of fire breathing and radicalism. At the 1950 Democratic convention, for instance, the rhetoric was grandiose, indeed. The keynote speaker greeted the delegates with these remarks:

I'll tell you what the Democrats can do. They will change the tax system and make a real American progressive tax based on the ability to pay. . . . On land, we will make available this land at auction in small parcels so that farms can be built up all over this beautiful land and people can own their own homes, grow their own vegetables and live as free Americans (*Honolulu Advertiser*, 30 April 1950).

All of this had a solid political logic: in attacking the territory's dependence on monoculture exports, the Big Five monopolisation of land, inequitable taxation, among other things, the young Democrats would effectively undermine the economic base of their political enemies while building a constituency among the society's many malcontents.

On a related level, the aspiring Nisei élite's own personal futures depended on a restructuring of the economy. As attorneys, realtors, life insurance agents, etc., they were in those sectors of the *petite bourgeoisie* that lacked their own base of capital accumulation and dearly needed a dynamically expanding economy. Meanwhile, the Big Five, never keen on diversified development in its domain and shackled by an elderly, ingrown, and fossilised leadership, showed little inclination to innovate new policies. Sugar and pineapple continually declined under the pressures of low prices and tough competition. A stagnant economy led to an annual net outflow of people to the mainland. To revive economic growth, the Nisei would open the huge estate lands to development, solicit outside capital, and erect new industries. To fund the modernisation of state services, especially education, the landed estates would be forced to bear a more equitable share of the tax burden.

The high-water mark of Democratic political radicalism occurred around the time of the 1954 election, in which the Democrats, promising "a new era of justice and fairness to all the people of the territory," scored an impressive sweep in taking both houses of the legislature. The Democratic party leader, John Burns, a former police captain who had cultivated strong Nisei ties during the war, announced, "We are going to change things in line with the platform. We have an outright mandate from the people to change the way of life down here" (*Honolulu Star-Bulletin*, 4 November 1954).

Had a prolonged economic crisis followed Democratic succession to political power and had the old ruling class remained unreconstructed, there may have been confrontation and further radicalisation of the Democrats. Timing, however, was critical. At precisely this time profound changes in Hawaii's political-economy were occurring that brought the old plantation era to a definitive close. The "New Hawaii," born of a composite of diverse but interlocked forces, was in formation.

The old *kamaaina* sugar agencies and banks, finally jolted out of stasis, underwent a significant transformation. The first notice of its coming, in the mid '50s, was the importation of managers trained in the most up-to-date techniques at mainland business schools. They rapidly streamlined operations, consolidated unwieldy holdings into subsidiaries, closed down marginal plantations, and sold off portfolio assets. Instead of an (ill-defined) intertwined corporate monolith, the Big Five and Dillingham evolved as six distinctive companies, each sporting a definite corporate character and goals.

With capital garnered from mainland money markets in the 1960s and 1970s, they effected a wave of overseas expansion into international agribusiness (Castle and Cooke and C. Brewer) and into diversified mainland enterprises (Amfac) and construction materials (C. Brewer). The logical consequence of this appeared by the '80s, by which time Amfac, Castle and Cooke, and Dillingham had moved their headquarters to the mainland, and Brewer and Theo. Davies were controlled overseas. What remained as a token of their Hawaiian past, however, was significant enough; they would seek to turn enormous acreages of prime landholdings into tourism-luxury residential developments (see Kent 1983).

Corporate rationalisation was accompanied by rationalisation of the state apparatus. Starting in 1957, during the administration of the Big Five lawyer William Quinn, the state played a much more active role in generating economic growth. New industries and a wider, more dynamic ruling class in Hawaii demanded a much greater governmental role. Government funds (gathered from mainland bond issues) paid for a costly physical infrastructure that included roads, airports, and sewerage facilities designed to accommodate a mass-tourism sector. The University of Hawaii, envisioned as the foundation for the education-think tank, high-technology centre Quinn thought Hawaii would become, underwent a substantial expansion. And in a historical reversal, Quinn and his Big Five advisers encouraged outside capital investment in essential island industries. For Quinn, movement from the constraints of a peripheral monoculture economy was to be accompanied by close linkage to centre-based companies. Hawaii would become a springboard for overseas and local multinationals to penetrate the Pacific Rim (Kent 1983: 122–27). In other words, the strategy held, by assuming the role of capital-technology export centre to the lesser developed regions of the western Pacific and South-East Asia, Hawaii would shed its peripheral status and would be the 50th state in reality and in name.

Overseas corporations responded well (if only to the lure of the profitable tourism-land development phase of the scenario). In 1961, a San Francisco stock brokerage firm described Hawaii as "a magnet for mainland capital . . . roughly one-third of Hawaii's total economy may be considered strongly dynamic, promising well above average growth in the sixties." By 1963, large mainland insurance firms had invested something in excess of $200 million in tourism-related projects (Kent 1983: 124).

Delivered en masse from North America and Japan by swift Boeing aircraft, the tourist horde made Waikiki one of the world's celebrated resort enclaves. Meanwhile, areas in Maui, west Hawaii, Kauai, and Molokai, close to the shoreline, were earmarked for large-scale "destination resorts" by overseas hotel interests and their Big Five hosts. Hawaiian tourism's consistently high profit rates made it enormously attractive to overseas investors, who erected scores of hotels and condominiums. This, in conjunction with Vietnam War related military spending, spurred a terrific economic boom. The '60s witnessed a 22 per cent statewide population growth, a steady rise in income levels, heady rates of annual economic growth, and a real estate market that was a speculator's dream come true (Kent 1983; Cooper and Daws 1985: 12).

As the boom gathered early momentum in the late '50s and early '60s, the Nisei political élite quickly abandoned its tepid commitment to restructuring the economy and adopted the conventional American approach; in the larger pie offered by economic growth lay the best solution to misdevelopment and imbalances. In fact, not only did this group enthusiastically support the Quinn programme, it even tried to claim credit for it. The Oahu Democratic Committee made the statement: "it is encouraging to note that a Republican governor appears willing to adopt and use the long-range development programme which we Democrats laboured to produce" (Honolulu Advertiser, 20 Sept. 1957).

Publication in 1985 of the meticulously researched Land and Power in Hawaii by Cooper and Daws revealed how the Democrats' programme was also on a deeply personal level. They write: "Within as little as three years after winning control of the legislature, major deals were being struck between Democratic developers and Republican landholders." Between the Big Five estates and ranches, still in possession of a near land monopoly, and Nisei politicians, land-less but now politically formidable, a symbiotic relationship materialised. The latter (in the name of rationality and public accountability in land-use changes) had established a complex series of state and county land codes and bureau-cracies to oversee the process. This gave the same men, who, as attorneys, de-velopers, investors, and realtors in private life, desperately needed developable lands and lucrative clients, the power in public life as legislators, councilmen, judges, and land-use commission officials to grant special design districts, de-velopment plan amendments, special variances, and rezoning permits to sud-denly enhance land values by 10 and 20 times. It was the basis for a thriving quid pro quo (Cooper and Daws 1985: 7).

Politicians such as Matsuo Takabuki, long-time kingpin of the Honolulu Board of Supervisors (later City Council) and lawyer for both the old-line Campbell estate and the new-line Asian financier Chinn Ho, a dominant power in the Democratic party, and key Oahu senator Mitsuyuki Kido were mar-velously placed to realise grand windfalls. They became central figures in the *huis* (partnerships) formed by investors to exploit development rights. Takabu-ki, in a most revealing 1961 statement, disclosed how wide his activities had become.

I have investments in corporations, partnerships and joint ventures in Waialua, Waipa-hu, Waianae, Kaneohe, Heeia, Makaha, Niu Valley, Moanalua, Waikiki, Airport area, Damon Tract, and Liliha, and I have clients in land and business in all parts of the city and county of Honolulu (see Kent 1983).

Kido used his privileged access to Cambell and Damon estate lands to emerge as a major developer-investor in the early '60s. Takabuki and Kido were merely early entrants into an immensely profitable real-estate development-speculation game that would possess the Asian élite through the next decades – the tip of an emerging iceberg. "A cascade of corruption, petty graft, influence peddling, land speculation, and favoritism in awards of government contracts" had begun that was to corrupt the political process and render Hawaii's people *defenceless against the inroads of overseas capital*. It is telling that as early as 1960, tax restructuring and land reform had lost their priorities on the political agenda. Democratic party reform leader Tom Gill, who knew the Nisei politicians well, noted that "making the old order over became less important than simply mak-ing it" (Kent 1983: 31).

By the advent of the 1962 election, which ushered John Burns into the governorship (along with a quarter-century of absolute Democratic political monopoly), a remarkable consensus reigned among the most powerful actors in Hawaii. Led by the Asian *petite bourgeoisie*, the Burns coalition also numbered in its ranks the government workers' unions and the declining but still politically useful ILWU (by now, long purged of its radical spirit and firmly integrated into the Democratic party). All these had good reason to give the New Hawaii model their abundant support.

Burns's inaugural speech, in which he pledged "to work for a more favourable climate of business, to encourage small business, to utilise the available offices of government for meeting the needs of business," might well have been uttered by the Republican Quinn. It set the tone of his administration. The Quinn period had taken Hawaii from an insular plantation economy to one ever more dependent on overseas investment in tourism-land development and military spending. Burns's 10-year tenure saw the model at full maturity, in a more complex situation demanding an intensification of public expenditures to attract investment and programmes aimed at stabilising a society rent by the social and economic contradictions accompanying the model's "success" (*Honolulu Star-Bulletin*, 4 Dec. 1962).

Massive new (publicly financed) projects were implemented to build the infrastructural setting modern tourism demanded and to steadily open new areas for resort exploitation. Official state delegations travelled to Japan to solicit investment capital from the Japanese tourism monopolies, and overseas investors received firm assurances of state support on every level. From 1963 to 1973, hotel rooms quadrupled to accommodate a visitor crush that increased from 429,000 to 2.63 million (State of Hawaii 1977).

The years from 1963 to 1973 were the era of Grand Illusions. Governor Burns talked incessantly about Hawaii's imminent birth as the "hub of the Pacific," "the Geneva of the Pacific," in what he assured everybody was "the era of the Pacific." The longer he stayed in office, the more pompously unreal his rhetoric became: "our horizons are limited only by our vision and by the depth of our desire to see the highest goals" (*Time*, 26 Feb. 1965). Burns and the Nisei political élite had certainly convinced themselves the new prosperity would be lasting and all-inclusive. The government's role was to pass enough social legislation to maintain a progressive, orderly, and decent society and to encourage "the magic of the marketplace" to accomplish the rest.

Without a doubt, *they* were doing well beyond their fondest dreams. Despite mounting internal factionalism in the political arena and intense personality struggles, the Nisei political-business class was firmly entrenched. Occupying twice the number of positions in the state legislature as the AJA proportion of the population and a slew of key bureaucratic posts in state and county governments, judgeships, and appointed positions on strategic state agencies and commissions, they were well-situated to pursue the politics of slf-aggrandisement. Strong alliances were fashioned with major local Chinese entrepreneurs such as Chinn Ho, Hung Wo Ching, and Clarence Ching, whose land development schemes required the ministrations of political insiders. In turn, as *Land and Power in Hawaii* elaborately documents, these rising capitalists provided their politicians with a generous piece of the action in their most lucrative development *huis* (along with sizable campaign contributions).

"By the 1970s," Cooper and Daws (1985: 122) argue, "every major political and administrative institution was dominated by, or contained, many who had been involved in land deals, individually or as members of *huis*." Bitter political rivals in public representing different Democratic factions were often connected privately as co-investors in the same *huis*; the maze of investment groups orchestrated by Clarence Ching around Oahu's Salt Lake perfectly illustrates this. No one enunciated this relationship between political influence and the rise of the developer class better than Herbert Horita, Hawaii's foremost builder, who had allied himself with senior politicos such as James Wakasuki in the legislature and George Akahane, power broker in the Honolulu City Council: "we used the political vehicle to create reforms and laws to change the regulations, laws, and business principles; so we had our own power structure" (Kent 1983: 150).

As "destination resort" complexes in the outer islands replaced Waikiki as the most dynamic area of tourism growth, opportunities arose for the Asian political class to play a mediation role *vis-à-vis* the incoming multinational corporations financing and operating these projects. It became the norm to employ "local boy" lawyers and consultants at hefty fees to facilitate business at the state and county levels. Weyerhauser, Boise Cascade, Cerro, Seibu, Rockefeller, Signal Oil, and Prudential Life, among others, found this policy expedient.

Land and Power in Hawaii, which furnishes a detailed recital of the myriad of the political-business interlocks, argues that interconnections were so extensive that such distinctions as public sector and private sector had no important meaning (Cooper and Daws 1985: 22). Indeed, the floating population of political insiders that flowed back and forth from the heart of the downtown business district around Bishop and King streets to the state and county office complex a few blocks away functioned as an integral component of a new power configuration in Hawaii. If its members lacked the landed interests of the old estates and the Big Five and the capital and sheer size of the multinationals, the political process was still theirs, and so was the ability to make or break a project. So, they had to be brought in.

By 1970, the New Hawaii model had been around for a dozen years, or long enough to generate some grave doubts. Despite the claims about Hawaii's emergence as a new Pacific centre, it was evident that what was being exchanged was one kind of peripheral status for another. Certainly, it was open season for Hawaii-based firms to exploit Pacific markets, resources, and labour, but investment penetration from the US mainland and Japan was overwhelming in comparison. Indeed, whereas in 1950 Hawaii residents held $44 million more in investment outside Hawaii than outsiders had in the islands, "by 1971 this situation was reversed and non-residents held $763 million more in investments in the islands than vice versa" (Stauffer 1985: 11).

As Quinn and Burns had foreseen, sugar and pineapple were being gradually phased out of Hawaii by the Big Five and Del Monte and moved to the third world, where labour was cheaper; but instead of a maturely diversified economy ready to take up the slack, there was only tourism-land development and the military. Rather than the "Geneva of the Pacific," Hawaii more closely resembled a "Miami-Puerto Rico of the Pacific."

By 1970, the contradictions of this kind of dependent development, both ecologically and in terms of race and class, were manifest. Sprawling subdivisions and cement-block flats made Honolulu an ugly city; there was pollution, traffic jams, welfarism, crime, and rising family disintegration. A low wage scale and a cost of living 25 per cent above the mainland's meant that only a bare one-third of Hawaii's families had the income to live at the official "moderate standard of living." Ominously, a definite chasm had opened between the mainly Asian-Caucasian *petite bourgeoisie* and stable working class and the predominantly Hawaiian-Filipino-Samoan marginal working class and welfare population. Tom Gill, lieutenant-governor and a liberal reformer long critical of the transformation of the Democratic party into a tool of unscrupulous land developers and financiers, said it best: "The sixties came to Hawaii with a shout and left with an ominous shudder" (Kent 1983: 147).

The 1970 gubernatorial election brought those critical of the model head to head with the newly entrenched élites. In midyear, Gill, attacking the "alarming friends" Burns had chosen to surround himself with, mounted an impressive primary campaign challenge for the governor's office. The class forces dependent on the state apparatus mobilised desperately. Gill, definitely no radical, represented, however, the impulse towards reform and restructuring frustrated by the corruption of the party leadership. A figure of integrity, he would certainly end the most glaring aspects of collusion.

On 30 July 1970, with Burns trailing Gill badly in the polls, more than 250 contractors and developers were brought together by Burns's top managers to discuss financing the campaign. Soon after, Department of Transportation Director Fujio Matsudo presided over a meeting attended by representatives of companies with state contracts in which demands were made for large contributions (in return for future contracts). Huge sums, unprecedented in Hawaiian politics, began flowing into Burns's war chest. The Dillingham Corporation, long a Republican pillar which had, however, received lucrative major construction contracts from Burns, pitched in from $150,000 to $300,000. In all, Burns spent $700,000 in the primary campaign alone (to $205,000 for Gill). His massively promoted television blitz was generally conceded to have provided the margin of victory (see Kent 1983).

When Burns fell terminally ill in 1973, his office passed to Lieutenant Governor George Ariyoshi, under whose guidance the state was to pass through the next 13 (more) troubled years. Since the New Hawaii model was tied to the fortunes of world capital, the economic downturn at the centre spelled an end to earlier euphoric projections for Hawaii's economy. Despite the social and ecological deterioration of the Burns era, there had been consistently high growth rates, employment, and state revenues. But the onset of stagflation, energy and monetary crises, deepening unemployment, and debt in the centre found its parallel in the islands, where joblessness, welfare dependency, and shortfalls of public revenues appeared as acute issues.

Tourism, projected to supply half the new jobs and generate income in the last quarter of the 20th century, quickly lost its inflation-proof reputation. At the depths of the 1976 mainland recession, when tourism stagnated, official unemployment mounted to 9 per cent, 2,000 workers a month were exhausting their unemployment payments, and the welfare case-load climbed to 15 per cent of the entire population. Three years of tourism prosperity followed (marked by wild, speculative sprees by overseas investors in Maui and Big Island luxury resort condominiums). But the boom and bust syndrome returned with a vengeance in 1980. For the first time since World War II, Hawaii's annual tourism arrivals declined in absolute numbers. Condominium units flooded a glutted market. Unemployment went double digit, and out-migration of locals soared. Residential housing construction nearly collapsed. After 1982, tourism experienced modest growth (topping 5 million in 1986), but not even tourism's most vociferous promoters would claim Hawaii was not dependent on a most highly volatile and unstable industry.

In George Ariyoshi one glimpses the Nisei business-political career writ large. Born in 1926 to an immigrant family of modest means, he was too young to participate in the 442nd's wartime exploits. He did, however, firmly hitch his star to theirs. First elected to the House of Representatives, when the "Democratic Revolution" came in 1954, he spent 16 uninspired years in the legislature, emerging in the mid-'60s as Senate majority leader. Meanwhile, in "private life" he had developed a thriving law practice serving both local developers and Big Five clients. His political prominence was rewarded with directorships in a bank, a utilities company, and an insurance firm. In conjunction with associates, he invested in several profitable developmental *huis*. His brother Jimmy became a leading condominium developer. Like other Nisei politicos, George Ariyoshi's sense of just who constituted the people was ethnically skewed: as a legislator, *all* 43 people he hired to work for him were AJAs (Cooper and Daws 1985: 392–99).

So the George Ariyoshi selected by a closed circle of party leaders for the lieutenant-governorship in 1970 had the approval of the old estates, the Asian entrepreneurs, local trade union leaders, and overseas investors as a most reliable fellow. He was also favoured by nearly half the electorate of Japanese descent, who provided him with large majorities in 1974, 1978, and 1982. His lavish, multimillion-dollar campaigns against mediocre foes did not hinder his fortunes either.

In 1986, commentators were referring to the approaching close of the long Burns-Ariyoshi era of modern Hawaii. The continuity is obvious: Throughout the Ariyoshi years, the commitment to the New Hawaii model – dependent on overseas investors, mediated by the local political-business class, and paved by government-financed infrastructure – remained intact. The number of arriving tourists doubled, and hotels and resort condominiums expanded enormously. Whole new areas, especially in Maui and west Hawaii, became major "up-scale" tourism centres. Military spending remained high, and, since the AJA-dominated Democrats never had less than a two-thirds majority in the legisla-ture, also keeping control of the county councils, insider manipulations and influence peddling could continue unbridled. The final touch was the gov-ernor's occasional insistence that Hawaii would yet become a Pacific centre.

But this was really a time of retrenchment and stasis, doubt and confusion about where the state was (and should be) going. The inflated "sky's the limit" ballyhoo that so dominated the Burns years fizzled out in the face of what Bob H. Stauffer has aptly called "the tragic maturing of Hawaii's economy" (Stauf-fer 1985: 1–8). And Ariyoshi's rhetoric changed accordingly. For instance, in his 1977 State of the State speech, Ariyoshi referred to "the financial crunch" and "heartbreakingly high unemployment." His rhetoric even touched on the issue of control: "We must shape our future, and not have it thrust on us by forces over which we have little or no control" (see Kent 1983).

And what was most noticeable about the Ariyoshi period was the AJA move-ment to a position of *defensive ethnicity* – ironically, the same position occupied by the *haole* élite *vis-à-vis* the Japanese before 1955.

The ethnic balance of power was shifting away from the AJAs, who num-bered a declining one-quarter of the population versus more than a third for the *haoles* and rapidly growing Hawaiian (18 per cent) and Filipino (12 per cent) populations. The AJA élite had committed two historic blunders: it identified itself too closely with an economic model that had brought uneven development and grossly disparate awards to Hawaii's different ethnic groups; second, it consolidated the ethnic cast of Hawaii's politics. Thus, it was inevitable that élite (and non-élite) Japanese came under attack from those who perceived them as "a successful monolith and arrogant power" (Odo 1985a: 1–3).

The prosperity of the Burns years had furnished the state with resources to paper over some of the ethnic rivalries. But given the realities of a declining economy, the Ariyoshi Democrats no longer had the luxury of pretending to function as *both* the party of the local *petite bourgeisie*-overseas corporations-Big Five and the party of the popular classes. Forced to choose, they chose their class base. This became abundantly clear as early as 1974 when the new governor called the legislature into special session to pass harsh new rules governing welfare eligibility. This marked the onset of a programme of state austerity directed against the working class and the poor.

Ethnic Hawaiians, constituting 40 per cent of the welfare population, were gravely affected by this. While the popular mythology had the Nisei displacing the *haole* élite, actually they had been *co-opted* by them, making the old *haole*-Hawaiian alliance redundant. This forced the Hawaiians out of the important segment of executive and rank-and-file public jobs they had occupied. So when the '60s boom came along, they lacked the political leverage, capital, or entrepreneurial skills to benefit from it. By the Ariyoshi period, their unemployment rates were twice those of the Japanese and their incomes half those of the Asians and *haoles*. In the New Hawaii, one Hawaiian scholar saw "land alienation, unemployment, ghettoization, the worst health profile in the islands, the lowest income level, a deep psychological oppression," as the lot of the indigenous people (Trask 1985: 11).

The Hawaiians now found the "upstart" AJAs confronting them nearly everywhere as authority – as school teachers, social workers, welfare case workers, and administrators. McGregor-Alegado expresses the widespread Hawaiian feeling against the AJAs' "racial exclusiveness in social relations and their patronage system." It was, she argues, the Japanese political-business class that rezoned and eliminated the "last remaining pockets of Hawaiian livelihoods based on farming and fishing utilising traditional Hawaiian cultural practices" (McGregor-Alegado 1985: 2). This was one of the issues in the early '80s, when the police, under command of top AJA state bureaucrats, evicted homeless Hawaiian squatters from public beach areas and arrested their leadership.

Indeed, in a stagnating economy where job creation was minimal (only 10,000 primarily low-wage jobs were created from 1980 to 1984 for a work force that increased by 50,000) and where home ownership was out of reach for at least 95 per cent of the renter population, the extremely high visibility of AJA power and success made them a very likely target. In his several gubernatorial campaigns against Ariyoshi, Frank Fasi, a *haole* and mayor of Honolulu, made a powerful bid for *haole*, Hawaiian, and Filipino votes against the "machine," a buzzword for Japanese political dominion.

The irony of all this is that the AJA élite has *never constituted a legitimate ruling class in Hawaii*. Instead, they have skilfully performed a multitude of roles – front men, middle men, mediators, agents, and power brokers – in the service of the authentic ruling calss, much of which does not reside in the islands and which prefers invisibility as one element of its power. Unseen forces wield immense control over Hawaii's economic life: the billionaire Bass brothers of Texas, who hold an important interest in Amfac and are in partnership with Chris Hemmeter in the $360 million Waikaloa Hyatt Regency, are one; Torray Clark, with its huge holdings in Amfac and Castle and Cooke, another; Philadelphia's International Utilities, parent company of C. Brewer; and Jardine Matheson of Hong Kong, owner of Theo. Davies. These overseas corporations, in conjunction with the more visible Prudential Life Insurance Company, Louisiana Land and Oil, Hyatt, Hilton, Seibu, Kokusai Kogyo, Marriott, Rockefeller, Northwest Mutual Life Insurance, Sheraton, and (above all) United Airlines, are the real power shaping the islands today.

Without doubt, the AJA élite has been well-rewarded for its services. The huge homes in Nuuanu, Makiki Heights, and elsewhere, the Mercedes and Porsches, the élite private schools for their children are all testaments to "American success." But they do not make the investment decisions that count. Only 7 of the top 50 companies within Hawaii are AJA-controlled. Nor do they occupy leading managerial positions within the Big Five firms or banks, much less directorships with overseas multinationals. Significantly, the Japanese, as an ethnic group, have higher incomes in the state sector than in the monopoly or competitive sectors. And after a generation of political dominance, the AJAs as a whole remain, curiously, a working class with the highest percentage of family members in the work force of any principal ethnic group.

A third of the state's construction workers, 40 per cent of the mechanics, 44 per cent of mail clerks and office messengers, 60 per cent of school teachers, 40 per cent of the computer programmers, and most secretaries and clerical workers are Japanese; many are in jobs vulnerable to automation and layoffs. Obviously, the AJA élite carried few of their compatriots with them on the journey into the upper reaches of the class structure (Kotani 1985: 108).

The "modernisation" of Hawaii's political economy over the past 30 years has really amounted to the transformation from a plantation to a tourism society, or a *limited* to a *complete* dependency. Whereas the old Big Five élite were masters in their domain, today's conglomeration of old banks and estates and the Asian *petite bourgeoisie* exist as little more than a comprador class to facilitate the entry of overseas capital into lucrative tourism-land development.

The responsibility of the political reformers who took control of the government apparatus a generation ago was to protect the integrity of the islands. As we have seen, their own vested interests subverted early commitments to land reform, tax reform, and a general economic restructuring. Instead of pursuing a policy of selectively building tourism-land development, they became accomplices in the erection of a Caribbean-style tourism society.

Nukolii represents the classic example of this dynamic. A 60-acre Kauai beach-front property sold by Amfac in the 1970s to a *hui* of prominent AJA politicos (headed by Maui real-estate speculator Masaru Yokouchi) became a *cause célèbre*. The Yokouchi *hui* sold the property nine months later for a $4 million profit to Hasegawa Komuten, Japan's largest condominium builder. Great opposition surfaced with this project, and it was rejected in 1980 by a 2-1 margin in an island-wide referendum. Undeterred, the Japanese corporation, aided by an assortment of Hawaii's top politicians, judges, and developers bided its time for several years until Kauai's sugar industry collapsed a bit more, then bankrolled a second referendum they won handily. Nukolii quite clearly illustrates "the extent to which overseas capital will go in utilising local allies and in corrupting the local political process to obtain objectives regarded as major." Local political collaboration with big outside investors made a mockery of the democratic process (Cooper and Daws 1985: 326–66).

The consequences of Hawaii's "soft state" have been calamitous. Misdevelopment of the kind usually associated with less-developed countries is present. Investment is wildly uneven; west Hawaii, west Molokai, and West Beach are inundated with hotels and condominiums, and east Hawaii, east Molokai, and Waimanalo are starved for capital. Overseas control of tourism means a crucial lack of spin-off activities; according to Stauffer, $1.4 billion was repatriated in 1980 out of the islands in fees and profits. Moreover, the "vast majority of Hawaii's people have seen a deterioration in their living standard in recent years." Tourism has created a huge servant class of menial employees; hotel wages, which averaged $234.57 weekly in 1984, have consistently been the lowest of any major industry in Hawaii. This has meant a more pyramidal class structure and a sharp income hierarchy: the top 3.1 per cent of state resident income earners received a gross income roughly equal to the bottom 43.4 per cent in 1979 (Stauffer 1985: 3–14).

And the cultural division of labour found in tourism bears an uncanny likeness to the plantations of old; in the deluxe resort areas, one sees *haole* expatriate managers, Asian clerks and supervisors, Hawaiian bellboys and cocktail waitresses, Filipino maids. All this contributes to the brittle social fabric that is Hawaii today.

Stanley Greenberg reminds us: "Capitalist development . . . both preserves and remakes the racial order, extending and reinforcing racial barriers, but also creating new contradictions that paradoxically threaten to dismantle them" (Greenberg 1980: 26). So there is the emergence of "localism" as a cultural-political force. Its unifying elements are the common idiom, music, surfing, local theatre, food, a sense of the "goodness of Hawaii," the wish to maintain what is truly distinctive *vis-à-vis* the mainland: a visceral resistance to complete assimilation. At the political level, localism manifests itself as grass-roots resistance to projects of overseas capital as discussions about "palaka power" among certain politicians. Provided it can locate a proper political vehicle (and is not reduced to merely an ethnic Hawaiian nationalist movement or an expression of anti-*haole*, anti-AJA rage), it may become a force to reckon with.

The luxury of a quarter-century of hindsight allows me to say, "No, James Michener was premature." The age of the "Golden Men" has not yet arrived. The context has been wrong. Such an age requires the *transcendence* of ethnic politics, of ethnic visions, of purely personal and communal agendas, not their glorification. The affirmation, rather than the negation, of integrity of place. A political leadership that intervenes not to support its overseas masters but to guarantee social equity. If the Hawaii model reveals anything to us, it is the limitations and pitfalls of ethnic élites pursuing the project of self-aggrandisement in multiethnic societies. And the limitations of what former US president Ronald Reagan has called "the magic of the marketplace."

REFERENCES

Beechert, E. 1985. *Working in Hawaii*. Honolulu: University of Hawaii Press.
Cooper, G., and G. Daws. 1985. *Land and power in Hawaii*. Honolulu: Benchmark Press.

Fuchs, L. 1968. *Hawaii Pono: A social history*. New York: Harcourt Brace Jovanovich.

Greenberg, S. 1980. *Race and state in capitalist development*. New Haven: Yale University Press.

Kent, N. 1983. *Hawaii Islands under the influence*. New York: Monthly Review Press.

Kirkpatrick, J. 1986. Ethnic antagonism and innovation in Hawaii. In *Inter-ethnic conflict: Myth and reality*, edited by J. Boucher, D. Landis, and K. Arnold. Los Angeles: Russell Sage Foundation.

Kotani, R. 1985. *The Japanese in Hawaii*. Honolulu: Hawaii Hochi.

McGregor-Alegado, D. 1985. *The Hawaiian perspective on Japanese in politics and business*. Honolulu: University of Hawaii. Unpublished paper.

Odo, F. 1985a. *A pictorial history of the Japanese in Hawaii*. Honolulu: Bishop Museum.

———. 1985b. *The meaning of the 100th anniversary of the Japanese in Hawaii*. Honolulu. Unpublished speech.

Porteus, S. D., and M. Babcock. 1976. *Temperament and race*. Boston: Richard Berger.

Reinecke, J. 1972. *Feigned necessity*. Honolulu: Vanguard Press.

State of Hawaii. 1977. *State of Hawaii data book*. Honolulu.

Stauffer, B. H. 1985. The tragic maturing of Hawaii's economy. In *Social process in Hawaii*, edited by S. Poolet and M. Sullivan, vol. 31, pp. 1–24. Honolulu: University of Hawaii Press.

Takaki, R. 1984. *Pau Hana*. Honolulu: University of Hawaii Press.

Trask, H. 1985. Hawaiians, American colonisation and the quest for independence. In *Social process in Hawaii*, edited by S. Pooley and M. Sullivan, vol. 31, pp. 101–36. Honolulu: University of Hawaii Press.

Wright, T. 1972. *The disenchanted isles*. New York: Dial Press.

Yamamoto, E. 1979. The significance of local. In *Social process in Hawaii*, edited by S. Pooley and M. Sullivan, vol. 27, pp. 104–16. Honolulu: University of Hawaii Press.

5

Aboriginality in a Nation-State: The Australian Case

JEREMY BECKETT

Benedict Anderson observes in his introduction to *Imagined Political Communities: Reflections on the Origin and Spread of Nationalism* that "The 'end of the era of nationalism,' so long prophesied, is not remotely in sight. Indeed, nation-ness is the most universal legitimate value in the political life of our time" (1984: 12). This phenomenon, so characteristic of Europe in the 19th century, manifested itself in Europe's colonies in the 20th century, eventually including island peoples of the South Pacific. It is now also to be found among the indigenous peoples of colonies of settlement, such as Australia and New Zealand. The difference, however, is that, as tiny minorities that are politically and economically dependent, they have no prospect of sovereignty. Their nationhood seems doomed to remain encapsulated within a nation-state that is not only differently constituted, but that sometimes seeks to appropriate the symbols of their aboriginality. What cannot be appropriated, however, is their descent from the original inhabitants of the country, which thus constitutes a problem for the nationalism of the settler society.

In this chapter, I shall be primarily concerned with the Australian Aborigines, although much that I say will also apply to Australia's other indigenous people, the Torres Strait Islanders.[1] Let me begin with the rhetorical proposition that, until the moment when the First Fleet landed in Australia, there were no Aborigines. There were aboriginal inhabitants; but my point is that – without in any sense questioning the claim of present-day Aborigines to be identified with them – Aboriginality must be understood as an artifact of the colonial encounter. Both native and settler began to articulate it in the process of coming to terms with one another's presence and redefined it as the local and global context of their interaction changed. Redefinition notwithstanding, it is a noteworthy fact that the idea of Aboriginality has persisted and been continually expressed in practice right up to the present: at any given time, people have been identified and identifying Aborigines.

118

This is not intended to imply that Aboriginality in its various definitions is a product of consensus. On the contrary, it is to be understood as a focus of conflict. It is noteworthy, however, that, although the political dominance of the settler majority has been almost total, its cultural hold has remained incomplete. Not only have Aboriginal people continued to reproduce Aboriginality for themselves, but they have reproduced it in ways that, for them at least, have contradicted the official definition. Sally Weaver's distinction between private and public ethnicity helps us to clarify this situation. The former she defines as

behavioural in that it is practised by groups or networks of aboriginal minority members in their daily lives. . . . In short, private ethnicity is defined and rationalized by the aboriginal groups, not the nation-state, and it is private because its content and use are not dependent upon public (non-aboriginal) debate and determination. Public ethnicity, by contrast, consists largely of symbols. It is part of the political culture of the nation-state, being determined in the public arena of relations between the nation-state and the aboriginal minorities (1985: 184).

Private Aboriginality is scarcely documented, but the conditions of its reproduction have generally favoured local and sectional variation. Public Aboriginality, with which this chapter is mainly concerned, strains towards unity, although there may be competing definitions at any given time. Until recently, however, the loci of its reproduction have lain beyond Aboriginal reach. Not only have Aborigines been a tiny percentage of the total population, but they have been dispersed, impoverished, and politically disfranchised. However, the settler population at large has not been directly involved either, for once the frontier moved on, the few Aborigines who survived massacre and exotic disease were made either physically or socially invisible, known to the majority only by report.

Although explorers, missionaries, scientists, artists, and photographers have contributed to the construction of Aboriginality, in this century the role of the state has been central. At different times and places, Aborigines have come into sustained client relations with employers; in some instances, missionaries have loomed large in their lives. Nevertheless, the prevailing mode of incorporation has been governmental, and the place of Aborigines in Australian society is that of a unitary minority managed through specialized institutional structures that can properly be termed colonial. Thus situated, the state has had the power to bring Aborigines some way towards external conformity with its constructions. In the past 20 years, Aboriginal people have been formally accorded a part in the process, variously designated self-determination or self-management, but this has been largely through government funded – and thus, in the final analysis, controlled – agencies.

As in other liberal democracies, the media, and in the past generation especially the electronic media, have played a part in the articulation of national consciousness and more generally "public opinion." They have also played a part in the construction of public Aboriginality, largely by commenting on government policies and programmes. At times, Aborigines have been able to use these outlets to tell their own story, but they have remained dependent on the goodwill of those who controlled the media and have in greater or lesser degree had to adapt their statements to these conditions. Again, in the last analysis the state has dominated the situation, first, because discussion has inevitably focused on its policies and practice, and second, because it has controlled much of the information and expertise.

Two points will be argued in the pages that follow. The first is that the state's definition of Aboriginality and, more broadly, its Aboriginal policies are to be understood in terms of its other concerns and objectives. The second is that the resulting definitions of Aboriginality must be understood against the background of its construction of Australian nationality. As one has changed, so has the other. I shall analyse these changes in terms of the concepts of citizenship and colonial status. Initially, Australian citizenship was reserved for people of European, especially British, descent; Aborigines were expected to die out, and while they lingered, they were a conquered people, deemed ineligible for either the privileges or the responsibilities of citizenship. When they seemed destined to survive and increase, their special status was reconstituted as a preparation for the citizenship they were still denied. In recent years, there has been an attempt to combine citizenship with a special status that has been shorn of its punitive and restrictive features. This is now under challenge.

COLONIALISM AND CITIZENSHIP

Although we seem unable to do without the term *colonial*, the multiplicity of even the analytical meanings given to it require that I make clear what I have in mind. Colonialism, as I understand it, refers primarily to the *political* outcome of European expansion into other quarters of the globe. The motivating force of this movement was economic and, at least in its later phase, was sustained by the dynamics of capitalism; but in particular places, military strategy might be the critical consideration instead of the exploitation of labour and resources or the security of markets. A colonial order arises when the state that has annexed a territory formally and systematically discriminates between the conquering invaders and the subject indigenes in such a way as to entrench the differences between them and to foster their economic, political, and cultural inequality. This discrimination is sustained by some form of ideology that justifies the domination of the indigenous population in terms of differences of race, mentality, moral qualities, cultural advancement, religion, or historic destiny.

Although the term is more often used in reference to the overseas possessions of some metropolitan country, it has also been applied to the position of people engulfed by national boundaries, as in the case of Britain's "Celtic fringe," and to the indigenous populations of colonies of settlement such as Australia, New Zealand, the United States, Canada, Mcxico, and Peru which subsequently became indepentent. But if the alternative for external colonies is sovereignty, what is the alternative for internal colonies? For Rodolfo Stavenhagen, whose writing on Mesoamerica has done much to establish the concept of *internal* colonialism, it is class. Emphasizing that "the class character and colonial character of interethnic relations are two intimately related aspects of the same phenomenon," he argues that "the colonial character of interethnic relations impress particular characteristics upon class relations, tending to stop their development" (1965: 76). These characteristics disappear with capitalist development, so that the interaction of persons holding opposed economic positions becomes increasingly independent of ethnic considerations (1965: 76). Thus, as the labour market expands, the Indian who has been tied to community and kept in semifeudal dependence on some Ladino patron becomes free to move and sell his labour.

Though colonial relations in the liberal democracies can at one level be opposed to class relations, they must also be understood against the complex of political and ideological constructions that are supposed to transcend or compensate for class inequalities. The British sociologist T. H. Marshall grouped these constructions under the heading of citizenship, which he divided into three stages: the civil, the political, and the social, the last being broadly conceived as "the whole range from the right to a modicum of economic welfare and security to the right to share to the full in the social heritage and to live the life of a civilized being according to standards prevailing in the society" (1963: 72–74). Tracing the development of citizenship in his native Britain from the 18th century, he located the social in the 20th century and especially in the time that he was writing, when the Welfare State was entering a new phase of expansion.

If capitalist development brings class into cultural dominance, peripheral areas may remain unaffected. But while the inhabitants of these areas may be excluded from class relationships and still locked into colonial structures, they are not thereby excluded from citizenship that, once it comes into existence, acquires a relative autonomy through its association with the state. Citizenship is defined in many different ways, to exclude and to include, but if it pretends to some universalistic principle, it must be at least formally extended to the enclaves of colonialism that linger on the periphery. However, citizenship without a place in a class system gives rise to some strange formations.

With the emergence of capitalism, the nation-state has become the typical form of polity, sustained by notions of nationhood that combine descent and culture in any uneasy embrace. When the emphasis is on descent, the rights of people of other descent to citizenship become problematic. They are either defined as transient, or, alternatively, as irremediably defective in their moral and intellectual endowments. When the emphasis is on culture, the nation may be represented as a melting pot, with the capacity to make people of diverse origins into citizens, all subscribing to the same cultural values. Alternatively, nationhood is conceived of in dynamic terms as integrating cultural differences and maintaining them in political equilibrium.

This is not to suggest that states remain forever committed to a particular definition of nationhood or citizenship. Such things are integral to the political and economic processes of development, and change accordingly. But they do not change reflexively. To the extent that an ideology is dominant throughout the society, the ruling class and party can change it only from within. Ideology can thus have unintended consequences.

One such consequence, exemplified recently in Australia and also in North America, is a need to extend citizenship to indigenous peoples whose relationship to the state is still colonial because of their peripheral situation in the economy. The outcome has been, by an irony, the rehabilitation of the old colonial structures: indigenous status takes on new ideological significance, and the old administrative apparatus is retooled for new tasks. As Beverly Gartrell puts it, "Indigenes can lay claim to payments both in their newly acquired rights as citizens, and in their old status as indigenes eligible for special benefits not open to other citizens" (n.d.: 30). The formation, which she notes (n.d.: 30) is found only in wealthy states with very small indigenous populations, has come to be known as Welfare Colonialism. Robert Paine coined this term in connection with the Canadian North, but recognized that it has wider application. Continuous with classic colonialism, it is solicitous rather than exploitive, liberal rather than repressive (1977: 3). However,

any decision taken by the colonizers has a basic flaw: a decision made for the material benefit of the colonized at the same time can be construed as disadvantaging them; a "generous" or "sensible" decision can be at the same time morally "wrong." This is so because it is the colonizers who make the decisions that control the future of the colonized; because the decisions are made (ambiguously) on behalf of the colonized, and yet in the name of the colonizers' culture (and of their political, administrative, and economic priorities) (1977: 46).

Welfare colonialism, then, is the state's strategy for managing the political problem posed by the presence of a depressed and disenfranchised indigenous population in an affluent and liberal democratic society. At the practical level, it engages in economic expenditure well in excess of what the minority produces. At the political level, it sets up machinery for the articulation and manipulation of minority opinion. At the ideological level, the "native" who once stood in opposition to the "settler" and outside the pale of society undergoes an apotheosis to emerge as its original citizen.

This is the situation of Australia's Aborigines today. But it has not always been so. In the early years, their distinctness was recognized, but it made the basis for exclusion from citizenship. Subsequently, they were "offered" citizenship as individuals on the condition that they abandoned their "distinctness." Only in the past decade or so has citizenship been declared compatible with indigenous status, and this doctrine is now under challenge. The rest of this chapter will be concerned with the interplay between economic and political and the cultural constructions of Aboriginality.

CITIZENSHIP AND COLONIALISM IN AUSTRALIA

Citizenship took much the same shape in Australia as it had in the "Mother Country." By the time the six colonies were brought together in a federation in 1901, the basic legal and political structures were in place and the first redistributive measures only a few years away. Despite some tendency to deride British social distinctions, Australian citizenship was primarily identified with British, including Irish, descent, being for many years the automatic entitlement of British immigrants as soon as they landed. It was open to persons of north European origin, less certainly to southern Europeans, and denied to other races, who were as far as possible excluded from entry. (Pacific island indentured labour was repatriated soon after federation.) Given Australia's explicit commitment to a white-Australian policy and its membership in a British Empire that ruled "native peoples," it is not surprising that the privileges and duties of citizenship were largely withheld from the indigenous population until the 1960s. They suffered varying degrees of legal disability, were politically disfranchised, and, apart from concessions during World War II, were excluded from the normal run of benefits that the state distributed to citizens.

The earliest colonial authorities came from Britain under instruction to establish friendly relations with the Aborigines and, if possible, to incorporate them into the labour force. However, they found it difficult to implement these instructions (Stanner 1977) and ceased to control the situation once settlers began to press into the interior. They did not fully regain control until the late 19th century, when they began integrating the surviving Aborigines as wards of special government agencies or officially supported church missions.

The dominance of these agencies can be traced to the special circumstances of colonization. Australia began as a place to off-load surplus population from Britain, either as convicts or as free settlers. Subsequent settlement took a pastoral form, with wool and meat as the staples of an export-oriented economy and gold as an occasional bonanza. Although sections of the economy were for periods dependent on cheap indigenous labour, the Australian economy as a whole was not. The incorporation of the indigenous population was incidental to other objectives, and those who needed labour could – at least in the long run – import workers who were healthier, more numerous, and more tractable (see Beckett 1986: 34).

Settler terror and exotic disease had combined to reduce the indigenous population to a tiny remnant. A few continued to sustain their traditional way of life in places still inhospitable to colonists, but most were to be found on the fringes of colonial society, sometimes as a reserve of cheap, casual labour, but often as paupers. As objects of pity or disgust, this latter group became the responsibility of the state. By degrees, however, the state extended its powers to all people of Aboriginal descent, constituting them as a "problem" group in need of special supervision.

From the turn of the century, government officials controlled the movement of Aboriginal people, confining many of them to reserves and, in increasing numbers, to supervised settlements more or less isolated from towns and cities. In the economic sphere, they served as recruitment agents for a labour force whose chief virtue was that it was cheap and easily controlled; or they were dispensers of relief, which, like the Poor Law in 19th-century Britain, was represented as an alternative to citizenship rather than an entitlement to it (Marshall 1963: 83). Required by the politicians to practise strict economy, they were often left otherwise free to follow their own notions of improvement and rehabilitation.

This regime, which might be called "protective segregation," was the institutional expression of a whole social and ideological structure that perpetuated the distinction between "native" and "settler" after the act of dispossession had been consummated. The social Darwinism that served as the ideology of an expansive capitalism designated primitive culture as an anachronism and even predicted the demise of its bearers. The virulent folk racism, through which white workers protected their relatively favourable conditions against cheap coloured labour, inevitably applied to Aborigines who, if they could not be excluded from the country, could at least be limited to the occupations that Europeans did not want.[2] Denied both the status of human being and worker, the only qualification that Aborigines had for citizenship was that they were permanent residents. Even this the settlers were able to negate, designating them historical transients in the sense that they were doomed by the laws of "progress" to pass from the scene.

Predictions of their demise continued long after the evidence for it had disappeared, but by the 1930s Australia's governments were obliged to recognise that, even if the so-called full-blooded Aborigines were to die out, there would still be a sizable and increasing population of mixed descent outside the pale of society. Since much of this population was in some degree dependent on the state, the Australian taxpayer could look forward to an increasing charge on the public purse. It was no doubt in recognition of this prospect that heads of the governmental agencies met in 1939 to frame the new assimilation policy. This policy, which after World War II included the now-increasing numbers of "full-bloods," had citizenship as its stated objective. However, it postponed realization until such time as Aborigines should fulfil the requirements deemed appropriate. Meanwhile, the assimilation objective provided legitimation for an intensification of state intervention, which, if anything, further curtailed the rights of Aborigines.

The wartime emergency, which brought national unity and the security of the northern coastline into doubt, had in fact resulted in a degree of enfranchisement through the inclusion of Aborigines and Torres Strait Islanders in the new provisions for old-age pensions and child endowment. This measure was a product of the heightened sense of social justice that emerged during the national emergency, but it was also a response to the fear that European abuses and Japanese contact had left a disaffected population along Australia's vulnerable northern coastline. It may have been a similar fear that prompted the military authorities to draft some 700 Torres Strait Islanders into the armed forces despite laws prohibiting them from military service (Hall 1980). In each case, however, the colonial authorities mitigated the effects of these changes by reducing the soldiers' wages to a fraction of the normal rate (Hall 1980) and taking control of the social service payments or holding them on their wards' behalf.

The cold war provided a new set of reasons for hastening the process of assimilation. As a small British enclave in the South Pacific, Australia found that it could no longer depend on imperial Britain for protection but must now cultivate the friendship of the United States. When it added its voice to American attacks on Soviet expansionism, however, it found itself embarrassed by references to its mistreatment of Aborigines, as a speech by Paul Hasluck admitted (Stone 1974: 192). Similarly, its reputation for racism hindered the cultivation of friendly relations with newly independent neighbours to the north such as Indonesia and Malaysia.

More or less simultaneously, the situation of the Aborigines became an issue for Australians outside the narrow confines of the church and minor political groups that had hitherto been the Aborigines' only advocates. Sympathy for the decolonization of Indonesia during the later 1940s did not immediately carry over to Papua New Guinea, still less to Aboriginal Australia; but the sentiment was kept alive by the decolonization process in Asia and Africa, the civil rights movement in the United States, and the emergence of resistance to apartheid in South Africa. A case can be made that it was only after this that the Aboriginal issue took hold, and white Australians began to talk of Australia's "Deep North" or "apartheid" in Queensland. Without doubt, the "Freedom Rides" that, for the first time, challenged local segregation in outback NSW took place in conscious emulation of the campaigns in Alabama and Mississippi.

As pressure mounted through the 1960s, the governments reduced the civil disabilities they had earlier imposed on Aborigines "for their own good" and extended to them more of the privileges of citizenship, such as franchise. The buoyant state of the labour market provided grounds for the belief that all but the remotest and most recently contacted Aborigines could be absorbed into the mainstream economy. The agencies charged with the management of Aborigines now declared that their task was to work themselves out of a job, and those of Victoria and NSW actually went into dissolution, handing over their functions to the agencies that provided health, housing, educational, and other services to the public at large. However, it was soon apparent that such "liberal" solutions did not solve the problem.

The newspapers of this period were "discovering" Aboriginal shanty towns on rubbish tips without water or sanitation, not in the remote outback but on the outskirts of prosperous country towns. During the 1930s, such poverty was unremarkable and was suffered by many whites as well as blacks; but by the 1960s, it threatened the doctrine, fostered by the long postwar boom, that a middle-class standard of living was within the reach of everyone in Australia. There was general agreement that "something should be done," but providing Aboriginal and Islander citizens with an acceptable standard of living was harder than legislating for civil or political rights. Although crash programmes could bring housing and medical care to the worst trouble spots, they could not generate employment in them or bring industry to places that were inaccessible or lacking in resources. Equal wage legislation in the northern cattle industry resulted in the dislodgement of Aborigines from a niche they had long occupied (cf. Kolig 1982: 52). High unemployment rates in the cities cast doubt on the value of relocation programmes, and though the development of the North provided Torres Strait Islanders with a brief period of prosperity, the mining industry proved to have little need for Aboriginal labour (Hinton 1968). The economic downturn of the early 1970s cast further doubt on the possibility of solving the problems of the Aborigines and Torres Strait Islanders through drawing them into the economic mainstream. The policy reversal and new initiatives of the mid-1970s must be understood against the background of this impasse.

In a referendum held in 1967, a large majority of the Australian electorate had accepted, at least in principle, that the indigenous population was a matter of national concern that should become the responsibility of the federal government. The conservative coalition then in office was nevertheless slow to exercise its new powers for fear of infringing on states' rights. However, one of the first actions of the federal Labour government, following its election in 1972, was to assume national responsibility for Aboriginal and Islander affairs. The newly constituted Department of Aboriginal Affairs immediately dispensed with the assimilation policy. It would continue to provide material assistance in the welfare mode, but progress towards assimilation would no longer be the touchstone: the goal was now community development, with the community itself as the final arbiter of its needs. In the words of the first report of the newly formed Department of Aboriginal Affairs:

Elements in the traditional Aboriginal culture and system of values may "impede" programs aimed at changing Aboriginals, but the aim is rather to help Aborigines achieve
their own goals as individuals and communities; such elements cease to be seen as obstacles and can be seen rather as factors for influencing the choice (1975: 7).

The application of such a policy to the great variety of situations existing in
Australia produced a broad range of programmes, from the funding of special
services in such areas as medical care, education, and legal aid to the comprehensive underwriting of remote communities. In the federally administered
Northern Territory and in some other parts of Australia, communities or community segments acquired rights over land and, in some instances, received
mining royalties. The Aboriginal world now embraced great diversity, but even
though overall they were more closely integrated with the non-Aboriginal
majority, the dominant mode of this integration was still governmental.
Whether they were seeking employment or economic assistance, claiming land,
defending civil rights, or practising traditional and modern arts, their point of
articulation was the state. The new national leadership and the emerging
"white collar" stratum directly or indirectly owed their existence to government.

The massive increase in government expenditure that the new strategy entailed must be seen as part of a general expansion of government redistributive
activity in the welfare field and, in a sense, continuous with it. Aborigines,
however, gained access to special benefits (besides the universal benefits distributed to the unemployed, the sick, the aged, and others) not available to other
Australians. Both types of benefits, however, were financed from the same
source and were thus subject to the same political processes.

When a liberal democratic state undertakes to redistribute part of its resources according to principles of "social justice," it brings into existence a
political arena in which concerned groups compete for public sympathy and the
support of legislators. At another level, bureaucrats compete with one another
to gain funds for their respective departments and clienteles. Which factors in
the equation are decisive varies according to the composition of the constituency and its standing in the society. Correspondingly, claimants adopt strategies
depending on their numbers, their political leverage, their access to the seats of
power, and their control of information. In so far as welfare politics engages the
public and the media, it generates its own discourse, in which special cases of
"need" are strategically linked to sacrosanct doctrines such as "social justice"
and "the national interest." Anyone wishing to compete in an arena of this kind
must be in control of these trophies, and the smaller, less-powerful claimants
may be largely dependent upon them.

On the face of it, Aborigines and Islanders were very poorly placed to compete in such an arena. Totalling less than 2 per cent of the Australian population, widely scattered, so that they rarely hold an electoral balance of power,

located far from the seats of power, poorly educated, and with meagre financial resources, their situation corresponded closely to Beverly Gartrell's profile of the Fourth World:

What power can a tiny minority wield? Unable to exert material control over the environment of the powerful, it can only challenge the self-concept of both bureaucratic and political office-holders, and the citizens of the nation, and appeal to the legal rights institutionalized in earlier phases. The resulting power is tenuous and fluctuating, for it is based on ideologies themselves changing, and it depends on the receptivity of some audience – elements in the wider society willing to listen to the message being sent by the dominated group (Gartrell n.d.: 28).

Considering their numbers and lack of political leverage, the Aboriginal movement was remarkably successful during the 1970s, both in terms of media interest and government response – even though basic problems remained unsolved. In the early stages, it relied heavily on "the politics of embarrassment." Thus, in a time when demonstrations were a frequent occurrence, it established the "tent embassy" on the lawn of Parliament House, attracting national and international media attention. At a later stage, it was able to use funds from the World Council of Churches to send groups overseas to publicize its cause. Government's response was to regularise political activity through the establishment of new structures that were amenable to control because it provided the funds. The policies of Aboriginalization and self-determination likewise resulted in the concentration of Aboriginal and Islander leadership around the bureaucratic apparatuses that extracted and administered these resources. This was especially so with the elected National Aboriginal Conference (Weaver 1983).[3] In sum, welfare colonialism perpetuated old structures and generated new ones whose purpose was the reconstitution of Aboriginal peoples as a national minority and whose function was their management as a national and international problem.

THE CONSTRUCTION OF ABORIGINALITY

Each of the policy shifts described here has been accompanied by a redefinition of Aboriginality, not *de novo* but through a reordering of established ideas. Framed by and for the dominant European majority, these definitions have reflected the cultural preoccupations and assumptions of the time, sometimes to the point where the ostensible objects appear almost incidental. I cannot conduct here the cultural analysis that a proper understanding of Aboriginality in Australia requires (for a pilot study see Beckett 1986), but will simply offer an outline of the positions that prevailed through the period reviewed.

From the beginning, European observers placed Aborigines outside the pale of civilization: without material possessions and especially without clothing; unresponsive to overtures of trade yet making free with the strangers' property. Settlers expropriating Aboriginal land found a ready justification in the occupants' nomadism and their failure to "improve" it. For the reflectively inclined, Aborigines could be seen as frozen in a prehistoric past – a stone age – from which the rest of humanity had progressed or – worse – a degenerate branch of the human race. Either perception effectively disqualified them from a place in the history of humankind.

Assimilationism gave Aborigines a future, at the price of surrendering their anachronistic culture and becoming apprentice Australians – a condition that left them effectively cultureless. Meanwhile, having separated Aboriginal culture from living people – or all but a few very old individuals who would "soon die out" – Anglo-Australians could enshrine it in museums and libraries as part of the national heritage they were "discovering" in the process of differentiating the Australian nation from that of the "Mother Country." Under such auspices, Aboriginality was celebrated in terms of its antiquity and reduced to a series of objects: the bark painting, the boomerang in its glass case, photographers of the "last" performance of this or that corroboree.

The reconstitutioning of Australia as a place without racial prejudice did not itself result in the rehabilitation of Aboriginality. Aboriginal people were rather identified with black Americans and other "coloured people" fighting for their rights. The early Aboriginal activists in the cities duly adopted the idiom of the Freedom Riders and, towards the end of the 1960s, indentified themselves with the North American Black Power movement. With the 1970s, however, the Aboriginal people were once again defined in terms of Aboriginality, which, however, was now regarded as having a valid place in contemporary Australian society.

This development coincided with an official recognition of the immigrant communities under the slogan of multiracialism. Australia was to accept this cultural diversity as integral to the emergent national identity. Aboriginality did not, however, become just another kind of ethnicity. Recognizing the danger of the possibility that Aboriginal bids for government funds could easily get lost in the general scramble for "special assistance," aboriginal spokespersons and their advocates insisted on their prior entitlement and special needs as the original inhabitants of the country.

The public aboriginality that emerged in this new climate could not simply be an externalization of private Aboriginalities. The experience of people of Aboriginal descent now ranged from the remote, "traditionally oriented" people of the centre and the north through the supervised communities of rural Australia to the growing ghettoes of the capital cities. As Jones and Hill-Burnett (1982) have remarked, "the common culture of diverse sub-cultures is not 'given' in a situation that is culturally diverse. The commonalities are first conceptualized and then constructed" – or, as Ben Anderson would say, "imagined." However, although those who did the imagining now included people of Aboriginal descent, the process of construction was subject to the constraints imposed by non-Aboriginal institutional structures, especially the media, and the strategies of welfare politics. The problem was that even though almost anyone who identified as Aboriginal was accepted as such by those whose business it was to assist Aboriginal people, it was the traditionally oriented Aborigines of the centre and north who held the public imagination and sympathy.

Like other Westerners, Australians in the early 1970s were ready to entertain criticism of "consumerism" and to take seriously a "counter-culture" that celebrated nature and favoured virtue, especially spirituality, in non-Western cultures. Whereas Australia had once swept away both wilderness and its "savage" inhabitants in the name of progress, it now attempted to conserve them both. The spirituality that anthropologists had reported in the Aborigines' relation with the land was now made the basis for land claims to enable them to perpetuate it. In the ambiguous field of tourism, Aboriginality was employed in tandem with wildlife and scenery as a lure for the overseas visitor, looking for "something different."

While this celebration of what Charles Rowley has called the "remote Aborigines" did much to establish the special status of Aborigines during the early stages of welfare colonialism, it cast doubts on the entitlements of those who had always thought of themselves as Aboriginal, but who, living in cities, practising no traditional arts or ceremonies and displaying some degree of European ancestry, failed to "look the part." The ways in which they had constructed their Aboriginality for themselves, primarily by reference to proximate ancestors and living kin, could not easily be made a basis for the construction of Aboriginality on a national scale. Their solution was to "enact" their Aboriginality in demonstrations and to project themselves through the media as Aboriginal representatives. By these means they were able, in some degree, to shift the emphasis away from the ungeneralizable particularities of "tribe" and "country" to land rights as a national issue around which all Aboriginal people must unite.

The federal government also gave salience to land rights in the mid-1970s, passing legislation that resulted in the transfer to Aborigines of a sizable area of the Northern Territory – albeit, much of it economically valueless. The states accepted in varying degrees the principle of land rights, but the actual transfers of land – especially productive land – were quite small. The Labour federal government, elected in 1983, pledged to implement Aboriginal land rights on a national scale. In the face of mounting political opposition and dwindling electoral sympathy, however, it delayed action and finally abandoned the proposal three years later. In the mean time, the special status of Aborigines was coming under challenge.

ABORIGINALITY OR CITIZENSHIP

By the mid-1970s, the long postwar boom had begun to falter, undermining the Whitlam Labour government's expansion of the welfare state. Australia's semi-peripheral role as a supplier of primary produce and raw materials has placed it in an increasingly disadvantageous position in international trade, but the social, political, and ideological concomitants of this downturn are much the same as those in North America and Britain. Wages have come under pressure while workers compete for a dwindling number of jobs. Government redistributive expenditure has been curtailed, intensifying the competition among the swelled ranks of claimants. This has been accompanied by the rehabilitation of economic growth as the paramount national goal and by scepticism about the value of the social engineering experiments of the early 1970s. Asian – specifically Indo-Chinese – immigration has been represented as a threat not only to the conditions of Australian workers but to the Australian "way of life." The doctrine of multiculturalism, which was supposed to have replaced the white-Australia policy, has been openly challenged.

This has been the political milieu in which the campaign against land rights and the special status of Aborigines has been conducted. However, to represent the campaign as a knee-jerk response to economic stringency is too simple. Although the end of the long boom brought the expansion of welfare spending to a sudden halt, it did not put an immediate end to the government's Aboriginal programmes. Indeed, it was a conservative government that passed and implemented the land rights legislation that its Labour predecessor had mooted. The bitter resistance this provoked from the premiers of Queensland and Western Australia, who stood at the same end of the political spectrum, draws our attention to the contrasting perspective of state governments, whose responsibility is mainly for internal matters, and the national government, whose responsibilities include foreign relations. Sympathy for Aborigines undoubtedly became a prime minister who was active in Commonwealth affairs, including the decolonization of Zimbabwe. His Labour successor has been more concerned with Australia's trading partners, who, with indigenous minorities of their own, are less concerned with the situation of the Aborigines. It is also worth noting that, whereas rural voters have the dominant voice in the governments of Queensland and Western Australia, urban voters have the larger say in the national government. Urban voters have had less to do with Aborigines face-to-face but were most heavily exposed to and presumably influenced by the sympathetic media presentations of the "Aboriginal issue" during the 1960s and 1970s. However, remembering that the media depend to a great degree on novelty for their appeal, it seems probable that Aborigines, with their seemingly insoluble problems, have, by the 1980s, lost some of their interest. As objects of pity and charity, the victims of famine in Africa are very likely to push them off the front page! Compared with the current struggles of Bantu against the government of South Africa, the grievances of Aborigines lack drama, and their threats of political reprisal ring hollow. Surprisingly, perhaps, the urban media have not subjected the government's Aboriginal programmes to sustained scrutiny, but they have featured special cases of alleged misappropriation of funds and dwelt on problems such as alcoholism and glue sniffing, which appear to the reader or viewer as self-inflicted.

The campaign against land rights was spearheaded by a powerful mining lobby and supported by the leaders of the Northern Territory, Queensland, and Western Australia and by farmer and right-wing organizations. It was widely and effectively publicized. Surprisingly, it did not encounter much in the way of public challenge, either because no opposing statements were made or none was published. The public opinion poll that the federal Department of Aboriginal Affairs commissioned privately in 1985 was rumoured to have revealed a widespread revulsion against land rights. In fact, the results are capable of other interpretation (Rowse 1986), but they seem to have been a factor in the federal government's decision not to introduce national legislation.

The campaign followed a pincer strategy, on the one hand questioning the authenticity of many who called themselves Aborigines, especially those of lighter complexion, and on the other questioning the value of traditional Aboriginal culture, emphasizing not its spirituality but its supposed practice of cannibalism, bodily mutilation, infanticide, and forced marriages between old men and young girls. Such sentiments had remained current among Anglo-Australians who lived at close quarters with Aboriginal people throughout the period of welfare colonialism; but the southern and national media rarely if ever reported them. They were now once again part of the public debate.

Land rights have also been subjected to the same liberal critique which is being applied to multiracialism in migrant affairs. Any measure that gives special groups or categories special status is represented as subversive of the equality that must prevail among Australian citizens, regardless of race, colour, and creed. This equality, however, is defined in terms of formal legal, political, and, less certainly, economic rights, disregarding and at times casting doubt on the inequalities that have been the consequence of conquest, dispossession, and forced segregation. In the future, if Aboriginal people are to qualify for assistance, it must be as individual citizens, disadvantaged through isolation, poverty, ill-health, and the like.

The stance of the federal government has been equivocal, reflecting both the longstanding policies with which Labour was elected in 1983 and the seemingly less sympathetic climate of the 1980s. In 1985, it transferred Ayer's Rock to the traditional owners in the teeth of opposition from the government of the Northern Territory and a press campaign insisting that what had become a national symbol should not be made the preserve of a minority. (In fact, the rock was immediately leased back to the government and has since been used in a succession of advertising and entertainment "events" that take no account of its Aboriginal ownership.) However, the abandonment of a national land rights policy followed within a few months. A little earlier, the National Aboriginal Council, composed of elected Aboriginal and Islander representatives, had been dissolved on the ground that it was not sufficiently representative. But after 12 months, no announcement of a replacement has been made, and Aborigines meanwhile lack an officially recognised body. Long used to government funding, the Aboriginal movement is probably less able to sustain an independent national organization than it was 20 years ago when it relied on church and humanitarian support.

In the closely settled areas, it would be practicable, if not politically easy, for government to dismantle the special agencies that have delivered aid and services to Aborigines. The clients would presumably join the ranks of the urban and rural poor, although they might well suffer from discrimination at the hands of officials and from antagonism from other groups. This is scarcely the case with the large settlements in northern and central Australia, which are funded largely if not wholly through direct government funding. They were established as instruments of the assimilation policy, but it was well understood they would exist for many years outside the normal flow of Australian life. Larger now as a result of population increase, they can scarcely be disbanded since there is nowhere for the people to go and no field of employment that can support them. Whatever the name of the policy, they will indefinitely remain a charge on the state. All that governments can do is to attempt to reduce them to a local problem sealed off from the rest of the Aboriginal population, which will be encouraged to forget its connection with them and its claim for special status.

The developments of the past 20 years, however, have given Aboriginal society a political intelligentsia, drawn from the ranks of rural and urban population. Though many of them have been absorbed into the bureaucracy and others have established themselves in the arts, almost all have made their ascent through the structures established for Aborigines during the recent period. Professionally identifying as Aborigines and often doubling as spokespersons for the Aboriginal cause, they are very likely to become the custodians of Aboriginality during the next period, articulating the more or less isolated communities in the absence of a formal structure. The eclipse of a national Aboriginality is thus by no means assured.

CONCLUSION

From the beginning of European colonization, the emerging Australian society has maintained the initial division between native and settler, although the former has always been a minute proportion of the whole and, in diverse ways, marginalized. Whether its dispositions have been kindly or, more often the case, unkindly, settler-Australian society has been unable to forget their existence. Even though they might be invisible and inaudible, they have continued to constitute an embarrassment – often economic and political, but always cultural and moral – to the society's sense of itself as a nation among nations. Thus, Aboriginality has been, by turns, represented as savagery, anachronism, local colour, "lost Eden," and liberal fiction. It is with these constructions that the Aboriginal people have had to come to terms to survive in a society whose recognition of them has been equivocal and shifting.

NOTES

1. The Torres Strait Islanders originate from the islands between Queensland's York Peninsula and the Coast of Papua New Guinea, but they are now to be found throughout Australia. Of Melanesian stock, their indigenous culture was closer to that of their northern neighbours than to that of Australia's Aborigines. Queensland administration institutionalized the distinction, and though federal policy has tended to merge the two peoples, Torres Strait political leaders have found it expedient to maintain a separate identity (see Beckett 1986).
2. Occupational boundaries have not been fixed. White workers have left the rough bush work, such as fencing and scrub cutting, to Aborigines when there is better to be had, but then returned when times became hard. The same has been true of seasonal work, such as fruit picking.
3. This body was originally formed in 1973 as the National Aboriginal Consultative Committee; it was reconstituted and renamed three years later, and it was dissolved in 1985.

REFERENCES

Anderson, B. 1984. *Imagined communities: Reflections on the origin and spread of nationalism.* London: Verso.

Beckett, J. 1982. The Torres Strait Islanders and the pearling industry: A case of internal colonialism. In *Aboriginal power in Australian society*, edited by M. C. Howard, 131–58. St. Lucia: University of Queensland Press.

———. 1986. *Uses of the past cultural construction of Aboriginality.* Paper presented at the Biennial Conference of the Australian Institute of Aboriginal Studies, Canberra.

Department of Aboriginal Affairs. 1975. *Annual report.* Canberra: Government Publisher.

Gartrell, B. n.d. 'Colonialism' and the Fourth World: Notes on variations in colonial situations. *Culture* 6(1): 3–17.

Hall, R. 1980. Aborigines and the army: The Second World War experience. *Defence Force Journal* 24.

Hinton, P. 1968. Aboriginal employment and industrial relations at Weipa, North Queensland. *Oceania* 38(4): 281–301.

Jones, D. J., and J. Hill-Burnett. 1982. The political context of ethnogenesis: An Australian example. In *Aboriginal power in Australian society*, edited by M. C. Howard, 184–213. St. Lucia: University of Queensland Press.

Kolig, E. 1982. *The silent revolution*. Philadelphia: Institute for the Study of Human Issues.

Marshall, T. 1963. *Sociology at the crossroads and other essays*. London: Heinemann.

Paine, R. 1977. *The White Arctic: Anthropological essays on tutelage and ethnicity*. St. Johns, Newfoundland: Memorial University, Institute of Social and Economic Studies.

Rowse, T. 1986. Land rights, mining and settler democracy. *Meanjin* 45(1): 58–68.

Stanner, W. 1977. The history of indifference thus begins. *Aboriginal History* 2: 3–26.

Stavenhagen, R. 1965. Classes, colonialism and acculturation. *Studies in Comparative International Development* 1.

Stone, S. 1974. *Aborigines in White Australia: A documentary history of the attitudes affecting official policy and the Australian Aborigine 1697–1973*. South Yarra, Victoria: Heinemann Educational.

Weaver, S. 1983. Australian Aboriginal policy: Aboriginal pressure groups or government advisory bodies? *Oceania* 54(1): 1–22.

————. 1985. Struggles of the nation-state to define Aboriginal ethnicity: Canada and Australia. In *Minorities and mother country imagery*, edited by G. Gold. St. Johns, Newfoundland: Memorial University, Institute of Social and Economic Studies.

6

Aboriginal Ethnicity and Nation-building within Australia

ROBERT TONKINSON

This chapter focuses on historical and contemporary aspects of Aboriginal ethnicity and nation-building in the context of the encapsulation of the Aborigines as a small minority within Australian society. Aboriginal ethnicity, expressed via appeals to the notion of "Aboriginality," can be understood only in relation to the experiences of European invasion, expropriation, oppression, and racial prejudice. And Aboriginal assertions of autonomy, self-determination, or nationhood must be read against Aborigines' extremely marginalised location in the Australian social formation, occasioned by historical factors and their continuing exclusion from access to significant economic resources. As Howard (1982: 1)has noted: "Aborigines lack both the ideological and economic bases of power in contemporary Australian society; for the most part, they control neither things or ideas."

Another source of difficulty for the Aboriginal "nation" is the great diversity in its members' experience of, and degree of absorption by, the dominant society and its values, which is relevant both to relationships among Aborigines and with the white majority. Mixed-race Aborigines, especially those in urban areas whose cultural heritage includes much of European origin, are subject to assaults on their Aboriginal identity by both conservative whites and, less commonly, by full-descended Aborigines living in rural areas. The perceived interplay of racial and cultural components in Aboriginal identity, by both Aborigines and whites, is extremely important. As M. Tonkinson (n.d.: 34, 35) states in an article on Aboriginal identity:

The Aboriginal emphasis on kinship and behaviour (culture) over physical features in determining identity is apparent in their analysis. But so too is the European notion that there is a strong biological component in identity, that hereditary behavioural tendencies persist through generations. . . . [Whites] see Aboriginality as resting in color (black), language and exotic cultural features such as religious practices totally different from those of Christians.

The challenge of Aboriginal ethnicity and self-identification is complex and has strengthened in recent years. As an emergent, solidarity-seeking Aboriginal "nation" sought to realise its legitimacy via a land rights movement, it encountered powerful capitalist interests that have successfully marshalled anti-Aboriginal prejudice to engender a severe backlash. This has seriously impeded, if not ended, the struggle to achieve nationwide land rights. State and federal governments, despite attestations to the contrary, have been party to the campaign by mining interests to ensure that their access to resources is not impeded by Aboriginal resistance. Federal policies aimed ostensibly at promoting national Aboriginal solidarity have at one level been important in providing Aborigines with avenues for "nation-building" activities and therefore in raising Aboriginal political and ethnic consciousness. But at another level, they ensure the continued encapsulation of an emergent Aboriginal élite within the structures of the state (Tonkinson and Von Sturmer 1983). This has prevented any concerted and resource-backed Aboriginal drive towards the attainment of a meaningful level of autonomy within Australian society at large. Here the situation is one of encapsulation, but without any concomitant integration, and the limitations of what Stavenhagen (n.d.: 43) terms "ethnopolitics" are clear.

Aborigines are a tiny minority, about 200,000 of 16,000,000, or 1.25 per cent of the Australian total, whose socioeconomic status, according to nearly all leading indices, puts them firmly at the bottom of the society (see Department of Aboriginal Affairs 1984). Their degree of embeddedness and "Fourth World" status, plus their near exclusion from the economy, guarantee their continued underdevelopment. The relationship of Aborigines to the economy is predominantly one of heavy dependence on social welfare payments; i.e., as inactive recipients rather than producers. The economic exclusion of Aborigines is especially marked in the current economic and political climate, where allegedly democratic socialist state and federal governments are in full capitalistic flight. In this atmosphere, concern for the disadvantage (both Aboriginal and white) is evinced largely in efforts to slash expenditure on them, whereas corporate profit-taking is being nurtured by every means possible.

Where the Aborigines have been successful in gaining rights to land and a share in mining royalties, as in the Northern Teritory, results have been decidedly mixed. The bureaucratisation of statutory bodies (e.g., land councils) to deal with such matters has led to a great deal of conflict and to rampant inequalities within the Aboriginal groups affected by these developments (cf. Von Sturmer 1982, 1984; Tonkinson and Von Sturmer 1983). Aboriginal achievements in the Northern Territory have no doubt provided inspiration for Aborigines elsewhere in Australia, but events there have proved more disintegrative than integrative for those directly affected by resource development. Also, the exercise by Aborigines and representative bodies of their veto power over proposed mining developments may have pleased most conservationists, but certainly not the resources lobby. The developers have sought, successfully, to have the federal government remove this power of veto from its planned national land rights legislation – which in any case is being steadily watered down (Altman and Dillion 1985).

Because Aboriginal ethnicity is essentially a product of colonialism, the history of government policies towards Aborigines is very important to this discussion. Such policies have largely been a prerogative of the various states, which were separate colonies before federation in 1901. Not until a referendum in 1967 overwhelmingly endorsed proposals to give all Aborigines citizenship and to empower the federal government to legislate with respect to Aboriginal affairs could steps towards uniform policies be implemented. Since then, however, some states have refused to surrender this control to the Commonwealth and have actively opposed federal initiatives in Aboriginal affairs. Queensland and Western Australia have both made frequent use of the "state's rights" appeal to oppose federal initiatives, with Aborigines often the unwilling victims.

State opposition notwithstanding, much of the impetus towards Aboriginal nation-building springs from steps taken by the federal government to promote nationwide Aboriginal unity and representation. The inception of advisory bodies such as the National Aboriginal Consultative Committee (later renamed the National Aboriginal Conference) provided Aborigines everywhere with a national focus. At the same time, however, these initiatives highlighted tensions between Aboriginal cultural diversity and an emerging pan-Aboriginal identity and revealed the difficulties of achieving a workable accommodation between local and national Aboriginal concerns and interests. So federal governmental initiatives have both promoted and challenged the growth of Aboriginality and the forging of an Aboriginal "nation" within the broader Australian society. Effective "national integration" (Stavenhagen n.d.: 31) has proved difficult to attain, and the emergence of an Aboriginal élite dominated by mixed-race Aborigines of predominantly light complexion has provoked severe criticism from white conservatives. They label such Aborigines as imposters and opportunists and question their authenticity and identity as Aborigines (English 1985). As M. Tonkinson (n.d.: 35) suggests, the antagonism of whites to people of Aboriginal descent is greatest where the distinguishing physical and cultural features are least evident.

In this chapter, I first consider briefly the historical development of Aboriginal ethnicity as a consequence of colonialism, then examine the influence of a succession of government policies concerning Aborigines, after which follows a discussion of important developments since the 1960s as a prelude to an assessment of "Aboriginality" and the contemporary and prospective situations of Aborigines with respect to nation-building. There is no question that, for Aborigines, the activation of ethnicity, via a stress on pan-Aboriginal identity and cultural distinctiveness, is simultaneously a consciousness-raising and a political strategy, not a return to "primordial sentiments" (cf. Stavenhangen n.d.: 43). What is notable is the way in which Aboriginal leaders are building on the notion of an Aboriginal ethnicity which their colonial masters originally imposed on them. This is a point made by M. Tonkinson (n.d.: 3); i.e., that Aboriginality is now viewed by its Aboriginal proponents as a positive force in their political struggle. Yet "this identity, negatively valued, was in the past defined and institutionalized by the dominant European society, enforced by legal codification and, at times, by force." Since identity is always constituted by both elements of self-identification and ascription by others, it is natural that Aborigines would seek to command the right to define themselves. This struggle is integral to the nation-building enterprise, which draws strength from a positively constituted Aboriginality. The problem remains, however, that the dominant 98.75 per cent of Australian society continues in many ways, both passive and active, to contest this positive self-evaluation and thereby to threaten the survival of the Aborigines as a viable cultural minority within the nation-state.

THE GENESIS OF ABORIGINAL ETHNICITY

Before the European invasion, Australia exhibited a great degree of cultural variation overlying several shared cultural themes (Berndt and Berndt 1985; Tonkinson 1978a). Local identities and ethnocentrism predominated despite a wide range of variation in the density of population, the extent of regional networks, and the significance of cultural boundaries. In such a situation, there could have been no notion of Aboriginality, only of much finer discriminations between groups and categories of people, largely on the basis of cultural differences that were validated in religious terms. The prevailing cultural ethos could fairly be called egalitarian, despite a conspicuous differentiation in all Aboriginal societies on the bases of age and sex. Therefore, nothing akin to classes existed, and people lived within universes of kin. Beyond the periphery were strangers who were often thought to be endowed with less than human propensities and attributes; i.e., it was normally only in relation to the category of "other" that biological differences, such as long fangs and huge genitalia, were sometimes imputed.

The British settlers clearly set the Aborigines apart from themselves and designated them in universalist terms as a category of very different, inferior beings – only arguably human and certainly not civilised. And once social Darwinist notions became entrenched in the latter part of the past century, the Aborigines were firmly placed at the bottom of the evolutionary ladder. Colour and culture were closely related in the European view, and it was thought that cultural characteristics, hereditary and immutable, were carried in the blood. The frontier of European colonialism in Australia lasted from 1788 until the 1960s (when almost all the remaining previously uncontacted groups of Western Desert Aborigines migrated or were taken into settlements), so a truly pan-Aboriginal identity could not have been realised until quite recently in Austra-

lian history; yet European assignations of such an identity had long been established and were dominated by negative valuations. The "noble savage" image
was at no stage in the ascendancy in Australia.

Certain chief homogeneous processes attendant on colonisation, such as expropriation, oppression, exclusion, and racial prejudice, laid the foundations for
an Aboriginality, or ethnic consciousness, constituted in shared experiences of
subjugation and deprivation. This awaited only the emergence of an awareness
of what had gone on all over the continent, of how, nearly everywhere, the
Aborigines have ended up as marginalised victims instead of active participants
in the nation-building activities of a long-since dominant majority. Even where
Aborigines have played a significant economic role, as station workers in the
north or as seasonal workers in settled Australia, credit for their contribution
has been largely denied them, as part of what W. E. H. Stanner has called the
"greater Australian silence" – the removal of the Aborigines from history,
which began in the past century and is only now being rectified by a new generation of historians. Aborigines have become active in this process of recording
and disseminating their history, and it is forming an important basis both for
their widely shared view of themselves as victims of prolonged and thoroughgoing oppression and for a positive pan-Aboriginality stemming from shared
cultural beliefs, values, and behaviours. Not all Aborigines are equally aware of
these broader historical and cultural similarities, and, especially for those more
tradition-oriented Aborigines in remote areas of the interior and north of the
continent, locally focused identities continue to take precedence, and there may
be no consciousness of pan-Aboriginality. Predictably, it is the urban-based
Aborigines, those most knowledgeable of and enmeshed within the dominant
society, whose political strategies frequently include appeals to the pan-
Aboriginal dimension of identity (cf. Jones and Hill-Burnett 1982).

GOVERNMENT POLICIES

For most of Australia's post-European-contact history, policies concerned with
Aborigines were decidedly negative in their rationales and their outcomes. The
dominant protectionist-segregationist policies of the colonies in the second half
of the past century, whose effects extended into the mid-20th century, were
based on firm convictions concernig the imminent extinction of the "weaker
Aboriginal race." Uniformly absent from such policies were any positive proposals aimed at involving Aborigines in the wider society or at facilitating their
movement from a marginal, deprived status to an integrated, productive one
(cf. Rowley 1970; Reynolds 1972; Broome 1982). When the Aborigines failed to
disappear as predicted (their population reached its nadir in the early 1930s),
the early "smooth the dying pillow" policies were replaced by an overtly assimilationist push, the intent of which was equally negative for Aboriginal identity,

since the apparent aim was to make all Aborigines become like whites in customs and behaviour. The state governments had long been applying assimilationist pressures to what had been identified as an embarrassing and increasing problem: that of the "half-castes," or mixed-race Aborigines. Depending on whether these people were thought to combine the best or the worst of the two races, measures were invoked to deal with the problem, including the large-scale removal of mixed-race children from their Aboriginal mothers and their placement in institutions. Hopes were widespread that light-skinned, mixed-race people would "pass" into white society, and in this way Aborigines would eventually be absorbed. The effect of these strong pressures, especially in states such as Queensland, is discernible in the fact that an estimated 30,000 to 40,000 people of mixed race do not identify themselves as Aborigines, despite improvements in the social climate for Aborigines since the late 1960s and a consequent increase in the number of people identifying as Aborigines for the first time in the federal censuses (see Smith 1980).

Aboriginal objections to the racist implications of the national assimilation policy (promulgated in 1959) led to a modification that allowed Aborigines a choice of whether or not to become like whites; however, the whole policy came under sustained attack from the mid-1960s as the voices of Aboriginal protest began to be heard and the first emulations of US black-power strategies began in Australia (cf. Lippmann 1981; Gurr 1982). In a period of continuing economic prosperity, general good will towards the notion of a "fair go" for the Aborigines on the part of Australian people and governments led to many positive changes. This was an era when assertions of ethnic identity and calls for political and economic reforms along ethnic lines were being made, and heeded, in many countries, where strong support came from elements of the dominant culture. By 1970, most of the restrictive legislation concerning Aborigines had been dismantled, including the various states' complex and largely biologically based definitions of Aborigines (cf. M. Tonkinson n.d.: 35–43). These had given strong support to the colour-culture equation that linked genetic and cultural distinctiveness and had disastrous effects on many mixed-race families that suffered disruption as a result of these restrictive and discriminatory policies. Current legal definitions of Aborigines are broad and weighted towards an inclusive category; e.g., those who claim Aboriginal descent and are regarded as Aborigines by the Aboriginal community at large.

Also by 1970, absorption had been replaced by more positive policies that emphasised Aboriginal self-management and the right of Aborigines to survive and prosper as a culturally distinct minority – but not in any sense as a separate "nation" within Australia. Conservative and racist whites have at times used Aboriginal land rights successes in the Northern Territory as a foundation for allegations of Aboriginal-initiated segregation, but there have been no national moves by Aborigines towards achieving nationhood in a geographical and a cultural sense. A change of federal government in 1972 signalled the full-scale inception of self-management policies for Aborigines and a great increase in the amount of attention and resources devoted to bringing about major social changes. These were aimed at improving Aboriginal living standards and, above all, at giving Aborigines a significant measure of control over their lives.

The now famous Aboriginal "tent embassy" of 1972 drew national and international attention to the indigenous minority's demands, which centred on land rights. For both black and white Australians, the embassy and associated protests would have made them aware of the existence of a national Aboriginal movement, which now had its own distinctive flag as a potent symbol of its unity, solidarity, and "nationhood." When the Labour party came to power shortly thereafter, this movement was given added momentum in all sorts of ways. Labour encouraged the creation of a host of Aboriginal voluntary organisations and representative bodies to serve local needs (e.g., in housing, health, and legal matters) and to unite communities and groups at regional and national levels. These have provided a training ground and power base for Aborigines, and the bodies that focussed on broader regional and national concerns have undoubtedly helped raise Aborigines' consciousness of their shared interests and identity.

The most prominent body created by the federal government to advise it on Aboriginal affairs was the National Aboriginal Conference (NAC, the former National Aboriginal Consultative Committee), made up of elected representatives from all over the country. It was an advisory body that lacked power, was subject to severe critcism from Aborigines and whites alike, and was finally disbanded in 1985 (to be replaced by some other national representative body at some future time). But the NAC was an important focus for Aboriginal national unity, and it achieved sizable media attention because of its criticisms of policies concerning Aborigines and its often radical calls for reform (cf. Weaver 1983). The NAC in turn was severely criticised for alleged shortcomings such as its supposed failure to adequately represent the range of opinions of its members or a national solidarity.

Predictably, the initiative and drive within the NAC came, in its formative period, from highly acculturated, urban, mixed-race Aborigines whose knowledge of the traditions and cultures of the remote-area representatives was minimal but whose knowledge of the wider society and its politics was extensive. Some of the more radical spokesmen received considerable media attention, which led to widespread questioning of their identity as Aborigines and therefore of their right to speak for this constituency. Caught tragically in the middle, they lacked "authenticity" as Aborigines in the eyes of many white Australians and also of fully descended Aborigines, both within and beyond the NAC. The latter, whose definitions of Aboriginality lean heavily on cultral characteristics, viewed these spokesmen as "white fellas" – not so much because of their skin colour but because they allegedly spoke, acted, and "thought" like whites rather than like Aborigines. White critics based their allegations of inauthenticity and opportunism on both colour and cultural criteria: many of the spokesmen were in physiognomy and skin colour not unlike whites, and none was believed to possess the skills that would make them "genuine" Aborigines (e.g., the ability to track, to make and use spears and boomerangs, and to speak an Aboriginal language and perform songs and dances).

ABORIGINAL ETHNICITY: ABORIGINALITY

It should be clear from the foregoing that the notion or concept of Aboriginality is not a uniform one and that Aboriginal and white perceptions of it vary enormously. Few people, Aboriginal or outsider, have attempted to state its constituents, yet its power as a symbol may relate to its very diffuseness. In an article on national identity and the problem of *kastom* in Vanuatu (Tonkinson 1982), I noted that the indigenous pro-independence movement leaders were careful not to attempt any specification of what they meant by *kastom* lest its power as a unifying cultural symbol be eroded by drawing attention to the negative and divisive aspects of *kastom* in its manifestations as signifier of local or regional differentiation of peoples. Perhaps the same sensitivities were at work in Aboriginal Australia with respect to pan-Aboriginal identity based on shared cultural characteristics. Aborigines have not been reluctant to specify the negative aspects of colonial domination and oppression as part of how Aboriginality is constituted, since these are widely agreed on and increasingly verifiable as Aboriginal history comes into its own. But the shared cultural constituents that stem principally from the "traditional" or pre-contact past are less easy to specify as universally integral to Aboriginality.

Certainly this topic has evoked a wide range of opinion among scholars of Aboriginal society. At one end of the spectrum of opinions stands that of Von Sturmer (1973: 16–7), who thinks that Aboriginality is "a fiction which takes on meaning only in terms of white ethnocentrism. . . . This identity can be nothing more than an expression of faith. It represents an ideological position far removed from the concrete situation from which it is presumed to have drawn its substance." Tatz (1979) deems it a universal Aboriginal quality or characteristic but refuses to attempt to define its constituents. Coombs, Brandl, and Snowdon (1983) make the fullest attempt to say what Aboriginality is; they list seven dimensions, a synthesis of which constitutes Aboriginality. Sansom (1982) argues for the persistence of pervasive "commonalities" in language use and culture and in modes of adaptation to Western influences, but notes that the same commonalities can work against wider solidarity; like *kastom* in Vanuatu, then, they may operate on different levels of inclusiveness in diametrically opposed ways.

For many Aborigines, especially those livng in urban areas and politically involved in Aboriginal nation-building, Aboriginality is real and very important to them even though its meaning remains imprecise. What is stressed most often is the blood tie to the past, to the original inhabitants and owners of the entire continent whose loss of their land has never been compensated for and remains as a giant moral debt owed to the descendants. The affirmation of Aboriginality is also the affirmation of nationhood, which requires or its realisation an end to Aboriginal powerlessness, via land rights and access to significant resources such as mining royalties. For those Aborigines who feel they have lost much of their traditional culture, Aboriginality also entails concerted attempts at retrieval and revival, thus the current emphasis on oral history and of obtaining from elderly Aborigines a record as full as possible of their memories of things Aboriginal and past and of their bitter experiences in an oppressive society. In Western Australia, for instance, one sees the active appropriation of elements of a still vibrant desert culture by coastal peoples whose much longer period of contact with whites led to great loss of valued religious lore.

In her analysis of Aboriginal identity, M. Tonkinson (n.d.: 34) maintains that Aboriginal activists are advocating a combination of Aboriginal and European ideas about it: they appear to be suggesting that "Aboriginal ancestry predominates over white ancestry, regardless of socialization and experience." In the face of colour prejudice and discrimination, the Aborigines are aiming to make a positive self-identification the dominant constituent of their identity. Aboriginal nation-building demands that the self-image be positive and widely shared by the Aboriginal society at large, so that in their political endeavours the leaders can use the claim of unity, of one nation, one voice, to extract the maximum concessions from the nation-state. The question I now turn to is what are the chances of success in this major aim?

ABORIGINES IN CONTEMPORARY AUSTRALIAN SOCIETY

The realities facing Aborigines in Australia today are such that, given the likelihood of continuing decline in an already shaky national economy and the extent and vehemence of the backlash against them, their major gains may already be behind them. (A poll conducted in 1985 for the Department of Aboriginal Affairs that was suppressed revealed a precipitous decline in white Australia's support for Aboriginal concerns, especially land rights). They still lack access to the means of production, and most are in fact divorced from the economy, unemployed, and therefore heavily reliant on social welfare income for survival. They are, it is true, no longer invisible and no longer silent, but they lack the political clout to impose their collective will on the society at large, whose members are increasingly convinced that as it is, Aborigines are getting more than they deserve and more than the nation can afford. Even in better times, Aboriginal wishes were ignored whenever governments decided that they conflicted with the "national interest" – defined by policy makers in the first instance but ultimately by corporate capitalism.

In theory, self-management policies have much to recommend them, though they rest on several unexamined assumptions regarding the nature and extent of shared Aboriginal interests (cf. Thiele 1984). In a sense, government policies reveal a greater willingness to assume pan-Aboriginality than the facts of cultural diversity would allow, but to ignore regional differences and need levels is always an easier strategy for policy makers. Government policies in practice reveal a different picture – mainly one of self-management constantly denied as a result of financial restraints and bureaucratic demands. Under these circumstances, it is impossible for Aboriginal communities to experience social and economic development as a vital learning process (Tonkinson 1978b). The priorities of state and federal governments can safely accord Aboriginal matters very low rankings because the Aboriginal vote hardly counts and because governments now know that anti-Aboriginal attitudes are in the ascendancy in the society at large; so the moral and humanitarian aspects of Aboriginal welfare carry less force today.

I have noted the proliferation of organisations that are either controlled by Aborigines or that have sizable Aboriginal representation in their decision-making structures. They have absorbed large numbers of better educated, mostly urbanised Aborigines – for whom employment opportunities have been good since the early 1970s. In the larger bureaucracies, such as the Department of Aboriginal Affairs and the Aboriginal Development Commission, Aborigines have experienced great vertical mobility. The makings of an Aboriginal bureaucratic élite can be discerned in these various organisations. But as long as Aboriginal relationships with Australian society continue to be mediated by power workers (black or white) in key positions, the attainment of meaningful self-management by Aborigines is unlikely (Tonkinson and Von Sturmer 1983: 2). It is clear that the involvement of Aborigines in a wide variety of bodies, from community councils to the NAC, has done much to raise their political consciousness and engender feelings of shared identity. Whites, too, have been affected by gaining an increased awareness of the implications of Aboriginal control over resources. Resource developers, for example, have mounted virulently anti-Aboriginal campaigns to prevent land rights from spreading into areas of interest to them, with unprecedented success in Western Australia.

When Aboriginal Australia is viewed as a whole, it is clear that enormous differences remain in levels of Aboriginal awareness, knowledge, and participation and in their access to the money and power disbursed in the pursuit of policy goals. Yet despite the great contrasts between the "colonial" north and the "settled" south, between urban and remote situations, and between the states, some important uniformities exist in the current situation of Aborigines. These derive from shared historical and socio-economic circumstances and at least in part from homogeneities in traditional Aboriginal culture, and they have combined to place most Aborigines in a similar situation *vis-à-vis* the white majority and the nation-state. In a discussion of Aboriginal political responses, Tonkinson and Von Sturmer (1983: 3) have outlined some of the major shared elements:

Nowhere is there significant Aboriginal input into the formulation and direction of state development policies; where there is Aboriginal opposition to policies affecting them, it has little force. The fact that Aboriginal responses much more often tend to involve reaction rather than the initiation of action is in significant measure a concomitant of their status as a dominated minority, but it may also reflect a political style that favours such reactive responses – and in some areas this could be seen as a continuity of 'traditional' worldview. Everywhere, it seems, politics for Aborigines means the ordering and reordering of relationships of power among Aboriginal individuals, groups and organisations, which appear to have greater import to them than their relationships with whites and the white world. Aboriginal political strategies, their 'ways and means', tend to focus on the indigenous areas of competition and conflict rather than on the implications of policy and its implementation.

Given the long history of extreme paternalism and exclusion of Aborigines from any voice in their political relationships with the white majority, it is not surprising that politics for most of them tends to be focused inwards, into local arenas where they feel they have some significant control over outcomes. At the community level, most institutional structures have remained much the same, and their foci have little to do with the economics of the marketplace or with the creation of productive relationships with the economy at large. Again, this is hardly surprising, given the marginalised situation of Aborigines in the social formation. Von Sturmer, in discussing the situation in Western Arnhem Land, notes that the Aboriginal affairs are increasingly concerned with means and modes of distribution instead of production. Given the current economic climate, there will be a further lessening of attention to productive relationships as unskilled labour, both Aboriginal and white, becomes increasingly unmarketable. The control and distribution of available moneys, in an era of budgetary cutbacks, especially in relation to Aboriginal concerns, remain a major concern of much current Aboriginal political activity, since the demand exceeds the supply by a huge factor.

In recent years the federal government has appointed many more Aborigines to senior and administratively powerful positions in bureaucracies such as the DAA and the ADC and it has increased their level of control over many financial resources. Since the disbanding of the National Aboriginal Conference, however, there is almost no representation at the federal level of the interests of rural and remote Aborigines. The latter are increasingly dependent on powerfully placed metropolitan Aborigines for access to needed developmental finance. In situations of tight money, many communities become susceptible to the overtures of powerful capitalist interests, such as mining and tourism concerns, which are increasingly viewed as a source of needed cash. In much of the continent, Aboriginal political responses are still mediated at some level or other by whites, whose interests are not necessarily congruent with those of the Aborigines for whom they act as advisors and spokesmen. And in the minority of cases where Aborigines act in the mediating role, their self-interest or compelling outside pressures may conflict with, or even define, the needs and wishes of the individuals or Aboriginal community in question.

Whether a unified Aboriginal "nation" can use its solidarity effectively to extract significant concessions from the nation-state depends to a great extent on the situation of its leaders and spokesmen. What we find is that in nearly every case, the power base of the most influential and prominent Aboriginal leaders is ultimately financed by the state, since Aborigines lack access to independent sources of wealth. This, then, is the essence of encapsulation. In so many matters, of which land rights is a good example, Aborigines must define their social fields in terms that oppose the imperatives of the society at large (Tonkinson and Von Sturmer 1983: 57). But in the absence of a secure and independent financial power base, there are clear limits to the rhetoric of opposition and separation. Because Aboriginal political action is subsidised by the state, Aborigines must understandably be mindful of the maintenance of the subsidy. The leaders are thus always on the razor's edge: they must command a political rhetoric powerful enough to satisfy their followers and indicate their responsiveness to Aboriginal aspirations and demands, but not so powerful that it is seen by the state as a revolutionary threat to the social order. Several formerly prominent Aboriginal nation builders have fallen silent as a result of pressure and threats from their superiors in government bureaucracies, and as long as Aborigines lack a significant presence in state or federal parliaments, they have few opportunities to engage in unrestrained criticism of the state and its continuing neglect of Aboriginal concerns.

Though it is true, then, that the establishment of a large number of Aboriginal bodies at local, regional, and national levels has been important for the realisation of some of the goals of self-management, the chief consequence throughout Australia has been to further marginalise Aborigines. People who identify themselves as Aborigines are obliged to operate through Aboriginal channels, such as the Aboriginal Development Commission or the Aboriginal Legal Service, which in effect assures their marginality (Tonkinson and Von Sturmer 1983: 59). Since such bodies must compete for scarce resources, this raises the possibility of conflict among Aboriginal organisations. These conflicts have occurred in many parts of Australia, and even if they are managed by the Aboriginal protagonists so that debate is confined within the Aboriginal polity, the divisions so created may be damaging for the Aboriginal national cause. Divide-and-neutralise tactics by the state are facilitated when conflicts among Aboriginal individuals and organisations are aired in the media. In Western

Australia, for instance, conservative politicians have funded an anti-land-rights movement, led by a prominent Aboriginal cleric and party member who has attacked the pro-land-rights Aboriginal majority as divisive of national development and unity.

One major phenomenon that has important implications for Aboriginal nation-building is the Aboriginal outstation movement, which, in the past decade or so, has seen the return of many Aborigines from large communities and townships in central and northern Australia to their ancestral homelands (cf. Gray 1977; Wallace 1977). This movement has many facets, but among the principal motivations for the reoccupation of homeland areas are: fears of disturbance and desecration of traditional lands by mining and other development activities; the strong desire of Aborigines to acquaint their settlement-born children with their cultural heritage as embodied in land, its economic resources, and its religious significance; and a pressing need for Aborigines to distance themselves from seemingly intractable social problems encountered in the town or settlement situation. This movement is not a return to the pre-contact way of life or a renunciation of Western society. The outstation dwellers continue to rely on modern technology and to seek medical, educational, and material assistance from the outside world; they also remain in touch with their settlements of origin via radio links, visits, and other means.

Despite an ambivalent attitude towards outstations on the part of governments and inevitable shortages of funding for their establishment, maintenance, and development, the movement has persisted and grown. Some observers would see it as antithetical to Aboriginal nation-building, in the sense that it has further distanced large numbers of Aborigines from access to any significant sources of power. This view, however, fails to take account of the strengthening of Aboriginal values and cultural identity that appears to have resulted from the outstation movement. If the move back to ancestral homelands also buys Aborigines extra time to adjust and react more effectively to the rapidly increasing pace of change, then it must be viewed as beneficial, in the long term, to the cause of nation-building.

Are there any alternative avenues for a nation-building Aboriginal élite to sustain itself independently of the state? This question needs to be considered on two levels: the level of the group and that of the individual. The experience of the NAC when it endeavoured to redefine its role as a pressure group rather than function as a mere advisory body contained clear lessons for Aboriginal leaders attempting to gain for their "nation" some genuine measure of power and autonomy. The attempt was firmly rebuffed, and one may ask where the NAC is today. The national voice of the Aboriginal people is defunct, put out of business by the nation-state. Prospects at the group level are thus not encouraging. In the case of individuals, for well-qualified Aborigines seeking to escape into the mainstream from the encapsulated Aboriginal political field, what opportunities exist? Any such movement would inherently be assimilationist in nature, unless it becomes possible for such people to create niches that are "Aboriginal" in character but also powerful in terms of access to resources. A few niches of this kind may be available, but alas, only in such areas as liaison and public relations in resource development companies. It would be impossible for an Aboriginal employee of a mining company, no matter how highly placed, to engage in effective political response or in the attempt to forge an oppositional Aboriginal solidarity. And since most major philanthropic concerns are funded by the profits of capitalism and used often in pursuit ultimately of capitalistic goals, Aboriginal leaders cannot look in that direction for the establishment of an independent power base.

Revolutionary action as an alternative appears never to have been seriously considered by the Aboriginal élite. This is not surprising because it is a totally unrealistic option. Protests have had limited success in the past. If the campaign mounted in 1983 by Aborigines opposing the New South Wales Land Rights Act is any indication, political protest is quite ineffective. The state Labour government ignored all the diverse and well-reported protests, which ranged from legal action of the highest level to sit-ins at government offices; and the legislation, considered by most Aborigines to be woefully inadequate, was passed. Because in NSW, where Aboriginal political responses are sophisticated and highly developed, their protests met with complete failure, the major contention of Gurr (1982) was borne out, that the gains achieved by Aborigines in recent decades are principally the result of changes in federal and state policies, which stemmed from a growing willingness on the part of white Australians and their governments to acknowledge the validity of Aboriginal claims. In Gurr's view, this willingness, more than Aboriginal activism and protest, was instrumental in generating policy changes. Now that the willingness is no longer present, Aboriginal nation builders are much less likely to succeed in their aims of coercing the dominant society into making important concessions. The numbers game certainly cannot be won by Aborigines on their own at the moment, and their non-Aboriginal support is small and weak and seems quite unlikely to grow much.

To conclude, it is clear that in the Australian case, ethno-development is severely limited by a great many factors and forces, despite the existence of an avowedly multicultural policy. Aborigines have strongly resisted any attempt to include them with other ethnic minorities, since they consider themselves to be "original" Australians, not "new" ones (as the postwar European immigrants were called) and to suffer more disadvantage and prejudice than any other segment of society. In Australia, the Aboriginal nation is deeply encapsulated and yet, not integrated into the nation-state, and it lacks the power base to achieve significant autonomy or socioeconomic integration, or both. When access to valued resources such as land has been achieved, as in the Northern Territory, this has led to accusations by racist conservatives that ethno-development entails Aboriginal-initiated "apartheid," a closing of geographical boundaries against white citizens of the realm. According to Stavenhagen (n.d.: 50–51), it might be argued that ethno-development could be used as an excuse for the dominant majority to maintain segregation and cultural oppression. In Australia, however, it is opposed on the basis that Aborigines are seeking to segregate themselves – and in so doing, they are attempting to "oppress" or exclude the dominant white majority. This is yet another case of "blaming the victim," but it reveals clearly the limited possibilities for any Aboriginal achievement of the kind of "nation" within the nation-state that would ensure the survival of the Aborigines as a distinctive and dynamic minority in times to come.

REFERENCES

Altman, J., and M. Dillion. 1985. Land rights: Why Hawke's model has no backing. *Australian Society* 4(6): 26–29.

Berndt, R. M., and C. H. Berndt. 1985. *The world of the first Australians*. Rev. ed. Adelaide: Rigby.

Broome, R. 1982. *Aboriginal Australians*. Sydney: George Allen & Unwin.

Coombs, H. C., M. M. Brandl, and W. E. Snowdon. 1983. *A certain heritage*. Canberra: Australian National University, CRES Monograph 9.

Department of Aboriginal Affairs. 1984. *Aboriginal social indicators*. Canberra: Australian Government Publishing Service.

English, P. B. 1985. *Land rights and birth rights: The Great Australian Hoax*. Perth: Veritas Press.

Gray, D. 1978. A revival of the law: The probable spread of initiation circumcision to the coast of Western Australia. *Oceania* 48(3): 188–201.

Gray, W. J. 1977. Decentralisation trends in Arnhem Land. In *Aborigines and change*, edited by R. M. Berndt, 114–23. Canberra: Australian Institute of Aboriginal Studies.

Gilbert, K. 1977. *Living black: Blacks talk to Kevin Gilbert*. Ringwood: Allen Lane (The Penguin Press).

Gurr, T. R. 1982. *Give us the means to the future: Aboriginal protest, political change and resource development in Australia*. Draft paper prepared for the International Studies Association, 23rd Annual Convention, Cincinnati, Ohio.

Hiatt, L. R. 1976. *The role of the National Aboriginal Consultative Committee: Report of the Committee of Enquiry*. Canberra: Australian Government Publishing Service.

Howard, M. C. 1982. Introduction. In *Aboriginal power in Australian society*, edited by M. C. Howard, 1–13. St. Lucia: University of Queensland Press.

Jones, D., and J. Hill-Burnett. 1982. The political context of ethnogenesis: An Australian example. In *Aboriginal power in Australian society*, edited by M. C. Howard, 214–46. St. Lucia: University of Queensland Press.

Lippmann, L. 1981. *Generations of resistance*. Melbourne: Longman Cheshire.

Reynolds, H. 1972. *Aborigines and settlers*. Sydney: Cassell.

Rowley, C. D. 1970. *The destruction of Aboriginal society*. Canberra: Australian National University Press.

Sansom, B. 1982. The Aboriginal commonality. In *Aboriginal sites, rights and resource development*, edited by R. M. Berndt. Perth: University of Western Australia Press.

Smith, L. R. 1980. *The Aboriginal population of Australia.* Canberra: Australian National University Press.

Stavenhagen, R. n.d. *Ethnodevelopment: A neglected dimension in development thinking.* Mimeograph.

Tatz, C. 1979. *Race politics in Australia.* Armidale: University of New England Press.

Thiele, S. J. 1984. Anti-intellectualism and the 'Aboriginal problem': Colin Tatz and the 'self-determination' approach. *Mankind* 14(3): 165–78.

Tonkinson, M. n.d. Is it in the blood? Australian Aboriginal identity. In *Cultural identity in Oceania,* edited by J. Linnekin and L. Poyer. Honolulu: University of Hawaii Press. Forthcoming.

Tonkinson, R. 1978a. *The Mardudjara Aborigines: Living the dream in Australia's desert.* New York: Holt, Rinehart and Winston.

———. 1978b. Aboriginal community autonomy: Myth and reality. In *"Whitefella business": Aborigines in Australian politics,* edited by M. C. Howard, 93–104. Philadelphia: Institute for the Study of Human Issues.

———. 1982. National identity and the problem of kastom in Vanuatu. *Mankind* 13(4): 306–15.

Tonkinson, R., and J. Von Sturmer. 1983. *Land rights, mining and self-management: Australian Aboriginal political responses (three case studies).* Paper presented at pre–ICAES Congress symposium on "The political responses of indigenous people to state development policies," Quebec City, Canada.

Von Sturmer, J. 1973. Changing Aboriginal identity in Cape York. In *Aboriginal identity in contemporary Australia,* edited by D. Tugby. Milton: Jacaranda Press.

———. 1982. Aborigines in the uranium industry: Toward self-management in the Alligator River region? In *Aboriginal sites, rights and resource development,* edited by R. M. Berndt. Perth: University of Western Australia Press.

———. 1984. The social impact of mining: Economic consequences – Residence, resources, and inequalities. In *Aborigines and uranium* (AIAS consolidated report on the social impact of mining on the Aborigines of the Northern Territory). Canberra: Australian Government Publishing Service.

Wallace, N. M. 1977. Pitjantjatjara decentralisation in north-west South Australia: Spiritual and psycho-social motivation. In *Aborigines and change,* edited by R. M. Berndt, 124–35. Canberra: Australian Institute of Aboriginal Studies.

Weaver, S. M. 1983. Australian Aboriginal policy: Aboriginal pressure groups or government advisory bodies? *Oceania* 54(1): 1–23; 54(2): 85–108.

7

Colonisation and Development of the Maori People

RANGIUNI J. WALKER

This chapter is predicated on the thesis that there are two basic cultures in the world, namely, the culture of indigenous people and the culture of metropolitan society.

The culture of indigenous people has a universal set of principles that distinguishes it from its metropolitan counterpart. Indigenous cultures are generally small, ranging from extended family units, subtribes, and tribes to tribal confederations. Their mythology and spiritual beliefs credit them with divine origins and descent through culture heroes. Although there was a ruling class of elders, chiefs, and priestly experts, the power they held was tempered by kinship bonds, the intense face-to-face relationships characteristic of small social units, and the need constantly to validate leadership by wise and generous rule. The microscale of indigenous cultures also facilitated consensus decision making as the *modus operandi* for the achievement of social and political goals. The distinguishing feature of indigenous culture is the relationship that the people have to the earth and its resources. The earth is personified as the earth-mother in union with the sun or the sky-father. Indigenous people think of themselves as an integral part of the natural order. Although tribal territories were demarcated for subsistence hunting, fishing, and horticultural activities, they characterised themselves as belonging to the earth and not its owners. They are the children of the earth, and the food that springs from the earth-mother, both wild and domesticated animals and plants, is for the sustenance of humanity. Generosity and sharing the bounty of nature from the harvest, a successful hunt, or a fishing expedition was a cardinal value of indigenous culture. Sharing and generous giving established a network of exchange relationships that strengthened group bonds. Indeed, the individual sought honour not by competitive self-aggrandisement, but by service to the people. The symbolism of the earth-mother and the mythology of divine descent with the reverence for ancestors were central to the spiritual beliefs of indigenous people. At death, the ancestors passed from the terrestrial to the celestial realm to dwell among the stars in a high state of perfection.

The culture of metropolitan society on the other hand is characterised by the macroscale aggregation of people into a nation-state. This culture has an infrastructure of centralised political power, legal system, judiciary, paramilitary and military enforcement agencies, and a bureaucracy through which power is devolved down to the parochial level of local authorities. With the exception of dictatorships, the legitimacy of government is founded on the democratic principle of one person, one vote, and the arbitrary convention of rule by simple majority. There is generally a separation between the secular state and the prevailing religious ideology. The spiritual beliefs of monotheism, as in the case of churches founded on the Judeo-Christian traditions, are so divorced from their pagan origins that they are disconnected entirely from the natural order and the earth-mother symbolism. This disconnection from nature is linked to the capitalist mode of production as the universal distinguishing characteristic of the culture of metropolitan society. Capitalism expropriates and commodifies the land, its resources, and people. Land, food, and human labour all have a price in the market place. The universality of metropolitan culture and the capitalist mode of production is attested to by the global spread of multinational corporations and the growth of an international network of transport and communication systems that makes the bearers of that culture portable and transposable. This means that migrants from Europe of French, German, Dutch, or English origin can settle in any one of the nation-states on the Pacific Rim half a hemisphere away with little sense of dislocation and cultural shock. The political infrastructure and mode of production are essentially the same; it is only local customary usages that are different, namely, language and the subtle imponderabilia of social life.

Metropolitan culture and indigenous culture are polar opposites in human organisation. The origin of metropolitan culture and its divergence from indigenous culture goes back to the beginnings of civilisation. The indigenous culture of tribal societies under favourable conditions, such as existed in the river valleys of the Nile and the Euphrates, led to the domestication of plants and animals. These achievements gave rise to specialisation and the development of city-states among the Sumerians and Egyptians around 3000 B.C. Over the next 5,000 years, city-states, nation-states, and empires rose and fell in the Old World; elsewhere, indigenous cultures continued their tribal way of life. But with the discovery of the New World in 1492, European expansionism, intensified by the industrial revolution, led to colonisation and the domination of indigenous cultures by the bearers of metropolitan culture. Indigenous cultures in the Americas and the Pacific were traumatised and transformed by the historic process of colonialisation. The process began innocuously enough with missionaries attempting to convert indigenous people to Christianity while traders introduced them to the cornucopia of material goods from the industrial complex of metropolitan culture. Transmigration of surplus population from metropolitan society, together with debilitation of the indigenous population by introduced diseases, facilitated hegemonic domination by the coloniser. Domination was achieved by diverse means according to local circumstance. These included treaty making, warfare, and termination of aboriginal title to land by fair purchase or simple expropriation of land by proclamation or legal strategem. Where genocide was not pursued as the solution to the problem of surviving indigenous populations, the answer was thought to lie in assimilation. To this end, the missionaries attacked the spiritual symbols of indigenous culture as ancestor or idol worship, and the secular state used schools to suppress indigenous languages and reproduce metropolitan culture in place of indigenous culture. The end product of this process is alienation, loss of identity, and marginalisation of indigenous people within metropolitan society. Yet, despite this transformation, clear evidence is emerging around the Pacific Rim that, in the past two decades, indigenous people have been recovering from the trauma of colonisation and that they are challenging the legitimacy and hegemony of metropolitan society.

COLONISATION OF NEW ZEALAND

The colonisation of the Maori people is a specific case of the general process described above. That process is well documented by Saunders (1896), Rusden (1974), Sinclair (1960), Ward (1973), Miller (1966), Scott (1981), and others, so only a résumé of its salient features will be included in this chapter to provide the historic setting against which contemporary Maori development might be examined. In the early 19th century, whalers, sealers, and traders began regular visits to New Zealand. The indigenous population, which was divided into 42 tribes (Buck 1950: 337), applied the word Maori (normal) to distinguish themselves from these visitors, whom they termed *pakeha* (white stranger). Thereafter, Maori and Pakeha define each other as the binary opposite of indigenous and metropolitan cultures locked in a struggle over land and its resources.

At first, Pakehas were welcomed for the trade goods they brought from metropolitan society. Chiefs competed with one another to have their own resident Pakeha as trade intermediaries by providing them with women and land. When the missionaries, under Samuel Marsden, arrived in 1814 (Sinclair 1960: 11), they too were taken under the protection of the chiefs in the belief they would attract more ships and enhance trading opportunities. Gradually, the control that Maoris had over these trading relationships was eroded by the corrosive effect of the presence of metropolitan culture. Men who had spent years on whaling ships returned home laden with material possessions as rivals to chiefly influence. Other men, trained in the mission schools, became the bearers of new knowledge to rival the *tohunga* (priestly expert). Pakeha sailors who raided *uru-*

paa (cemeteries) for their grave goods without any adverse consequences raised doubts concerning the laws of *tapu* (sacred prohibitions).

In warfare, chiefs were levelled by commoners armed with muskets. The musket wars of the 1820s ushered in the most debilitating phase of Maori tribal history. Casualties were high, and possession of muskets became necessary for survival. Whole tribes were mobilised to cut and dress flax growing in swamps, with dire consequences to their health from alien diseases. A ton of dressed flax fibre was the going rate for a musket.

After a decade of this necrotic behaviour, a relative balance of power was achieved and the tribes longed for surcease. By the 1830s, the chiefs had lost the initiative and turned to the missionaries as the peacemakers. It is truly written in the Bible "blessed are the peacemakers for they shall inherit the earth," because in New Zealand, they did. After 1835, whole tribes converted to Christianity, with Catholic and Protestant churches carving out respective spheres of influence. Missionaries in many instances acquired land holdings ranging up to 50;000 acres in extent (Grace 1966: 424–5). The missionaries undercut the power of chiefs by insisting they free their slaves and give up polygamy as a precondition for baptism. With the assurance of their new-found influence, the missionaries symbolically emasculated Maori people and their culture by cutting off the genitals of ancestral carvings in meeting houses. The art of carving disappeared altogether in Northland, where the misionaries gained their first foothold.

At the instigation of the missionaries, the chiefs petitioned Great Britain to intervene in New Zealand to establish law and order over the tribes and British residents. There was the additional fear of a takeover by France or some other alien power. Under the Treaty of Waitangi signed on 6 February 1840, the country was annexed by Great Britain and systematic colonisation begun by the New Zealand Company and the Crown (Ross 1972: 20).

At first, the chiefs were willing sellers of land. They coveted trade goods and thought they were dealing only with the 2,000 or so Pakehas who had settled among them. They did not realise that the governor's land-purchase commissioners were systematically extending the beach-heads of British sovereignty into native districts by the device of extinguishment of native title by fair purchase. But as shiploads of settlers arrived, reaction set in. From 1853 on, the *Kotahitnaga* (Unity) Movement held a series of intertribal meetings to discuss the encroachment of Pakeha settlement and the need to control it by withholding land from sale.

By 1858, through the process of transmigration of surplus population from metropolitan England, the indigenous people were outnumbered (56,000 against 59,000) in their own country (Miller 1966: 221). The chiefs attempted to counter the enormous inertia capable of being generated in metropolitan culture by unifying the tribes under a Maori king. Ideologically, this was a difficult accomplishment for an indigenous people whose political relations were defined by segmented tribal structures. Yet, despite ancient animosities, the first Maori king, Te Wherowhero, was installed in 1858. The king symbolised *mana whenua*, or sovereignty over land held in tribal districts, and his embargo on land sales was binding on all (Jones 1959: 196).

In electing the Maori king, the chiefs envisaged a *modus vivendi* with metropolitan society of a conjoint dual administration: the king would preside over native districts and the governor in territories acquired by the Crown. Both were to be united under the sovereignty of the queen and the law of God. So effective was the king's prohibition on land sales that the governor's despatch to the Duke of Newcastle in 1859 noted that only 7 million of the 26 million acres in the North Island had been acquired for colonisation (Walker 1985: 252). He considered that the Maoris had more land than they needed and the Europeans were determined to get those lands "recte si possint, si non quocunque modo" (Miller 1966: 30).

Since expropriation of the land by metropolitan society could not be accomplished fast enough to satisfy settler demands because of Maori resistance to land sales, the settler government (established under the New Zealand Constitution Act of 1852) resorted to a war of conquest. Under the New Zealand Settlement Act of 1863, approximately three million acres of Maori land was confiscated by the Crown for military settlers. But the Maoris were not easily subdued. According to Belich (1986), the stout resistance and brilliant military strategy of Maori leaders brought fighting with the British army to a standstill. In the end, the government had to borrow 3,000,000 pounds (Miller 1966: 133) to field an army of 18,000 men armed with rockets, howitzers, and the 118-pound Armstrong gun to subdue the tribes. Yet, despite the superiority of numbers and weaponry, General Cameron suffered a heavy defeat in the penultimate battle of the wars at Gate Pa. After a minor victory in the next battle, peace was made.

A less costly and more efficient method of expropriating land came in the form of a legal stratagem created through the Native Land Court established in 1867. The court functioned to transform tribal titles into individual titles. Initially, the court was obliged to record only 10 names on the court order issuing a Crown grant. These "owners" of tribal land were suborned into conveying the freehold to lawyers, land sharks, and storekeepers. By 1900, more than 95 per cent of Maori land had been alienated. The cumulative effects of introduced European diseases, musket wars, land wars, and the operations of the Native Land Court pushed the Maori population into a sharp decline. In 1845, it had stood at 109,500; by 1900, it had fallen to 45,000. Sorrenson (1956: 183–99) apportions much of the blame to the operations of the Native Land Court.

Loss of land, of connectedness with the earth-mother, almost killed off the subsistence economic activities that are a hallmark of indigenous culture. The Maori were progressively transformed into a brown proletariat seeking wage labour in the market economy of metropolitan culture. At first, only seasonal labour was sought to supplement subsistence activities. But by World War II, when the population had recovered and almost doubled – to 82,326 in 1936 (N.Z. Year Book 1977: 68) – the subsistence economy was no longer viable on the remnants of Maori land.

In 1867, an education system of public schools was introduced, ostensibly to provide the indigenous population with access to metropolitan culture. Its hidden agenda was assimilation. Schools became the instrument to subvert indigenous culture and replace it with the culture of metropolitan society. In 1900, more than 90 per cent of Maori school entrants spoke their mother tongue as their first language. But because teaching was conducted in English, progress was slow. Thereafter, schools became an arena of culture conflict when a policy of language suppression was introduced. Within six decades, the number of children speaking Maori had dropped to 26 per cent (Biggs 1968: 75).

Another mechanism introduced in 1867 that further undermined the Maori politically was the Maori Representation Act, which created four Maori seats in Parliament. Maori leaders did not seek representation in the House because they wanted their own council. Instead, they were given four seats in a house of 70 members, when, on a population basis (56,049 to 171,009), they were entitled to 20 seats. Such a large minority would have been inimical to Pakeha designs on Maori land (Walker 1985: 254).

MAORI RECOVERY AND DEVELOPMENT

The recovery of the Maori from the trauma of colonisation occurred in two phases. The first began in 1900 and the second after World War II. The population recovery appears to have been a spontaneous phenomenon, with an 8.18 per cent intercensal increase recorded in 1901. This recovery peaked at 29.3 per cent in 1936 and declined thereafter to 13.35 per cent in 1976 (N.Z. Yearbook 1977: 68).

The resurgence of Maori population coincided with the emergence of the first generation of Maori graduates trained in law (Ngata) and medicine (Buck and Pomare). From 1905 to 1911, these men were elected to Parliament in the Maori seats. Whereas the chiefs in the preceding century sought recognition of *mana motuhake* (Maori sovereignty), this new generation of leaders was concerned with physical and cultural survival. They worked through mainstream politics to get a better deal for the Maori people. Their achievements included health reforms, such as better drainage and pure water supplied for tribal *marae* (a courtyard and ancestral meeting house); the revival of the Maori cultural arts of singing, dancing, carving, and weaving; and the building of meeting houses as the focus for communal activities.

In the 1930s, Ngata, as minister of native affairs, instigated Maori land de-

velopment schemes. Many of the landholdings were too small to be economically viable. Most of the income from dairy farming went into paying mortgages.
Ngata's most successful enterprise was the establishment of Maori land incor-
porations among his own tribe on the east coast. But, as for the basic issue of
control over Maori land, Ngata was powerless to stop the erosion of the Maori
land base. The remaining five million acres of Maori land was being alienated
at a rate of more than 72,000 acres per annum. With 2.8 million acres leased by
the Maori Trustee to Pakeha farmers, that left only 20 acres for each man,
woman, and child (McClean 1950: 61), and much of that was marginal land.

THE URBAN MIGRATION

Before 1936, 81 per cent of the Maori population lived in rural poverty in their
tribal areas. Belshaw (1939: 1) reported to the first Young Maori Leaders' Conference at Auckland University in 1939 that the Maori faced serious social and
economic problems and their resolution would be of profound importance to
both Maori and Pakeha. Belshaw anticipated the inevitability of an urban
migration. The catalyst for the migration was World War II, during which the
Manpower Act directed non-combatants to work in essential industries in
towns and cities. After the war, many returned servicemen also moved to cities
in search of work. In 1960, the Department of Maori Affairs organised an urban
relocation programme for 399 families over a five-year period and assisted 485
other families in finding employment and accommodation (Rose 1967: 38).
Countless others found their own ways into towns and cities by using kinship
networks to find shelter and employment. Metge (1964: 128) points to the primary motivating factors among the migrants as the "Big Three" of work,
money, and pleasure. By 1971, more than 70 per cent of the Maori population
was urbanised (N.Z. Yearbook 1977: 65).

   The Maori migrants into the urban milieu had to accomplish three basic
developmental tasks. These involved learning the necessary survival skills in
metropolitan society, maintenance of cultural continuity, and a political response to Pakeha domination.

   Urban living nearly precludes the subsistence economy of indigenous culture.
Hunting, fishing, and the gathering of native foods are relegated to an occasional activity on weekends. The primary adaptation is to regular employment and
complete dependence on the cash nexus. Wage earnings, rents, mortgages,
rates, hire-purchases, and time payments lock Maoris into the universal culture
of capitalism and consumerism within metropolitan society.

   Although urbanised Maori in the main constitute a brown proletariat, their
success in the second developmental task of transplanting their culture to ensure cultural continuity in towns and cities differentiates them from their Pakeha counterparts. The two basic mechanisms for cultural transmission consist of

kinship organisations and voluntary associations. Metge (1964: 164–70) has commented on the function of family *komiti*, or family clubs, in urban life for mutual support at funerals, weddings, and other life crisis rites. But for individuals who lack a sufficient number of kin in the same suburb or town, voluntary association on a multitribal basis substitutes for kinship. Banton (1957: 168) and Little (1955: 222) have both stressed the importance of the integrative function of voluntary associations in a multitribal situation. For many people, urbanisation leads to dispersal of kin. Some are left behind in the rural hinterland, and others are scattered in different towns or across different suburbs of a metropolis, such as Auckland (Walker 1975: 167–68).

Some of the earliest voluntary associations to integrate Maoris across tribal affiliations were culture clubs, Maori sections of orthodox churches, Maori protest religions, and Maori sports clubs. In 1951, the Maori Women's Welfare League was established as the first national Maori association with branches throughout the country. Although the league was primarily concerned with family care, health, and housing, its annual conferences became an important platform for airing Maori grievances. In 1962, the Maori Council was established as a statutory organisation to formulate Maori policy and negotiate Maori rights with the government and departments of state. As a pan-Maori organisation, the Maori Council replaced the earlier tribal committees based on the 1945 Maori Social and Economic Advancement Act.

Although kinship and voluntary associations provide integrating political mechanisms for cultural transmission, the symbolic focus of Maori social and cultural life is the *marae*. In the rural hinterland, the *marae* complex of an open courtyard in front of a carved ancestral meeting house with a dining and general purpose hall is the property of a kin group, such as a *hapu* (subtribe) and *iwi* (tribe). The kin group is responsible for its maintenance and all ceremonial activities that take place there.

The *marae* is the most appropriate venue for rites of passage such as birthdays, weddings, and the *tangi* (funeral). In this respect, the *marae* is the bastion of cultural conservatism. In the absence of *marae*, the urban migrants converted their private homes to serve as a "mini *marae*" for the *tangi*. The living room was cleared of furniture for the lying in state of the deceased while kinsmen and friends came to pay their respects. Some families erected double garages on their house lots to provide dining space for their guests. In most cases, corpses were returned to their tribal *marae* for completion of the mortuary rituals. In time, as the migrants put down roots in the cities and suburbs where they lived, they began building urban *marae*.

The urban *marae* is a symbolic statement of the successful transplantation of Maori culture into the heart of metropolitan society. But it is not a static symbol locked in the past by tradition. It is a dynamic symbol expressing both tradition and transformation in response to changing human needs. In fact, four types of urban *marae* have evolved in response to new circumstances:

1. First, there is the tribal *marae* of people whose territory has been engulfed by urban growth. Within this category are *marae* built by groups outside their own tribal area. The unifying principle underlying both is kinship. These *marae* are made available to other groups who have no *marae* of their own.
2. The second type of *marae* to emerge in response to urban needs is the church-based *marae*. Members in this type are drawn from many tribes. In this case, a common religion is the basic unifying principle instead of kinship.
3. The third type of *marae* in urban areas is the multitribal *marae* controlled and operated on the basis of communally recognised leaders who form a *marae* committee. In the first instance, the initiators of a *marae* building project are usually elected to a steering committee. Successful performance in the steering committee in most cases leads to confirmation of leadership roles when the project is completed.
4. The fourth and most recent type of *marae* to emerge is the on-campus *marae*, which caters to the social and cultural needs of students in educational institutions, including secondary schools, teachers' colleges, and universities.

POLITICAL DEVELOPMENT

In the 19th century, Maori leaders resisted cultural invasion from metropolitan society by a series of dynamic responses. These included electing a Maori king, defending their lands from armed invasion, resorting to resistance movements led by prophets to drive out the invaders, and, when that failed, turning to pacifism and coexistence on the basis of separation of the races.

In 1892, the chiefly leaders formed two independent bodies to preside in native districts to formulate Maori rights as guaranteed under the Treaty of Waitangi and to negotiate those rights with Parliament. These were the *Kauhanganui* (Great Council), formed by the King Movement, and *Kotahitanga Mo Te Tiriti o Waitangi* (Unity under the Treaty of Waitangi, commonly known as the Maori Parliament), formed by tribes outside the King Movement. Both movements were expressions of *mana motuhake* (Maori sovereignty) attempting to establish a *modus vivendi* with metropolitan society. Both were legitimate attempts at self-government under Section 71 of the New Zealand Constitution Act of 1852. The colonial government, on the other hand, was so confident of its dominance that both bodies were treated with disdain. Even when the Maori Parliament, through the member for Northern, succeeded in introducing a Maori Rights Bill into the House in 1894, it was ignored for two years before being rejected in 1896 (Walker 1984: 272).

After the turn of the century, when the *Kotahitanga* and *Kauhanganui* became moribund, the co-option of educated Maori leaders into the political mainstream appeared to have resolved the "Maori problem" for metropolitan society. The policy of assimilation was being vindicated, and in recognition of their services to the state, Buck, Ngata, and Pomare were awarded knighthoods. In the four decades leading up to World War II, the bulk of the Maori population lived out of sight and out of mind in impoverished rural enclaves. The co-operation of the Maori élite and the spatial separation between the Maori people and metropolitan society helped the government to project an image of racial harmony to the rest of the world.

Even as the myth of harmony was being promulgated, it was contradicted by the prophet-leader Ratana, who got a petition with 30,128 signatures to have the Treaty of Waitangi tabled and ratified in the House in November 1932. For the coloniser, it was business as usual. The petition was held over for 13 years and finally fobbed off in 1945 with a resolution to have the treaty published and hung in the schools of the nation as a "sacred reaffirmation" (Henderson 1963: 88–89). Ratana made one last attempt at co-operation with metropolitan society when he aligned the brown proletariat with the Labour party. From 1932 to 1943, the Ratana Church captured the four Maori seats and delivered them into a 40-year alliance with Labour. Nothing substantive was achieved by this alliance apart from the general benefits of social security and pensions that accrued to all New Zealanders.

In the two decades after the war, the Maori Women's Welfare League and the Maori Council became the mediating bodies between the Maori people and the Crown. These bodies operated in the conservative mode of heading deputations to ministers of the Crown and making submissions to parliamentary select committees. Both organisations and the tribal authorities failed to modify the two oppressive clauses in the 1967 Maori Affairs Amendment Act whereby the Maori Trustee for Maori land could acquire compulsorily small parcels ("uneconomic shares") to the value of NZ$50 (Kawharu 1977: 291–93). For indigenous culture, a share in Maori land, no matter how small, represented *turangawaewae* (standing) in the tribal estate as the spiritual connection with ancestors. But in metropolitan society, land is treated as a commodity. If it is "uneconomic," then it must be sold to aggregate it into economic units, and hence into Pakeha hands. These conflicting views over land underline the ongoing binary opposition between metropolitan society and indigenous people.

Up to 1967, all the creative Maori responses to cultural invasion and oppression by metropolitan society appear to have been negated by the government. The contradiction of Pakeha dominance and Maori subordination was masked by New Zealand's ideology of egalitarianism, the "we are one people" myth stated by Hobson at the signing of the Treaty of Waitangi in 1840. An ideology of equality and one people is, in Larrain's view (1979: 46–49), a distorted "solution in the mind to contradictions which cannot be solved in practice. The sharper the contradictions become, the more ideology descends to the level of mere idealizing." In the next decade the illusion was shattered by a new wave of urbanised Maori leaders. The urban experience for the Maori has, in Freire's terms (1973: 148), culminated in knowledge of the alienating culture, which leads to transforming action, resulting in a culture being freed from alienation. One consequence of this knowledge is diversification of Maori leadership, whereby youthful activists create space for themselves outside traditional tribal structures and orthodox leadership roles to initiate radical transforming action. This diversification makes it more difficult for metropolitan society to co-opt Maori leadership. Furthermore, the exposure of the contradictions in New Zealand society by radical action makes it possible for those at the conservative end of the political spectrum to win some concessions from metropolitan society.

The first portent of contemporary Maori activism took the form of a radical newsletter in 1968 named *Te Hokioi*, which characterised itself as a "*taiaha* (weapon) of truth for the Maori nation." This was followed by a similar newsletter from the Maori Organisation on Human Rights (MOOHR). These movements called for unity to organise the downfall of those sections of New Zealand society that oppress and exploit the Maori nation. Although there appeared to be a connection with the trade union movement in the tenor of these newsletters and the alignment of the Maori struggle with the class struggle, the two are not synonymous. The Maori struggle is distinguished from the latter on the basis of the status of Maori as *tangata whenua* (people of the land) and all that that implies in terms of aboriginal title to the land and what was conceded to the British Crown under the Treaty of Waitangi. Both groups looked to the treaty to redress Maori grievances and pledged to uphold it. In 1970, the Young Maori Leaders' Conference on urbanisation held at Auckland University precipitated the formation of Nga Tamatoa (the young warriors) as a leadership outlet for Maori youth. The instigators were former students who wanted to recover their own sense of identity and to challenge hegemonic domination of their lives by metropolitan society.

At its inception, there was a division in Nga Tamatoa between conservative students at the university and radical elements. The radicals brought adverse publicity to the movement in the form of revolutionary rhetoric of brown power, Maori liberation, separatism, and even a separate foreign policy. Eventually, the more level-headed leaders became the dominating force in Nga Tamatoa and embarked on a positive programme of Maori self-development.

Nga Tamatoa opened an office in Auckland to interview new arrivals and find them jobs. Members also monitored the courts to provide assistance to Maoris in need of advice and legal aid. A similar service was also started in Wellington. A petition calling for the inclusion of the Maori language in the education system collected thousands of signatures. In answer to the challenge that insufficient teachers were available to deal with the nationwide introduction of the language, Nga Tamatoa called for the inception of a one-year teacher training course for native speakers of Maori. To prove its seriousness, it took parties of urban youth to rural *maraes* to learn the language from elders. In 1974, the "link system" of teaching Maori between primary and secondary schools was established, and the one-year Maori language teacher-training scheme was introduced. This scheme trained approximately 40 teachers per annum over a four-year period.

Perhaps one of the more important contributions of Nga Tamatoa was the protest activity it mounted in 1971 against the Treaty of Waitangi celebrations. It was argued that only fools would celebrate their own downfall, an allusion to the 63 million acres of land in Pakeha ownership as against the three million acres left in Maori hands. Nga Tamatoa proclaimed 6 February as a "day of mourning" for what was lost. Stung by this challenge, the government sought advice from the Maori Council. The council responded with a submission by Ngata citing 14 statutes that contravened the Treaty of Waitangi, ranging from the Mining Act to the Town and Country Planning Act (Ngata 1972: 19–28). It took four years before the government responded with the establishment of the Waitangi Tribunal to hear Maori grievances under the treaty. But like all previous responses, the tribunal was a cosmetic change; it was non-retrospective and had no power to make awards.

By the mid-'70s, the creative burst of Nga Tamatoa had come to an end and the movement went into recess. In retrospect, Nga Tamatoa was the portent of more vigorous Maori activism to come. The erosion of Maori land rights by a century of colonising legislation under the Maori Land Court, the Public Works Act, the Town and Country Planning Act, and others fuelled Maori anger as these laws continued to bite into what was deemed to be the "last three million acres" of Maori land. In 1975, Matakite o Aotearoa (the seers of prophetic vision) organised a potent Maori land rights movement of 30,000 people in a land march to Parliament under the slogan of "Not One More Acre of Land" (to be alienated). The nightly stops at *marae* en route down the centre of the North Island served to politicise rural hosts and the alienated urban brown proletariat, such as former inmates of penal institutions.

Pakeha bemusement over the Maori land march had hardly subsided when 280 hectares of Crown land at Bastion Point in Auckland was ocupied in 1977 by 200 protestors supporting the Orakei Maori Action Committee's contention that the land ought to be returned to the control of the *tangata whenua* (tribal owners). The protesters defied the government and the Supreme Court for 507 days until they were removed by 600 police on 25 May 1978. In the same decade, there were occupations of land at Raglan and Awhitu. In all three cases of occupation, the Maori right was recognised and the land returned.

The uneasy peace between Maori and Pakeha was disturbed a year later when a new wave of young activists emerged to carry on where Tamatoa had left off. These activists were known under various guises as He Taua (avenging party), Maori Liberation Movement of Aotearoa, Black Women, and Waitangi Action Committee. All these groups were domiciled in Auckland and had overlapping personnel.

In May 1979, He Taua had a physical confrontation with students of the engineering school at Auckland University over their parody in the Capping

Parade of the Maori *haka* (war-dance). Five minutes of direct action stopped this gross insult to Maori culture where 25 years of patient negotiation had failed. He Taua carried contemporary activism to a new level by putting its members at risk with the law. Fourteen were apprehended and charged with rioting. The following year Maori activism took a new turn when a group called Maranga Mai (arise) toured the country with a play dramatising Maori grievances.

As the decade of the 1970s drew to a close, the Maori activism that characterised the period culminated in the resignation of Matiu Rata from parliament to found the Mana Motuhake (Maori sovereignty) movement. The name of the movement revives in limited form the concept of Maori sovereignty. The essence of its policy is to wrest the four Maori seats away from Labour as a form of self-determination outside party politics and to assert Maori control over their own future within a dual or bicultural society. At the by-election for Northern Maori in 1980 following Rata's resignation, Mana Motuhake put up a respectable showing by taking 38 per cent of the vote. This was a clear signal to the Labour party that the Maori vote should no longer be taken for granted.

In 1980, the broad thrust of Maori activism of the previous decade was refocused on the Treaty of Waitangi by the Waitangi Action Committee. The group mounted strong protests against treaty celebrations. Each year as their protest became more vehement, the state responded by increasing the police presence to curb them. Undeterred by arrests and charges of rioting in 1981, members of the group adopted the new tactic of defending themselves in court, challenging the legitimacy of the state to try them and challenging the veracity of the judicial system itself. Their acquittal more than nine months after the event vindicated their actions. In the following year, church leaders began siding with the Waitangi Action Committee by proclaiming Waitangi Day as a day of repentance for the part missionaries played in encouraging the chiefs to sign a document that stripped them of their land and humanity. Pre-emptive arrests by police of peaceful demonstrators, including Pakeha activists, liberals, and church leaders who had sided with the protesters, exposed the repressive use of state force to enforce a celebration that, in the changing social climate, was no longer tenable. In 1983, the churches refused to sanctify the occasion by their presence, and the Minister of Maori Affairs, B. M. Couch, an elder of the Mormon church, had to conduct the service at the celebration.

Contemporary Maori activism, represented by the efforts of the Waitangi Action Committee and Mana Motuhake, has reopened the question of Maori sovereignty. Donna Awatere (1982: 38), a foundation member of Nga Tamatoa and the most articulate advocate of Maori sovereignty, defines it as

the Maori ability to determine our own destiny and to do so from the basis of our land and fisheries. In essence Maori sovereignty seeks nothing less than the acknowledgement that New Zealand is Maori land. At its most conservative it could be interpreted as the desire for a bi-cultural society, one in which *taha Maori* (Maori culture) receives an equal consideration with *taha Pakeha*. It certainly demands an end to monoculturalism.

Awatere's definition of Maori sovereignty is clearly rooted in the long tradition of Maori activism in the century and a half since the signing of the Treaty of Waitangi. Whereas the original proponents of Maori sovereignty sought its establishment by coexistence, Awatere's advocacy (1982: 42) takes on a hard and even desperate edge in reaction to the dominance of metropolitan society:

For the Maori, without sovereignty we are dead as a nation. It is not sovereignty or no sovereignty. It is sovereignty or nothing. We have no choice.

CONCLUSION

The publication of *Maori Sovereignty* has heightened Pakeha consciousness and brought about the realization that Maori activism concerns them directly as the beneficiaries of a colonial legacy, and in this respect, they know that the Maori people occupy the moral high ground. The issue turns on the Treaty of Waitangi, what it conceded to metropolitan society and what it promised the Maori people. Under clause 1, the chiefs of New Zealand conceded *kawanatanga* (governance) of the country to the Crown. The missionary translators distorted the meaning of the treaty by avoiding the word *mana*, the authentic Maori equivalent to sovereignty. But *kawanatanga* has been consistently interpreted by the coloniser as sovereignty. It is very likely that had the word *mana* appeared in the treaty, no chiefs would have signed the document. This calls into question the very legitimacy of New Zealand as a nation-state, since the Maoris did not concede sovereignty, nor were they conquered. The treaty is the basis on which governance is founded, and yet it has not been ratified by Parliament, and all subsequent laws passed by Parliament have contravened it.

Under clause 2 of the treaty, the Crown promised to recognise the *rangatiratanga* (chieftainship) of the Maori people over their lands, homes, and possessions. Maori leaders have interpreted this clause to mean the right to self-determination in Maori districts, and their attempts to establish a conjoint administration through their own institutions of a Maori king, the Kauhanganui, and the Maori Parliament were consistent with this clause of the treaty and with Section 71 of the New Zealand Constitution Act. But the numerical, economic, and political domination of metropolitan society at the turn of the century allowed the power brokers to override these Maori efforts to establish a *modus vivendi* between the two cultures. The openly avowed goal was for indigenous culture to be assimilated by metropolitan culture.

Metropolitan society, on the other hand, did not reckon on the resilience of indigenous culture as it pursued its goal of assimilation. The contemporary

resurgence of Maori culture has negated that policy and its more recent sani-
tised cognate of integration. The bastion of indigenous cultural conservatism is
the *marae* and its associated rituals and mortuary practices. A total of 464 *marae*
reserves throughout New Zealand are the well-spring of Maori cultural integrity that have been transplanted through the process of urbanisation into the very
heart of metropolitan culture. The agenda of contemporary Maori activism is
recognition of Maori sovereignty, recovery of the Maori language through the
450 *kohanga reo* (language nests) established in the past four years, and the transformation of all social and political institutions to incorporate biculturalism. In
education, this means the establishment of bilingual schooling and independent
Maori schools based on total immersion in the Maori language. The same
moves towards institutional transformation to incorporate the values and procedures of Maori people are also occurring in other bureaucracies, such as the
Department of Social Welfare. The Rangihau Report (1986: 9) accepts
unequivocally the Maori agenda of biculturalism for future nation-building in
New Zealand.

The case of the Maori as an example of the conflict generated in the process of
nation-building between the bearers of metropolitan culture and indigenous
culture has its parallels in Australia, Hawaii, Tahiti, New Caledonia, Canada,
the United States, and Latin America. In all these places, nation-building began with the destruction of the aboriginal (first) nations. Surviving populations
were marginalised in their own lands and subjected to enormous assimilationist
pressures by the dominant group. But the resilience of indigenous people has
been underestimated. In Australia, Alaska, Canada, New Caledonia, New Zealand, and elsewhere, indigenous people are claiming aboriginal title to the soil.
That claim must be dealt with.

Berger argues that, with the decolonisation of third world nations, the time
has come to reassess the position of indigenous people who are locked into nations that they can never hope to rule because of the numerical dominance of
metropolitan society that colonises their countries.

Indigenous people do not usually struggle to separate from the nation-state nor to
achieve independence within national boundaries; they want mainly to retain control
over their own lives and their own land. Fourth World (indigenous) claims are claims to
limited sovereignty, but they have not achieved the same recognition as Third World
claims to full sovereignty (Berger 1985: 76).

The Maori and Pakeha in New Zealand are at present in the painful throes of
grappling with the concept of Maori sovereignty, whether it is paramount,
limited, or co-equal with the sovereignty of metropolitan society. The answer
lies somewhere in the future, and all the nation-states of the Pacific Rim that
share the same problem have a role to play in its resolution on an international
basis.

REFERENCES

Awatere, D. 1982. On Maori sovereignty. *Broadsheet*, no. 100 (June).

Banton, M. 1957. *West African city*. London: Oxford University Press.

Belich, J. 1986. *The New Zealand wars*. Auckland: Oxford University Press.

Belshaw, M. 1939. Preface. In *Report of Young Maori Conference*. Auckland: Auckland University College.

Berger, T. R. 1985. *Village journey*. New York: Hill and Wang.

Biggs, B. E. 1968. The Maori language: Past and present. In *The Maori people in the nineteen sixties*, edited by E. Schwimmer, 65–84. Auckland: Blackwood and Janet Paul.

Buck, P. H. 1950. *The coming of the Maori*. Wellington: Whitcombe and Tombs.

Freire, P. 1973. *Education for critical consciousness*. New York: Continuum.

Grace, J. 1966. *Tuwharetoa*. Wellington: A. H. & A. W. Reed.

Henderson, J. M. 1963. *Ratana*. Wellington: A. H. & A. W. Reed.

Jones, P. TeH. 1959. *King Potalau*. Wellington: Polynesian Society.

Kawharu, I. H. 1977. *Maori land tenure*. Oxford: Clarendon Press.

Larrain, J. 1979. *The concept of ideology*. London: Hutchinson.

Little, K. 1955. Structural change in the Sierra Leone Protectorate. *Africa* 25: 217–33.

McClean, S. 1967. *Maori Representation 1905–1948*. M. A. thesis, University of Auckland.

Manuel, E. 1972. *The Fourth World*. London: Minority Rights Group.

Metge, J. 1964. *A new Maori migration*. London: Athlone Press, University of London.

Miller, H. 1966. *Race conflict in New Zealand*. Auckland: Blackwood and Janet Paul.

Newsletters. 1979–80. *Maori Organisation on Human Rights*. Wellington, deposited in Auckland University Library.

Newsletters. 1980–84. *Waitangi Action Committee*. Auckland, deposited in the Auckland University Library.

Ngata, H. 1972. *The Treaty of Waitangi and land: Parts of current law in contravention of the Treaty, Te Maori* (Journal of the N. Z. Maori Council). Wellington.

N. Z. Yearbook. 1977. *New Zealand year book*. Wellington: Government Printer.

Rangihau, J. 1986. *Puao te atatu: Report of the Ministerial Advisory Committee on a Maori perception for the Department of Social Welfare*. Wellington: Government Printer.

Rose, W. D. 1967. *The Maori in the New Zealand economy*. Wellington: Department of Industries and Commerce.

Ross, R. 1972. The Treaty on the ground. In *The Treaty of Waitangi: Its origins and significance*. Wellington: Victoria University Extension.

Rusden, G. W. 1974. *Aureretanga: Groans of the Maoris*. Wellington: Hakaprint.

Saunders, A. 1896. *History of New Zealand 1642–1861*. Wellington: Whitcombe and Tombs.

Scott, D. 1981. *Ask that mountain*. Auckland: Heinemann.

Simpson, T. 1979. *Te Riri Pakeha*. Martinborough: Alistair Taylor.

Sinclair, K. 1960. *A history of New Zealand*. Harmondsworth: Penguin Books.

Sorrenson, M. P. K. 1956. Land purchase methods and their effects on Maori population. *Journal of Polynesian Society*: 183–99.

Walker, R. J. 1975. The politics of voluntary association. In *Conflict and compromise*, edited by I. H. Kawharu. Wellington: A. H. & A. W. Reed.

———. 1984. The genesis of Maori activism. *Journal of Polynesian society* 93(3): 276–82.

————. 1985. The Maori people: Their political development. In *New Zealand politics in perspective*, edited by Hyam Gold. Auckland: Longman and Paul.

Ward, A. 1973. *A show of justice*. Auckland: Oxford University Press.

W. C. I. P. 1975. *Charter of the World Council of Indigenous People*, declared at the inaugural conference of WCIP, Port Alberni.

8

From Race Aliens to an Ethnic Group — Indians in New Zealand

JACQUELINE LECKIE

Studying history, and especially that of "God's own nation," was an established part of the school curriculum in New Zealand for most students during the 1960s and early 1970s. The indoctrination began at a young age, when almost every child learnt of the peopling of Aotearoa. Enthusiastic teachers would recount romantic tales of the great Maori migrations from Hawaiiki and then proceed on to "real history," the heroic voyages of the "discoverers," notably captains Tasman and Cook. Older students were expected to have plodded their way through the Eurocentrically labelled Maori Wars of the 1860s and the settlement of the confiscated land by British settlers. Little attention would be paid to the economic and political dynamics of this transformation from Aotearoa to New Zealand, or to the significance of this region in the world economy. The emphasis of most high-school social studies programmes was on the conscious shaping of a humane, egalitarian society. Young New Zealanders were encouraged to be proud of their nation, which enjoyed one of the highest standards of living in the world. Although in many other parts of the globe during this period people were engaged in radical debate or in the throes of unprecedented conflict, in New Zealand criticism of this kind was limited and more subdued. Orthodox history paid some lip-service to past problems and struggles, but still placed this within the evolutionary context of the rise of a democratically endorsed welfare state. Racial problems and race relations had some place on the agenda, but invariably they were narrowly defined as Maori-Pakeha relations, with the emphasis being on the "Maori problem."[1] Nevertheless, students were expected to submit answers in their state-regulated examinations that pointed to a future in which racial disharmony would be eradicated through "progressive" state institutions, such as the newly constituted Race Relations Act of 1972 (see Trlin 1982). Though all students learnt that there had been hardship in New Zealand, such knowledge tended to pivot around the 1930s' depression, for which populist-based state management was presented as the solution. The result is that, even after New Zealand suffered the full effect of the 1970s' recession and after protests over continued Pakeha dominance, certain well-sung myths about New Zealand's population and the benevolence of the "people's state" resound in the 1980s.

This version of New Zealand's history exhibited little interest in ethnic groups other than the Maori except when they constituted a problem or were in conflict with other sectors of society.[2] The dominant ideology perpetuated was that of a unique and progressive egalitarian welfare state, but one that could be maintained only with a homogenous population. Caucasian migrants who were not of British descent were unwelcome, but they were tolerated if they could be readily assimilated into white New Zealand society.[3] It was never clear who this society represented (see de Lepervanche 1984: 29), although assimilated immigrants were typified as those with nuclear families, owning a house in the suburbs, and with the male head being fully employed, "respectable," and fitting into a "Kiwi life-style." Immigration restrictions in 1921 required a permit for all persons intending to visit who were not of British birth and parentage; behind this requirement, however, were confidential orders stating that distinctions were to be made between different nationalities and races.[4] All non-Europeans (except the very wealthy, diplomats, or visiting athletes) were required to have permits before embarkation, although "persons of foreign nationality but of European race and colour" from, in particular, France, Belgium, Italy, Denmark, and the United States were almost always issued with an entry permit on arrival. There had been some settlement of Yugoslavs in New Zealand since the 1890s, but generally migration from Southern Europe and Eastern Europe was not considered desirable. On the other hand, from 1950 to 1964, a total of 6,261 Dutch people were given subsidised passages under the New Zealand Assisted Passage Scheme. Up to 1968, approximately 23,879 Dutch emigrated to New Zealand, resulting in Europeans of Dutch and Indonesian birth constituting the largest group of non-British residents there (Thomson 1970). This migration was promoted not only because of demands in the labour market, but also because the Dutch were considered culturally very similar to the most favoured group of immigrants, the British.

INDIANS AS "RACE ALIENS"

This was in complete contrast to Asian, and in particular Chinese and Indian immigrants, who were classified as "race aliens" until 1926 and then still perceived as another "race" as late as the 1970s by official statisticians in New Zealand. Ironically, although Indians and their descendants today are probably more conspicuous than before in dress, customs, and religion, they attract less attention than when they constituted only .05 per cent (or 671) of the total population in 1921. Yet, such a trickle was enough to give fire to a white New

Zealand immigration policy (see Leckie 1981: 241–47, 342–52, 371–82; O'Connor 1968; Spoonley 1982). The roots of this policy were laid in the 19th century, and, although immigration barriers were drawn in 1921, anti-Asian hostility continued to be one of the effective means through which racial and economic hegemony of the white *petite bourgeoisie* could be voiced. Such rhetoric was frequently much more overt and vehement than that which could be publicly expressed with regard to Pakeha hegemony over Maoris.

White racism directed against Indians assumed its prominence in the decade after World War I. Having achieved self-governing dominion status in 1907, New Zealand was fully integrated within the capitalist world-economy and shared both the economic insecurity and racist ideologies in which fascism thrived in the years after World War I. The most notorious expression came from growers in the Franklin district, near Auckland, when they founded the White New Zealand League in 1925 (Leckie 1985). This was in response to Asian competition in potato and onion farming, but the league soon spread grossly exaggerated and unrealistic xenophobic fears throughout New Zealand.

The serious danger with which civilisation is threatened does not come from actual savages or even those of a little plain [sin], who may be called barbarians. The peril is from those dark-skinned races which have long ago put on a thin veneer of semi-civilisation, but have remained for centuries without rising any higher – are really constitutionally incapable of rising any higher. No better example of this class can be found than the Hindus . . . "mentally and morally incapable of real civilisation" (*Franklin Times* 18.1.26)

This period also gave rise to attempts at drafting legislation that would reflect dominant interests in the young nation. The 1921 Immigration Restriction Amendment Act alluded to the pressures the postwar government was under to adopt policies that would apease populist demands.

The Bill is the result of a deep-seated sentiment on the part of a large majority of the people in this country that this Dominion shall be what is often called a "white" New Zealand, and that people who come here should, as far as it is possible for us to provide for it, be of the same way of thinking from the British Empire's point of view (*New Zealand Parliamentary Debates* 1920, vol. 187: 905).

Returned servicemen were the most vocal group urging government to introduce a white immigration policy. These men were also severely hit by the postwar economic slump, and though government measures to alleviate this were not effective, the introduction of immigration controls suggested to contemporaries that steps were being taken to reduce unemployment and other problems. Nevertheless, the 1921 act also revealed that New Zealand did not want to jeopardise its participation in the Commonwealth and so could not ignore resolutions adopted at the 1917 and 1918 imperial war conferences that had endorsed a principle of reciprocity of treatment between India and the self-governing dominions.[5] The compromise reached was that, after 1921, any prospective migrant of non-British birth and parentage required a permit before entering the dominion, but nearly unlimited access was maintained for the children, wives, and fiancés of Indians resident in New Zealand before 1921. This assured that Indians could remain as a small minority and that its size would still be permitted to undergo a slight increase. Later government policy indeed encouraged the immigration of immediate families. Ostensibly this was because the nuclear family was integral to the New Zealand "way of life," which meant that ethnic minorities were expected to follow the same pattern. Thus, although the 1916 census recorded only 181 Indians in New Zealand, by 1981 the official statistics noted 11,244.

What constitutes the ethnic group called Indians? This identity has been partly adopted by those it covers in response to both negative and, more recently, positive categorisation by the dominant society in New Zealand. Indians as an ethnic group appear to assume reality with, for example, the presence of a national New Zealand Indian Association or in glossy and superficial articles such as one that appeared in the *Auckland Metro* in December 1983. The "Indian community" may warrant a few lines in the newspaper when it pressures the minister of immigration, celebrates Indian Republic Day, or has members who have represented New Zealand in international sports, such as when a gold medal was won in hockey at the 1976 Olympic games. "Evidence" of a significant ethnic group of Indians is produced every five years with the census, which records birthplace and ethnic origin. The latter mainly applies only to non-European minorities and represents a new label for groups that were categorised as "race aliens," then "other races," until the 1971 census (see Brown 1984). The erroneous confusion between perceiving those who may wish to be classified as a separate cultural and historical entity with those of a biologically separate race has been rooted in both the official record and the popular stereotypes in New Zealand. Further, although the entity may be "Indian" and be referred to by both Indians and others, the term does not necessarily have much meaning for its internal relationships.

The term Indian or New Zealand Indian (hereafter referred to as Indo-New Zealander) is appropriate only in certain contexts. Most fourth generation New Zealanders of Indian descent consider themselves to be New Zealanders by virtue of history, nationality, and identity, but they are still conscious of their ancestry from the subcontinent of India. More specifically, most Indo-New Zealanders, when referring to their ethnicity or identity, stress the region from which they or their ancestors originated. McLeod (1980: 113) has also noted:

The very word "community" is, in fact, a thorough misnomer, for there are actually two separate communities of Indian origin in New Zealand together with a heterogeneous remainder belonging to neither. Separated by language, tradition, occupation, and (in most instances) conscious religious affiliation they constitute two distinct identities.

Although mutual advantage draws them together in the Central Indian Association this organisation exacts a very limited involvement from most of its members, and even within its organisational bounds the fundamental difference can be clearly perceived.

Of these two communities, the one of greater number has roots in the former Surat District and the state of Baroda, both of which today fall within south Gujarat. The other community (today comprising about 600), are of Punjabi descent from villages in the Jullundur and Hoshiarpur districts. The heterogenous remainder include more than 2,000 Indians from Fiji who gained entry to New Zealand through professional, study, or work schemes, or by marriage. Also about 200 Indians from Uganda were given refuge in New Zealand following the expulsion orders of Amin in 1971. A few Indian professionals have also settled, either temporarily or permanently, in New Zealand, following the government's selective "liberalisation" of its immigration programme in 1974. In this chapter, I will focus on the established Indian community of several generations of residence in New Zealand, that is, Indians of Punjabi and especially Gujarati origin.[6]

Distinctive regional cultures and languages have reinforced awareness of regional differences as most families have attempted to maintain speaking Gujarati or Punjabi in their homes and, if self-employed, in their businesses. With the Punjabis, Sikhism contributes to a further separateness from other Indo-New Zealanders. However, not all Punjabis are Sikhs. Consequently, if asked about origins, many Indians would refer to the region, but when further pressed, it is the locality, village, and kin relationships, and with the Gujaratis also caste, that are relevant. These networks do not extend only to New Zealand and India, but are part of a world-wide pattern of social and economic links stretching from New Zealand to Australia, South Africa and East Africa, Britain, Europe, India, the United States, Canada, and Fiji. These networks are historically grounded, reflecting both local and wider political and economic developments in the British empire and on the Indian subcontinent. As outlined below, with Gujarati migration and increasingly with the capitalisation of agriculture, caste and kin links became more advantageous and lucrative for both survival and profit maximisation. To an extent, this throws light on why some of these villagers ended up in the far reaches of the empire. Equally, however, the migration and settlement of Indians in New Zealand are centred within the changing demands for migrant labour and the "nation building" of New Zealand (see Miles 1984; Miles and Spoonley 1985).

THE ROOTS OF AN "ETHNIC" COMMUNITY: MIGRATION

The Punjab and Gujarat home regions are both centres of global emigration that began in the late 19th century. British imperialism and market relations had also penetrated into these regions to the extent that the rural areas were

undergoing marked transformations during this period (see Breman 1985: 14–
23; Chua 1986; Guha 1985; Kumar 1982; Leckie 1981: 41–189; Mishra 1983;
Raj et al. 1985 especially 51–162 and 210–46).

Before this, Gujarati merchants had a long history of travelling and settling in
East Africa, the Middle East, and South-East Asia. Later within New Zealand,
the stereotype of the Indian migrant, that of the petty, avaricious businessman,
fitted in with the so-called "typical" Gujarati, the Bania. In fact, Banias did not
sail to New Zealand; the overwhelming majority of Gujaratis there were descendants from farming families from Jalalpore and Bardlo talukas in the Bombay
Presidency or from Navsari mahal in the former princely state of Baroda. Employment opportunities in New Zealand available to the early migrants generally would not have appealed to Indians from well-established urban mercantile
families. Contrary to popular assumptions, Gujaratis in New Zealand did not
possess an "innate ability" to accumulate money and establish businesses over-
night. For many, their situation in Gujarat had been precarious.

Investigations have shown that the migration to New Zealand from this region was part of an increasingly accepted and necessary strategy for economic
survival or improvement (see Breman 1985: 52–61, 100–114; Leckie 1981: 105–
89). This process was well entrenched by the early 20th century.

Gujarati migration involved two main castes from different areas of South
Gujarat. One was the southern coastal region, where the Koli caste predominated in numbers. By the late 19th century, they faced a severe shortage of land
for further cultivation. Further inland, Kanbis were an increasingly powerful
agricultural caste centred around Bardoli. Land here was more valuable and
productive, especially after the 1860s with the introduction of cash crops.
However, with a rising population and competition for resources, almost no
more land was available by the late 19th century for extending cultivation.
Other pressures that contributed to existing economic insecurity in South Gujarat were the prevalence of small, scattered landholdings, severe famines that
occurred towards the end of the century, rising costs, and indebtedness through
mortgages and loans being contracted to meet other expenses. Families were
aiming either to prevent further loss of land and proletarianisation or to extend
agricultural holdings. This exerted pressure to seek additional income. Costs
also rose with changing consumption patterns, which were partly induced by
the penetration of mass-produced, usually imported, goods. Changes in practices related to caste mobility and caste assertion necessitated greater conspicuous consumption for religious and family ceremonies, which contributed
further to the need for a greater income.

Since the turn of the century, Kolis had been seeking to strengthen their
economic and political power and caste status in the Surat district. In talukas
such as Jalalpore, the Anaval Brahmans dominated the ritual hierarchy and
filled élite and powerful positions in the local political hierarchy. With the
strengthening of capitalist relations in rural Gujarat, Kolis faced marginalisa-

tion if they did not seek outside sources of income. The Talabdas, in particular, the subcaste that settled in New Zealand, were prominent in adopting strategies to ameliorate their position. One means was migration, both within and outside of India (see Leckie 1981: 62–75). This also eased pressure on landholdings, as more family members came to reside outside the village. Later, Talabdas Kolis were able to take advantage of land reforms after 1939 and, more recently, of land development and irrigation programmes to consolidate their position (see Shah 1975: 8–21).

Economic improvement was simultaneously linked with claims to higher status, which effectively also helped to reinforce access to more political power in Gujarat. Changes in the caste status involved Kolis distancing themselves from any tribal origins. This resulted in a preference for the category Talabdas rather than Koli and increasingly the adoption of the more ambiguous surname Patel. Kolis also pursued ways of life and amended religious ceremonies to advance claims to higher Sanskritic status. Migration and earnings from New Zealand contributed to these increasingly expensive religious and marriage ceremonies. However, the nationalist movement also played a role in advancing Koli claims to power and respectable status. Gujaratis in New Zealand still proudly boast of Gandhi's presence in their villages. Many migrants attended or gave financial support to *rashtriya*, or nationalist schools. "Freedom fighters" now settled in New Zealand have special status conferred on them, while the myth persists of these peaceful, cooperatively run villages where old heroes can spin and wear khadi.

Talabdas Kolis in New Zealand therefore still identify and focus on a cluster of villages in South Gujarat. Relatives there draw on the resources of an octopus of Gujaratis settled in New Zealand, Fiji, South Africa, East Africa, Britain, Canada, and the United States. A similar pattern applies to the Kanbis around the sugar centre of Bardoli (see Leckie 1981: 71–82). Superficially, they appear to have much in common with Kolis, but these two castes are quite aware of their separateness, especially in terms of their access to local power structures and of their caste identity. Although in a few villages and occasionally in the district centre of Surat there is some competition and antagonism between these two castes, geographical distance keeps the Kolis and the Kanbis apart. This has not been possible in New Zealand, where some degree of caste competition has been transferred. Stereotypes between Kolis and Kanbis have also developed as much in the New Zealand context as in Gujarat.

This competition between castes in New Zealand results partly from the economic advantage Kanbis had earlier in the century. Most Kanbi migrants originated from families with holdings of at least a few acres. Though few could claim to equal the powerful Patidars of Charotar (see Pocock 1972), Kanbis from Bardoli generally were under less threat of proletarianisation than Koli migrants were. Nevertheless, within Kanbi circles were differentiations in status, and this was in part reflected in the locale and subcaste to which the Kanbis belonged. Earlier in this century, Kanbis from Bardoli were not dominant, but they were able to take advantage of changes in land tenure and the declining stranglehold of the old feudal élite, the Desais. Although their position was further enhanced by the extension of cash-crop farming, not all villages or families could immediately take advantage of this; therefore, outside earnings were used to consolidate existing wealth and to extend capitalist agriculture in these villages. Migration was also linked to Kanbi attempts to raise their status and to shake off Shudra origins (see Breman 1985: 363–461): greater expenditure was necessary, especially in house building and marriage dowries. Like Kolis, Kanbis also sought to change their categorisation and surnames. While all Kanbis can use the surname Patel, for many, a more important goal is to aspire to recognition as Patidars. The latter category implies success, power, and high status. Kanbi status and access to political power was also enhanced by involvement in the nationalist movement, the Bardoli satyagraha of 1928, and the rise of Sardar Patel, the "Lion of Baroda" (see Hardiman 1981). As with Kolis, these memories have become part of Kanbi mythology and identity in New Zealand.

The forces behind external migration and its timing are rooted in the transformations in rural India since the late 19th century. The direction of international movement from both the Punjab and Gujarat reflected shifts in the colonial political economy and the circulation of labour within it. Gujarati migration to the South Pacific was preceded by that to South Africa (Leckie 1981: 154–69), but once restrictions and discriminatory policies were implemented in 1897, potential migrants began to search for other destinations. Simultaneously, news was filtering through to the Gujarati villages of employment being available in the South Pacific. Family and village networks soon became important in adapting to and utilising shifting economic circumstances and migration possibilities to either Australia (de Lepervanche 1984), Fiji (Gillion 1962: chap. 7; Prasad 1978: chap. 2) or New Zealand (Leckie 1981: 214–47). Once they were settled, many migrants encouraged and assisted friends and relatives in joing them. Although thousands of miles from the Punjab and Gujarat, "home" continued to mean the village; thus deprivation and hardships of the early migrants were endured because of the goal of improving the economic and social positions of their kin in India. Most of these pioneering migrants did not leave to escape rural society but to strengthen their base within it.

SETTLEMENT IN NEW ZEALAND: TOWARDS "ASSIMILATION"?

Stereotypes about ethnic groups have been as prevalent in New Zealand as elsewhere. Indians have not escaped being typified at varying periods in New Zealand's history as hawkers, greengrocers, and, more recently, as dairy (shop)

owners.[7] Higher proportions of Indo-New Zealanders have been involved in
such pursuits than the general population has, but this does not suggest that all
Indo-New Zealanders follow the same trends.[8] A persistent feature of Indian
businesses has been to aim for self-sufficiency, in the sense that labour, capital,
and advice should be, preferably, confined within the kin or caste community.
Such *petit-bourgeois* ideals, be they of the independent yeoman, artisan, or shopkeeper, were an integral feature of New Zealand society (see Fairburn 1975).
This throws some light on the resentment that the "placid" New Zealanders
vented against Asian competition in small businesses and farms. During the
earlier years of Indian settlement in New Zealand, marked opposition was also
shown towards Indian labourers.

Although some 94 per cent of Indo-New Zealanders today live in urban
areas, before 1920 they were almost equally resident in rural (46 per cent) and
urban (54 per cent) regions. Questions about "Hindoos" roaming the country-
side and selling the "most worthless Brummagem stuff imaginable" began to be
raised in Parliament during the 1890s (*New Zealand Parliamentary Debates* 1896,
vol. 95: 597). These men were frequently lumped together with "Assyrians"
(probably Lebanese and Syrians) who also initially found work as hawkers of
trinkets, pots and pans, fabrics, and other items in scarce supply around the
remote areas of New Zealand. Besides cries of economic competition, a persistent theme in Asian phobia was of exaggerated notions of the moral and sexual
threat itinerant migrants presented.

At the outset, most Indian hawkers were Punjabis (McLeod 1980: 115–16).
During the 20th century, their numbers were swelled by Gujaratis, who increasingly tended to specialise in hawking fruit. As business and commerce
expanded within the New Zealand economy, restrictions crept in to control
these aliens, who were reputedly evading overheads such as taxes and rents.
Attempts were made to introduce nationwide restrictive legislation during the
1890s. The link between racial exclusion and nation-building in New Zealand
was clearly spelt out:

We are engaged in a great experiment in State Socialism if we may use the word. . . . The
object of that legislative experiment is to raise the staus of the people. . . . Therefore the
Government is bound to keep out of the new partnership all who are likely to take
everything and give nothing in return (*New Zealand Times* 4 Oct. 1894)

While New Zealand's colonial dependency on Britain meant that efforts to exclude Indians could be met with only limited success, local bodies such as the
Wellington City Council responded to pressure from white shopkeepers and
passed regulations to standardise fruit hawking through licensing and inspec-
tion.

These restrictions did not deter Indians either from working in rural areas or
from penetrating into the expanding retailing sector. This provided ample fuel

to stoke the embers of the always-present fire for a white New Zealand. The establishment of Indians in rural regions, not only in the arena of hawkers and retailers, but also in other agricultural and rural-based industries, continued to attract sizable numbers of new migrants up to the 1920s. Usually, they found work as ditch-diggers, "scrub-cutters," road labourers, or farmhands with the intention of eventually either securing employment in an Indian business or starting their own enterprise.[9] Such work became more difficult to acquire as the New Zealand economy underwent a series of recessions during the 1920s and early 1930s (see Brooking 1981).

Indian immigrants were also able to seize the opportunities presented by the opening up of new rural towns in early 20th-century New Zealand to purchase or open new fruit and vegetable businesses. If the surrounding population was too small to support a specialised business, an alternative investment might be in a general store. General stores tended to be in the very remote areas of central North Island, which did not attract the larger commercial enterprises.

Despite intense opposition, some Indians were able to purchase land during and after the 1920s. Many Punjabis established themselves as dairy farmers in the rich farming land of the Waikato. A smaller proportion of Gujaratis were centred around Pukekohe as potato and onion growers where, against the continued hostility of the White New Zealand League, they were able to build up lucrative farms. This partly reflected the subsequent expansion of Auckland City and the high value of land in its vicinity. Opposition to Indians was couched there and elsewhere in terms of a perceived economic and moral threat to both white and Maori society of Asian "non-assimilability." A letter to the minister of immigration in 1953 exemplifies the prevailing sentiment:

Indians are quite unassimilable nationally and have no loyalty to their land of adoption. The cling together, quite understandably, in sealed-up coteries and take little part in national life, and for their habits, unpleasing personality and incivility are cordially disliked by most of their neighbours. . . . They breed like rabbits.[10]

Ironically, when Indians did pursue goals held dear to New Zealanders and sought to assimilate through acquiring property and economic security, they were rebuked. Jelal Natali found that attempts to acquire and farm property in the King Country were rejected because "he was not a farmer himself and he was not a suitable man to own property such as this."[11]

As New Zealand society became increasingly urbanised in the 20th century and the population drifted north to follow employment opportunities, Indians followed. To a large extent, changes in occupation, investments, and location have been in response to maximising opportunities presented by shifting economic and geographical patterns, especially in the capital city of Wellington and the expanding commercial and industrial centre of Auckland. Earlier in this century, the newly arrived Indian migrants in the cities tended to work as

hawkers, fruiterers, and bottle collectors, either in self-employment or in partnership with another Indian. Others found domestic work in the many hotels
and boarding-houses that filled the centres of New Zealand cities. These
occupations appealed more to Indians who did not have wider kin, village, or
caste contacts in New Zealand. Working in service, however, was always perceived as a means to self-employment. A Gujarati who followed this path for
more than 50 years in New Zealand recalled his goals:

I always remember the advice, given to me by my Greek employers, not to work for
wages for long but to branch out on our own account, as soon as one has saved enough to
get a start (J. K. Natali, press cutting of an address at a farewell function in his honour,
Waimiha, n.d., c. 1946).

Opportunities for establishing and investing in businesses grew as suburban
development spread. This was especially so in Wellington and Auckland.
Therefore, in contrast to the earlier years, when some streets in the inner cities
were referred to by contemporaries as Asiatic ghettos, after the 1940s, Indian
settlement became scattered as opportunities for small retail businesses opened
up in the suburbs, where the bigger stores found it unprofitable to operate. In
any case, apart from fresh fruits and vegetables, the larger national, and today
multinational, wholesalers supplied the small shops owned by Indo-New
Zealanders. Although they were residentially dispersed, family links and a sense
of "ethnic identity" were maintained through economic and business networks,
institutions such as the Indian associations and sports clubs, and cultural links
through marriage, religion, and caste. The focus of this maintenance of links
was the continued ties with the family and village in India and with Indian
communities from the same locality now scattered around the globe.

Family and village networks, especially links through *falias* (separate residential areas in villages), were precipitant in the migration process. These relationships continued to be a main determinant in occupations and accommoda-
tions in both rural and urban areas (see de Lepervanche 1984: 140). Assistance
would range from sharing news o employment opportunities to providing substantial loans for setting up an independent business. During the initial period
in New Zealand, financial and other assistance, especially advice, was invalu-
able to adjusting to the new society. When the Indian community was still
small, this help was often offered to those who were not related or who were
from a different province of India, but more selective networks became the norm
in later years. The goal was always to acquire enough experience and capital to
invest in a business, either as a partner or independently. After the 1920s, more
and more new migrants were offered positions as shop assistants in established
fruit and vegetable businesses. This was partly a response to New Zealand's
deteriorating economy, which limited the options available to all unskilled
workers. Also, as more enterprises were set up by Indians, the capacity to offer

work to others was greater. Many of the larger fruit retailing businesses used family members to establish branches throughout the North Island.

This preference to hire workers from a similar background has remained a striking characteristic of Indo-New Zealand businesses to the present day. Kin were usually the first choice, then offers of employment would normally be extended to those from the same village or caste. Relatives were expected to repay the debt of being brought to New Zealand through their labour and by showing acquiescence and deference to their sponsors. Other New Zealanders frequently complained about how this facilitated the means for Asians to circumvent labour laws. Attention was drawn by the Fruit Marketing Committee in 1937 to the high percentage of Indians classified as business partners who were really shop assistants. Indian businesses were accused of paying rates below the minimum wage and of working employees excessively long hours (Fruit Marketing Committee 1937). Indian businessmen would have justified this by highlighting the long-term incentives offered to many of their employees, such as partnerships, finance to establish a separate business, or support in securing a favourable marriage. This patronage system worked on the principle that eventually the dependent would acquire security and status to patronise others. As the following quotation from Natali (from his Waimiha speech, c. 1946) reveals, such ideals have been propagated by references, made not only by the wider society but also by Indians, to "rags to riches" scenarios: "With ambition, incentive, thriftiness and by giving service to the public everyone has an opportunity to make a sucess of life in this wonderful country."

These "typical" success stories start with memories of a grandfather arriving in a foreign, hostile land with only sixpence in his pocket, hawking fruit in a hand-barrow and enduring hardship so that his son might one day own a chain of supermarkets. The son in turn "typically" is able to finance his own sons (and maybe daughters) through law school. Power and status accrue to such individuals within the Indian associations and possibly also in other civic and professional bodies. It is this small élite that is frequently held up as an example to others and cited as evidence of the successful formula of what is given as Indian (or Gujarati) values. Acquisitiveness and ambition are not confined to any one ethnic group, but the use of family, regional, and caste ties within New Zealand and between India and elsewhere is marked among Indo-New Zealanders.

These links foster dependency, especially when a new migrant has been sponsored by an employer. Illegal immigrants, posing as the sons of Indians who are already permanent residents of New Zealand, were open to exploitation, to working long hours for inadequate wages in fruit shops. One case brought before the courts concerned an illegal immigrant who had been forced to relinquish all his wages from factory work to his "adoptive father" for five years.[12] A contractual agreement involving a fee had been made between the real father and the bogus father, who in turn signed false declarations to the immigration authorities. Other successful entrepreneurs employing several Indian shop assistants frequently acted as the fathers or as a sponsor or go-between in illegal immigration. Many of these businesses were in rural areas where it was difficult to obtain labour. Unpaid wages and labour were important components of Indian family enterprises in New Zealand. This was especially significant once women and children began to migrate to New Zealand after the 1940s. Indeed, the boom in small Indian-owned businesses in the cities during the '60s and '70s was heavily dependent on this labour.

The attraction to and relative success in small-scale business on the part of Indo-New Zealanders should be considered against the changing circumstances faced by these migrants and their descendants. The entrepreneurial aptitude especially of Gujaratis has gained popular credence both within New Zealand and in other parts of the world. As noted, however, both the early and more recently arrived migrants were not Banias with cultural traits promoting hard work, thriftiness, and accumulation. Newly arrived migrants generally seized available opportunities, which was partially facilitated by village contacts from India. To attribute contemporary Indo-New Zealand concentration in small businesses, especially dairies, to cultural characteristics alone might imply that other New Zealanders do not possess the skills of small-scale entrepreneurship. On the contrary, outside the main centres of Auckland and Wellington, especially in the South Island, the Pakehas and the Chinese are the ones who mainly control the small businesses.[13] Responses to shifts in the wider market economy and the concentration of capital within this also need to be considered. As supermarket chains found it profitable to expand into the suburbs of Auckland and Wellington during the 1970s, it then became less lucrative for the independently owned fruit and vegetable businesses. Many Indo-New Zealand greengrocers responded by investing in dairies that returned small but steady profits by remaining open for extended hours to sell a wide variety of goods. Again, the utilisation of family labour was an important factor.

The foregoing discussion suggests that consciousness as a separate ethnic group became reinforced through distinctive occupational patterns and especially an involvement in small family businesses. The maintaining of small family businesses in turn helped maintain kin networks through the accumulation of capital, for example. Migrants were thus able to improve their own economic security and status and that of the wider kin group within both New Zealand and India. However, though it could be argued that the structure of small enterprises contributed significantly to family and caste cohesion in New Zealand, it does not follow that "ethnicity" was weakened when employment became more diversified. Indeed, today most Indo-New Zealanders do not follow the stereotype of either the small shopkeeper or the dynamic young executive. About 34 per cent (compared with about 11 per cent in 1921) are employed as factory workers, skilled trades people, and labourers. Though in 1921 few migrants were able to secure white-collar employment, approximately 14 per cent

today is engaged in clerical work and 15 per cent are professionals and techni-
cians. Obviously, in the bulk of the industries that employ Indo-New Zealanders, family or caste networks are rare. Diversified employment has been
much greater among Indo-New Zealanders born in New Zealand who have not
faced the same kind of language and educational limitations as newly arrived
migrants did.[14] Also, opportunities to work in factories and the public sector
developed in New Zealand mainly after World War II.

Some descendants of the first migrants indicated they preferred employment
outside the family business because this offered greater immediate financial re-
turns, career opportunities, and the possibility of economic and social independence from the family. On the other hand, outside incomes frequently are
included in the family budget, which means that additional and usually regular
contributions are encouraged. Many migrants also recognise that professional
occupations are accorded high status within both wider New Zealand society
and the Indian community there. The high status associated with professional
occupations may be an important consideration in marriage negotiations with
Indian communities in other parts of the world.

Common occupations with a shared, almost corporate, goal of economic and
social advancement within the New Zealand and Indian context appear to have
been fundamental to Indian and specifically Gujarati or Punjabi cohesion in
New Zealand. This reflects not simply a sense of a shared community but also a
common past rooted in the migration process and the experiences of settlement
abroad. On one level a united Indian community presents itself on occasion to
the New Zealand public, but relationships within this community are much
more complex. The reality of being an Indian, Gujarati or Punjabi, Talabdas
Koli, Kanbi, Sikh, Muslim, or Hindu is of little relevance to the dominant New
Zealand society largely because of the racist or assimilationist restrictions it has
imposed. Nation-building in New Zealand was based on egalitarian principles,
but in practice, class differentiation and conflict were not eradicated. As with
egalitarianist and assimilationist policies in Australia (see de Lepervanche
1980; McQueen 1978: 42ff.), in New Zealand, colour consciousness was a
powerful ploy masking class consciousness. Racism in New Zealand was only
slightly less overt than in Australia and was complicated by the presence of a
proportionately larger population of indigenous people. Their cultural, physical, educational, and economic conditions continued to worsen while most
white New Zealanders had no qualms about discrimination in both words and
actions towards Maoris. However, anti-Asian phobia was always a safe focus
for extremist racism, especially with the possibility that recent migrants could
be evicted from the country.

In the face of such threats and with very small numbers, expressions of solidarity among Indo-New Zealanders were a means of protest and survival.
Working, living together, and relaxing together as an Indian community was
far more common during the early years of settlement. However, links with

family and villages in India meant that such solidarity as an Indian community was restricted to the specific conditions in New Zealand. In the decades following World War II, the Indian community became recognised as constituting some kind of ethnic group. Egalitarianism now implied assimilation, so the strategy adopted by most Indians was to quietly accumulate and establish a secure financial base while confining "culture" to the family business or Indian association halls. Clearly, this "don't rock the boat" formula elicited approval from outside the community, as evidenced by a report in the *New Zealand Herald* of the opening of Nehru Hall at Pukekohe on 17 August 1953:

They had a series of common denominators – pride in achievement, an emphasis on the fact that the hall had been built for the whole community and not just for the Indian folk, the importance of becoming good citizens of their country of adoption as well as unofficial ambassadors of their country of ancestry, plus gratitude for being permitted to settle in a country of peace and plenty and live in unity with Maori and Pakeha alike.

The ambiguities of such expressions of egalitarianism and harmonious race relations in New Zealand were brought to a head during the 1970s with, for example, dawn raids to round up overstayers from the Pacific islands for deportation and police and state opposition to Maoris reclaiming land from which their ancestors had been dispossessed. The year 1981 was one of intensive protests against apartheid, and a visiting South African rugby team precipitated considerable soul searching about the kind of nation New Zealand really was and would be during the following decade. Not surprisingly, multiculturalism has assumed great respectability, which may, paradoxically, as Jacubowicz (1981) and de Lepervanche (1980) note, serve once again the interests of dominant class interests in the same way the old white racist rhetoric did. Ethnicity is now promoted by progressive public bodies, which, at least, has given more scope for Indians to practise their religious and other cultural ceremonies. A certain residue of being a cultural show-case persists, and references such as that made by an Auckland city councillor, Jolyon Firth, to "curry munchers" in 1983 appear to be a part of a national racist consciousness that has not disappeared (*Auckland Star* 1 June 1983).

ETHNICITY AND THE LINKS WITH INDIA

To a minor degree, the "Indian community" has taken shape in response to threats and perceptions by the New Zealand public, and, as will be discussed, they have been especially instrumental in the formation of Indian associations. However, as noted, occupational patterns and kin-village networks are central to many of the internal relationships and survival of this community. They also help sustain economic and social differentiation within it. The continued relationship with villages in India is also very significant to many Indo-New Zealanders. Migration may have opened the doors to some economic success, but evidence and recognition of this, especially in the ealier years, was displayed in the villages. Conspicuous consumption in the form of purchasing land, house building, marriage arrangements, and fulfilling other ceremonial obligations to kin was taken by many Indians, especially Gujaratis, as an indicator of social status and influence. Today such expenditure may also be found within New Zealand. Though lavish displays were a very overt statement of the migrant's success, there were other means through which an individual, and consequently the family, was acknowledged to be of higher status and influence. "Correct behaviour," usually through religious devotion or involvement in the national-ist cause, was not totally dependent on financial success, but it could confer status in the village. Nevertheless, emigrants were obligated to contribute to their family and the caste's economic enhancement and social position by pro-viding finance for both necessities and displays of affluence. Ascetics certainly were idealised, but devout Hindus who were also prosperous wielded more power in the village and within local caste and intercaste politics.

Indians in New Zealand therefore remained part of a wider network centred on the village in India. This applied especially to the first generation because very few of their wives accompanied them overseas. Even when the migrants requested their sons to join them, it was still assumed that their marriages would be arranged in India. Daughters only emigrated when their mothers did, and in New Zealand this was after World War II. Even then, for many years the practice continued of arranging marriages in India. With such pressing finan-cial and social obligations, it was essential that the migrants maintained links with their villages. The first requirement was to repay immediate debts in-curred by the migrant or his family. Then it was mandatory to send regular remittances to support dependent family members. Failure to do so could make it difficult for other members to contract favourable marriages or to secure alliances for future migration.

Support was not limited to cash, but also to offering advice and participating in family ceremonies. Visits to India became essential, although the frequency was constrained by finances, business commitments in New Zealand, and, to some extent, the relationship with the family in India. Costs included not only travel; migrants were also expected to shower their relatives with money and gifts, and their return usually coincided with a costly family ceremony. Visits by first and second generation migrants were more frequent and longer than those of their children. Men who had spent their childhood in India had much strong-er ties to the locality than those raised overseas. Longer sojourns were also easier when most migrants were self-employed or in casual work. Today, many younger Indo-New Zealanders claim that they limit their visits partially be-cause of boredom with the village life-style, but also because of leave restrictions or business commitments that cannot be left unattended for long periods.

Before World War II, most returning migrants preferred and felt compelled to spend periods of up to five weeks with their families. Overseeing the construction of a house was a major priority. This was literally concrete evidence of the migrant's success and his family's material security in the village. Also, because almost all first and many second generation migrants anticipated retirement in India, house building was an investment for retirement.

Overseas earnings also were invested in acquiring land and in agricultural development, especially following land reforms after World War II and the extension of migration during the 1970s. Indeed, outside capital has been important in raising the economic standing not only of the migrant's family, but also that of the village and the caste. Overseas migrants have made sizable contributions to the construction of schools, roads, nationalist memorials, religious buildings, and to development projects, such as afforestation and land reclamation schemes. In the case of the Kolis of South Gujarat, therefore, migration has contributed not only to their overall economic improvement, but also to the reinforcement of differentiation within this caste and its consolidation as a class of comparatively secure small landowners in relation to other, landless castes and tribal peoples (see Breman 1985).

A major influence, therefore, in sustaining ethnicity organised around region, caste, and village has been continued ties with India. In the past, direct economic links, the main force in emigration, formed the basis. During the past few decades, financial investment in India has been secondary to that in New Zealand, although cash remittances, house construction, and some support of village projects has continued. Marriage arrangements continue to be a major social and economic link between the villages and New Zealand. However, though many Indo-New Zealanders continue to discuss their plans to retire in India, few actually fulfill this. Financial security in New Zealand, in the form of housing, business investments, superannuation and other social welfare benefits, and family commitments are some of the chief influences in the decision of where to retire. This dilemma was not faced by most of the first migrants, because even though their goal was clearly to accumulate wealth in New Zealand, they planned to retire to their home villages.

The early Indian immigrant was an adult who had migrated in search of an El Dorado. Although he found one in New Zealand his outlook at that time was to regard his stay here as a means to an end – that retirement in his own motherland was his ultimate aim.[15]

Many second-generation migrants have preferred to keep a foot in both societies, travelling between India and New Zealand while remaining in both places for periods of several years.

Economic and cultural networks between India and New Zealand sustain consciousness of being part of a particular caste, family village, region, and religion. This awareness is not perceived by most New Zealanders. Indo-New Zealanders have tended to be reluctant to publicise their cultural links, especially with regard to caste. Recently, the greater acceptance of alternative religions and ways of life within New Zealand has meant that Indo-New Zealanders are discussing more openly their cultural and religious differences. But categorisation as one ethnic group continues to be dominant in government policy, as exemplified by the census. The categories adopted also contribute to the masking of class differentiation within ethnic groups.

AN INDIAN COMMUNITY?

The labelling as Indian and consciousness as an Indian community have been facilitated through other means. Discrimination that lumps all Indians together has been a catalyst of Indian solidarity and organisation as a distinct ethnic group. Formal Indian associations began in 1918 in Auckland to provide support against racist attacks. The formation of the New Zealand Indian Central Association in 1926 was in direct response to the support the White New Zealand League elicited throughout the country. The constitution of the Indian body clearly demonstrated that the association intended to act as a pressure group:

To seek the redress of wrongs affecting the Indians in New Zealand . . . to watch and consider proposed changes in law relating to Indians and to make representations to the authorities in connection with the existing law and any such proposed changes and to take such other steps in relation thereto as may be expedient.[16]

During this period, most of the association's members were greatly limited in their fluency in both written and spoken English. They were also timid about overtly criticising as individuals the laws and behaviour of New Zealanders. Added to this was the fear of jeopardising their rights of domicile in New Zealand or prejudicing any future immigration applications of their families. More open criticism could be made through the Indian associations, especially because most of the leaders were self-employed. Many of the leaders were also more proficient in writing and speaking English, which made it easier to defend causes on behalf of members. The Auckland Indian Association, for example, forwarded a telegraph in 1937 to Peter Fraser, the acting prime minister of New Zealand. In it, they urged him to reject proposals for the compulsory registration of the thumb-prints of all Asians:

This meeting of the Auckland branch of the New Zealand Association views with grave concern the thumb prints recommendation made by the Fruit and Vegetable Committee for all Asiatics engaged in the fruit and vegetable trade. If put into operation, this unjust recommendation will be most humiliating to our nationals, and we have not the slightest doubt that the fair-minded legislators of this wonderful Dominion will not pay any serious attention to this un-British suggestion.[17]

Besides protesting other existing or proposed discriminatory practices, the Indian associations opposed or suggested amendments to immigration legislation and policy (see Leckie 1981: 650–58).

Today, the main role of the Indian associations is to promote cultural and religious activities. Because no mandirs were built in New Zealand, the Indian associations provided the sites for religious celebrations and meetings. They have also undertaken the screening of Hindi and Gujarati movies. Attendance at these and at sporting events organised by the Indian sports clubs are probably the most regular means through which Indo-New Zealanders stay in contact with one another and identify as a community. Playing hockey or cricket was the main leisure activity for the migrants; later, sports provided a means of interaction with other New Zealanders. In particular, in a society like New Zealand, where sports assume compulsive devotion above most other pursuits, participation and success in representative sports have encouraged public acceptance, showing that this ethnic group is assimilating into a Kiwi life-style (see Sedgwick 1984: 56).

Studies undertaken some years ago of Indians living in societies outside of India (de Lepervanche 1984: 167–84; Desai 1963: 108–21; Dotson and Dotson 1968: chap. 7; Morris 1959: 787) have noted the scope that ethnic organisations have given for the formation of factions and conflict, especially in situations in which the ethnic group is not organised along political lines or is lacking an effective political voice. It is not entirely clear whether such factions within the New Zealand Indian associations are formed along caste, village, or class lines. However, groupings based on separate networks and their dominance of the executives of the associations appear to be more rigid than in earlier years. The growth of the Indo-New Zealand population and emergence of greater economic and occupational differences within it has permitted more room for factionalism. Simultaneously, religion, language, and regional ties to India have been replicated in the composition of the Indian associations. Although their constitutions prohibit any restrictions on communal grounds, there have been frequent complaints that these are "Gujarati associations" because most of the meetings are conducted in Gujarati. Also, almost all religious functions and festivals celebrated are Hindu and tend to be those popular in South Gujarat.

The few Muslim migrants from Gujarat were active members, notably in the years when both the associations and the Muslim community in New Zealand had fewer members. Esup Bhikoo, for example, served as one of the first secretaries and presidents of the Waikato Indian Association, and his brothers were founders in 1950 of the first New Zealand Muslim association. As the numbers of Muslims grew, especially with emigration from Fiji after 1965, to the current estimate of more than 2,000, other Islamic associations were founded (see Shephard 1985). Links with selected international Muslim bodies are more common today, with overseas funds recently contributing to the erection of mosques in Auckland and Christchurch. This will probably serve to further separate the descendants of earlier Muslim migrants from the Indian associations. Nevertheless, they continue to maintain strong links with villages in India and continue to be passive members of the Hindu-dominated Indian associations. Muslims linked especially with Gujarat remain a small religious minority within the Indian community, but they are still part of its largest regional and linguistic group. They are no longer as dominant among Muslims in New Zealand as in previous years.

Communal and regional affiliations with India in the associations are clearly evident in the Country Section, a branch of the New Zealand Indian Central Association that has almost exclusively Punjabi membership. Its headquarters is in the Waikato, a province that also supports the Gujarati-dominated Waikato Indian Association, founded in 1945. Communal ties were further reflected in the formation of the Sikh Society in 1964. Ostensibly it aimed to facilitate the organisation of religious gatherings and festivals, or *gurpurabs*, which led to the erection in 1977 of a gurdwara where these could be held.

McLeod (1980: 120) notes that the Sikh society reinforces social needs to a much greater extent than the "male dominated Country Section." Male hegemony of the associations is by no means exclusive to the one under Punjabi control. Very few women are registered members of any Indian association, but they are considered to be affiliated through their husbands or fathers. Even fewer women have served as executive members, although recently a few have been able to break this pattern. Women have almost no direct input, therefore, into committee meetings, but they do participate fully in the religious functions organised by the associations.

Religion regional ties to India, and gender divisions have thus meant, especially at the executive level, that associations are dominated by male Gujaratis. Class divisions are not quite so clear, with both leadership and general participation reflecting the predominantly *petit bourgeois* character of the Indo-New Zealand population. The associations do not openly express a preference for any political party in New Zealand, but it is no secret that most of their members from varying class backgrounds support Labour for such reasons as its relatively more liberal immigration policies towards Asians and an avowed policy of multiculturalism. Previous Labour governments also pursued economic programmes that were especially favourable to small shopkeepers and wage earners.

Caste, or, more explicity, *jati*, affiliations would appear to have no relationship to political adherence in New Zealand. Although Indians have not expressed political views in the Indian associations, many observers have suggested that factional grouping, loosely centred around caste, has permeated the associations. These factions also have taken on a parochial nature by being linked to particular localities and branches of the Central Association. I am not suggesting here that caste ties are prominent in the associations, but they do have importance, especially because of the strong links between caste, village, and kin. Publicly, most Indo-New Zealanders deny the maintenance of caste with such statements as "there is no caste now." Many denounce caste in general, as did Natali in a letter to the *Auckland Star* on 17 February 1955:

The caste system, which even the British rule did not correct, is the curse of modern India and has existed for so long that it will take years for it to disappear. . . . Indians who believe in the caste system are to be pitied and guided, not condemned for their ignorance.

It comes as little surprise, then, that in a society such as New Zealand, where Indians were a small minority, caste as a rigid hierarchical system of social and economic relations was not reproduced (see Grimes 1957: 23; McGee 1965: 140; Taher 1965: 230–31). The selectivity of castes that migrated to New Zealand reinforced this. As noted, most of the Gujaratis were Kolis and Kanbis, along with a few representatives from artisan castes such as Sutars (carpenters), Kumbhars (potters), Darjis (tailors), Dhobis (washermen), Khatris (weavers), and Hajam (barbers). No brahman religious officiates emigrated, although a few Bhatelas who were attempting to validate their brahman status did. Some Harijan families of Mochis (shoemakers) and Khalpas (tanners) settled in New Zealand earlier in the century. However, all these castes originated from different localities in South Gujarat, which made it impossible to replicate a local caste hierarchy. Of more significance is that migration was effectively a means to avoid rigid relations between castes. Kolis and Kanbis were primarily concerned with the economic and social security of their own subcaste and the family and village ties within that subcaste. Because Kolis were numerically a dominant caste in the villages from which migrants stemmed and because migration was a major means through which to secure wealth, these villages could become less dependent on higher castes such as the Vanias and Desais.

Similarly, Kanbis have operated primarily as a caste advancing itself, and they focused on their own economic and social position (Breman 1985). Finance derived from emigration and the expansion of profitable commercial agriculture meant that many families were able to be relatively independent of the once-dominant castes, such as the Anavalas and the Banias. Caste identity was not cemented in the form of a hierarchical "ladder" but has become linked with kin and village social networks. Because of such strong ties, caste has been an important component of ethnicity in New Zealand; non-Indians are not usually aware of this. Either they perceive a blanket homogenous Indian community or, as outsiders, look for the model brahmanical caste system.

Most Gujaratis in New Zealand are aware of their caste origins, although increasingly younger people tend to be vague about the meaning of such categories as Koli, Kanbi, Patel, or Patidar. Nevertheless, stereotypes persist, and especially in relation to the two main Gujarati castes of Koli and Kanbi. Accusations flare up from time to time of snobbishness or greediness or that one group is pursuing the practices associated with low castes, such as eating meat or drinking liquor. Some Kanbis refer to differences of dialect ("those people don't speak sweet Gujarati") and an inadequate knowledge of Hindu ceremonies as implicating caste differences. Although caste does not determine social networks, remarks such as these help to reinforce some degree of exclusivity. Indo-New Zealanders generally do not overtly acknowledge caste to be significant in their social interaction, but instead would argue that village and kin networks are the determining factors. Even this should not be exaggerated, as certainly, among those born in New Zealand, socialising is increasingly outside family, village, and caste circles.

As noted, migration and the greater wealth it brought permitted more elaborate ceremonies, especially those related to marriage and dowries. This meant higher status, which, for Kanbis, presumably opened the door to acceptance as a "twice-born" caste and adoption of the name Patidar. Identification with part of the powerful rural bourgeoisie in Gujarat is still of significance to many Kanbis, both Indian born and New Zealand born. The acquisitive, capitalistic spirit "concerned with the here and now" (Breman 1985: 389–90; see also Bates 1981: 785, 813) but also imbued with a "strongly religious tinge" noted by Breman and Pocock (1973) could be equally descriptive of many Kanbis in Gujarat or in New Zealand. Validation of power and status within a *jati*, or subcaste, of Kanbis is reflected in the practice of parents choosing marriage partners for their children from among equals or among those from a higher *jati*. The search for an appropriate partner may take years, necessitate world-wide travel to Gujarat and to other countries where Kanbis have settled, and may or may not involve the full consent of the marriage partners.

The status and power of Kolis, especially Kolis from villages of high emigration, are also much greater than in comparison with 50 years ago. Caste solidarity, but more important, that organised around villages, reflected the growing affluence and access to economic and political resources by Kolis in Gujarat. Emigration did not necessarily weaken this because overseas migrants remitted substantial sums of money towards village projects that benefitted their kin and caste associates. Moreover, older Gujaratis in New Zealand remained members of caste organisations, such as the Dikrana Gujarat Koli (Patel) Samaj (South Gujarat Koli [Patel] Society), which attempted to standardise religious and cultural practices and to raise and lobby for funds for various projects. But it is quite likely that younger generations will show less interest in direct involvement in caste-based organisations.

Most young Gujaratis born in New Zealand, however, still marry not only another Gujarati, but one of the same *jati*. Parents maintain that marriages are not strictly arranged, but that they will "gently pressurise" a child to marry someone who meets the prescribed criteria. Caste is not the only consideration. The village and family backgrounds are scrutinised, along with considerations of wealth, education, health, occupation, and future migration links. With a larger Indo-New Zealand population, it is possible for some to find suitable partners in New Zealand, but a greater proportion of young people are sent on a "world tour" to meet relatives settled in such places as South Africa, East Africa, Britain, Canada, North America, and Fiji. The main object is to find an appropriate spouse who will settle in New Zealand.

The Indian community, and in this case, specifically the Gujarati community, is reproduced to an extent through these marriage migrants. These reinforce caste links, especially when the arrangements have been made with a partner from Gujarat. Great sums of money, up to tens of thousands of dollars, are spent on what becomes an investment for the family both in India and in New Zealand. This does not mean that the immediate happiness of the partners was not perceived as an important consideration. However, we can also note that marriage between people descended from different *jatis* or linguistic regions of India has been less common than marriage between Indians and Europeans or between Indians and Maoris. Though these so-called inter-racial relationships have not always been condoned by the relatives of those involved, the high number of mixed births relative to the total Indian population suggests that both marital and extra-marital liaisons were not that uncommon (see Leckie 1981: 542–48).[18] Nevertheless, the persistence of marriage within the *jati* indicates that caste, village, and family social and economic networks are still highly relevant to many Gujaratis and other people of Indian descent in New Zealand today.

CONCLUSION

Since British colonisation in the 19th century, the population of New Zealand and its labour force has been built up by migrants. Among these were Asians who were never welcomed, so that by 1921, their entry into the young nation was severely restricted. As noted, various provisions and already-existing ties with India ensured that the Indian community was renewed and that it grew in size. Identification of the community as one ethnic group was problematic because it threw together those of differing and frequently conflicting regions, languages, religions, and castes. Continued external links helped to reinforce an identity strongly centred on developments in the villages in India. The stability and comparative security the Indian community has in New Zealand today has been part of the economic, social, and political consolidation of sections of castes, especially (as discussed here) in Gujarat. Furthermore, to draw the boundaries of ethnicity at New Zealand's shores for the descendants of the Indian migrants is difficult when marriage, religious, and economic networks span the Pacific, India, North America, Britain, and parts of Africa. On the other hand, Indo-New Zealanders visiting their ancestral villages can be almost fervently patriotic about their "home" in the Pacific, desiring to be recognised as Kiwis, distinct from other Indian migrants.

What does this mean in the New Zealand context, especially when New Zealand increasingly is described as "two nations" of Maori and Pakeha? The name New Zealand is no longer acceptable to some people, who demand that it be restored to Aoteoroa. Nation-building has resulted in the subjugation of one nation by another, Maori by Pakeha (see Walker 1984). This has assumed different guises, from the white racist egalitarianism that lashed its tongue especially at Asians, to the slightly more accommodating but equally patronising assimilationist policies that sought to swallow up ethnic diversity into one Kiwi mass. By the 1960s, ethnic minorities were grudgingly accepted as "there to stay," but with the provision that they "hurry up and merge into" the dominant society. McGee's observations (1965: 246) about Indians in Wellington reveals this: "The question now is, How soon can the community throw off its 'ghetto' attitudes and begin the long struggle for assimilation into New Zealand society?" What constituted this New Zealand society would become a central issue of conflict by the 1980s.

During the past 10 years, a more liberal and tolerant multicultural ideal has been offered in various contexts as a desirable path for New Zealand to take. This more tolerant ideal has not been acceptable to many Maoris and Pakehas, who consider that the most immediate steps are to recognise Maori sovereignty. Government interventions in Maori policies and programmes, and through the Race Relations Conciliator, have been perceived as "disorganising Maori interests" (Wilkes 1983: 13) while giving effect to the state's claims that it is concerned about equality and is instigating appropriate policies. In reality, the state's support for multiculturalism has been a critical factor in dissipating opposition while encouraging specific ideological and political forms that are in the interests of the dominant factions (Miles and Spoonley 1985: 17).

The present Labour government has tended to emphasise biculturalism, and public interest has grown in not only Maoritanga but also Pakeha ethnicity (King 1985; *Sites* 1986). The bicultural debate, especially in more populist forums, has led to New Zealand history being dichotomised into Maori and Pakeha. This tends to overlook both the presence of other ethnic groups and class formation and its dynamics within New Zealand (see McDonald 1985, 1986; Wall 1986). A further sinister development has been the racial connotations characterising the Maori-Pakeha debate with, for example, Wall's description (1986: 35) of Pakeha resurgence. He argues that some Pakehas "want their own racial identity and they are going for it with some gusto." Almost predictably, in recent months there has been a "Pakeha backlash" against Maoris, although evidence increasingly suggests that this "anti-Maori campaign" is a vehicle for a right-wing resurgence intended to topple the present Labour government (see *New Zealand Monthly Review* 1987: no. 296).

In the mean time, only a few citizens ask about the future and place of those other ethnic minorities who, more and more, are establishing historical roots in New Zealand but who still retain a cultural distinctiveness and ties to their ancestral homes elsewhere. As with most of the nonwhite minorities, Indo-New Zealanders continue to be classified as an ethnic group. As this chapter has attempted to delineate, identity as an Indian community has had some utilitarian advantages, but it has also skimmed over the linguistic, caste, regional, and religious divisions amongst Indo-New Zealanders and also their relationship to the economic, political, and social histories of New Zealand and perhaps to the Aotearoa of the future. Indo-New Zealanders are not Maori or Pakeha, but were migrants and settlers in a nation where debates of ethnicity continue to be couched in racial terms and overlook the intra- and interethnic economic and political inequalities within that nation.

NOTES

1. The Interdepartmental Committee on Resettlement (Department of Labour), in *Immigrants and ethnic minorities: What words should I use?* (quoted in *Sites* 1986: 19) give the following definition:

   Pakeha: this term is in common usage, but many have difficulty in defining its meaning. From early records it is clear that the term was used in New Zealand before 1815 to mean "white person." Initially the Pakeha was the person who came from England, and settled or worked in New Zealand. With time, the Pakeha was the fair-skinned person who was born in New Zealand. Later, the term became even more general. It was applied to all fair-skinned people in New Zealand, no matter what their ancestry or place of birth.

   According to this definition, therefore, Indian migrants and their descendants would not be classified as Pakeha. Note that this chapter does not deal with recent migration from Fiji to New Zealand by people of Indian descent.
2. Useful sources for further information on immigration into New Zealand are Spoonley et al. 1980; Spoonley and Trlin 1986.
3. Immigration facts and fallacies No. 3, *Labour and Employment Gazette.* 4(3): August 1954: 45.
4. C33/25. Memo no. 1925/35, Notification for shipowners, Immigration Restriction Act 1920 (Amendment), 23.7.25, New Zealand National Archives. The terms race and race relations are taken as a social construction. See Miles 1982: 7–92.
5. Note on emigration from India to the self-governing dominions, *Proceedings of Imperial Conference 1917*, India Office: 22.3.17, reprinted in Ollivier 1954, pp. 262–65.
6. The substance of this paper is based on my doctoral thesis (Leckie 1981), where more detailed references can be found.

7. Hawkers usually operated from small mobile carts and sold fruits and vegetables. In New Zealand, the term "dairy" refers to a small shop that sells dairy products, newspapers, cigarettes, and a wide variety of other everyday goods.

8. For example, according to the 1921 census, 33 per cent of the male Indian population was working in commerce, compared with 14 per cent of European males. By 1981, about 24 per cent of male and female Indians was engaged in the wholesale and retail industry, compared with about 15 per cent of the European population of New Zealand.

9. Scrub-cutters were employed to clear the growth of secondary vegetation or bush that had to be removed if the land was to be cultivated or used for grazing. Information for this section has been taken from immigration records and interviews.

10. C33/156M; 122/1/134. Policy files and records – Indians, New Zealand National Archives.

11. Judgement of the Crown Court, October 1944. Source: undated newspaper cutting from Jelal Natali's memorabilia.

12. Immigration records, see Leckie 1981.

13. For example, in *Better Business* April 1984: 8–9, L. D. Nathans Associated Wholesalers notes that in Auckland, Indian-owned businesses comprise 60 per cent of their listings. About 70 per cent of the dairies in Wellington are owned by Indians.

14. The 1981 census recorded about 46 per cent of "ethnic" Indians born in New Zealand.

15. I22/1/134, New Zealand Indian Central Association to Minister of Immigration and Minister of External Affairs, 18.3.54.

16. New Zealand Indian Central Association Incorporated, Hamilton: 1927/8, Constitution, objects 1 and 2.

17. Newspaper cutting from Natali. Probably *Auckland Star* or *New Zealand Herald*.

18. For example, the 1976 census noted that, of the Indian population, 21 per cent was classified as of European and Indian descent. Seven per cent returned themselves as of Maori and Indian descent. In 1926, 30 per cent of Indians were of "mixed blood." This census did not separate those of Maori descent. It should also be noted that some of the latter could have been classified under the Maori census. Several of those returned under European/Indian descent included Anglo-Indians and others born outside New Zealand.

REFERENCES

Awatere, D. 1982–83. Donna Awatere on Maori sovereignty. *Broadsheet* June 1982: 38–42; October 1982: 24–29; January/February 1983: 13–19.

Bates, C. 1981. The nature of social change in rural Gujarati: the Kehda district 1818–1918. *Modern Asia Studies* 15: 771–821.

Bellara, A. 1986. *Proud to be white? A survey of Pakeha prejudice in New Zealand*. Auckland: Heinemann.

Breman, J. 1985. *Of peasants, migrants and paupers. Rural labour circulation and capitalist penetration in West India*. Delhi: Oxford University Press.

Brooking, T. 1981. Economic transformation. In *The Oxford history of New Zealand*, edited by W. H. Oliver, 226–49. Wellington: Oxford University Press.

Broomfield, J. H. 1973. C. F. Andrews in New Zealand. *New Zealand Journal of History* 7(1): 70–75.

Brown, P. 1984. Official ethnic statistics in New Zealand. In *Tauiwi: Racism and ethnicity in New Zealand*, edited by P. Spoonley, C. Macpherson, D. Pearson, and C. Sedgwick, 159–71. Palmerston North: Dunmore Press.

Census of India. 1902. *Census of India, 1901, Bombay*, 9–10 (1–3). Bombay.

Chua, C. 1986. Development of capitalism in Indian agriculture: Gujarat, 1850–1900. *Economic and Political Weekly* 21(48): 2092–99.

de Lepervanche, M. 1980. From race to ethnicity. *Australian and New Zealand Journal of Sociology* 6(1): 24–37.

———. 1984. *Indians in a white Australia*. Sydney: George Allen & Unwin.

Department of Statistics. 1916–81. *New Zealand census of population and dwellings*. Wellington: Government Printer.

Desai, R. 1963. *Indian immigrants in Britain*. London: Oxford University Press.

Dotson, F., and L. O. Dotson. 1968. *The Indian minority of Zambia, Rhodesia and Malawi*. New Haven: Yale University Press.

Fairburn, M. 1975. The rural myth and the new urban frontier: An approach to New Zealand social history 1870–1940. *New Zealand Journal of History* 9(1): 3–21.

Fruit Marketing Committee. 1937. *Report*. Wellington: Fruit Marketing Committee, General Assembly Library, 23.1.37.

Gillion, K. L. 1962. *Fiji's Indian immigrants*. Melbourne: Oxford University Press.

Grimes, E. 1957. *Indians in New Zealand: The socio-cultural situation of migrants from India in the Auckland province*. M. A. thesis (anthropology), University of Auckland.

Guha, S. 1985. *The agrarian economy of the Bombay Deccan 1818–1941*. Delhi: Oxford University Press.

Hardiman, D. 1981. *Peasant nationalists of Gujarat: Kheda district 1917–1934*. Delhi: Oxford University Press.

Jakubowicz, A. 1981. State and ethnicity: Multiculturalism as ideology. *Australian and New Zealand Journal of Sociology* 17(3): 4–13.

King, M. 1985. *Being Pakeha*. Auckland: Hodder and Stoughton.

Kumar, D., ed. 1982. *The Cambridge economic history of India. Volume 2 c.1757–c.1970*. Cambridge: Cambridge University Press.

Leckie, J. 1981. *They sleep standing up: Gujaratis in New Zealand to 1945*. Ph.D. diss. (history), University of Otago.

———. 1985. In defence of race and empire: The White New Zealand League at Pukekohe. *New Zealand Journal of History* 19(2): 103–29.

McDonald, G. 1985. *Shadows over New Zealand*. Christchurch: Chaston Publishers.

———. 1986. *The Kiwis fight back*. Christchurch: Chaston Publishers.

McGee, T. 1965. *The Indian community of Wellington City*. M. A. thesis (geography), Victoria University, Wellington.

McLeod, W. H. 1980. The Punjabi community in New Zealand. In *Indian in New Zealand: Studies in a sub culture*, edited by K. Tiwari, 113–21. Wellington: Price Milburn.

———. 1986. *Punjabis in New Zealand*. Amritsar: Guru Nanak Dev University.

McQueen, H. 1978. *A new Brittanica*. Harmondsworth: Penguin.

Mayer, A. C. 1957. Factions in Fiji Indian rural settlements. *British Journal of Sociology* 8(4): 317–28.

Miles, R. 1982. *Racism and migrant labour*. London: Routledge and Kegan Paul.

———. 1984. Summoned by capital. In *Tauiwi*, edited by P. Spoonley, C. Macpherson, D. Pearson, and C. Sedgwick, 223–43. Palmerston North: Dunmore Press.

Miles, R., and P. Spoonley. 1985. The political economy of labour migration. An alternative to the sociology of 'race' and 'ethnic' relations in New Zealand. *Australian and New Zealand Journal of Sociology* 21(1): 3–26.

Mishra, S. C. 1983. The state and the agrarian economy of Punjab and Bombay before and after independence. In *South Asia research paper 1*: 132–64. Norwich: University of East Anglia, Development Studies Occasional Paper No. 22.

Morris, H. S. 1959. The Indian family in Uganda. *American Anthropologist* 61: 779–89.

New Zealand Monthly Review. 1987. The Anti-Maori campaign. No. 296.

O'Connor, P. S. 1968. Keeping New Zealand White, 1908–1920. *New Zealand Journal of History* 2(1): 41–65.

Ollivier, M. 1954. *The colonial and imperial conferences from 1887–1937*. 3 vols. Ottawa: Queens Printer.

Pocock, D. 1972. *Kanbi and Patidar – A study of the Patidar community of Gujarat*. Oxford: Oxford University Press.

———. 1973. *Mind, body and wealth. A study of belief and practice in an Indian village*. Oxford: Oxford University Press.

Prasad, K. K. 1978. *The Gujaratis of Fiji, 1900–1945: A study of an Indian immigrant trader community*. Ph.D. diss. (history), University of British Columbia.

Raj, K. N., S. Bhattacharya, S. Guha, and S. Padhi, eds. 1985. *Essays on the commercialisation of Indian agriculture*. Delhi: Oxford University Press.

Sedgwick, C. 1984. The organisational dynamics of the New Zealand Chinese. In *Tauiwi*, edited by P. Spoonley et al., 44–67. Palmerston North: Dunmore Press.

Shah, G. 1975. *Caste association and political process in Gujarat: A study of the Gujarat Kshatruya Sabha*. Bombay: Popular Prakashan.

Shepard, W. 1985. The Islamic contribution – Muslims in New Zealand. In *Religion in New Zealand society*, edited by B. Colless and P. Donovan, 181–213. Palmerston North: Dunmore Press.

Sites. 1986. *Being Pakeha*. Palmerston North: Massey University.

Spoonley, P. 1982. Race relations. In *New Zealand sociological perspectives*, edited by P. Spoonley, D. Pearson, and I. Shirley. Palmerston North: Dunmore Press.

Spoonley, P., and A. D. Trlin. 1986. *New Zealand and international migration: A digest and bibliography No. 1*. Palmerston North: Massey University, Department of Sociology.

Spoonley, P., K. A. Carwell-Cooke, A. D. Trlin, and Department of Labour (Research and Planning Division). 1980. *Immigrants and immigration: A New Zealand bibliography*. Wellington: Department of Labour.

Taher, M. 1965. *Asians in New Zealand – A geographical review and interpretation*. Ph.D. diss. (geography), University of Auckland.

Thomson, K. W., and A. D. Trlin, eds. 1970. *Immigrants in New Zealand*. Palmerston North: Massey University.

Tiwari, K. N., ed. 1980. *Indian in New Zealand: Studies in a subculture*. Wellington: Price Milburn.

Trlin, A. D. 1982. The New Zealand Race Relations Act: Conciliators, conciliation and complaints (1972–1981). *Political Science* 34(2): 170–93.

Walker, R. 1984. The genesis of Maori activism. *Journal of the Polynesian Society* 93(3): 267–81.

Wall, C. 1983. The Indians. *Auckland Metro* 30: 66–80.

———. 1986. Te Pakeha. The search for white identity. *Auckland Metro* 6(65): 34–48.

Wilkes, C. 1983. *The state*. Paper presented to New Zealand Sociological Association Conference, Auckland.

9

Banabans in Fiji: Ethnicity, Change, and Development

HANS DAGMAR

Eighteen years ago the Government allowed the Company to make its own initial terms with a handful of ignorant and illiterate natives. A child wrote down the name of the "so called King" and Chiefs who were equally ignorant of the purpose of the document. . . . This agreement has never been questioned by the Government. Years later the Government greatly improved conditions for the landowners and it is now necessary, if the phosphate of Ocean Island is to be worked to advantage, to remove the Banabans.[1]

In 1945, some 1,000 people of Micronesian origin arrived on the island of Rabi in Fiji. They were the former inhabitants of the island of Banaba, also called Ocean Island, situated between Nauru and the string of islands that now, together with Banaba, form the nation of Kiribati. The I-Banaba, as they call themselves, had to leave their own home territory because of intensive phosphate mining, and in this respect, they are a classic example of a community whose way of life has been fundamentally disrupted by colonial expansion. Their case also illustrates the saliency of ethnicity in postcolonial nation-building. The Banabans are now citizens of Fiji and have special provisions made for them in the Fijian constitutional legislation. But through their ownership of Banaban land, they also retain an interest in the state of Kiribati, a fact that is similarly recognized in the constitution of that country.

In this chapter, I will address issues of Banaban ethnicity and socio-economic development, and I will argue that appreciation of the interrelation of the two asks for a historical and cultural approach. From this point of view, attention is paid to the broader political and economic structures within which Banaban community life has evolved, but it also focuses on the special way in which the Banabans have perceived and reacted to these external constraints.

A GLIMPSE OF BANABAN HISTORY

The quotation opening this chapter is taken from a Colonial Office document of 1919. It is from a text by the resident commissioner of the Gilbert and Ellice Islands Protectorate, Edward C. Eliot, in which he considers the "difficult question" of the future of the Banaban people. Eliot criticizes the Pacific Phosphate Company for its way of obtaining initial "permission" from the landowners of Ocean Island in order to begin its mining operations. He paints a picture of the government as a protector of the interests of the Banabans, but leaves no doubt that, in the last instance, the needs and interests of "the Empire" should prevail. And it was seen to be in the interest of the Empire to get revenues from phosphate mining to support the imperial administration of the Gilbert and Ellice Islands Protectorate and, later, to subsidize Australian and New Zealand farming. Thus the position of the Banaban landowners was a delicate one, to say the least. Eliot's text is not unique; in the Colonial Office files one finds similar documents, all dealing with impediments to mining by the Banaban presence on the island and all searching for more or less elegant means to get the Banabans out of the way.

In view of the later British denials of Banaban claims of being an independent ethnic group or nation and of having, therefore, primary rights to the phosphate wealth of their island, it is interesting to note Eliot's contemplating purposefully blurring the Banabans' ethnic boundaries as a means of weakening their hold on Ocean Island phosphate. Explicitly, in relation to their removal from the island, Eliot recommends that, "to effect a transfer of the Banabans with the least shock will be to continue on the present lines, namely that of intermarriage with natives from other parts of the Colony." Assistance in promoting this aim was seen to be provided by the acquisition of a government steamer, breaking the Banabans' isolation and, it was hoped, leading to their swift integration into the larger population of the Gilbert Islands. Eliot is most apprehensive about the old generation, who might not be so willing to leave the island in this manner. Eliot warns that great care should be taken not to alert them to any government plans for the Banabans' departure, for there are "sufficient still alive . . . who would devote the rest of their lives to endeavouring to persuade the younger generation to continue their 'opposition to removal' after they had gone." However, Eliot says, if some patience would be exercised, it may be expected that when, in "5 or 6 years time" this "old Brigade" has passed away, "a less unreasonable spirit of opposition will be found to exist among the remainder." When that time would arrive, Eliot expected the Colonial Government's officers to use their position of trust *vis-à-vis* the Banabans and to persuade them finally to leave their home.

I do not wish to simplify or caricature Banaban colonial history. One can easily do so when using one or two documents to make a point. However, it cannot be denied that the text referred to above gives, in a nutshell, some of the fundamental facts of the issues involved. It does, in particular, reveal the role of the government and its officers. Strictly speaking – and this certainly holds for the early period of mining – it was not the government that dug up the Banaban soil and made the island uninhabitable; it was not the government that tried to keep the monetary compensation for Banaban loss of home territory and traditional social and cultural life to a minimum. But the government did assume a mediating and, therefore no less crucial, role, admittedly sometimes to the benefit of the Banabans. Such rule is almost by definition double-faced and certainly ambiguous. On the one hand, government officials had to convince the Banabans that they would act in their best interest; on the other, they had to see to it that the commercial exploitation of Banaba was carried out to the bitter end. A poignant example of this position can be seen in the infamous "Buakoni-kai letter" in which Resident Commissioner Grimble threatened the people of Buakonikai Village with possible destruction of their village should they remain unwilling to give up more land for mining; Grimble signed this letter with "your old friend and father"![2]

The files of the Colonial Office abound with documents illustrating the ambiguous position of the colonial government and its officers. Apparently they often succeeded in gaining the confidence of the Banabans. In their struggle against the phosphate mining company, the Banabans had no one else to turn to for support; moreover, the government carefully tried to build up an image of being in no way associated with the company. Thus, when, in 1913 the resident commissioner was negotiating with the Banabans to give up more land for mining, he felt his work to be seriously obstructed by a company official who urged people to accept the terms proposed by the government. This, according to the commissioner, led to great distrust among the landowners "as it seemed evident to them that if the Company urged them to accept the terms offered they could not believe that such terms were made in England in their own interests."

All in all, government officials engaged themselves in sometimes clever psychological manipulation of those whom they saw as little more than children. To break the resistance of the old people to releasing more land for mining, a local government official urged his superiors not to put all the revenues of rent and royalties into a trust fund, but also to allow a sum to be spent at the "community's pleasure." As he explained: "A trust fund, remaining for an indefinite period in the control of the Secretary of State, cannot be expected to appeal forcibly to octogenarians who, at times, are hard pressed to buy a little tobacco, or to find funds for other small luxury such as an evening's enjoyment at the Company's cinematograph exhibitions."[3]

As noted above, it was understandable that the Banabans, in their uncertainty over everything that happened to them, turned to government officials for support. When they considered the purchase of a new island, they asked for a government official to go with them as their adviser, should they make the move (see Silverman 1971: 145). Consequently, when building up a new community on Rabi after 1945, they were accompanied by a colonial officer, paid by the Banabans, who assumed the role of Banaban adviser.

There was certainly ambiguity also towards the colonial government on the part of the Banabans. But it was the Banabans themselves who put an end to this, thereby automatically ending the double role of the British colonial government. As the Banaban community on Rabi gained self-confidence, it required the Banaban adviser wholeheartedly to support the Banaban cause. In their eyes, the adviser was paid with Banaban money and therefore they expected him to work in the Banaban interest only, regardless of the colonial government's wish. One Banaban leader later explained: "We could not stand paying someone whom we trusted that he should look after our interest and yet he did not."[4] Relationships with the government changed dramatically when, in the late 1960s, a large group of armed Banabans threatened the adviser and demanded his immediate departure. With this they put an end to direct government interference in the spending of Banaban funds and in local political matters on Rabi.

To understand the Banabans of today, one must know their history and most certainly one must understand their relationship with the British colonial administration. Although the imperial political machinery did not reach out for Banaba until after the mining company had established itself there, once it arrived, it did become a very important party in the exploitation of Banaba's phosphate wealth. In 1920, the mining operations were taken over by the British Phosphate Commissioners. The United Kingdom, Australia, and New Zealand appointed one commissioner each, and together they held the undertaking in trust for the three participating governments. From that moment on, the colonial government had a very direct interest in phosphate mining, but it is interesting to see how, even after the take-over, the government and its officials strictly tried to maintain an image of three parties involved in Ocean Island mining: the company, the government, and the Banabans. The double role of the government was glaringly illustrated in 1946 when Maynard, the British Phosphate Commissioners' representative, negotiated with the Banabans on Rabi over releasing more land for mining and the royalties to be paid for the phosphate from these lands. The high commissioner instructed the Banaban adviser that he "should of course take no part whatever in Mr. Maynard's land negotiations."

Consequently, the Banabans, who, out of their own pocket, paid for a European adviser, were left without his help in a matter with far-reaching consequences. In the 1947 agreement resulting from the above-mentioned negotiations, the Banabans signed away the largest piece of their land up to that point, and they did so at a rate of royalty that was fixed, no matter how long the phosphate extraction took.

In consideration of the above, it is not surprising that, gradually, the Banabans came to appreciate the government's direct involvement in the mining operations. When, in the early 1970s, the Banabans instituted legal proceedings against the British Crown, it was the logical culmination of their growing awareness of the government's role. The verdict of the judge confirmed them in their stand. As the judge said: "The obligations of the Crown in respect of phosphate royalties were governmental obligations. . . . There have been grave breaches of these obligations."[5]

BANABANS ON RABI: A REDEFINED IDENTITY

About one year after the Japanese invasion of Ocean Island in 1942, the Banabans were deported from their home island and distributed over the islands of Kusaie, Tarawa, and Nauru. When the war was over, it was deemed inexpedient by both the phosphate company and the government to allow them to return to Ocean Island, and, initially for a period of two years, they were taken to Rabi, an island in the Fiji group bought with Banaban funds accumulated through payments for mining.[6]

The group that arrived in 1945 consisted of 1,003 people, 703 of whom were Banaban and 300 Gilbertese (I-Kiribati). An indication of the growth of the Rabi population since then is given in table 1.

The move to Rabi was a drastic change, not only in the Banabans' material environment, but also in their mental environment. As Silverman (1971: 105) noted of the Banaban community on Ocean Island, it "became more of a self-conscious and political community, as it became less autonomous." It is most interesting to see what became of these characteristics on Rabi.

First of all, it is necessary to see what, at present, constitutes "the Banaban community." As the Banabans themselves see it, being Banaban is equal to being an owner of land on Ocean Island or being entitled to inherit land there. In the latter category, we find not only unmarried children of Banabans, but also adults who have founded a family of their own and whose landowning parent(s) have not yet subdivided their landholdings and given their children a share. Ocean Island land is obviously no longer used by Banabans to produce food and materials, and therefore parents possibly postpone subdivision longer than was customary on Banaba (see Maude 1932). Land is bilaterally inherited, and, in principle, equal shares go to sons and daughters. It is obvious that, in this system, everyone who has at least one Banaban parent (and this includes adoptive parents) is entitled to a share in Ocean Island land, and in this sense the dividing line between Banabans and non-Banabans is a distinct one; there are no part-Banabans!

In defining the Banaban community, the position of the I-Kiribati people is of special significance. As indicated above, almost one-third of the "pioneers" who arrived on Rabi in 1945 were I-Kiribati. But that in itself does not make the place of the I-Kiribati a special one; for this, there are other historical and

Table 1. Population figures for the Banaban community in Rabi

	1945	1956	1965	1976	1985
Households	—	238	—	313	495
Females	—	616	889	1,143	1,990
Males	—	670	963	1,160	2,074
Total	1,003	1,286	1,852	2,303	4,064

political reasons. As Banabans became more sophisticated with regard to the phosphate revenue, they increasingly began to contest not only the amount of revenue gained from phosphate mining, but also its distribution. Of the total royalties and other payments for mining rights until 1973, 15 per cent went to the Banabans and the remaining 85 per cent to the Gilbert and Ellice Islands colony. This was seen to be an injustice by the former, who felt they "were born with a blessing" (the phosphate wealth) and that control of this wealth should be primarily in the hands of the Banaban landowners. During the 1978 constitutional conference for the Gilbert Islands, the Banabans argued for secession from the new nation of Kiribati. They felt supported in this by evidence given by H. E. Maude to the effect that the Banabans had probably had a language of their own and were a distinct ethnic group, although with cultural influence from the Gilbert Islands groups. It was also brought up that Banaba was not included in the Gilbert and Ellice Islands Protectorate until after phosphate deposits had been discovered. Thus Grimble (1921: 53–54) wrote that early information about Banaba led the English to believe "that this island was more of a burden than an asset to the Gilbert and Ellice Island Colony, also too far away from it, so it was rejected by the colonial government."

It is not my intention to repeat the arguments pro and contra Banaban independence. What the above indicates, however, is that the friction between Banabans and I-Kiribati must be understood in terms of colonial exploitation and colonial and post-colonial state formation.

But viewing Banaban ethnicity in only these terms is too simple. The attitudes of the Banabans towards the I-Kiribati may be much in line with the "very strong individual islands' patriotism," which Teiwaki (1983: 3) notes for the Kiribati cultural area as a whole. That the Banabans set themselves apart from the I-Kiribati also finds expression in their religion. Thus, according to informants, their most important goddess, Nei Tituabine, protected the Banabans against the Gilbertese and "killed them if they tried to hurt the Banabans."[7]

However, though in Banaban history there has been a most distinct anti-I-Kiribati sentiment, it must be noted that on Rabi there is absolutely no sign of prejudice against the I-Kiribati members of the community. The Banabans apparently distinguish very clearly between the Kiribati nation as a competitor for phosphate money and control of Ocean Island on the one hand and individual I-Kiribati on the other. Clearly, this supports the view that Banaban-Kiribati conflict is a colonial and post-colonial issue with a strong economic overtone. This was emphasized when, after the Banabans failed to achieve independence during the constitutional conference, Banaban leaders called on everyone of "Banaban descent" living in Kiribati to come to Ocean Island and join in peaceful resistance against further mining operations.

As a macroeconomic issue, the conflict with Kiribati is one of a higher political level. It is regularly brought up in the discussions of the Rabi Council of Leaders, but it does not seem to draw much attention in the affairs of daily living. It must be admitted that this is not lastly due to the I-Kiribati members of the Banaban community fully accepting their contemporary status. Inequalities are without doubt present in this status. For instance, the I-Kiribati do not get annuity or bonus payments, they do not get a quarter-acre residential block of land, and they are not entitled to a share of copra land; further, they cannot vote in the elections for the Rabi Council of Leaders.[8] It is probably part of a general Pacific cultural complex that the I-Kiribati do not complain about this. Rabi is seen as a Banaban island, and a Pacific islander fully recognizes the right of the local population to control affairs on its own island. During a project of collecting data for a sociography of Rabi households, it was found to be common that a Kiribati husband would point out that his wife was considered the head of the household. In such cases, even though the husband willingly provided information on all sorts of matters, he would categorically refuse to answer questions dealing with Banaban land and political matters. When asked some questions about the situation on Rabi and his views of the future, one informant stated:

I am not in a position to reply to this, because I am not a Banaban by birth; it is more appropriate for those who are Banaban to speak on their future. If I say anything myself I am told off by Banabans who say I have no right to say anything; at the moment it is my wife who should speak on Banaban matters.

It must be added that in everyday life the behaviour and attitudes of the Banabans towards the I-Kiribati is accommodating and relaxed, thus contributing to the latter's acceptance of their position. The best evidence of this is the frequent intermarriage between I-Kiribati and Banabans. Of all contemporary marriages of heads of households on Rabi, 44 per cent are between Banabans and I-Kiribati, 51 per cent are between two Banabans, and 5 per cent are other mixed marriages, usually involving Fijians or Tuvaluans. If we remember that everyone who has at least one Banaban parent is considered to be a Banaban, it is clear that, without further immigration on Rabi, the I-Kiribati element in the Banaban community will gradually disappear, at least in name. Presently, of all those who are members of the Banaban community, either by descent or marriage, or who are incorporated in a Banaban household in another manner, 92 per cent are Banaban, 7 per cent I-Kiribati, and 1 per cent belong to other ethnic groups (Fijians and Tuvaluans, mainly). But undoubtedly, the Banaban community today is suffused with an I-Kiribati "tradition." A second thing that softens the Banaban-I-Kiribati relationship is that, although the I-Kiribati can never own Banaban land, they are entitled to the use of land on Rabi. This applies even when a Banaban spouse has died. Moreover, I-Kiribati spouses of Banabans will share in the Banaban communal funds through their children, who will later, through their other parent, become Banaban landowners.

Thus, although there is a political conflict with Kiribati and although there are strict and formal distinctions between the Banabans and the I-Kiribati, the latter are well and truly accepted as members of the Banaban community. When discussing the position of the I-Kiribati with Banaban informants, I got the impression that some of them could not help feeling slightly embarrassed about the element of contradiction in the I-Kiribati position: that of close kin or well-esteemed community member on the one hand and being without basic political and land rights on the other. When inquiring about the rights of I-Kiribati on Rabi, slightly less than half of the respondents (45 per cent) said that no distinction should be made and that I-Kiribati should be able to share in Rabi land rights. Of these, some 15 per cent of the total number of respondents felt this should apply to every I-Kiribati resident; the rest stipulated that, for equal rights, they should be married to a Banaban or should have resided on Rabi since the pioneering days of 1945, or both. Half of all respondents were against the I-Kiribati getting land rights.

That nearly half of the respondents, although with some qualifications, were prepared to grant land rights on Rabi to I-Kiribati people is a major breakthrough and shows that increasingly the Banaban community is becoming a Rabi community.

I cannot do full justice to the complicated subject of Banaban community identity in the limited space available. It is certain, however, that the process noted by Silverman on Ocean Island of the Banabans becoming a self-conscious political entity was continued on Rabi. Maybe the process reached its zenith in the 1970s, when the Banabans fought the mining company and the British government in court and the young nation of Kiribati in the constitutional conference. In the period leading up to this, the Banabans kept a long distance from the former colonial government of Fiji, not in opposition, but carefully to guard their independence. Most of the infrastructure on Rabi was built up by the Banabans themselves, who did not want the Fijian government to become involved in their business. But all this is changing now. Relationships between the Rabi Council of Leaders and the government of independent Fiji are cordial, and Banabans are eager to receive Fiji government support. The attitude towards Kiribati has also changed. The Banabans seem resigned to Ocean Island not being under their own sovereign authority, but a part of the nation of Kiribati. The Rabi Council of Leaders has accepted the recommendations of the 1985 Independent Commission of Inquiry Relating to the Banabans. Following these, the Banabans are now prepared to "work with the Kiribati Constitution" and will appoint a nominated member of Kiribati's "Maneaba ni Maungatabu," who will take up a seat reserved for a Banaban-nominated representative. In August 1985, the president of Kiribati paid a historic first visit to the Banabans on Rabi.

Given the above, it may be said that Banaban community identity is no longer dominated by attitudes of political-economic opposition. Traces of it are still there, and Ocean Island matters are still important, but increasingly the Banaban perception of its community revolves around issues of the development of the island of Rabi itself. Given the safeguards of the so-called Banaban Settlement Act and the attitudes of the Fiji government, the Banabans have regained a degree of autonomy that, as noted by Silverman, they were losing on Ocean Island. Under these circumstances, they have not lost their identity of a self-conscious political entity, and in Fiji, the Banabans are strongly aware of being a separate ethnic group. But the sharp edges of opposition have worn off, and as Rabi matters are beginning to take precedence, internal differences in the community are getting more exposed. Thus, in mid-1985 political opposition to the Rabi Council of Leaders became vocal and even led to the damaging of council property.

But even though the Banabans increasingly focus on their future on Rabi, the past cannot be wiped out and still looms large over everything the Banabans undertake.

ISSUES OF SOCIOECONOMIC AND
POLITICAL DEVELOPMENT ON RABI

When the Banabans finally agreed to their removal to Rabi in 1945, there were elements in their considerations that foreshadowed important issues of their future life on Rabi. Silverman (1971: 146) notes that Rotan Tito, the most prominent leader of the Banabans, indicated that the reason behind their move to Fiji was to be close to the high commissioner for the Western Pacific (whose office was in Suva at that time) so that the Banaban political fight would be facilitated.[9] In consideration of developments since 1945, this statement appears to have been an accurate representation of Banaban intentions. The past 40 years on Rabi have been dominated by the struggle of the Banabans to get justice and what they thought was due to them in financial terms. Closely involved in this was the Banabans' concern not to lose contact with their homeland of Ocean Island. To some extent, this was taken care of by having their permanent representative on Ocean Island. Their concern was furthermore expressed by their wish to remain under financial responsibility of the Gilbert and Ellice Islands Protectorate, not that of the Fiji colonial government.

Another consideration of the Banabans to agree to their removal was their fear of completely losing their own cultural identity. In the face of an over-whelming European presence on small Ocean Island, there was probably little room for Banabans to maintain their own life-style. This, at least, is how Bana-bans themselves saw it, and it is interesting to note that they considered the disappearance of their "native crafts" as a major factor in the process leading to their being "compelled to habituate European ways of living."[10] Rotan, who expressed this fear, also mentioned the wish of the Banabans to be near trading stores giving access to European goods, and, as Silverman (1971: 146) writes, a major theme in Banaban culture apparently was "remaining distinctly Bana-ban and having the benefits of modern Europeanized life."

The aspects mentioned above are not unique in the development process of non-Western peoples, but some characteristics of the Banabans' situation may be more pronounced than in other cases. This is true of the long campaign of the Banabans to seek justice from the British, leading to a climax in the 1970s in the famous lawsuits of "Rotan Tito and others versus Sir Alexander Waddell, K. C. M. G. and others" and "Rotan Tito and the Council of Leaders versus Her Majesty's Attorney-General," as the legal proceedings of the Banabans against the phosphate company and the British Crown were called. I cannot adequately deal here with the reasons why this small group of people fought with so much determination against so powerful an adversary. What concerns me is that it is impossible to understand socioeconomic development on Rabi without taking into account this special concern of the Banabans.

One need not refer to outsiders' opinions to discover this all-pervasive theme in Banaban life. As an informant told me: "Development seems to be so late here, it should have been picked up long ago. We Banabans have looked to the past so much, everything seemed to revolve around the court case. I remember the British did a study on development on Rabi but nothing really came of it. In those days the Council was concentrating on getting justice."

Indeed, the Banaban leaders devoted much energy to the lawsuits, and when they were over, their attention was drawn to disputing the incorporation of Banabans into the new nation of Kiribati. Thus, Banaban leaders focused on the world outside Rabi, the chief subject of their attention being justice, inde-pendence, and control over Banaban resources. The last was expressed in terms of money, and in this sense the Banabans were good pupils of the mining com-pany and the British government.

The attitude of the Banabans towards money is an issue in itself and deserves wider treatment than I can give it here. A few comments, however, are neces-sary to give the reader understanding of the special problems of development on Rabi.

The transformation of the Banaban economy from one dominated by subsis-

tence fishing into one based on royalty payments has deeply affected the Banaban mentality. The peculiar nature of this monetary income has not given the
Banabans, as a group, much experience with working for money. The rising
expectations of a steadily growing number of Banabans have mainly been satisfied by their leaders' fighting for a larger share of phosphate income and
distributing this to the community. Development in the Banabans' eyes was
associated with improving the cash flow to the Rabi Council of Leaders.
Through this, the option of building up the community step by step, by means
of small-scale local projects, has not been given the attention it needed. The
typical emphasis on development in money terms was underlined as late as
1984, when the Rabi council appointed a university-trained Banaban as its
adviser, whose task it was to prepare a case for claiming war reparation money
from the Japanese!

That the Banabans came to equate development, Westernization, or progress, or whatever other meaning they attached to the process of change, with
control of money is not surprising. One of their more important native categories, land, became a source of direct monetary income.

The flow of payments for phosphate stopped after the mining company's
operations wound up in 1979. But the Banabans still receive today money "from
Ocean Island" in interest paid on a sum awarded to them as an "*ex gratia
payment*" by the British government after the court case. [11] This interest is now
almost the only source of income of the Rabi Council of Leaders and is used by
the council to pay for the administration (in a wide sense) of Rabi and Ocean
Island households. Part of this is distributed on an equal basis in the form of
so-called annuity payments: that is, periodic payments to every member of the
Banaban community. Another part goes to the households in the form of so-
called bonus payments, the amount of which varies according to the size of
one's landholding on Ocean Island. The continuing importance of the Banaban's former homeland is emphasized by these bonus payments. Since land
means money, there is a continuing and lively debate on land issues. The council employs four people (one from every Rabi village) on the "land tribunal,"
who, with the island magistrate, deal with all land matters, many of which are
cases of Ocean Island land inheritance and disputes.

But, as noted above, not all phosphate revenue was and is distributed directly
to community members. A great part falls under the control of the council. The
former British colonial government always showed a preference for payment of
phosphate money into a community fund (see Silverman 1971: 193). Much can
be said for this approach, but it did present the Banabans with two problems.
First, it put large sums into the hands of the council, the members of which did
not have a great deal of experience in handling such sums and certainly not in
investing them in a profitable manner. During the 1970s, when the phosphate
income was at its highest, the council ventured into large-scale business, Rabi
Holdings Ltd. As the council saw it, the purpose of the company was manifold:

To improve economic and social services on Rabi Island; to create employment; to make money; to be an investment company for the Banaban landowners; to ensure a source of income when their phosphate royalties income ceases after the completion of mining on Ocean Island (Rabi Council of Leaders, n.d., p. 1).

The company ended in financial disaster in the late 1970s, losing an estimated F\$5–6 million, but, nevertheless, emphasized the Banabans' reputation in Fiji of having plenty of money. It also made Banaban leaders anxious about undertaking further commercial ventures.

A second drawback of the council controlling the larger share of the phosphate revenues is that (and I paraphrase the words of a council member) it created a tendency among the Banabans to expect everything from the council and to take little individual initiative. What the people expected from the council was money in the first place. Just as their leaders concentrated on getting money from the mining company and the British government, the individual Banabans approached the council for money. A whole complex of "claims" and payments has arisen, sometimes of exaggerated proportions. Thus, according to informants, when the council set up a cattle-raising project and the animals broke through the fence and strayed into nearby *babai* fields, the owners of the fields lodged claims to a total of F\$60,000.[12] As a public relations instrument, the council set up a near-professional singing and dancing group, and every performance and rehearsal was being paid for. People got paid for carrying banners at demonstrations on Ocean Island. Money eventually also penetrated into local politics.

It is easy to criticize the Banabans for their ways of handling money. It must be remembered, however, how they became involved in a money economy. In the opening section of this chapter, we saw how the colonial government manipulated monetary rewards to break the resistance of Banabans to giving up more of their land for mining. When Banabans came to Rabi, they were used to buying most of their food in the company stores, and because they had almost no knowledge of agriculture, it was extremely difficult for them to provide their own food in the foreign environment of a Fiji island. It was only logical that community members continued to rely on what they saw as *their* money.

The issue of distribution of Banaban funds is a crucial one and is closely related to the views that Banabans have of the development of Rabi: should this be a collective or an individual matter, or is there an intermediate solution. Silverman (1971: 164) broached this subject in terms of the Banabans initially attempting to solve their organizational problems on Rabi by way of an "integral model," a single system with political, economic, and religious units. The integral model, according to Silverman, ultimately failed, but in his discussion of Banaban society, he also notes how the Banabans seemed to hesitate between forms of individual (household) development (1971: 168) and efforts "to mobilize support for community action in development" (1971: 195). More than 20 years after Silverman completed his research on Rabi, this element of indecision is still prominent. While I was carrying out research on Rabi in 1985, the people pressed the council for paying the larger share of the Banaban fund directly to the households. But, at the same time, answers to questions in survey interviews and informal discussions made it clear that an overwhelming majority of Banabans expected major improvements of life on Rabi to be initiated and accomplished by the Rabi Council of Leaders. Without any doubt, the council occupies a central place in Banaban thinking, and from that point of view, the integral model still lingers on Rabi. From a development perspective, this can be both a weakness and a strength.

THE RABI ECONOMY

To quickly characterise the contemporary Rabi economy, one can call it a subsistence economy with some extra input from wage labour, copra cutting, commercial farming and fishing, and payments from the phosphate fund. Table 2 summarises the situation in terms of average annual household income through these vaious sources.

A more accurate impression of Rabi incomes is gained when we separate the households into those in which one or more persons earns wages from those that have no income through wages. Of all Rabi households, 70 per cent are not supported by a wage earner. As shown in table 3, in these families the average annual income and the average annual per capita income are dramatically lower than in wage-earning households (for comparison, the table also includes the per capita income of Fiji as a whole).

It is not satisfactory to compare figures of Banaban per capita income, as based on a household survey, with those calculated for Fiji as a whole. A further regional differentiation and direct comparison with household survey figures is more enlightening. Tables 4 and 5 compare the average annual household incomes of wage- and non-wage-earning families on Rabi with figures obtained in the 1977 Fiji Household Income and Expenditure Survey.[13] The regional category "Isles/other" is the one most directly comparable with Rabi.

If we consider that since 1977 urban incomes in Fiji have risen about 3.5 per cent annually, the highest income-earning group on Rabi does not appear to be much better off than the average urban household in Fiji. Furthermore, the large group of non-wage-earning households on Rabi (70 per cent of the total) can be counted among the poorest in the Fijian nation. Clearly, the myth of Banaban richness may be readjusted, and a more realistic image of the Banaban financial situation is timely, not in the least from a development perspective.

About half of all the jobs on Rabi are provided by the Rabi Council of Leaders; the other half are Fiji government jobs. Taking wages paid by the council

Table 2. Average annual household income from various sources (in F$)

Income source					
Wages	Copra	Fishing/farming	Annuity	Bonus	Total
1,590	298	132	347	163	2,530

Table 3. Average annual household and per capita income of households with and without wage earner(s) (in F$)

With wage income		Without wage income		
Average household income	Average per capita income	Average household income	Average per capita income	Average per capita income of Fiji[a]
6,306	712	908	113	1,564

[a]Current Economic Statistics, Bureau of Statistics, Suva, Fiji, Oct. 1984. The figure given is an estimate for 1982; Rabi figures pertain to 1984/1985 and are based on field-work.

Table 4. Average annual household income of non-wage-earning households in Rabi (1984/85) and of village households in various regions of Fiji (1977) (in F$)

Rabi	West	Central	Northern	Isles/other
908	1,010	1,300	1,417	824

Table 5. Average annual household income of wage-earning households in Rabi (1984/85) and of urban households in different regions of Fiji (1977) (in F$)

Rabi	West	Central	Northern	Isles/other
6,306	4,921	4,552	4,671	3,969

and annuity and bonus payments together, 43 per cent of the total income of all Rabi households stems from the phosphate fund. Next to this, 40 per cent of Rabi household income is accounted for by salaries paid by the government of Fiji. The rest (17 per cent) is made up of earnings from copra cutting (15 per cent of the total), sales of farming products (2 per cent), and fishing (3 per cent).

A drastic increase of wage labour, either provided by the council or by the Fiji government, is not to be expected. It is also clear that copra must not be counted on to bring much more income to Rabi households soon. The figures on copra income given here are from 1984, a year during which the council still subsidised copra earnings. Since then, following the advice of a "Management Effectiveness Review," the Rabi council has stopped this subsidy, and consequently income in this sector has decreased. The present state of the Rabi coconut groves is poor, and future yields can only be expected to decrease further. According to a report of the second half of the 1960s, 44 per cent of the coconut palms on Rabi were planted between 1880 and 1910, and the remaining 56 per cent were planted between 1911 and 1929. Since then, no replanting scheme of any significance has been successful. Because the prime productive life of a coconut tree usually does not exceed 60 to 70 years, most coconut trees have passed their best productive period or are very close to the end of it. A replanting scheme carried out under British development aid has failed. A brief look at the lack of results of this project will convey some of the problems of Rabi economic development.

The money of the grant was used to buy tools, fertiliser, and planting materials, but the bulk of it was spent on wages for those working on the scheme. This work involved not only the preparing of the soil and the planting itself, but also periodic cleaning and weeding around the young trees and generally controlling the undergrowth. When the grant money ran out, the council (for reasons not altogether clear to my informants) no longer paid the labourers for their maintenance work; consequently, the young groves soon became overgrown and many of the young trees died. One main reason for the project's failure was that the replanted groves were on communally owned land (controlled by the council) and thus nobody wanted to take the responsibility for their maintenance on an unpaid basis. Here we come across one difficulty of agricultural development on Rabi: uncertainty as to the rights of people to land. As we saw before, all the land on Rabi is owned collectively and therefore, as a rule, people are reluctant to invest work in agricultural development when, as they see it, they are so unsure as to who will benefit from the fruits of their labour. [14] The Banabans, of course, are not unique in this. All over the world one sees evidence that in commercial agriculture, the household is the central economic unit and that people judge economic improvement in terms of benefit to this unit. Other, equally important, impediments to rural development on Rabi, as revealed by this case, are the dependence of Banabans on their political authority, the council, and their narrow conception of the council's task as being basically one of chanelling phosphate funds to the community members. Development is seen as primarily a council task, and participation in council projects must be paid for in cash.

It must be remembered that the failure of the coconut replanting scheme occurred when the Banabans were still receiving payments for phosphate mining and when the "fight" against the British was at its peak. But, although a new situation has arisen and although the Banabans are on a course of changing attitudes, it is obvious that the mentality that took shape in the preceding decades is still a relevant factor in Banaban development. A good indication of the Banaban stance during the 1960s and 1970s is given by a statement of their leader Rotan, who said: "We did not come to Fiji to be workers on the land but to get our money" (quoted in Silverman 1971: 195).

Returning to the present situation, I repeat that it is unlikely that copra will play a leading role in improving Rabi household incomes. Leaving aside the fact that the future prospects for copra on the world market are difficult to judge, the rehabilitation of the exhausted coconut plantations would require so much money, determination, and organisation that, even should the Banabans accept the challenge of such a project, it would be many years before the first effects of it could he expected.

Given the difficulties of improving copra income and the improbability of the growth of a manufacturing sector, except, perhaps, one of processing primary products, the expansion of Rabi's economy must, in the first place, be sought in agriculture, fishing, and the exploitation of timber resources. I cannot deal with this at length here, but must limit myself to some brief comments.

The figures above indicate that both fishing and agriculture obviously are in their infancy as commercial ventures. Basically, Banabans are not agriculturalists, which soon also becomes obvious in a comparison of their agricultural knowledge and skills with those of the native Fijians and Indo-Fijians. But agricultural skills can be learned, and there are indications that, given the declining phosphate income, the Banabans are willing to learn. An obstacle to agricultural development still remaining is that Rabi land is communal land. In a household survey, a large majority of informants expressed a preference for working the land on the basis of individual productive household units, and consequently there is also a general preference for land subdivision. However, this will be not only a costly operation but also a most difficult one because of the desire of many people to maintain the Ocean Island land division. This division has big differences; for instance, in one village the smallest individual landholding is 0.025 acres and the largest 13.169. Data on the preferences of the Banabans for specific types of subdivision of Rabi lands are available, but not yet fully analysed. A provisional count, however, shows a large proportion of respondents in favour of a subdivision on the basis of equal shares, and this will almost certainly cause a conflict with those who prefer a division according to Ocean Island landholdings.

Besides these internal organisational problems, Rabi faces many more obstacles in setting up a viable agricultural structure. Many are in the technical sphere – Rabi does not have fertile soil; the land is hilly and parts of it suffer from seasonal droughts – others are in marketing: problems of choice of crops, long supply lines, and a lack of commercial experience.

As for fishing, this fits in better with the Banaban traditions. Banabans are expert fishermen, and with good organisation and appropriate equipment, they may be able to build up a sound structure of commercial fishing. However, this will offer employment only to a few people.

But the discussion of Rabi's economic potential and its special strengths and weaknesses is a task in itself that I can touch on only lightly here.

CONCLUSION

Where earlier this century the Banabans moved from subsistence fishing into a form of peripheral capitalism, the community is now going through a reverse process in which subsistence fishing and agriculture play an increasingly important role.

Within the Fijian nation, the Banabans form a distinct ethnic community with language and cultural characteristics of their own. To a large extent this hinges on and is continued by a strong territorial segregation. Less than 10 per cent of the total Banaban population in Fiji lives outside Rabi, mostly in the capital city of Suva. The existence of some form of boundary between the Banabans and the rest of Fiji is also evident in the under-representation of Banabans in the higher income-earning and professional groups. But the separate identity of the Banabans is certainly not a source of feelings of ethnic antagonism among them.

The Rabi council faces the difficult task of building up a new economic basis for the community on Rabi. In this, it feels the weight of external structural disadvantages of a remote region in a third world nation. But there are also other, internal, obstacles to the development of Rabi, partly a consequence of past socioeconomic structures and occurrences. These internal and external impediments are two dimensions of a process to which they also contribute by way of a dialectic of action and reaction. To define the ethnic dimension of development, must we consider this internal component? But allow me to specify what I mean by internal and, in doing so, try to get closer to the ethnic dimension.

When calling attention to internal impediments to Rabi development, I mean those aspects that are characteristic for the Banabans as a group, those influences on the development process that can be seen as the Banaban input. This includes thinking, behaviour, and products that are part of a Banaban tradition, but also phenomena that stem from other traditions. Thus, the belief in the goddess Nei Tituabine is characteristic for the Banabans, but so is the belief in Jesus Christ and Christianity that can now be considered part of the Banaban tradition. This shows that traditions merge and are not necessarily unique. But there is a third group of phenomena that must also be counted among the internal aspects of the Banaban situation: ways of thinking and bahaviour that developed in reaction to the typical history experienced by the group.

This, then, is what I mean by the internal aspect of the Banaban situation: the complex and more or less unique whole of Banaban behaviour, thinking, and products. In describing its origin, I hope to have demonstrated that in no way do I see this as something static or unchangeable; neither do I see it as an ephemeral factor of negligible importance in considering the future development of the Rabi community. We may also refer to this whole as the culture or ethnic dimension of the Banaban community, and it is this perspective from which to consider the community in terms of ethno-development.

To show that studies of processes of ethno-development deal not only with patterns of behaviour of long, traditional standing, let me end by going back briefly to some internal aspects of Banaban development: the Banabans' attitude to and use of money and the relationship between the Rabi Council of Leaders and "the people."

For a long time, the Banabans have focused their attention exclusively on getting a larger monetary share of their "blessing," the phosphate wealth of Ocean Island. But there is a very strong awareness now of the necessity of building up an economic structure in which they can become more self-supporting, instead of waiting for money to drop into their laps. The people realise that to achieve this, the council needs funds to spend on community projects. In the past, they have made money available for this. It should be remembered that Rabi Holdings Ltd. was financed with millions of dollars from the landowners fund. Even after the financial disaster of the company, the council was left in control of more than two-thirds of the phosphate fund. The council, for its part, has tried to do what it can to make the capital "work" instead of consuming it. But so far, in the eyes of many Banabans, the council has been unable to show satisfactory results, and consequently the pressure has grown to distribute a larger share of the phosphate income directly to individual households. This came to a head when, during village meetings, the people forced the council to hold a referendum on the distribution of funds. The result of the referendum, held in 1985, was that most voted in favour of alotting two-thirds of the fund to the households, leaving a third for the council. Given the large debts of the council, this will nearly rule out any significant spending by the council on structural improvements of the Rabi economy.

Any consideration of future economic development on Rabi must take these local attitudes into account. The council faces not only external constraints on economic growth; it must also convince the Banabans that, in the long run, communal spending may be more beneficial (given that this is true; the people at present do not think so). The case becomes even more interesting when we remember that the leaders of the Banabans have a long history of pushing for individual distribution of funds against the colonial government's emphasis on

communal investment. After the referendum, some members of the council expressed satisfaction at the result: it would decrease the dependence of the people
on the council and (this is my own interpretation) relieve the tremendous pressure on the council to show clear results for its spending.

   In the above, I have been able to reveal only a glimpse of the complexities of
the Banaban story. Undoubtedly, it can only be understood by taking into
account the macroeconomic and macropolitical aspects of colonisation, decolonisation, and world capitalism. But equally important is the anthropological
perspective that focuses on the ethnic dimension. Nothing may illustrate better
how subtle the truth is and how much we need constant referral to the "internal
aspect" than the words of Rotan Tito. Rotan spent a lifetime leading the Banabans in squeezing money from the mining company and the British government. After the Banabans lost their legal case against "the British," in which
they asked for F\$80 million compensation, he told his son Tebuke Rotan:

It is good that we did not get all that money. It would not have been good for the people.
After all, I fought for justice. Why did the British have to take our land? We did not grab
it from anybody! The British misunderstood us all along. We were forced to be generous
to the Gilbertese. We Banabans do not mind being generous . . . we just don't like to be
forced, that's all.[15]

                                    NOTES

1. Western Pacific, CO 225/164, High Commissioner despatches Jan.–March 1919,
   conf. desp. 25/3/19; Public Records Office, London.
2. See also Silverman (1971: 124); files of the Rabi Council of Leaders.
3. Western Pacific, CO 881/14, Affairs of Ocean Island 10/1/1914–4/1/1915, enclosure
   B, report of negotiations 7/11/13–17/11/13; Public Records Office, London.
4. Tebuke Rotan, giving evidence in the lawsuit of the Banabans against the British
   Crown. See Judgement no. 2, Royal Courts of Justice, 30/11/1976. Before the Vice-
   Chancellor: Rotan Tito and the Council of Leaders versus Her Majesty's Attorney-
   General.
5. From the Vice Chancellor's judgement in "Ocean Island no. 2." Royal Courts of
   Justice, 1976. Before the Vice-Chancellor: Rotan Tito and the Council of Leaders
   versus Her Majesty's Attorney-General.
6. Rabi was bought from the firm Lever Brothers, which maintained coconut groves on
   the island. There was at that time no longer a native population on the island, only
   some families of Fijian and Solomon Islands plantation labourers.
7. It is arguable that this belief has developed after the beginning of mining on Ocean
   Island and thus is merely a reflection in the religion of aspects of economic competition. However, it must be noted that when informants speak of Nei Tituabine, they
   refer to a period that at least predates their arrival on Rabi in 1945. The belief in Nei
   Tituabine has now weakened very much, and initially the Banabans were not even
   sure their goddess had accompanied them to Rabi.

8. These are payments to Banabans of monies connected with phosphate mining; a further explanation of this will be given below.

9. Rotan later (in 1972) told the lawyer Richard Brown that "at one time he approached Major Kennedy to try and find a way of getting a lawyer to take up the Banaban case. The advice Rotan was given was that they should buy an island in Fiji where they would be closer to the Governor and Major Kennedy would approach the Governor to help Rotan find a better way of presenting their case. Major Kennedy was the first Banaban adviser on Rabi." From Rotan Tito and others versus Sir Alexander Waddell K. C. M. G. and others. Joint Advice on Oral Evidence. Davies, Brown, and others.

10. Letter of Rotan Tito to the Secretary of State for the Colonies, files of the Rabi Council of Leaders; see also Silverman (1971: 146).

11. This money is included in this chapter under phosphate revenue or phosphate fund.

12. *Babai* is a wild species of taro that would easily have grown again after having been damaged in this way.

13. Figures for Fijian household income are taken from the Household Income and Expenditure Survey 1977. See Fiji's Eighth Development Plan, 1981–1985 (Suva, Central Planning Office, 1980), p. 12.

14. There is one exception: the coconut lands of two of the four Rabi villages have been subdivided on the basis of one acre per head (*te aba ni maiu*: the land for living). Although this subdivision is registered, the legal ownership of the land is still unclear.

15. From Rev. Tebuke Rotan, personal communication.

REFERENCES

Grimble, A. F. 1921. From birth to death in the Gilbert Islands. *The Journal of the Royal Anthropological Institute* 51: 25–54.

Maude, H. E. 1932. The social organisation of Banaba or Ocean Island, Central Pacific. *Journal of the Polynesian Society* 41: 262–301.

Rabi Council of Leaders. n.d. *A 6-year progress report on the operations of the Rabi group of companies prepared for the information of Mr. R. Posnet, a British government representative on a fact-finding mission to the Banabans on Rabi island, Nuku, Rabi.* Suva.

Silverman, M. G. 1971. *Disconcerting issue: Meaning and struggle in a resettled Pacific community.* Chicago and London: The University of Chicago Press.

Teiwaki, R. 1983. Kiribati: Nation of water. In *Politics in Micronesia*, edited by R. Crocombe and A. Ali, 3–28. Suva: Institute of Pacific Studies, University of the South Pacific.

10

Race, Class, and Ethnicity in Western Samoa

PAUL SHANKMAN

In the final paragraph of *Samoa mo Samoa*, the definitive book on Western Samoan independence, J. W. Davidson comments on the growing unity of the Samoan population. This increasing unity between Samoans and part-Europeans leads Davidson to conclude that "custom has been transformed. Samoa has become a nation" (1967: 430). Although Davidson reviews earlier conflicts and possible schisms between Samoans and part-Europeans, their seeming resolution at the time of independence in 1962 provides an upbeat finale to an occasionally problematic past.

Davidson is largely correct that, in contemporary Western Samoa, ethnic relations are stable, bearing little resemblance to other parts of the South Pacific, where circumstances differ and tensions are greater. This was not always so. Ethnicity, or "race" as it was then conceived, was an issue throughout the 19th century and was the partial basis of the Mau (1926–1935), the South Pacific's most successful anticolonial political movement. The mobilisation of ethnicity was essential in the process of nation-building for Western Samoa, the first independent country in the South Pacific. More traditional than any other people in Polynesia, Western Samoans pride themselves on the retention of *fa'asamoa*, or the Samoan way. Also, Western Samoa has accommodated its small but prominent part-European citizenry.

Does the relative ethnic harmony that exists in Western Samoa indicate an absence of ethnic and class interests? And if differing interests exist, how have they been articulated in an independent Western Samoa? In this chapter, I will argue that part-European economic interests and external economic interests exist and remain very influential in the economy of Western Samoa and that Samoan political representation in parliament has not significantly compromised these interests. Moreover, the patterns of dependency that have developed over the past century have favoured and continue to favour part-European interests and external interests. Political circumstances and governmental reforms have minimised conflict and have modified ethnic relations, but they have not altered the basic pattern in which part-Europeans and external interests control much of the economy.

DEFINITIONS AND CATEGORIES

Although Western Samoa is overwhelmingly Samoan and relatively homogeneous as South Pacific countries go, some ethnic categories require definition and clarification before we can examine the relationship between ethnicity and economy. In this chapter, the term part-European refers to some, but not all, of the descendants of Samoan-European marriages during the colonial period (1830–1962). Several of today's part-European families are related to the Europeans seen in the 1907 *Cyclopedia of Samoa*, and they retain their European surnames. Part-European designates people who are known elsewhere in the literature as "local Europeans," "mixed bloods," and "half-castes." Though the term part-Samoan is probably the most common designation in the literature, part-European has been chosen to highlight the contrast between "part-Samoans" and "real" Samoans, as they sometimes designate themselves. It is not a term commonly used by any ethnic group in Western Samoa; it is simply one that may help avoid some past confusions.

The distinction between Samoans and part-Europeans is complicated by the overlapping of biological, cultural, and legal categories. During the early colonial period, there were frequent cross-ethnic unions. Felix Keesing cites a study indicating that by the 1930s, much more than 30 per cent of the Western Samoan population had "mixed blood" (1934: 456). Yet biological heritage and cultural heritage are quite different. Using self-identity as expressed in the islands' census between 1906 and 1966 (see table 1), we find that the percentage of the population labelling itself as part-European only recently exceeded 10 per cent. Thus, most who could claim to be part-European have, in the past, identified themselves as Samoans. Those legally registering themselves as part-Europeans are an even smaller percentage. To have "European" rights in

Table 1. Self-identification of ethnicity in the census of Western Samoa (1906–1966)

	1906	1936	1945	1956	1966
Samoans	89.8%	90.9%	90.7%	90.4%	88.5%
Part-Europeans	2.4	6.2	7.4	8.1	10.1
Other Pacific islanders	3.6	1.2	0.9		
Chinese	3.0	1.0	0.5	1.5	1.0
Europeans	1.2	0.7	0.5		

Source: Stanner (1953: 331), Census Commissioner's Office (1968: 3).

colonial and postcolonial Western Samoa, part-Europeans had to register with the government and not merely identify themselves as part-Europeans in a census. There are fewer part-Europeans legally and politically than there are culturally and biologically.

To further complicate matters, there are Europeans who are expatriates and Europeans who are not part-Europeans but Europeans who have become Samoan citizens. Moreover, not all people categorised as part-Europeans are biologically part-Europeans. This category as a legal designation has included non-Samoan Pacific islanders and part-Chinese residents in Western Samoa. The potential for confusion here is expressed in the following passage from the well-known study, *Western Samoa: Land, Life and Agriculture in Tropical Polynesia*:

Of the total population of 97,327 in September 1956, 88,036 or 90.4 percent were Samoans; part-Samoans numbered 7,900 or 8.1 percent; and Europeans 662 or 0.7 per cent. In addition there were living in the territory 531 other Pacific islanders, 49 people who failed to give the full information required, and 149 "others" of mixed blood. In terms of legal status, however, these figures must be modified to indicate 91,833 "Samoans" and 5,494 "Europeans." The former category therefore included more than those of Samoan "physiological descent," and the latter embraced a number of part-Samoans and others who desired to retain some claim to European status (Fox 1962: 112).

Problems in categorisation arise because there has been a degree of choice of ethnic and legal identity. Part-Europeans can opt for either a part-European or a Samoan identity. Some part-Europeans choose to live as Samoans, speaking Samoan, living as Samoans on Samoan land, holding Samoan titles, and voting as Samoans. In family affairs, Samoan and part-European members of the same family may share the same interests and maintain close family relations. On the other hand, part-Europeans may choose to retain part-European privileges, living on freehold land, voting as individuals, and living a more European lifestyle. Other permutations of legal status and life-style are also possible. The extent to which Samoans and part-Europeans consciously and legally identify with one ethnic group or another depends, to some extent, on circumstances.

If there is some legal and cultural blurring of ethnic categories in Western Samoa, in the economic realm part-Europeans are often quite distinct from Samoans. They control many of the commercial establishments in the port town of Apia, large and small, and are highly visible as village traders. They are also well placed in the public service. A representative survey conducted in 1972 by the Western Samoan government found that the average part-European family had a higher income than the average Samoan family (Department of Statistics 1972). Part-Europeans were also more likely to engage in wage labour instead of village agriculture, to live in European-style houses, to own cars, to live in and around Apia, and to own freehold land as opposed to Samoan communal land.

Individually, there was a wide range of individual and family variation; part-Europeans were a category instead of a well-defined class. Nevertheless, part-Europeans as a group tended to occupy a very different economic niche than most Samoans, and some part-Europeans belonged to an élite class.

These economic data suggest that Western Samoa is not simply a plural or multicultural society with different ethnic groups; it is a stratified society in which class and ethnicity have been closely related in the past. There is ethnic stratification in which Europeans and some part-Europeans are at the upper levels, and there has been economic discrimination against Samoans. Social discrimination against Samoans was evident well into the 1970s at social clubs in town and on social occasions. Although Samoans remain proud of their cultural heritage, to the point of sometimes being labelled ethnocentric, they are not as influential in economic matters as their less numerous European and part-European counterparts.

The differing economic roles of part-Europeans and Samoans are the products of the colonial period. Tracing the historical basis of ethnicity and its relationship to economic dependency and political development is the primary subject of this chapter. In the first part of the chapter, the origin of ethnic groups and their interests during the early colonial period and during the critical years under New Zealand colonial rule are reviewed. The chapter also deals with the transformation of ethnic or racial categories into contemporary, legal categories of citizenship during the period just before Western Samoan independence in 1962 and the outcome today. The growing ethnic unity in recent decades referred to by Davidson may mask important class-related phenomena; in this chapter, therefore, ethnic relations will be viewed less in cultural terms and more in economic and political terms.[1] As Davidson himself comments, "In Samoa the distinction between custom and vested interest is a delicate one" (1967: 327ff.).

THE EARLY COLONIAL PERIOD (1830–1900)

Economic stratification and the emergence of ethnicity in Western Samoa have their bases in the colonial period. Before the 1830s, contact with the West was sporadic, and the part-European political and economic systems remained intact. In aboriginal Samoa, the islands were rarely if ever unified as a group. The usual political condition was internecine warfare between rival chiefdoms with shifting alliances that did not lead to a permanent, centralised state-level political organisation. Kinship and territory were the core of organisation and identity. An ancient enmity with Tonga also provided Samoans with an identity.

The period from the 1830s through the 1870s was marked by increasing internal warfare related to changing Samoan alliances with different groups of European settlers – German, English, and American. The emergence of a colonial agricultural export economy of the plantation variety was just as significant. Great tracts of Samoan land were alienated to large German plantations and also to smaller European plantations. By the 1850s, most Samoans had become involved in the copra trade as small-scale village producers. The islands' economy was thus moving from an undeveloped state in which local factors of production and distribution were dominant to an underdeveloped state in which external factors were dominant.

The establishment of a European export enclave in the mid-19th century with new land and labour interests brought numerous changes to the Samoan economy (Gilson 1970; Lewthwaite 1962; Davidson 1967), although the consequences of German, British, American, and finally New Zealand colonial influence in Western Samoa were not as damaging as in other parts of the world, including the Pacific. The Samoans were never defeated in battle, and largely because of the existence of an indigenous hierarchical structure and the exigencies of indirect rule, an early, if troubled, mutual accommodation was worked out.

The Samoans were incorporated into an unstable colonial polity and a growing agricultural-export economy. Rapidly expanding Christian missions were also influential. The durability of the initial Samoan adaptation to the wider world has given this relatively recent configuration an aura of tradition. Although Samoans continue to identify with Samoan custom, or *fa'asamoa*, a closer look reveals that *fa'asamoa* is more an ideology of tradition than a behavioural replica of pre-European society. What is referred to as *fa'asamoa* today probably had its basis in the Samoan-mission-trader adaptation that developed between 1830 and 1870 (Keesing 1934: 467; Stanner 1953: 305–23).

By the 1870s, Apia had become the second most important port in the South Pacific after Honolulu. Germans dominated this era, with British and American traders vying for influence. In the mid-1870s, an American-inspired revolt by Samoans against German control exacerbated local tensions. Although the islands were not central to international concerns – a "footnote to history" in the words of Robert Louis Stevenson – a "Great Power" territorial dispute nearly erupted into a major naval confrontation involving Germany, Great Britain, and the United States just off the coast of Upolu in 1889. The conflict was avoided only after a violent storm scuttled most of the warships. At the turn of the 20th century, a territorial division of the islands peacefully resolved the hostilities, with the United States acquiring what was to become American Samoa, while the large islands of Upolu and Savai'i fell under Germany's dominion.

In the latter half of the 19th century, in conjunction with the plantation economy, a new set of ethnic groups emerged with a new social order in which race and class were nearly synonymous. On the one hand were the Samoans, the overwhelming bulk of the population, rurally based and marginal to the plantation system proper. Although the Samoans did grow coconuts for conversion into copra, they were not part of the plantation labour force, remaining in villages based on communal land tenure. On the other were the Europeans, numbering only a few hundred, but they were the main economic presence, controlling the privately held plantation lands and the commercial businesses on the waterfront in Apia. Indentured Micronesians and several hundred Melanesians worked the plantations during the latter part of the 19th century. By the end of the century, there were also about 500 part-Europeans.

Ethnic categories were reinforced by law, dispensed largely by European consulates employing a 19th century view of racial differences. The principal cleavage between the "European beach" at Apia and the rest of the islands under Samoan control was complicated by cleavages within the European and Samoan groups, but these were shifting, and the Europeans could coalesce if common interests required unity. Conflict, political intrigue, and intermarriage were major components of interethnic relations (Hempenstall and Rutherford 1984: 18–43).

In the 1840s and again in the 1850s, the parents of the first part-European children became concerned about their education and requested that the London Missionary Society construct a special school for European and part-European children, fearing that they would grow up to be "just like Samoans" without proper instruction (Gilson 1970: 241). The church complied with this request, and the educational system came to reinforce pre-existing divisions between Samoans and Europeans. It also provided the educational basis for part-European participation in commerce and government during the later colonial era.

Intermarriage during the 19th century was almost always between European men and Samoan women. Most part-European offspring could not become members of the Samoan traditional élite because high-ranking Samoan families would not allow their senior women to intermarry, or if they did, they would not allow transmission of high titles. Nevertheless, given the sharp economic differences between Samoans and Europeans and the educational advantages of the Europeans, part-Europeans came to play important, if sometimes dubious, interstitial roles in European government and commerce. As Gilson recounts in his history of Samoa in the late 19th century, they were often viewed as "troublemakers":

Some of these locally-born people performed their vital functions without unduly abusing the trust placed in them, and there were a few able and consistent ones who spent their working lives in devoted "public service." But many others, succumbing to temptations put in their way by bribery and personal ambition or frustration, took advantage of the obvious opportunity to manipulate forces and events. Indeed, the history of Samoa in the latter part of the nineteenth century is studded with "incidents" set off by the unauthorised acts of various scribes and other go-betweens. The few of these officeholders who bore chiefly titles were not, it should be mentioned, among the more unreliable. Those most complained of – and the complaints grew more numerous as the century wore on – were in fact part-Samoans, from which general class also came other elements reported as troublesome. Among the latter were experts in the handling of firearms who were welcome and privileged recruits to any war party. Nevertheless, part-Samoans were seldom prime-movers in any affair of great moment; and if they were rather given to turbulence and treachery, it must be remembered that they often had little credit, status or resourçe, apart from their personal knowledge and wits, upon which to depend for the achievement of their aspirations, whether these were European- or Samoan-oriented (1970: 341–42)

THE GERMAN COLONIAL PERIOD (1900–1914)

By 1900, the pattern of plantation-oriented agricultural export economy was firmly established. The frontier period had waned, and under German rule through 1914 there was relative political calm and economic prosperity, especially for the planters. Exports of copra and cocoa boomed as Western Samoa became the prized jewel of the German protectorates. Part-European commercial ventures and inherited properties also flourished.

In 1904, Samoans launched the Oloa movement to gain a stronger foothold in the commercial economy. Organised as a co-operative enterprise, Samoan chiefs hoped to produce and market village-grown copra, paying higher prices than white traders. But the German administration forbade Samoan participation, and when Samoans openly defied the governor in a related matter, he fined, imprisoned, or deported the chiefs involved. Even more dramatically, the governor dispersed Samoan governmental representatives to their villages and prohibited the use of titles and privileges by the great Samoan orators. The political repercussions of the suppression of the Oloa movement would surface later in the 1920s; for the time being, the monopoly of the Europeans and part-Europeans was preserved.

From its inception, the German regime was concerned not only with economic control, but also with the "racial purity" of Samoans and Germans. At the same time, it was necessary to secure more indentured labour to satisfy the labour demands of plantation owners. In 1903, the importation of more than 2,000 male Chinese indentured labourers began, but the administration placed severe restrictions on liaisons between indentured Chinese men and Samoan women.[2] The administration also frowned on European-Samoan unions. Yet it had to accept existing cross-ethnic marriages. When Germans in Europe heard of "race-mixing" in the colonies, they wanted to make such marriages illegal. In Samoa, however, German settlers with part-European children were quick to protest, pointing out that Samoans were not racially inferior and that many part-Europeans were prosperous planters. German parents, fearing prejudice in their home country, refused to send their part-European children back to Europe. According to one account:

The exasperation. . . has now advanced to such an extent that it threatens to be prejudicial to the progress of German ideals, and several German parents have sent their children to America and New Zealand to be educated, not only for reasons of convenience, but also to protect them from insults in Germany (Keesing 1934: 454).

Although the Germans were unsuccessful in banning intermarriage, they did establish the legal categories of "European" and "Samoan" that would pervade ethnic relations for the next six decades. Before German rule, the colonial convention had been that part-European offspring would inherit the legal status of their fathers, who were almost always European. But over time this convention led to problems:

Serious legal difficulties were arising in German Samoa in connection with succession to property, in cases where Europeans had been married under Church auspices but had not completed a civil registration, and regarding the admission of part-Samoans to buy liquor in the hotels. The authorities were also faced with the problem of dealing with "a particularly rowdy half-caste population" and a rapidly increasing group of "waif and stray" children of non-legitimate ancestry, hence presumably of Samoan nationality that were congregated around Apia. Some redefinition of the status of mixed bloods thus became urgently necessary (Keesing 1934: 452).

In 1903, the colonial regime passed a law that allowed "any illegitimate half-caste" to apply through the local police to the high court to become a "European." The court would examine each case on its individual merits, taking into account the "worthiness" of the applicant for the "superior" classification. In less than a year, 263 individuals had changed their status; this figure is significant because there were only 599 part-Europeans to begin with in the census of 1903. Children born of "European" parents automatically inherited European status, enabling the families of such children to change legal and ethnic categories.

Because the number of part-Europeans was rising rapidly, local authorities passed a law to counteract this trend. The new law of 1914 stated that illegitimate children of mixed unions could not take the name of a European father and that they legally belonged to the mother's family (fathers were required to pay for the child's welfare through age 14, including education). In this way, the Germans hoped to reduce the increasing and problematic group of part-Europeans. However, the law did not go into effect because the German colonial period ended with the islands' loss at the outset of the Great War.

THE NEW ZEALAND COLONIAL PERIOD (1914–1962)

World War I came to Western Samoa without a shot fired on either side. The loss was a blow to German pride, since the islands were the first German possession relinquished in the Great War. The occupying New Zealand government had few problems, and its military garrison of 300 men had little to do for the duration of the war. German plantation owners and traders were allowed to retain their holdings, but the war and policies of the new colonial regime led to problems for which New Zealand was unprepared.

The war interrupted trade; costs escalated as duties on copra, cocoa, and rubber increased. Shipping was difficult, and copra prices fell catastrophically. Meanwhile, the new government began forcibly to repatriate indentured labour. During the war, Chinese and Melanesians were returned to their home countries; the number of Chinese fell to 838 in 1918, from 2,184 in 1914; Melanesians decreased to 201, from 887 (Lewthwaite 1962: 161). The prevailing assumption was that Samoan labourers would fill the labour requirements of the plantations; but this assumption was faulty, because Samoans could make more cutting copra on their own land than as plantation workers for Europeans or part-Europeans. Even worse, the islands were decimated by the great influenza epidemic of 1918–1919, in which an estimated 19 per cent of the Samoan population died (Field 1984: 49).

All these circumstances left the commercial economy devastated. The large German plantations were hardest hit, especially the cacao plantations that relied on semiskilled imported labour. Some German planters abandoned their substantial holdings, which were then taken over by the New Zealand government as trust estates. The remaining planters were displeased with the new administration's seemingly irrational repatriation schemes. Although Samoan village agriculture was less vulnerable because it was not geared to full-time cash cropping, the loss of Samoan lives in the epidemic and the New Zealand government's mishandling of this tragedy left Samoan resentments that smouldered for decades.

Western Samoa recovered quickly from the epidemic and the financial disasters of the early post-World War I years. By the mid-1920s, the plantation system had been restored, and exports of copra, cocoa, rubber, and bananas were healthy. Chinese labour, still under severe restrictions, was again imported. The New Zealand administration, now under the League of Nations mandate, launched a set of new social policies designed to improve Samoans' health, education, and welfare. Public works were initiated, and a series of economic measures were undertaken to invigorate the village agricultural sector. Copra marketing schemes for Samoan villagers were introduced by the government to alter what was perceived as price-fixing by local trading companies. Diversification of crops, including bananas, for example, was also encouraged to reduce dependency on copra. Going even further, Governor Richardson (1923–1926) wished to provide individual Samoans with bank accounts, the leasing of land to individual untitled males, and even individual land ownership, putting them on a more competitive economic basis with Europeans and part-Europeans.

Along with these economically progressive measures, the administration sought to restrict Samoan social customs that were believed to have a debilitating effect on agricultural production. With the consent of a government-controlled Samoan advisory committee, Richardson attempted to limit village cricket, the number of lengthy holidays, ceremonial visitations, and fine-mat exchanges, all of which were viewed as time-consuming and wasteful. These social measures were resented by most Samoans for obvious reasons. European and part-European businessmen were also disenchanted with administrative policies that explicitly favoured the Samoans in the economic sphere. The prohibition of alcohol fueled these resentments. While on the surface the New Zealand colonial regime seemed progressive in the economic and social realms, it was gradually alienating almost all the ethnic groups and economic classes under its jurisdiction.

When O. F. Nelson, a part-European and the most prosperous trader in Western Samoa, went to New Zealand in 1926, he met with the prime minister and the new minister of external affairs in Wellington, and the raised grievances about "interferences by Richardson in fa'a Samoa, prohibition, administrative expenditure, the lack of proper representation despite high taxation, and copra maketing" (Field 1984: 72). Assured that an investigation would ensue, Nelson returned to the islands and, in a series of meetings, prepared his case. These meetings were initially only a forum for complaint, but when they were vigorously opposed by Richardson, they formed the basis of a national resistance to the New Zealand administration. As the colonial government became more heavy handed with arrests, banishments, and deportations, the Samoans withdrew and set up a parallel government in the late 1920s and 1930s, rejecting most of the economic and social measures that the New Zealand colonial regime had fostered. The movement was called the Mau ("opposition"; see Field 1984: 85) and had as its rallying cry Samoa mo Samoa, "Samoa for Samoans."

The extent and intensity of support for the Mau was unanticipated. In 1929, hostilities between the colonial regime and the Mau erupted when a peaceful demonstration by Mau followers was fired on by colonial police, leading to the deaths of 11 Samoan leaders, including Tupua Tamasese Lealofi III, one of the two most important leaders of the movement. The incident was known as "Black Saturday." The reaction to these killings furthered the cause of the Mau and increased nationalistic sentiments.

The Mau, however, did not lead to separatist *economic* sentiments against the Europeans and part-Europeans who controlled the commercial sector. Indeed, Europeans and part-Europeans were able to use the Mau to retain their economic interests while fostering Samoan nationalism. Lewthwaite has analysed the economic considerations involved:

The Mau arose from a partially incompatible conjunction of European and native grievances. The white and mixed-blood groups remained profoundly unhappy with a policy which frankly subordinated their interests. Part-Samoans, sensing a measure of discrimination, transmitted their resentments to the Samoan communities with which they increasingly merged. The white planters shared with them a legacy of political and economic grievances crystallised by the lack of political power and the chronic labour shortage, the latter being accentuated by economic recovery and the irritations of the "free labour" system. Even more resented was the prohibition of liquor.

The running sore of financial grievance was still more effective, for the weight of customs duties and taxes fell naturally upon the commercialised rather than the subsistence sector of Samoan economy, while the receipts were expended to a growing civil service, on public works and on Samoans whose contribution was disproportionately small. Thus, when the administration launched a copra-buying scheme that posed an incipient threat to the profits and perhaps the livelihood of middlemen, the trading community swiftly reacted. Under the leadership of O. F. Nelson, appropriately enough the leading copra-trader and a part-Samoan, they determined to marshall Samoan support in defence of their own interests (1962: 168–69).

For these reasons, the political conflict between Western Samoa and New Zealand did not manifest itself in an internal class conflict or as an ethnic conflict.

The colonial regime under Richardson had attempted to promote a schism between the Samoans on the one hand and the Europeans and part-Europeans on the other. And this was done in the name of the Samoans. It was a critical juncture in the history of the islands because if Richardson's policies had succeeded, the tradition-based communal land tenure system of the Samoans would have become more individualised, the authority of the *matai* would have been undermined at the local and national levels, and the Samoan sector of the economy would have become more commercialised with more equitable competition between Samoans, Europeans, and part-Europeans. Ethnic and class relations would have been altered. But this did not occur. Instead, Richardson's heavy-handed tactics led to an unlikely alliance between the different ethnic groups against New Zealand colonial rule. "*Samoa mo Samoa*" had originally been a slogan used by the New Zealand colonists to drive a wedge between the Samoans and Europeans and part-Europeans, but it was appropriated by the Mau to mean "Samoa without the New Zealanders" (Davidson 1967: 122).

The New Zealand regime sparked a remarkably united anticolonial political movement that posed no challenge to existing internal or external economic relationships. The Mau supported European complaints for the most part. As Davidson states:

In the circumstances of general disaffection that prevailed, the alliance between the laissez-faire conservatism of the Europeans and the tradition-based conservatism of the Samoans was scarcely ever an easy one.

In political matters and in those relating to custom there was, on the contrary, no important divergence of outlook even at the theoretical level (1967: 125).

Thus, anticolonial politics led first to resistance, next to political separatism with continuing mass disobedience, and later to the quest for political independence. In each of these periods, common political interests prevailed over divergent economic and ethnic interests. It was the most successful anticolonial movement in the South Pacific.

Political relationships between the Mau and New Zealand were in crisis from 1929 to 1935. A temporary improvement accompanied a change in the New Zealand government in 1935, but by the mid-1930s, the goal of the Mau was no longer simply the peaceful registration of complaints or the repeal of unpopular laws and policies. It was instead self-government for the islands. The actual demands of any one period varied between 1929 and 1941, and there was some internal debate about the best strategy to pursue. Given the overall colonial situation and the Samoans' successful resistance, the depression, and World War II, there was a long period of marking time waiting for political opportunity. A major consideration was having firm leadership in place so that when the movement for self-government resumed, Samoans would be prepared.

ETHNICITY AND LAND UNDER NEW ZEALAND COLONIAL RULE

The political turmoil caused by the Mau and its aftermath drew attention to the role of the part-Europeans, but their status was already an issue that the New Zealand regime had addressed well before the Mau arose. Like the German administration before it, the new government was concerned with the rising number of part-Europeans. In 1920, a law was passed requiring all residents claiming European status to register. If a person had been classified as a Samoan but was not of "pure" Samoan descent, he or she could apply for European status by passing a reading test; the high court would then consider whether a change in legal status was in the individual's personal and the public's interest, and, where appropriate, place the person on the European register. The chief advantages to such a change were social status and legal and political privilege.

Just as under the Germans, the part-European population grew under the New Zealanders. Self-identified part-Europeans, often unregistered, were becoming numerically significant. They were the most rapidly growing segment of the population, and their power in and around Apia was a source of concern both to colonial administrators and to Samoans. However, the part-Europeans of the 1920s were not a cohesive group in political or economic terms. Although some were affluent and influential, owning land and trading companies, most were poor and actively discriminated against. Their image among the colonial administrators was as negative as it had been in the late 19th century. As one high-ranking New Zealand official stated:

Half-castes form the great social problem of the country; their number rapidly increases
. . . they are almost without exception unemployable except in low grades of work. It is
apparent that the problem of the half-caste will become increasingly acute, and a class of
poor half-castes already in existence and growing in number will develop and exist on the
borderline of extreme poverty – a menace alike to the Samoan and the European. At
present food is plentiful and living easy, but as the population grows and brings about
economic pressure the position of the half-caste is not enviable.

I cannot suggest a remedy for this. It would not be fair to the Samoan in whose
interests the islands are governed and the preservation of whose race is considered to be
our duty, to give the half-caste the same status as the native with regard to land. On the
other hand, the half-caste can never be expected to rise as a class to the ordinary European level. . . . The half-caste must be left to sink to his own level in the scale of humanity and become in time a hewer of wood and a drawer of water for the rest of the community (Keesing 1934: 463).

A major problem was that most urban-based part-Europeans were landless,
and they could not obtain Samoan land, which was inalienable. Most land was
in Samoan hands; there was also Crown land or Reparations Estates, the former
being largely German plantations that the colonial government had taken over
to help Samoans. There was also a third land tenure system, freehold land on
which private commercial plantations were located, including part-European
plantations.

If landless part-Europeans were to get land, the government would have to
make it available from the Reparations Estates. During the 1920s and early
1930s, the New Zealand regime refused to consider part-European petitions for
leasing land on the Reparations Estates. Samoans were favoured, and most
part-Europeans were viewed as undesirable. But in the 1930s, there was a policy change that allowed part-Europeans continuous leasehold rights to some
Crown land. The first leases were given in 1939. Large blocks of government
land also were granted to Samoan villages to improve village agriculture. By the
late New Zealand colonial period, roughly 8 per cent of the islands' land was
freehold land, a small but proportionate percentage in relation to the part-
European population that held it. This land would become more significant
after independence.

ETHNICITY AND ECONOMY AT MID-CENTURY

As World War II came to an end, there had been a period of political calm for
10 years. The war had led to greater prosperity for Samoans because of the
American presence, and to a great extent, it marked the end of the large foreign-
owned plantations, which continued to be run by New Zealand for the benefit of
the Samoans. The production of copra and cocoa – agricultural staples of the

export trade – was gradually shifting to Samoans who grew these crops on communal land, including small-scale commercial ventures. Bananas were another village-grown economic bright spot in the 1950s. The distribution and export of these staples, however, remained in the hands of Europeans, part-Europeans, and international trading firms.

Although Samoans had been drawn increasingly into the cash economy as primary agricultural producers, the economic niche they occupied was still controlled by a small urban élite. As previously noted, most part-Europeans were not members of the élite. In fact, at midcentury there was much cultural diversity even among part-Europeans with "European" status. As Davidson, who knew the community well, commented:

There were few things that could be said, for example, about all the members of the local European community. They possessed in common their separate legal status, a general tendency to wear European dress, and a fairly general – though not universal – ability to speak the English language. But, in almost all other respects, they were characterised by wide differences of background, of interest and outlook. Most were, in fact, part-European by descent; but, since the essential requisite for the possession of European status was to be partly of non-Samoan descent (in accordance with a complex and curious legal definition of the term "Samoan"), some were Chinese-Samoan and a few others of different but also wholly non-European origins. Among the European ancestors of the part-Europeans, the largest numbers had been British or German; but Americans and Danes, Frenchmen and Swiss and persons of other European nationalities had also settled in the country. Many of the local European families had been established in Samoa for several generations, some for almost a century. The national origins of many of them had thus become, through intermarriage, extremely complex. For similar reasons, some local Europeans were of predominantly Samoan descent, some half-Samoan and a small proportion predominantly European. Many – particularly among the better educated – prided themselves on retaining the full rights of citizens or nationals of the country from which the founder of their family had come. A fair number had, in fact, retained such rights. Many others, however, were merely cherishing an illusion; and these, like the Samoans, possessed the national status of British protected persons (1967: 194–95).

Just as earlier in the century there was an economic diversity of occupations and income levels among part-Europeans, ranging from well-to-do business families who moved comfortably in international circles through families who were less prosperous and less well-connected but who were nevertheless upwardly mobile. A larger group of part-Europeans were shop assistants and lower-level civil servants, and there were still others whose economic status was more marginal. The economic and social divisions among part-Europeans and various divisions between them and the Samoans were sources of frustration and resentment.

Amidst this diversity, though, the dominance of the large firms in the port town continued. Based on his work in the early 1960s, David Pitt found what seems to be an influential European and part-European *class* with commonly articulated interests:

The most important reasons for failure or low profits (by Samoans) result from the monopolistic position of the big firms in Apia who ultimately control the buying and selling of most goods and many services. . . . The big firms are able to perpetuate this monopoly by excluding Samoans from the European social group. This social group is an important reason, in fact, for the part-European and European success (1970: 259).

Furthermore, this economic élite engaged in discriminatory practices, as referred to by Pitt:

Many overseas Europeans and local part-Europeans tolerate a handful of high ranking Samoans or Samoans who stay "in their place," i.e., in the village. But they intensely dislike and actively discriminate against Samoans and other Polynesians or Melanesians who aspire to urban residence. There is little the Europeans can do to stop Samoans acquiring the outward signs and symbols of European life if the Samoans have the money to purchase goods. But Europeans can, and do, restrict other forms of communication (1970: 184).

Samoans were further constrained by the nature of credit available to them. Small-time traders offered Samoans credit at high interest rates. As Pitt explained:

Many of these traders and money-lenders are considered credit-worthy by the trading bank and are able to borrow money at around a 6 per cent interest rate, which is promptly lent to Samoans at interest rates of between 15 and 80 per cent. Again many Samoans, especially those dependent upon a fluctuating cash crop income, are forced to pledge their season's crops to traders and storekeepers at even higher interest rates. The result of this credit dependence on high interest, unofficial sources is indebtedness, defaulting, and possibly the origin of the myth that Samoans are not credit-worthy (1970: 211).

Samoan capital formation was also discouraged by credit practices that favoured consumption activities instead of capital investment. Pitt notes:

The traders, or at least the back-street or village traders who always give credit, concentrate on the sale of consumer luxuries. Much capital equipment, especially the more expensive technological capital, can only be acquired from larger merchants or the Government who are very much more reluctant to give credit. . . . Many Samoans feel that if capital formation is not possible, any savings should be used directly to secure status through ceremonial disbursement. "If I cannot get a ladder to pick all the breadfruit on the tree, I will stand and pluck the lower branches," as one chief put it (1970: 211–12).

Most Samoans were thus effectively excluded from large-scale, capital-intensive ventures. Exceptions such as Va'al Kolone have been cited in the literature, but they were not typical.

While the economic relationships of the colonial period were modified to some extent over a century between the 1850s and 1960s, the fundamental structure of the agricultural export economy and ethnic stratification remained intact. Perhaps as important as the agricultural economy in maintaining ethnic stratification was the development of the civil service bureaucracy. At midcentury, most of the top-ranking civil servants in the colonial government were Europeans and part-Europeans. With the public-service sector providing many of the wage labour opportunities in Western Samoa, bicultural and bilingual part-Europeans had employment advantages over most Samoans. The New Zealand regime had specifically favoured them for these positions since the mid-1930s. A cursory review of top-ranking servants during this period suggests a part-European role in government akin to their role in commerce. Within the first half of the 20th century, several part-Europeans had become part of an important class within the New Zealand colony. Most other part-Europeans of lower socio-economic status were part of a category, recognised by Samoans and Europeans, as below the élite but above most Samoans.

INDEPENDENCE AND CITIZENSHIP

With the promise of independence following World War II, the United Nations and New Zealand began carefully to investigate economic conditions in the islands. One of the first of Western Samoa's postwar observers, W. E. H. Stanner, reported that the basic tools for assessing the state of the economy – a reliable census and economic survey – were lacking. More disturbingly, he noted that while the territory was politically quite advanced, according to the available economic evidence, it would have to be put "in a subclass so 'backward' that the problem is still one of creating most of the conditions precedent to development" (Stanner 1953: 409).

As information became available through policy-oriented studies conducted in the 1950s (Stace 1956; Fox 1962), it was generally agreed that Western Samoa could face increasing economic hardship in future decades. Although some observers emphasised population constraints on development (Pirie and Barrett 1962) and others emphasised social and institutional barriers (Ala'ilima and Ala'ilima 1965), there was a broad consensus as to the underdeveloped state of the economy. However, at this time, little economic planning could be done, and there was very little that could be contemplated in terms of altering the system of ethnic stratification. A recommendation to "Samoanise" the public service in the 1950s was implemented at a glacial pace.

The political realm was more amenable to change. Independence would insure Samoan governance of a new nation. The task would not be an easy one, though, since it called for the dismantling of the moribund New Zealand colonial administration, including the Department of Samoan Affairs, and the framing of a new constitution, the structuring of a parliament that would adequately represent Samoans and part-Europeans, and the defining of citizenship itself.

Throughout the colonial period, racial categories had provided a system of differential privileges. The very terms Samoan (or "Native") and European formed the legal basis of discrimination in many areas of society. In the late 1940s and early 1950s, as the legislative groundwork for an independent Western Samoa was being laid, Samoan legislators discussed obvious examples of discrimination. Not only were there differential economic opportunities and different land tenure systems for the different groups, there were also different wage scales, different schools, different courts, and different hospital wards assigned on the basis of race. During legislative discussions, past reasons of differential privileges were aired and there was discussion of practices applicable to Samoans but not Europeans. For example, although the Department of Samoan Affairs would allow the Samoan custom of banishment for certain village crimes, this punishment could not be applied to Europeans.

The existing racial system of legal categories was obstructing progress toward a uniform definition of Samoan citizenship. In his role as constitutional adviser in the independence process, Davidson hoped to develop a common domestic status for both Samoans and part-Europeans, believing that it was not only desirable, but necessary, to abolish racial distinctions before self-governance. Such divisions had led to resentment in the past, and future relations would not be helped by the preservation of this colonial legacy. Unity was to be the watchword of decolonisation, and "Samoanisation" the desired trend.

The key issues in the legal transformation of racial categories were suffrage and representation. As the legislative efforts toward independence proceeded in the 1950s, these issues were discussed at length. Universal suffrage for all of Western Samoa's future citizens was promoted by several Samoan representatives, just as more traditional views emphasising exclusive suffrage for titleholders or *matai* were also articulated. The existing composition of the legislature, which consisted of 41 Samoan, 5 "European," and 2 official members, acted as a brake on a more universal conception of suffrage and representation. A similar brake in the consideration of head of state also assisted in the maintenance of the *status quo*.

The result was that part-European and Samoan representation and suffrage remained separate. In independent Western Samoa, all citizens would have voting rights, but there would be two different voting rolls. There would be a district roll corresponding to the Samoan territorial seats of the past and an individual voter roll corresponding to the part-European seats. In theory, ethnic categories had been abolished, but in practice there would be 45 district seats representing the 100,000 Samoans under *matai* suffrage at that time and two individual seats representing about 6,000 part-Europeans, voting individually.

In 1957, a preview of the new parliamentary system occurred when the new assembly met in November. Fully half of the Samoan representatives were political novices in national politics, including some successful Samoan planters, businessmen, and public servants. More "modern" Samoans were seeking representation in the legislature. At the same time, some part-Europeans were becoming more "traditional," taking Samoan names and titles, being represented through district rolls, and being elected to serve as district representatives. This cross-over phenomenon was not a political idiosyncrasy.

Opting for Samoan status had been a legal possibility for many citizens who were part-European, although it was historically rare. The changing of ethnic identity for legal purposes had been going on since the inception of German rule at the turn of the 20th century. During the German and New Zealand regimes, legal and economic circumstances favoured part-European status, and so their numbers increased. The reverse was also possible. Under New Zealand rule, part-Europeans with European status could elect to become Samoans, but very few had done so "because of a reluctance to yield the prestige and other associations of the former status, and some of those who have tried have had their status reversed again" (Keesing and Keesing 1956: 199 ff.). However, as independence for Western Samoa approached, being Samoan no longer meant being a second-class citizen.

The new law concerning citizenship in independent Western Samoa was phrased in such a way that a person could not hold individual and district status simultaneously. Any individual voter could be disenrolled if he or she exercised "any privilege in relation to a *matai* title or to Samoan land or to a person who was doing so" (Davidson 1967: 378). The explicit, long-term objective of this policy was to gradually assimilate part-Europeans so that they would become "more Samoan." The policy was ratified by vote in 1960, when the new constitution was overwhelmingly accepted. A substantial proportion of part-Europeans (20 per cent to 35 per cent in the Apia area) voted against the constitution and independence, fearing that independence would harm the economy, that their personal position might worsen, that they would be unable to migrate to New Zealand in the future, that there would be no universal suffrage, and that New Zealand might cut off foreign aid to Western Samoa. Nevertheless, the new order was clearly favoured by most part-Europeans and Samoans.

Some influential part-Europeans understood the political opportunities in the new order. In the new Parliament elected in 1961, the effects of the assimilationist policy became even more apparent as several part-Europeans were elected as members of Parliament on the district rolls. They had become, for political purposes, Samoans:

Nine of the members elected by territorial constituencies had formerly possessed European status, including two who had sat in previous assemblies as European members and one who had served as head of a government department (Davidson 1967: 425).

In a by-election later that year, a tenth part-European member was added, so that when independence arrived in 1962, almost 25 per cent of the assembly had a part-European background. The new constitution had not hindered part-European political participation at all, but instead had channelled it into new forms of representation, and this pattern has continued and increased to the present. The consequence of assimilationist policy was to increase parliamentary representation of part-Europeans who had formerly been individual voters. To the extent these members of the legislature retained previous economic interests, their contribution to the legislative process did not hamper part-European interests in commerce and public service.

But assimilationist policy did not lead to most part-Europeans becoming Samoans. The shift was confined to a very small segment of the part-European élite. Ths rest of the part-European population who were legally registered as individual voters retained that status. Although politically significant, integration of Samoans and Europeans has been largely limited to the élite; most extended family members of part-European legislators who have taken Samoan titles have kept their individual voting status. Indeed, far from assimilating, individual voters have grown rapidly in numbers since independence, as table 2 indicates. Because the number of seats in the legislature for individual voters is regulated by a formula that allows for more seats as the number of individual voters increases, if the present trend continues, individual voters will add one more seat within the next 20 years, possibly earlier. If this happens, the persistence of individual voter status and, by implication, part-European separateness will be highlighted, even though the occasionally acknowledged political influence of part-Europeans who have become Samoan legislators is more important.

Table 2. Individual voters registered for general elections, 1960–1985

1960	829
1964	1,230
1967	1,285
1970	1,329
1973	1,376
1976	1,432
1979	1,307
1982	1,702
1985	2,023

Source: Register of Electors and Voters.

THE POSTCOLONIAL ERA

Although the electoral process had increased élite integration between Samoans and part-Europeans, leading to greater political homogeneity on the surface, it did not make governance easier. The late 1970s and 1980s was a period of political unease and difficulty; the Western Samoan economy also entered a period of deepening crisis at this time. Concomitant with these changes, there was an internal weakening of the *matai* system. To increase the number of *matai* that could elect a representative, families began splitting titles, undermining the traditional criteria for titleholding. New titleholders were younger and had fewer rights over the control of land and family labour. Tim O'Meara (1986) found that by 1984, nearly 70 per cent of all male Samoans 25 years or older held titles, double the percentage of 30 years earlier.

A near-universal franchise for adult Samoan males had been nominally achieved by the mid-1980s, but at the expense of the *matai* system itself. As O'Meara stated:

Today, these titles are losing their contemporary power and material importance, leaving only prestige based on historical legacy, and simple paternal dominance. Without a foundation of real power, the lingering prestige of the *matai* is likely to diminish further (1986: 144).

The major reason for the increase in titles and weakening of the system was the law restricting Samoan suffrage. O'Meara notes:

The main cause of the proliferation of *matai* titles is undoubtedly the law that restricts voting in parliamentary elections to *matai*. Because of this law, political candidates often strive to appoint as many new *matai* as possible among their supporters. It is now common for politically united families to create dozens, even scores of new titleholders in preparation for an election. . . . Influential Samoans now widely abuse these traditional prerogatives for political gain, and it is the most honoured, highest status *matai* who lead the way (1986: 136).

In 1982, title-splitting violations led to the ouster of a prime minister and the questioning of other election results.

The character of district elections also changed during the 1970s and 1980s. The election of *matai* to the national legislature was ideally supposed to represent family, district, and rural Samoan interests. However, Samoans and part-Europeans who were elected tended to come from the ranks of the urban-oriented, better-educated, politically well-connected, and economically affluent. Urban dwellers were running for rural seats. Furthermore, as Meleisea and Schoefel (1983: 99) observe, the merchant community in Apia was able to wield influence through financial contributions to *matai* in the district constituencies who could represent their interests. National party formation, an incipient trend, is also very likely to perpetuate the interests of the political and economic élite.

The cost of standing for election can be very high, ranging into the tens of thousands of dollars per candidate. Election "presentations" or gifts to constituents by a standing member of the Parliament can reach as high as 100 kegs of beef, 100 cases of tinned fish, S$1,000, and many fine mats per village, there being several villages in each district (*Samoa Times*, 4 January 1985). Potential abuses were so serious that a ban of these presentations went into effect in 1984. Occasions on which such presentations could be made, such as weddings and title installations, were also banned for the period just before elections. Nevertheless, the cost of political candidacy remains high and favours the well-to-do.

Trends in land ownership also tended to strengthen the economic position of wealthy part-Europeans and urban-based *matai*. In the 1970s, urbanisation increased pressure on land in and around Apia. The declining economic fortunes of the Reparations Estates (or WESTEC) led the government to sell off parcels of this and to offset the WESTEC debt. Other freehold land was also being sold. Since the value of freehold land had increased dramatically because of its strategic location and extreme scarcity, when the new parcels were sold off, they could be purchased only by those who already owned freehold land and could mortgage it and those who were commercially or financially successful. That is, mainly only the wealthy part-European, urban-based *matai* and overseas immigrants could afford the land.

P. Thomas has summarised these long-term economic and political trends as follows:

Considerable changes are taking place in the distribution of wealth and access to political power. . . . As the village agricultural and economic situation declined and as many high ranking, politically important *matai* moved to Apia, the locus and base of power shifted. Simultaneous with the urbanisation of the political elite, many urban part-Samoans strengthened their identification with indigenous Samoan culture and, while maintaining a European life-style, activated links with their Samoan families and in time accepted *matai* titles, foregoing their rights as individual voters. This allowed them to stand for election in the constituency from which they derived their title and gave them a numerically greater opportunity of election. It also provided the opportunity for more part-Samoans to be represented in parliament. Bestowing titles on the economically influential provided mutual benefits. The *aiga* gained access to cash and goods and the new *matai* access to the status and rank that has traditionally been necessary for political success. A *matai* also gained access, should he wish to achieve it, not only to the family lands pertaining to his title, but also the family labour force, while he could direct to work where he chose.

Although these events seem to be leading toward a more homogeneous society with greater urban-rural linkages and a more equitable distribution of assets between urban and rural families, this has not yet emerged. Political and economic power is aggregating to an urban elite comprising a disproportionately larger number of part-Samoans who not only control inherited freehold land and business interests but have also achieved integration into the traditional system, with its specific political advantages. As values change, rank is less important than wealth in determining status and authority (1984: 17–19).

Apart from these changes, there was a formidable challenge to the two-constituency electoral system itself. In 1982, a challenge was brought by several part-Europeans to the Electoral Act of 1963. A politically active individual voter, Georgina Moore, was deprived of her individual voting status after her husband had taken a *matai* title. Although this action was legal under the assimilationist policy, it seemed to contradict another law that guaranteed equality and protection for all citizens under the law. The ensuing lawsuit went to the Supreme Court and was heard on appeal in different forums. An early decision by a New Zealand judge called for abolition of the two-constituency system and establishment of a universal suffrage for all Samoan citizens, male and female, over the age of 21. This opinion was overruled in late 1982 by three judges from New Zealand. They recommended that Samoans over 21 should vote, but that candidacy be restricted to *matai*. This recommendation was narrowly defeated in the Western Samoan parliament, leaving the earlier system in place. Some legislators felt that universal suffrage could lead to an even further erosion of the district constituencies.

The nature of Western Samoan citizenship itself was raised as an issue in another volatile context during the overstayer crisis in New Zealand, also in 1982. By the 1980s, more than 40,000 Western Samoans were living in New Zealand, most on a permanent basis; by then, almost a quarter of the Western Samoan population resided in New Zealand, with thousands of others living in American Samoa, the United States, and Australia. Foreign citizenship, or at least access to other countries, had become economically vital for Samoans, including those remaining in the islands, since remittances sent or brought back constituted a large percentage of both national and personal income. Although most Samoans overseas were legal migrants, some temporary migrants to New Zealand had overstayed their visas and were defined as illegal aliens. During the first overstayer crisis of 1976, Samoans were threatened with deportation, or they were actually deported. But in the second crisis of 1982, a Samoan woman appealed her deportation, and the Privy Council of the United Kingdom ruled that Samoans born between 1924 and 1949 and their children were New Zealand citizens.

Had this ruling been implemented, thousands of Western Samoans would have left for New Zealand; there were already long waiting lists for visas well before the crisis. But before further migration could take place, New Zealand curtailed temporary visas and threatened to restrict other visa allocations for Western Samoans. The New Zealand government and public were quite hostile to the idea of New Zealand citizenship for most Western Samoans. Under New Zealand pressure, representatives of the two governments promptly signed a protocol that disallowed the right of immediate New Zealand citizenship for the Western Samoans in question, while allowing overstayers the opportunity of citizenship. Thousands of Samoans in Western Samoa and New Zealand protested the protocol, but to no avail.

Although the crisis passed, it was another reminder of just how fragile the notion of citizenship was for Western Samoans and how their relationship with the wider world could be a significant determinant of their legal status. At independence, the meaning of Western Samoan citizenship seemed clearly defined and secure. Within two decades, this was no longer the case because ethnicity overseas had become a factor in the islands' political economy.

CONCLUSION

On the eve of independence for Western Samoa, constitutional planners anticipated an internal reduction in the legal and political salience of ethnic categories. In a limited sense, this has occurred. As in the Caribbean, there has been ethnic integration among the élite. Moreover, the categories formerly used to identify ethnic differences did not even appear in the 1976 and 1981 censuses. Yet, part-Europeans have not stopped living part-European life-styles and identifying themselves politically as part-Europeans. Nor have Samoans, who increasingly live part-European life-styles, stopped identifying themselves as Samoans. What has happened is that with independence, Samoan culture has become the dominant political idiom. For part-Europeans to overtly contest Samoan political and cultural hegemony would be counter-productive. The electoral and citizenship crisis of the early 1980s did not challenge Samoan political and cultural hegemony directly, nor were they perceived as doing so. Instead, part-Europeans and Samoans have adapted to new circumstances with part-Europeans preserving their economic interests in an occasionally problematic accommodation.

As the political system changed following independence, giving Samoans more power and overt representation, so did the economy. During the 1960s, 1970s, and 1980s, the new nation's economy moved from an agricultural foundation to one based on a mix of agriculture, remittances, and foreign aid. There has been greater urbanization, and cash incomes outside of agriculture have increased. Samoans are more visible in the economy. Yet the *structure* of the economy has not changed markedly; it has merely become more complex. Although the political and social orders have been modernized, part-Europeans, Europeans, and international interests have remained in control of the commercial economy, with government involvement increasing and often complementing the private sector. And while independence fostered a pragmatic political amalgam of wealth and power for both Samoans and part-Europeans, the emerging "neotraditionalist" political culture has not been able to reduce the pressing problems of economic decline (Nakata 1982). In this context, the "Samoanization" of a colonial social and political system has not led to solutions to the problems of underdevelopment in contemporary Western Samoa.

During the first half of the 20th century, Samoan ethnicity was successfully mobilized for political resistance and nation-building and was mobilized again in 1982 during the immigration crises. But it will be difficult to mobilize ethnicity for genuine economic development given the kinds of external dependency that Western Samoa is enmeshed in and given a class system that employs tradition as a metaphor in political and economic life. The past century of Western Samoan history suggests that although ethnicity may be a valuable resource in some situations, it is also changeable and negotiable as political and economic circumstances vary. Thus, ethnicity is not necessarily a permanent, primordial state of being (Patterson 1975), nor has it been in Western Samoa.

ACKNOWLEDGEMENTS

I am indebted to several colleagues for sharing their knowledge of Western Samoa and the South Pacific with me, including Cluny Macpherson, Pamela Thomas, Michael Howard, Michael Bellam, John Connel, and Martin Kleis. Tim O'Meara provided valuable comments on an earlier draft of this paper. These individuals are not, however, responsible for the contents of this paper.

NOTES

1. Finney's work in Tahiti (1970) uses this same perspective. Some of the historical framework for this essay is drawn from Shankman (1976).
2. Among the best reviews of the Chinese in Western Samoa are Haynes (1965) and Tom (1986). The Melanesians are the subject of Meleisea's short book (1980). The most useful early histories of the part-European population are found in Davidson (1967), Gilson (1970), and Keesing (1934), and I have drawn heavily on these sources. Malama Meleisea's forthcoming Ph.D. dissertation contains a chapter on part-Europeans that will provide additional data on this influential minority.

REFERENCES

Ala'ilima, V., and F. Ala'ilima. 1965. Samoan values and economic development. *East-West Center Review* 1(3): 3–18.

Census Commissioner's Office. 1968. *Population census of Western Samoa.* Volume I. Apia, Western Samoa.

Davidson, J. W. 1967. *Samoa mo Samoa: The emergence of the independent state of Western Samoa.* Melbourne: Oxford University Press.

Department of Statistics. 1972. *The report of the survey of household living conditions in Western Samoa, 1971–1972.* Apia: Department of Statistics, Western Samoa. Mimeograph.

Field, Michael J. 1984. *Mau: Samoa's struggle against New Zealand oppression.* Wellington: A. H. and A. W. Reed.

Finney, B. 1970. Race and class in the Society Islands of French Polynesia. In *Proceedings of the 7th International Congress of Anthropological and Ethnological Sciences* 9. Moscow: Academy of Sciences.

Fox, J. W. 1962. Population and settlement. In *Western Samoa: Land, life and agriculture in tropical Polynesia,* edited by J. W. Fox and K. B. Cumberland, 130–76. Christchurch: Whitcomb and Tombs.

Gilson, R. P. 1970. *Samoa 1830 to 1900: The politics of a multi-cultural community.* Melbourne: Oxford University Press.

Haynes, D. R. 1965. *Chinese indentured labour in Western Samoa 1900–1950.* M. A. thesis, Victoria, University of Wellington.

Hempstall, P., and N. Rutherford. 1984. Protest and dissent in the colonial Pacific. Suva: Institute for Pacific Studies, University of the South Pacific.

Keesing, F. 1934. *Modern Samoa.* Stanford: Stanford University Press.

Keesing, F., and M. Keesing. 1956. *Elite communication in Samoa: A study of leadership.* Stanford: Stanford University Press.

Lewthwaite, G. 1962. Land, life and agriculture to mid-century. In *Western Samoa: Land, life and agriculture in tropical Polynesia,* edited by J. W. Fox and K. B. Cumberland, 130–76. Christchurch: Whitcomb and Tombs.

Meleisea, M. 1980. *O Tama Uli: Melanesians in Samoa.* Suva: Institute of Pacific Studies, University of the South Pacific.

Meleisea, M., and P. Schoeffel. 1983. Western Samoa: "Like a Slippery Fish." In *Politics in Polynesia,* edited by R. Crocombe and A. Ali, 81–114. Suva: Institute of Pacific Studies, University of the South Pacific.

Nakata, K. 1982. The costs of fa'a Samoa political culture's complementarity with the modern world system. In *The Politics of Evolving Cultures in the Pacific Islands,* 321–57. Laie: Institute for Polynesian Studies, Brigham Young University.

O'Meara, J. T. 1986. *Why is village agriculture stagnating? A test of social and economic explanations in Western Samoa.* Ph.D. diss., University of California, Santa Barbara.

Patterson, O. 1975. Context and choice in ethnic allegiance: A theoretical framework and Caribbean case study. In *Ethnicity: Theory and experience,* edited by N. Glazer and D. Moynihan, 305–49. Cambridge: Harvard University Press.

Pirie, P., and W. Barrett. 1962. Population, production and wealth. *Pacific Viewpoint* 3: 63–96.

Pitt, D. 1970. *Tradition and economic progress in Samoa: A case study of the role of traditional social institutions in economic development.* Oxford: Clarendon Press.

Shankman, P. 1976. *Migration and underdevelopment: The case of Western Samoa.* Boulder: Westview Press.

Stace, V. D. 1956. *Western Samoa – An economic survey.* Noumea: South Pacific Commission, Technical Report No. 21.

Stanner, W. E. H. 1953. *The South Seas in transition*. Sydney: Australasian.

Thomas, P. 1984. *Society, land and law: Land policy in Western Samoa*. Manuscript.

Tom, Y. W. 1986. *The Chinese in Western Samoa 1875–1985*. Apia, Western Samoa: Western Samoa Historical and Cultural Trust.

11

Ethnicity and Nation-building: The Papua New Guinea Case

RALPH R. PREMDAS

Papua New Guinea (PNG) is a small, multiethnic state in the south-west Pacific and inhabited by about 3 million people. It shares the island of New Guinea with Irian Jaya, which is an Indonesian province. PNG became independent in 1975 after six decades of colonial control by Australia. The Melanesian peoples of PNG speak about 715 languages and live in small-scale, decentralised communities. In its task of national development, the PNG government faces formidable difficulties of disunity, much of this derived from its ethnolinguistic and ethnoregional fragmentation. Colonial control imported both new ethnic vertical cleavages and horizontal class formations (see Howard et al. 1983). Especially after World War II, the country was dramatically transformed as Australia, in hurried frenzy, pumped millions of dollars into the economy to prepare for self-government (Brookfield 1972). Large numbers of Papua New Guineans were caught up in this radical transformation process that would modify and recast their ethnic and class identities. From a simple traditional society, a complex and highly differentiated social and economic order had emerged. Ethnic claims to new identities, malleable and improvised, became pervasive, serving as defence mechanisms and stabilisers in a turbulently changing world. The ethnic dimension emerged as a salient prism through which most development efforts were interpreted and directed. In some instances, the ethnic factor became a formidable force in defining national issues and allocating scarce resources.

In the decade or so since independence in 1975, what have become of development and identity in PNG's ethnicised environment? Has ethnicity retarded or facilitated desired social goals? Has the ethnic dimension in intergroup relations been modified by class cleavages? Can ethnic identity be superseded by class claims? Or does it overwhelm and reshape class? Or do the two factors coexist, each asserting its separate pre-eminence in different circumstances? Clearly, the interface between ethnicity and class raises a fierce volley of vexing questions and issues. For the student of Marxist analysis, other critical questions are also germane (Bonacich 1980). Is ethnicity a reactionary and destructive force *vis-à-vis* the task of nation-building? Is ethnicity a primitive phase in development that will be superceded eventually by other social and economic relations as PNG moves towards fuller capitalist maturity? Is ethnicity only a capitalist phenomenon that will in time wither away with the state? In this chapter, only a few of these questions will be investigated; others will be touched on briefly. My concern will be focused more especially on the issues of ethnic formation under colonial rule, the emergence of an ethnic map, and the general effect of ethnicity on nation-building. On the larger canvass, I shall seek to address the issue related to public policy: Can the PNG experience be generalised both practically and theoretically? I shall begin by a brief discussion of the key concepts: ethnicity, nation-building, and class.

NATION-BUILDING, ETHNICITY, AND CLASS

Political scientists use the term "nation-building" in a specific way, usually in contradistinction to "state-building." The latter term points to the problem of establishing authority and control, penetrative bureaucracies, and security forces. State-building, then, has a regulatory aspect about it and is usually connected with extracting resources and exacting compliant behaviour. Nation-building, on the other hand, refers to the moulding of a common set of outlooks, orientations, and loyalties towards an integrated national community. The task of nation-building in this context is to recast the particularistic and parochial orientations of the subgroups in the multiethnic state so that a new unifying consciousness and commitment is erected around national symbols, myths, and aspirations. What is wrong with the political scientist's definition of nation-building is that it suggests that the task is value-free and is a mere technical exercise. What is often true is that it tends to conceal Western modes of nation-building fashioned from European history. Every definition of nation-building implicitly or explicitly embodies values and institutions. PNG, for instance, is a facsimile of the European state that embodied an institutional freight of a parliamentary system, such as Western laws, courts, and bureaucratic practices.

A few years before independence, an opportunity was offered to PNG leaders to design a framework of government reflecting local ways and interests. The task was entrusted to a Constitutional Planning Committee (CPC), which propounded a blueprint for nation-building and national transformation (Final Report 1974). Called the eight-point development programme, it was passed by the PNG parliament in March 1973; the ideas contained in it promised a significant disjunction from the past. The eight aims included policies on localisation, more equal distribution of economic benefits, decentralisation of government activities, reliance on small-scale business activity, a more self-

reliant economy, equal participation of women in all forms of activity, and government control of strategic sectors of the economy. If PNG could implement
even a small but sizable part of these aims, it would achieve a sharp break with
a colonial legacy of inequality, uneven development, discrimination, centralised
bureaucratic domination, and embedded economic dependence. In the end,
when the eight-point programme was implemented, it was anticipated to lead to
"integral human development, liberation, and fulfilment of every citizen, so
that each man and woman will have the opportunity in improving himself or
herself as a whole person and achieving integral human development" (Final
Report 1974: 21). This was the fundamental aim of nation-building in PNG; it
was incorporated into the country's constitution. Further, it prescribed that
"true nation-building can only come through the active and meaningful involvement of people in their own development" (Final Report 1974: 1–3).

Standing between the aims of nation-building and their actualisation are
many hurdles, including one that is as formidable as it is intractable: ethnicity
and ethnic fragmentation. PNG is a multiethnic state suffused by discrete sub-
state ethnonationalist entities, each representing its claims as a terminal community. A larger PNG consciousness that transcends ethnic particularism is
still to evolve. Ethnic identities have proliferated, and their pervasiveness has
inserted a major parameter in social planning. Public policy aimed at nation-
building must be refracted through the ethnic prism.

Ethnicity can be analytically conceived to contain two dimensions: objective
and subjective. In this chapter, ethnicity is defined as a sense of collective consciousness (the subjective factor) shared by a group whose members may also
be bound by a common language, religion, region, values, etc. (the objective
factors). The objective factors may be fictional, but because group members
perceive them to be factual, this imparts solidarity to a group's activities. It is
the subjective factor, the beliefs of group members, that serve the critical function of establishing group identity, uniqueness, and boundaries. Most groups in
competition or conflict with others develop collective ethnic consciousness. Despite ethnic group loyalties, ethnic group boundaries are notoriously unstable
and tend to change and be manipulated over time and even situationally. In
PNG, all persons are carriers of multiple ethnic identities.

Since colonial contact with the peoples of PNG, an ethnic map has emerged
around artificial administrative boundaries and townships. Hence, there are
Chimbus, Tolais, Madangs, Sepiks, North Solomon Islanders, Motus, Waghis,
and Engas. The same person may be a Hanuabadan at one level of organisation
and a Papua at another, with each entity converting friends to enemies in different contexts. These are colonial tags that have become literally alive in governing intergroup relations. Thus, the word *wantok* need not refer only to a kins-
person who shares a *ples tok*, or village language, but it can embrace others
sharing common economic, geographical, and even political boundaries. In
PNG, people relate to one another through what the late Sevese Morea

called their "ethnic belly button." During the colonial period in PNG, not only were large numbers of ethnic groups formed, but in relation to privileges, power, and prejudices, an emergent informal hierarchy stratifies their relative significance.

Colonial contact did not spawn only new ethnic identities in PNG, but it also stimulated new socioeconomic formations. In the colonial order, Europeans were occupants of privileged positions and owners of productive assets. Papua New Guineans were subordinate persons in the employment of colonial authorities and settlers. Europeans acquired land by dubious methods and established plantations on which they recruited PNG villagers to serve as indentured labourers (Rowley 1965). The labour indenture system, carried out extensively over PNG for a prolonged period, would commence the dramatic disruption and decay of PNG social systems. A monetised economy was established, and qualitatively new instrumental material definitions in interpersonal evaluations were implanted. The new extensive monetised order was a capitalist system that progressively integrated all Papua New Guineans into a common grid of economic relations. Whereas language, culture, and topography divided the population, the emergent capitalist economy with the money medium, profit motive, and materialist quest would unify the socially fragmented system in a network of producers and consumers, workers, and owners. If ethnicity was pervasive and divisive, the monetised economy was equally powerful in forging new definitions of self around property and employment. In effect, the influence of capitalism and the money market would create incipient horizontal economic cleavages and formations, in contradistinction to vertical divisions pertaining to ethnic bonds. In the personal lives of Papua New Guineans, class and ethnic identities would periodically collide. The evidence is becoming abundant that dissonance and ambivalence created by competing class and ethnic loyalties are growing in PNG, especially in urban areas, where second- and third-generation Papua New Guineans lose their intimate links with their villages. But just how far the clash has gone in influencing behaviour is unknown.

The question of class defined as a relationship between wage and capital raises fundamental issues about liberation and integral human development in PNG's quest to build a nation. Is the persistence of terminal assertive ethnic communities antithetical to equality and freedom? Is there any consistency between ethnic pluralism and classless society? The framers of the PNG eightpoint programme did not sort out this problem. In fact, they spoke positively of both ethnic particularism and economic universalism in their vision of nationbuilding. They did not suggest that equality is inconsistent with capitalism or ethnonationalism. The eight-point programme is as poetically elegant as it is institutionally and ideologically obscure. In this situation, the chances are excellent that the state will flounder on its own ambivalences, in the end surrendering to the inherited capitalist institutions while merrily parroting the song of the eight-point programme.

COLONIALISM AND ETHNICITY: CREATION OF AN ETHNIC MAP

Before the conquest of PNG, the indigenous people lived in small, decentralised, economically self-sufficient communities. Members were bound by kinship connections, a common language, and communal landholdings. Except for a few places, PNG societies were meritocratic systems lacking highly differentiated Polynesian-type hierarchies. "Big men" acquired power and prestige by personal achievements; community decision-making was reached after discussion and consensus. Taken as a whole, the pre-contact map of PNG societies pointed to the proliferation of small-scale settlements with about 50 to 300 persons that were dispersed widely over the New Guinea archipelago, on the coast and inland alike. In the jargon of the anthropologist, PNG was a "stateless society." Linguistic diversity was expressed in more then 700 languages; personal identity was kinship and clan-based.

Colonial intrusion would radically transform the economy, polity, and society of PNG. All definitions of the pre-existing order were altered. This included definitions of the indigenous peoples: the creation of new ethnic formations, the assignment of new ethnic names, the delineation of new ethnic boundaries, the implanting of a new interethnic hierarchy, and the evolution of new stereotypical perceptions in intergroup relations. Colonialism entailed the forcible acquisition of indigenous land, the virtual enslavement of a people to provide cheap labour, the systematic extraction of resources, and the reshaping of the economy aimed at export production for foreign investor and imperial gain. Expatriate coffee, cocoa, coconut, and tea plantations were the main means of exploitation of external resources. The material foundations of the indigenous order were being altered with the introduction of cash crops, a large-scale monetised economy, and new technology.

To attain their ends, the colonial administrators, settlers, and missionaries superimposed a new social order with its own hierarchy of ethnic rankings. European values and ways were now the measure of excellence; the European occupied the top tier in the new order. Papua New Guineans, black and unfamiliar with European ways and called "kanakas," "manki," "boys," and "meri," were institutionally and permanently inferior in this scheme of things. Even when a Papua New Guinean acquired European education and acculturated to European ways, he or she was still inferior to any white person.

As a result of contact, a new ethnic differentiation (an ethnic map) would emerge among the indigenous tribes, reflecting the interests and activities of European traders and administrators. Papua New Guineans on the Papuan coast and New Guinea islands were the first "beneficiaries" of imported European values. They were first "civilised" and assigned the highest rung in the indigenous hierarchy. Over the period of colonial history, it was inevitable that coastal Papua and New Guinea islanders acquired most and the best jobs in government and business. In turn, this differentiated, endowed with unequal advantages, consolidated, and perpetuated the privileged positions of certain groups, planting the seeds of invidious interethnic jealousy of competition among Papua New Guineans. In the contemporary scene, these early ethnic divisions reverberate in demands for equal development, proportional representation in the public service, local autonomy, and even self-determination and continuous claims and counter-claims of discrimination and prejudice. It would be useful to sketch how some of these new ethnonationalist divisions were created by colonial practice.

The scramble for colonial territory by the Dutch, Germans, British, and Australians was insensitive to the patterns of indigenous cultural organisation. When New Guinea was colonised, imaginary longitude and latitude coordinates bearing no relationship to natural or social boundaries were drawn, dividing the island into two halves. The Dutch acquired the western half by this imaginary act in the 15th century. In the eastern sector of the island, colonial boundary demarcation would not be much different from that in the west. The British formally acquired the southern and south-eastern part of the island in 1884, calling it British New Guinea. At about the same time, the Germans laid claim to the nort-east section of the island, creating German New Guinea. The two imperial powers lacked precise information of the peoples and the terrain in their territorial areas. Like the Dutch in the west, the Germans and English used their imagination to delineate boundaries. In the scramble for territorial real estate, they unknowingly planted flags on each other's claims (Nelson 1972: 18).

From the scramble for territory and the indiscriminate process of boundary demarcation, the first new identities for Papua New Guineans would be fabricated. These colonial boundaries created "Papuans," embracing a diversity of peoples with the absurdity of the South Highlands included in the package; they would also create the category "New Guineans," which covered an area stretching from the New Guinea Highlands to the New Guinea islands and contained an even more diverse set of groups than in Papua. Papuan and New Guinean would remain as colonial artifacts. Although artificial, imported, and imposed, the peoples would develop collective attachment to these appellations over time. Social content would breathe life into these ethnic names. Stereotypical behavioural traits in antagonistic contradistinction to New Guineans would soon be ascribed to the Papuans (Premdas 1977b).

A Papuan identity, then, has emerged from colonial practice, reinforced by behavioural perceptions assigned to Papuans by others and which Papuans themselves have come to accept. Colonial practices have encouraged and fortified Papuan distinctions from New Guineans. Under Australian administration, Papuans were proto-Australian citizens and New Guineans Australian-protected persons. Papua and New Guinea were administered by different Australian governors and bureaucracies until World War II. The lingua franca in Papua was Police Motu, and in New Guinea it was pidgin. During

WWII, separate Papuan and New Guinean battalions were maintained (Nelson 1972; Premdas 1977a).

Colonial strategies of development would also deepen the wedge between Papuans and New Guineans. A 1965 World Bank report recommended that "to obtain the maximum benefits from the development effort, expenditure and manpower should be concentrated in areas and activities where prospective return is highest" (IBRD 1965: 35–36). Colonial administrators and investors determined that these areas were in New Guinea. More roads and other infrastructure were established in New Guinea than Papua. This uneven development would prompt Papuans to fear domination by New Guineans (Abaijah 1975: 8)

From their colonially instilled differences, Papuan and New Guinean "nationalists" were created, and they went at each other's throats as if their colonial identities were God-given and natural. The colonial birthmarks, "Papuan" and "New Guinean," would be infused with fictional social meaning and instigate furious antagonistic relations between the two groups.

Colonial boundaries thus became ethnic boundaries, bearing a fiction that became imbued with bitterness that Papuans were different from New Guineans. Colonial administration and private business investment consolidated the cleavage. From the small, decentralised communities spread over the island of New Guinea, new ethnic collectivities were created, becoming a source of strife. The ethnic animosities would be the cause of secessionist movements at a later date (Premdas 1977a, 1977b, 1977c). Papuans, fearful of New Guinean domination, sought an independent state. The Papuan movement, called Papuan Besena, activitated and intensified its demands when PNG was about to become independent in 1975. Secessionist threats would be the cause of an enormous waste of resources because they came not only from Papua, but from other parts of the patchwork colonial ethnic mosaic.

The effect of colonialism in PNG has worked to redefine ethnic identities and relations not only regionally between Papua and New Guinea, but also interprovincially. The country was divided into administrative districts reflecting the imperatives of colonial control. Like the Papua New Guinean boundary, provincial divisions have created new regional and ethnic consciousness where none existed before. In contemporary PNG, certain provincial ethnoregional boundaries have become deeply embedded, such as Chimbu, Enga, North Solomons, Sepik, and Madang. For certain purposes, Papua New Guineans define themselves in these terms. But the typical Papua New Guinean will also maintain other ethnic identities connected to a main town, subregion, or village. What the colonial legacy has bequeathed is a new array of categories that have added to divisions and jealousies in PNG. The creation of some of these categories has facilitated colonial control through divide and rule tactics. In the post-independence period, the colonially implanted ethnic categories would be manipulated by PNG ethnonationalists for their own narrow political ends.

ETHNICITY, DEVELOPMENT, AND DECENTRALISATION

Suffusing almost all aspects of intergroup life, ethnic identity has become a pre-eminent influence on national policy formulation and implementation. The PNG leaders who spearheaded the independence movement were evaluated by Papua New Guineans from the standpoint of ethnoregional and ethnolinguistic perspectives. Although periodically a few outstanding leaders, such as Michael Somare, have transcended ethnic loyalty to mobilise a cross-section of voters, the general electoral pattern since the introduction of universal adult suffrage in 1964 and through subsequent elections in 1968, 1972, and 1982 has underscored unequivocally that ethnic identity, usually at the *ples tok* level, is the foremost determinant of voter preference (Bettison et al. 1965; Epstein et al. 1968; Stone 1976; Premdas 1978; Premdas and Steeves 1983; Hegarty 1983). An over-arching set of national values and leaders with widespread cross-ethnic and cross-regional support have yet to evolve in PNG. National policy makers and parliamentarians whose primary impulse is to acquire and retain power are fine-tuned to ethnic sensitivities and claims. The problem of political allocation of values and resources central to the political process substantially revolves around ethnic calculations. It is distorted through the prism of ethnic consid-erations that can become so powerful, such as the threat of secession, that ordi-nary economic sense in public expenditures is sacrificed at the altar of ethnic accommodation. How costly the ethnic factor has been in budgetary terms is hard to state precisely. What is certain is that the huge aid package of more than A$300 million offered by Australia to PNG annually is partly consumed by accommodation to the particularistic claims of assertive ethnonationalist groups created in colonial times. Ethnicity has meant waste, duplication, and inefficiency in the allocation of scarce national resources. It has deepened divi-sions during the process of modernisation and stimulated the evolution of polit-ical and social organisations and micronationalist movements that have been rewarded for their ethnic militancy and blackmail of national and provincial governments (May 1982; Premdas 1977a). A poor country needs all its re-sources and leadership capabilities to address issues of scarcity, uneven de-velopment, and inequality. The colonially created created ethnic map throws an immense distortion into the allocative process and it often must come to dominate it. Vital time and resources are lost to feed and appease the appetite of the ethnic monster, whose size continues to grow and whose needs have come to define much of PNG's political and social reality.

In this section of the chapter, I will briefly examine one chief policy-making area, local autonomy and decentralisation, to demonstrate the role of ethnicity in the devolution of power to local authorities to promote development.

The establishment of a highly centralised and hierarchical administrative machinery by the Australians to facilitate control and resource extraction in PNG followed two stages. In the period before World War II, the administrative system was weak, skeletal, and sporadic in comparison with the massive and comprehensive hierarchical bureaucracy that would be constructed after the war. It would take the massive upheaval of the war to transform the system into a new, dynamic order. The thrust of Australian efforts in transforming PNG was fashioned on the doctrine that eventual political independence first demanded a viable economic structure. The emphasis on economic development hampered the transfer of political power at all levels of government: it led to centralisation of the public service, which increased to 18,000 in 1968, from 1,687 in 1949, more than 1,000 per cent. Even then, the public service was short-staffed. Nearly all public servants were Australian; it was not until 1955 that a Special Auxiliary Division, composed of Papua New Guineans, was created (Parker 1966: 193). For the most part, development programmes were executed by expatriate staff concentrated in urban centres. A great many Papua New Guineans were not admitted to the middle and upper levels of the public service until the mid-1970s. An uncompromisingly steep, hierarchic administrative structure evolved (Tordoff and Watts 1974).

A World Bank report in 1965 recommended against "the concentration of decision-making in the headquarters staff at Port Moresby" (Parker 1966: 203). Despite such admonitions, Australia had become obsessed with laying out an infrastructure to sustain stability. The defence of Australia's northern flank required a stable and dependent neighbour. The massive infusion of aid and investment meant that Papua New Guinea would become dependent on Australia for its survival. If centralisation was an inevitable concomitant of rapid economic change, it was also an excellent device for welding the Papua New Guinea economy and society to Australia. After independence in 1975, Papua New Guinea received a phenomenal A$200 million a year of foreign aid from Australia (Premdas 1976). To be effective, decolonisation would need to reverse the embrace through diversification and decentralisation.

To prepare the country for independence, a Constitutional Planning Committee (CPC) was appointed by the House of Assembly in 1972 to seek public opinion on the structure of the future government. The CPC toured extensively and found that there was "a widespread discontent with the present distribution of power in our country" (Final Report 1974: 1–2). It described the government as "highly centralised." Consultants to the CPC confirmed this view, stating, "in our experience of political systems in Asia, Africa, and the Caribbean, we have not come across an administrative system so highly centralised and dominated by its bureaucracy" (Tordoff and Watts 1974: 2).

The CPC had made a convincing argument that the administrative structure installed by Australia was centralised, oppressive, and alienating. It legitimised its demands for decentralisation by consulting the PNG people and reflecting their views. The CPC wanted "to return power to the people" via decentralisation. What would, however, cloud the thinking of the CPC was the ethnic map that the colonial power had drawn for PNG. It was through dictates of the design of the artificial and incongruent boundaries that had come to assume irrational collective loyalty that the experiment in devolution was to be implemented (Tordoff 1981: 1–27). The provinces were not to follow new economic and planning criteria or characteristics of a new social order; instead, they were to reflect and reinforce the administrative boundaries drawn during the colonial period. As pointed out earlier, the administrative boundaries had stimulated new ethnoregional formations based on fictional premises.

The dominance of ethnoregional consciousness is best illustrated by the North Solomons Province (formerly Bougainville) case. It was the attempted secession of the Bougainville ethnonationalists that triggered the final adoption of the system of provincial decentralisation, not only in Bougainville (renamed the North Solomons), but throughout PNG (Okuk 1980; Premdas 1977c). The claims for provincial autonomy followed the ethnic map drawn by PNG's colonial masters at a different time and for different purposes.

Provincial government quickly became a fact of political life in PNG. The Organic Law entrenched the decentralised system of local autonomy into the legal system, imparting to the institution the force of a constitutional law. John Momis, a North Solomons Roman Catholic priest who had resigned from Parliament and joined forces with his ethnonationalist compatriots to force the central government to concede provincial government, became the minister of decentralisation in the new Somare government. Within two years, Momis had moved rapidly to scrap the old local government system and supplant it with provisional forms of the new decentralised structures. Each province was to have a premier, a cabinet, a parliament, and a bureaucracy. There were 19 such provinces.

In terms of nation-building, the system of decentralised provincial government was supposed to perform several positive roles simultaneously. The most important of these was integration, the forging into existence of new loyalties from the provinces to national symbols and objectives. In fact, the CPC, in advocating provincial decentralisation, viewed it as a device for national unification by accommodating PNG's cultural diversity. Said Momis:

The case for provincial government recognises the diversity of our people. The CPC believed that it was important to find institutions which give expression to the richness of our institutions, which give expression to the richness of our cultures, and the diversity of our people. We were not impressed by arguments that decentralisation would mean the end of PNG as a nation. We believe that a national constitution and national government would be more acceptable if they respected rather than repressed the search for identity which must begin in the locality and the district before it encompasses a nation. People need to feel secure in their home environment before they can make a commitment to a larger entity (1980: 10–11).

In this vision of decentralisation, local level integration, once established, would have a "trickle up" effect; local pride would spill over and mature into national loyalty. This is a speculative hope bearing as much validity as the argument that the concession of provincial government would encourage outright secession. Local pride can in fact breed national animosity (Premdas and Pokawin 1980). After a decade of the provincial government experiment, sparse evidence exists to uphold the conclusion that decentralisation has encouraged loyalty beyond the village to a broader PNG nationhood. A better case can be advanced for the opposite inference.

At two levels in particular, provincial government has added to national alienation. At one level, provincial government has permitted an intraprovincial ethnic élite to seize control of the provincial bureaucracy, thereby excluding or discouraging other ethnic representatives from the advantages of employment, access to services, credits and loans, and development projects. Provincial "wantokism" is now widely practised. It denies fair expression and full opportunity to the diversity of groups that live in each province. The capture of a provincial bureaucracy by an ethnic élite and the practice of wantokism have had at least other grave repercussions for national unity and nation-building. First, throughout PNG, numerous alienated ethnic groups that have suffered discrimination have demanded their own provincial government. Militant subregional ethnonationalist movements for self-determination have become rampant. In some cases, even in the national public service, networks of wantoks dominate certain critical posts and simultaneously facilitate access to services such as credit or project clearance to their ethnic relations while denying similar access and services to ethnic strangers (Premdas 1980b). Carried to its logical extreme, concessions to each subprovincial group for its right to self-determination could utterly dismember the PNG state.

The second effect of provincial wantokism has been the creation of a self-perpetuating ethnoeconomic élite. A class of educated and well-placed persons belonging to a particular linguistic group or a small combination of them has entrenched its privileges and position by cultivating and manipulating ethnic divisions in many provinces. There has been the occurrence at both the national and provincial levels of an ethnic élite attempting to maintain and perpetuate itself by deliberately stressing the importance of language and cultural divisions. Often the demands for additional provinces are made by intraprovincial élites excluded from access to the privileges of an established province. In this sense, provincial decentralisation has contributed to both deepening ethnic divisions and to the entrenchment of ethnic élites and the perpetuation of inequality. In the long term, another sort of inequality is generated by provincial wantokism. This takes the form of differences in the availability and distribution of provincial élites across PNG's 19 provinces. Specifically, because each province has tended to attract its own people away from the national public service and because some provinces have been notably advantaged by early colonial contact (so they have a larger contingent of skilled and educated people), provincial and regional inequality have been accentuated. Hence, provinces such as Enga and the Southern Highlands, because of late contact, suffer the disadvantage of having fewer skilled and educated persons to direct and develop provincial resources. When this unequal provincial distribution of skilled and educated people is combined with the practice of intraprovincial ethnic élite wantokism, the availability of trained personnel for provincial development narrows. Overall, then, provincial wantokism, in relation to nation-building, fosters alienation and demands for more provinces, the entrenchment of provincial élites in positions of power, and causes continued inequalities between the provinces.

At another level, provincial government has accentuated intraregional animosities. Elections for provincial office have generally been fought along clan and ethnic lines. With the transfer of major functions and funds to the provinces, these local bodies have become a veritable repository of patronage opportunities. Capturing a provincial government entails access to large amounts of revenues apart from the symbolic prestige bestowed on the victor over ethnic adversaries. Elections for provincial office, therefore, are fought bitterly. This conflict is intensified by an electoral system based on the zero-sum principle of winner-takes-all, as against a system of proportional representation that would have encouraged provincial ethnic co-operation and coalition arrangements. In summary, provincial elections have tended not to impart constructive conflict and discourse over issues of development, but instead have instigated and accentuated ethnic rivalries, some old and others new.

Provincial government, it was also argued by its proponents, would bring power closer to the people. It would stimulate participation in community decision-making, imparting a sense of belonging among citizens. This was in contrast to the centralised colonial government, which was nonparticipatory and remote from the people. Momis argued that the central government bequeathed by Australia "resulted in the disenfranchisement of the people at the provincial and other levels so that they had little to say in decisions that affected them in their everyday lives" (Momis 1980: 7). In theory, decentralisation was supposed to reverse this. Momis argued:

True democracy will not work until our people in every village and hamlet accept that they cannot be free and independent unless they actually say something, think something, and take action about what should happen to their own lives and those of the people of our country. It was in keeping with the CPC's emphasis on human development and on the taking of responsibility for one's future that we came out in favour of establishing responsible political bodies in the provinces. We believed that administrative organisation at a provincial level responsible to provincial elected bodies was more likely to be more responsive to the people. It was also likely to be more accountable for its actions, since power would be closer to the people (1980: 9).

In other words, decentralisation would more than likely lead to democratic participation in decision-making by devolving political and administrative powers from a highly centralised system to one physically and geographically closer to the people at the provincial level. Provincial government would be closer to the people; it would be simpler and easier to understand. Hence, nation-building was equated with political participation.

The realities of provincial government after a decade of implementation all point indisputably to continued separation of people from decision-making. In part, this happened because each provincial government was still far away from most villagers in a country that is very rugged and topographically chopped up and in which settlements are widely dispersed, with poor communications linking them to provincial headquarters. The charge has become widespread that provincial governments have become new centralised seats of power situated at the periphery. The pyramidal structure of government and its characteristic bureaucratic ways of operating have remained intact at the provincial level. But these points aside, what has been even more damaging to decentralisation as a nation builder is that each province contains numerous ethnolinguistic groups. Political participation in such a culturally and linguistically variegated setting is alien to the traditional Papua New Guinea mode of decision-making conducted in small, face-to-face communities. The dismal record of local government before provincial government can in part be assigned not only to the Westernised councils and their procedures being alien institutions, but also to their tendency to embrace a wide assortment of villages, languages, and customs (Fenbury 1981). To many observers, the crisis in political participation at the local level could be resolved by establishing community governments smaller in scale and closer to the people (Salisbury 1985). Even though this format will be built on microethnic identities and will probably deepen them, many other factors impede the practice of vibrant personalised local-level democracies, including illiteracy, poverty, leadership, and a weak economic base for revenue raising.

There are limits to building provincial governments around ethnoregional claims for maximum internal autonomy. One is performance measured in waste and corruption. Today, PNG's provincial governments cost annually K$100 million to maintain. This is the cost of salaries and allowances for the premiers, cabinet members, parliamentarians, political appointees, and the local bureaucracies. Poor accounting practices and extravagant expenditures have led the central government to suspend several provincial governments that raise only 10 per cent to 20 per cent of the revenue each spends. The central government, to appease militant ethnoregional claims and intimidated by threats of secession, has paid dearly for a system of provincial government that is destroying a nation.

CONCLUSION

Does ethnicity reflect a deeper reality, such as class interrests, in PNG's continuing transformation from simple societies to a complex, highly differentiated captialist state? This is one of the wider issues this study raises. There is no question that ethnic formations have facilitated colonial control by impeding the evolution of cross-cultural socio-economic organisations among Papua New Guineans. The objective of nation-building is liberation and integral human development, as the CPC emphasised, but ethnicity has clearly thwarted these aims, adding instead new divisions, waste, and distorted national priorities and policies. In the postcolonial state, almost every main office holder built his or her political success by mobilising ethnic wantoks. Built on fictive premises instead of real interests, ethnic formations beyond the village have proven incapable of supporting and sustaining collective, co-operative efforts for equitable development. The masking of dominant interests behind provincial ethno-nationalist militance for autonomy does not solve the problems of equality and participation. Ethnic mobilisation conceals the internal contradictions of intragroup exploitation and élitism.

The introduction of cash crops, a monetised economy, private property for profit maximisation through exploitation, and a wider political arena have, however, released new dynamic forces in PNG society. Though ethnic identity has so far defined most interpersonal and intergroup relations in this early capitalist phase of PNG development, below the surface of ethnic assertion resides emergent socio-economic formations, which from time to time break out from the constraints of their ethnic boundaries and explode into strikes and demonstrations. The Rabaul strike of 1928 stands as an eloquent symbol of the power and potential of these emergent forces against growing inequality, uneven development, and the citadels of privilege in PNG. When the strait-jacket of ethnicity is destroyed – and this will require a fundamental change of PNG's economic structure – then and only then will the first step to liberation and to integral human development be realised.

REFERENCES

Abaija, J. 1975. *Papua's colonial experience with Australia and New Guinea.* Paper delivered at the New Guinea Research Unit, Waigani, Port Moresby. Mimeograph.

Bettison, D. et al. 1965. *The Papua New Guinea election.* Canberra: Australian National University Press.

Bonacich, E. 1980. Class approaches to ethnicity and race. *The Insurgent Sociologist* 10(2): 9–25.

Brookfield, H. C. 1972. *Colonialism, development and independence.* Cambridge: Cambridge Univerisity Press.

Epstein, A. L. et al. 1968. *The politics of dependence.* Canberra: Australian National University Press.

Fenbury, D. M. 1981. *Practice without policy.* Canberra: Australian National University, Development Studies Centre, Monograph No. 13.

Final Report. 1974. *Final Report of the Constitutional Planning Committee, Part I.* Port Moresby: Government Printery.

Hegarty, D., ed. 1983. *Elections in 1977.* Waigani: University of Papua New Guinea Press.

Howard, M. et al. 1983. *The political economy of the South Pacific*. Townsville, Queensland: James Cook University, South-East Asian Monograph Series No. 13.

IBRD. 1965. *The economic development of Papua New Guinea*. Baltimore: Johns Hopkins University Press.

May, R., ed. 1982. *Micronationalist movements in Papua New Guinea*. Canberra: Australian National University, Department of Political and Social Change, Research School of Pacific Studies.

Momis, J. 1980. Decentralisation and development. In *Papua New Guinea: The experiment in decentralisation*, edited by R. Premdas and S. Pokawin, 15–20. Waigani: University of Papua New Guinea Press.

Nelson, H. 1972. *Papua New Guinea: Black unity or black chaos?* London: Penguin Books.

Okuk, I. 1980. Decentralisation: A critique and an alternative. In *Papua New Guinea: The experiment in decentralisation*, edited by R. Premdas and S. Pokawin, 21–25. Waigani: University of Papua New Guinea Press.

Parker, R. S. 1966. The growth of territory administration. In *New Guinea on the threshold*, edited by E. K. Fisk, 187–220. Pittsburg: University of Pittsburg Press.

Premdas, R. 1976. Papua New Guinea foreign policy options. In *Oceania and Beyond*, edited by F. P. King, 37–158. Boulder, Colo., Greenwood Press.

———. 1977a. Secessionist movements in Papua New Guinea. *Pacific Affairs* 50(1): 64–85.

———. 1977b. Secession and political change. *Oceania* 48: 265–83.

———. 1977c. Copper, ethno-nationalism and secession on Bougainville. *Canadian Review of Studies in Nationalism* 4(2): 247–65.

———. 1978. Papua New Guinea: The first elections since independence. *Journal of Pacific History* 13(1, 2): 77–90.

———. 1980a. Review of *Race, class and rebellion in the South Pacific*, edited by A. Mamak and A. Ali. *Pacific Studies* 3: 68–74.

———. 1980b. Decentralisation: A compendium of problems and opportunities. In *Papua New Guinea: The experiment in decentralisation*, edited by R. Premdas and S. Pokawin, 369–74. Waigani: University of Papua New Guinea Press.

———. 1983. Political science in the South Pacific. *The Journal of Pacific Studies* 9: 172–218.

Premdas, R., and S. Pokawin, eds. 1980. *Papua New Guinea: The experiment in decentralisation*. Waigani: University of Papua New Guinea Press.

Premdas, R., and J. Steeves. 1983. Papua New Guinea: The return of Pangu to power. *Asian Survery* 23(8): 991–1006.

Rowley, C. 1965. *The New Guinea villager*. Melbourne: Melbourne University Press.

Salisbury, R. 1985. *Decentralisation and local government*. Montreal: McGill University, Department of Anthropology. Mimeograph.

Stone, D., ed. 1976. *Papua New Guinea: Prelude to self-government*. Canberra: Australian National University Press.

Tordoff, W. 1981. Decentralisation in Papua New Guinea. In *Manchester papers on development*, edited by M. Minogue. vol. 3: 1–27.

Tordoff, W., and R. C. Watts. 1974. *Report on central-provincial relations: Papua New Guinea*. Waigani: Government Printery.

12

Independence and Ethnicity in New Caledonia

DONNA WINSLOW

In November 1984, the native peoples of New Caledonia (the Kanaks) boycotted the territorial elections, set up their own provisional government, and demanded freedom from French rule and a "Kanak Socialist Independence."

This chapter examines the causes of the independence movement and the French response. France has committed itself to institute several economic, social, and cultural reforms aimed at remedying "the social and economic inequalities of the Territory" while securing France's strategic interests in the South Pacific. The independence movement can be linked to the historical circumstances that have led to the formation of a Kanak ethnic identity. The formation of a Kanak ethnic identity is tied to the economic and political domination of the native peoples of New Caledonia by French colonialism.

New Caledonia and its dependencies are not only 20,000 kilometres from France; they are also relatively isolated in the south-west Pacific. They are 1,500 km east of Australia, 1,700 km north of New Zealand, and 7,000 km south-east of Japan. Historically, there have been two forms of articulation of the Kanak economy to the larger New Caledonian and French economy: petty peasant production and forced or wage labour. The importance of one form over another has varied through time and according to region. However, both forms have been present since early contact, and each has produced certain contradictions within Kanak society.

Contact with European and American merchants and Christian missionaries began in the 19th century. After New Caledonia was annexed by France in 1853, tribal lands were expropriated for the establishment of a penal colony, settler colonialism, and nickel mining. The indigenous population, which formerly had no common national identity, was perceived and treated as one homogenous group, although divided into collaborators and resisters. By the end of the century, Kanaks were confined to native reserves and compelled to do corvée labour on French plantations, ranches, and public works.

259

Ethnic boundaries between the Kanaks and the rest of the New Caledonian population were established and reinforced by a colonial division along racial lines and by segregation. The Kanaks were confined to the rural reserves and worked mainly in agriculture and public works, while contract labourers were brought in to work in the mines and urban centres. The Kanaks were further isolated by having a separate status and a native administration to implement native policy.

After World War II, there was a liberalisation of colonial policy, and forced labour was abolished. Kanaks were no longer confined to the reserves, and health and education services were improved. In the 1950s, the Kanaks continued to be marginalised economically as the financial gap between them and the rest of the New Caledonian population continued to widen. Ethnic differentiation continued to be reinforced by occupational specialisation and regional segregation. The majority of Kanaks continued to live in the underdeveloped rural areas, practising agriculture and working as unskilled manual labourers, and most of the whites and other ethnic groups occupied semiskilled, skilled, and management positions in the urban areas.

The early 1970s were a boom period for New Caledonia because of the rise in world nickel prices (New Caledonia is the third largest producer of nickel in the world). Urbanisation increased as the rural areas were drained of workers. The collapse of the nickel boom in the late 1970s led to unemployment and economic recession. At this time we see an increase in Kanak demands for participation in economic and political decision-making and a growth in the Kanak independence movement. Since then, politics in New Caledonia have become increasingly polarised in autonomy versus dependency and in ethnic terms – with whites and other urban ethnic groups standing for continued French presence and Kanaks for social independence.

TRADITIONAL KANAK SOCIETY

There are many sources of information on traditional Kanak society (Benza and Riviere 1982; Doumenge 1975, 1982; Leenhardt 1930, 1932, 1937, 1947; Lenormand 1953; and others). In this chapter, I will draw largely on the most recent work by Benza and Riviere (1982) and Doumenge (1975, 1982).

The exact population of New Caledonia at first contact is unknown, and the estimates run from 40,000 to 60,000 (see Doumenge 1982: 148–49 for details on the debate). The Kanaks were distributed along the river valleys and coastal areas in groups defined by Benza and Riviere (1982) as "small."

The Kanaks cultivated tubers, yams and taro being the most important. Yams are a dry crop, and their annual cycle determined the Kanak year. Taro is an irrigated crop that, in the past, was cultivated on mountainside terraces with elaborate irrigation works. The Kanaks also hunted and gathered food in the forests and fished along the riverbanks and seacoast.

Each family cultivated its own plots. The family members co-operated in daily activities following a sexual division of labour. Men did the heavy labour, such as clearing the land and breaking the soil for planting, besides hunting. The women did the repetitive tasks, such as weeding, besides caring for the children and preparing the food (see Doumenge 1975: 34–39). The nuclear families were patrilocal. A single male belonged to his father's family, and when he married, he formed another family unit that maintained ties to his father's unit. The father and the eldest son occupied the dominant positions in the family.

Families were united in a blood line that was usually three generations deep. A blood line linked several unclear families, acknowledging a common ancestor considered to be the oldest known representative of the line. Members of a common blood line did not necessarily live near one another, but if they did, they co-operated in certain collective activities such as construction, large agricultural works, hunting, and fishing. Blood lines were incorporated into a lineage through reference to a common ancestor and place of origin. The lineage was patrilineal and exogamous, and the elders controlled a relatively rigid marriage system.

The clan, an exogamous ensemble of lineages, was the largest patrilineal grouping. Its members did not co-operate in domestic activities; however, they did co-operate in wars against other clans. The clan had a hierarchy of chiefs who played important roles during wars and in alliance formation. Reflecting the structural model of the family, the clan was based on the notion of the service of the cadets towards their elders, and conversely, the sense of responsibility of the elders for the cadets. The relationship between elders and cadets, chiefs and servants, and the general subordination of the latter to the former constituted the central notion of Kanak chieftainship.

According to Kanak tradition, land was the exclusive and immutable property of the first cultivator of the land and his descendants. As such, land was considered to be collective family property. The first cultivator of the soil was regarded as the master of the land, even if the land was no longer cultivated by him. Using a piece of land gave nonowners the right to its crop, but not to the land, to which they enjoyed only seasonal rights of cultivation (Doumenge 1975: 58).

Land was much more than a means of subsistence; it was (and still is) part of the structural whole of Kanak society, an integral part of kinship, religion, cosmology, and custom. Land claims are a central issue in New Caledonian politics.

It is important to note that, although many similar cultural features were evident among the Kanaks of New Caledonia, there was no sense of a collective

Kanak identity in precontact times. According to Lenormand (1953: 245), New Caledonia had 36 distinct dialects. Many groups could not even communicate with one another. The clans were organised into tiny independent states. They lived in relative isolation from one another in the transversal valleys dividing La Grande Terre and its satellite islands.

THE COLONIAL PERIOD

The first contact with merchant capital took place in the 19th century. Whalers were among the earliest to use Kanaks as ships' crew and shore labourers (see Howe 1978: 25). Sandalwood trade boomed in the early 1840s, when the forests of the Solomon Islands, New Hebrides, and Fiji were becoming depleted. Shineberg (1967) shows how ships' captains were quick to take advantage of native labour to cut and carry sandalwood to the beaches and to provide crews for ships and longboats. Traders were especially dependent on local labour during the Australian gold rushes, when European workers were scarce. "Hundreds of Melanesians might be employed at any one station" (Howe 1978: 24).

The Kanaks also worked as seamen. Charles Pigeard (quoted in Howe 1978: 23) reported in 1846 that every English vessel he saw in New Caledonian waters had Loyalty Island crew members. Natives from the Isle of Pines "who only a few years since considered the most savage and treacherous of any (were) rapidly acquiring the English language and seeking employment as seamen" (Capt. Erskine, 1849, quoted in Howe 1978: 23).

Contact with the traders, although limited and sporadic, did have some effect on Kanak society. There was the gradual adoption of new techniques of production (metal tools and organisation of labour, for example), new weapons (guns, knives, and others), new habits (imbibing alcohol, for one), and new methods of exchange. During this early contact with a money economy, missionaries came. As they spread the word of God, they also spread new values, such as a respect for private property and law and order. Land and labour were being treated as commodities.

The territory was annexed by France in 1853. And even if this brought little change to the Kanak way of life at that time, it established French dominion over the territory. Sovereignty over the land passed from the Kanaks to the French state:

The uncivilised inhabitants of a country have over that country only a limited right of domination, a sort of right of occupation. . . . A civilised power on establishing a colony in such a country, acquires a decisive power over the soil, or, in other terms, she acquires the right to extinguish the primitive title (French minister of the navy and colonies to Foreign Ministry, 1854, quoted in Ward 1982: 1).

In 1868, a new system of native reserves was set up based on the concept of communal property. Land was no longer held individually by families, but collectively by a unit artificially defined by the administration as *tribu* (tribe). Except for waste and unoccupied lands, Kanak property had never been held collectively. Kanak property rights were administratively overridden:

The traditionally scattered pattern of settlement, based on the family unit and centred on the garden lands of particular clans was to be formally replaced by concentration in villages based on the artificial administrative unit of the tribe (Douglas 1972 quoted in Ward 1982: 3).

The French governor could define tribal territory and regulate native affairs concerning land. Reserve boundaries could be easily modified by the administration. The governor also had the power to apply disciplinary measures such as fines, prison, and confiscation of property and could even impose collective sanctions on a tribe if he wished (Lenormand 1953: 267).

In 1870, the main island of La Grande Terre was divided into four *arrondissements* (regions). This reform was aimed not only at land expropriation, but also at facilitating the use of native labour in case the manpower from the penal colony proved insufficient (Doumenge 1982: 98).[1] The territory had served as a penal colony since 1864 for France's criminals and politicos.[2]

The convicts far outnumbered the settlers. For example, of 15,500 Europeans in New Caledonia in 1875, 10,500 were convicts (Dornoy 1984: 38). They provided an important source of labour for the growing colony. It was convicts who drained the land for the establishment of the territory's capital, Noumea. They built roads, set up telegraph lines, and worked for the settlers.

An insurrection broke out in New Caledonia in 1878. It was a revolt by the native people against the French society trying to dominate them. It called for a renewal of Kanak society after the whites were gone. There had been many rebellions before 1878; however, the 1878 revolt differed from previous uprisings because it was a concerted effort by many tribes acting together. In this way, it is seen by the Kanaks as the first nationalist struggle.[3]

What were French attitudes towards the Kanaks? According to Dousset-Leenhardt (1976), racism was present in all levels of French society. The French considered the Kanaks to be savages. As a matter of fact, the idea that the Kanaks could be intelligent enough to organise themselves in a revolt was so foreign that the French believed the Kanaks were being led by whites – missionaries, convicts, or most probably the English.

From their actions it is evident that the Kanaks had spent much time planning the revolt: they had amassed guns, performed systematic reconnaissance of the military outposts and telegraph lines, and established guerilla camps with gardens to where the rebels could retreat. In this respect, it is clear that the Kanaks saw the necessity for planned, unified action.

The revolt marks the beginning of the development of a collective identity on the part of the Kanaks as a result of a common colonial experience. This is not to say that all the Kanaks came together to fight the French (the revolt actually failed because of the key role played by Kanak collaborators). It was the central tribes of La Grande Terre who formed the core of the rebellion and fought from the beginning to the bitter end. As Maurice Leenhardt (quoted in Dousset-Leenhardt 1976: 97) points out, it was the central tribes who had suffered the greatest effect of colonialism and who had the greatest contact with white society.

Following the brutal suppression of the 1878 revolt, the French embarked on a cleanup campaign. Any village suspected of having supported the revolt was burned to the ground. Gardens were destroyed and native lands expropriated. Captured rebels were executed or deported to neighbouring islands. In a report to Paris, a visiting vice-admiral condemned the atrocities committed by the French at the time (quoted in Dousset-Leenhardt 1976: 151).

The remaining Kanaks were herded into overcrowded, infertile reserves. Although approximately 21 hectares are required for the traditional Kanak system of crop rotation, the reserves were calculated at 3 hectares per person (Thompson and Adloff 1971: 262). Whereas 852 hectares were alienated in 1859, by 1882, a total of 26,700 hectares of native land had been expropriated (Saussol 1986: 16).

It was the dream of the territory's civilian governor, Paul Feillet, to establish settler colonialism in New Caledonia. In the late 1890s, the flow of convicts was stopped, and 525 French families were encouraged to settle in the territory and take up coffee, cattle, and other agricultural production. To replace the convicts, contract labourers were brought in for the settlers and the growing nickel industry. Native labour was also used by the settlers, although for the most part the Kanaks were not willing participants in the European economy.

The French administration played a key role in recruiting Kanak labour. The recruitment was at times a tenth, sometimes even a fifth, of the active population. The administration enlisted the chiefs' co-operation by offering them a tenth of the salaries of the workers they supplied (Doumenge 1982: 113). If the chiefs refused to supply labourers, they were imprisoned until they complied (Gasher 1975: 9). Latham (1978: 12) tells us that the Kanaks were paid half or a quarter the salary they normally would have received on the open market. If a Kanak was fined and could not pay in cash, he or she had to pay in labour on public works or for individual farmers and mine owners.

Also, Governor Feillet reorganised native administration and resettled the Kanaks into new villages (termed "tribes"). What had formerly been a tribe became an *arrondissement*. All the *arrondissements* were placed under the authority of *syndics des affaires indigènes*, who were responsible for law and order and "paternalistic guidance." After 1900, the *syndics'* duties were carried out by the *gen-*

darmes: "One of their principal duties was to provide native labourers for the colony. Each tribe was obliged to supply workers according to its population" (Lenormand 1953: 263).

The decree of 1897 gave the colonial administration the right to expropriate Kanak land and to relocate the natives on other, designated plots. Native reserves went from 320,000 to 120,000 hectares between 1895 and 1903 (Saussol 1986: 16). By 1902, reserves on La Grande Terre totalled less than a tenth of the island (Ward 1982: 5). The parking of Kanaks on reserves was accompanied by a demographic decline. The Kanak population, estimated at 42,000 in 1887, was at an all-time low of 27,768 in 1901 (Ward 1982: 4).

Besides the loss of their land and a demographic decline, the Kanaks came under the *Régime de l'Indigénat*, a code of "native regulations" established in 1887. Considered to be noncitizens, the Kanaks were outside of French common law and were subject to the laws and disciplines (whims) of the local administration.[4] Curfews were established and the Kanaks were not allowed to leave the reserves except for work. They were required to do compulsory labour on roads and other public works, and through the levy of a head tax, natives were obliged to work for the settlers.[5]

Refusal to work, or "insubordination," resulted in sentencing to an *atelier de discipline* (discipline workshop) or prison and fines or confiscation of property, or both. Acts against "public security" were punished with up to 10 years in prison and confiscation of property.

The "prisoners" of a discipline workshop worked from 5am to 8pm breaking stones for roads – without a salary of course. In the case of insubordination they were imprisoned. If they were ill, the time spent in the infirmary was not counted towards their sentence which they continued serving once cured (Leenhardt 1978: 16).

Further amendments to the *Régime* added to the list of infractions for which a Kanak could be sent to an *atelier* or prison and/or fined. These included:

the refusal to give information to government agents, a disrespectful attitude towards a representative of French authority, a public speech made with the intention of weakening respect for French authority or France's representative (Lenormand 1953: 273).

The aim of the *Régime* was to supply a regular and controlled labour force to the settlers, although the overt ideology was to "protect" the Kanaks. Kanaks were limited to 10 hours of work per day; however, building maintenance, caring for livestock, and domestic service were not considered work. So the Kanaks had to put in their regular 10 hours plus several hours of "non-work." Leenhardt (1978: 16) writes that many Kanaks preferred discipline workshops rather than working for the settlers.

Kanak labour was used primarily for public works and in agriculture; the colony used mainly immigrant contract labour in the mines. It was the New Caledonian immigration bureau that negotiated on behalf of the settlers and miners with the administrations of neighbouring countries for contract labourers. New Caledonia became an ethnic mosaic of contract labourers, French settlers, and Kanaks (see Winslow 1986).

In 1892, the first group of 600 Japanese contract labourers arrived to work for the French mining company – Société le Nickel – and, according to official records, 6,880 Japanese arrived in New Caledonia between 1892 and 1919, when the immigration stopped (Kobayashi 1980: 64).

Indonesian (primarily Javanese) labourers were also recruited for the expanding nickel industry and for the large agricultural (particularly coffee) plantations. The number of Javanese workers in New Caledonia reached a peak of 7,602 in 1929 (Thompson and Adloff 1971: 447), and, according to Dornoy (1984: 78), there were 7,735 Indonesians in the territory in 1939. The Javanese were the most popular labourers and were considered to be the most "docile, orderly and adaptable."

New Caledonian authorities also recruited under contract a large number of Tonkinese coolies from Indochina.[6] The flow of Vietnamese labourers soon became a flood, and by 1929 the 14,535 Asians in New Caledonia outnumbered the European population (Dornoy 1984: 45).

The depression of the early 1930s put an end to the labour traffic between Indochina and New Caledonia. Many Vietnamese were repatriated, and on the eve of World War II, only 3,471 Vietnamese labourers and 285 free residents remained (Thompson and Adloff 1971: 451); in the postwar period, most remaining Vietnamese were repatriated.

It is important to note how colonial policy functioned to keep the different ethnic groups distinct. They lived in separate areas, worked in separate jobs and under separate conditions, and lived under different laws. The Kanaks were restricted to the rural reserves and allowed out only for work. In 1936, only 732 Kanaks had been granted permission to live and work in Noumea (Connell et al. 1985: 3). The immigrant labourers were working under contract mainly in the mines and urban centres. There was also, and still is, a judicial separation under French law whereby French and other non-Kanak minorities live under the *droit commun* and the Kanaks under the *statut particulier*.

The settlers continued to increase their demand for tribal land after World War I, and at first the administration complied, legalising settler encroachment on native reserves and recruiting native labour for the settlers. But as the Kanak demographic decline came to a halt and their numbers began to increase, the administration began to realise that the natives would not just fade away and began to take some steps to promote native welfare. The Kanaks benefited from a lightening of the *Indigénat*, but as Doumenge (1982: 114–15) points out, the period between the wars was characterised by the continued subjugation of the

Kanaks. Feillet's strategy remained the norm: almost all Kanaks continued to pay a head tax, gave up a certain number of days as prestation to their municipality, worked for neighbouring settlers, and served an increasing number of days in the local administration's public works programme.[7]

Government officials began to encourage the Kanaks to remain on the reservations and increase agricultural output. Coffee production especially was emphasised. The introduction of coffee, a perennial crop, disrupted the Kanak system of annual crop loans. According to custom, each farmer is the owner of his crop, and coffee cultivation implies a long-term occupation of the land. This situation led to disputes between people who were masters of the land and those who had rights to occupy the land on which their crops grew (see Doumenge 1975: 204).

What were the reasons for this change in native policy? It would seem that most of the infrastructure permitting the implementation of capitalism was in place and required mainly maintenance work; therefore, some Kanak labour could be released for agriculture. Moreover, coffee production had not been a success with white settlers, who seemed to prefer cattle ranching; therefore, there was an interest in developing coffee production in the reserves. Also, there was the British example in West Africa (especially the Gold Coast), which demonstrated that it was possible to develop intensive market agriculture among the natives.

With the outbreak of World War II, New Caledonia was cut off from all metropolitan goods upon which it had become dependent. The territory was able to survive by selling its nickel matte to the United States and its crude ore to the Japanese up to 1941. The Vichy government was rejected, and New Caledonia supported Free France and General DeGaulle (see Thompson and Adloff 1971: 267–89).

American troops began to arrive in New Caledonia in 1942. The economic boom that followed lasted for four years and brought a prosperity the territory had never before known. It is not certain whether the Kanaks benefited materially from the American presence. Without doubt, the colony experienced unprecedented prosperity, but the extent to which any of this trickled down to the Kanaks is unknown. According to Guiart (1954: 115), Kanak labour continued to be requisitioned, but, although the Americans were willing to pay two to three times the regular salary, the local colonial administration was reluctant, fearing that this would drive up the price of labour in the mines and agriculture. This viewpoint is supported by information obtained from the US government:

A seaman informant did not know the exact wages which the American government paid to native longshoremen. He was informed, however, that while the scale was adequate, this sum was paid to the French and only a small portion of it ever reached the natives themselves (O. S. S. Document No. 25183).

THE POSTWAR PERIOD

The postwar French government liberalised France's colonial policy, although it did not relinquish its control over the territory. In 1946, the French Assembly adopted a proposition in which "forced labour is absolutely forbidden in overseas Territories," and the *Régime de l'Indigénat* came to an end.

By 1951, some of the Kanaks were enfranchised (universal suffrage would have to wait until 1956). The first organisers to effectively mobilise the Kanaks were mission-based organisations set up in part to fight the "Red Menace" that was threatening the territory.[8] During and after World War II, attempts were made to establish a Communist party in New Caledonia that apparently received strong support from the Kanaks (see Dornoy 1984). The churches were mobilised to neutralise the Communists. The church organisations were set up to direct and control Kanak political aspirations. Their policies were paternalistic and assimilationist. According to Apollinaire Anova Ataba, a Kanak priest, the objective of these religious organisations were

to slow down the decolonisation movement in New Caledonia and to work towards integrating the Blacks and the Whites, a necessary precondition for the continued colonisation of the island (quoted in Kermel 1986: 24).

Land claims became a central issue, and because the reserves were no longer prisons, they became bastions of traditional culture. There was a demand for the return of lands partially in response to demographic growth and economic needs and to the recovery of traditional territories.[9] As Ward (1982: 8) and Doumenge (1975: 196) point out, the economic and psychological claims were mixed from the beginning.

The Union Calédonienne (UC) was formed in the early 1950s. It drew its support from the early mission-based organisations, but it also had support from urban progressives who favoured redistribution of the land of the large pastoral companies and absentee landowners. From the beginning, the UC was a multiracial party; its slogan was: "Deux couleurs, un seul peuple" (two colours, one people).[10]

The early UC programme was also assimilationist and was aimed at a greater inclusion of Kanaks into white institutions. With Kanak and *petit blanc* support, the UC won a majority in the Territorial Council in 1953 (nine Kanaks were elected). In 1956, a Socialist government in France developed a *loi-cadre* for all overseas territories to decentralise administrative power. In other French colonies, this was a prelude to independence. In New Caledonia, it led to the creation of a Territorial Assembly and a Governing Council. France still appointed senior government personnel and retained power (e.g., mineral rights) over the colony's important resources.[11]

The UC attempted many land reforms (see Ward 1982: 9–13), but some sections of the UC felt that these piecemeal efforts were too limited. They proposed a more thorough transfer of land based on higher land rents or taxes and on powers of pre-emptive purchases and expropriation of unused or under-used settler land.

The *grands colons* were already nervous about the threat to their primacy, apparent in the growing success of the Kanak-based UC and the adoption of the *loi-cadre*. In 1958, the Rassemblement Caledonien (Caledonian Assembly) was formed to represent settler interests and, with DeGaulle recently gaining power in France, armed settlers caused disturbances in Noumea and threatened the UC. The governor regained control, and DeGaulle's referendum followed, in which the overseas territories voted whether or not to stay in the French union. New Caledonia had to vote "yes" or be faced with immediate and total independence without any financial assistance. The UC opted for the *status quo*.

In the late 1950s and early 1960s, the alliance between the right and the centre in France was established with the settler right in New Caledonia. France needed the settlers to retain French presence; and the settlers needed France to preserve their privileges against the Kanaks. The 1963 Jacquinot revision of the Territorial Statute sharply reduced the size and the power of the Governor General (see Thompson and Adloff 1971: 317–18). Effective power lay with the governor, his secretary-general, and the army and the police. Paris controlled the budget, appointed officials, and supervised all territorial development.

The postwar period was a time of industrial expansion in New Caledonia. The Doniambo nickel smelter was renovated, the Yate dam was built, and new mining sites were opened at Poro and Nepoui. Nickel production sizably increased.[12]

New Caledonia's economy has been dominated by the nickel industry. Nickel is removed by opencast bulldozing in the mountainous areas. This leaves a badly scarred, eroded, and polluted landscape. The territory has almost half the nickel resources of the non-Communist world. The French company Société le Nickel (SLN) is the largest mining interest in New Caledonia and has always maintained close ties with the French government. From 1958 to 1969, the French government paid a subsidy on refined nickel that helped the SLN through a period of extensive development and investment in New Caledonia. In 1962, the governor, an appointee from France, supported SLN's request to have its produce exempted from territorial export duties (McTaggart 1976).

Although agriculture supports 38 per cent of the population, it has represented only 3 per cent of the GDP since 1975, compared with 10 per cent from 1960. From 1956 to 1981, the proportion of the work-force engaged in agriculture fell from 50 per cent to 15 per cent (Connell et al. 1985: 5). Four per cent of the Europeans work in agriculture, opposed to 60 per cent of the Kanaks; yet two-thirds of the arable land is in the hands of 1,000 French settlers, and more than half is controlled by a small élite (4.5 per cent) of landowners (AISDPK 1985: 10–11).

The agricultural economy is divided between Kanak producers, who are primarily involved in subsistence agriculture supplemented with some coffee and copra production, and non-Kanak producers involved primarily in commercial production both in large cattle stations and market gardens (Connell et al. 1985: 5–6). The government had previously made several attempts at rural development. A development aid fund (FADIL) had been set up in 1975. This was replaced by ODIL in 1983 (see Connell et al. 1985), but neither enjoyed great success. Doumenge (1982: 345) writes that massive injection of capital, such as that occurring under FADIL and ODIL, is not a solution to New Caledonia's rural problem and that small-scale, appropriate technology projects are better adapted to the territory's needs.

Tourism, New Caledonia's second industry after mining, is concentrated in Noumea. Few tourists venture away from the large hotels to the rural areas, "hence almost all the domestic revenue generated from tourism remains in the capital" (Connell et al. 1985: 5). The Pisani/Fabius Plan also hoped to create a rural counterweight to Noumea in the lopsided New Caledonian economy.

The heavy dependence on nickel emphasised the growing dualism in New Caledonia – the separation between the rich, white, urban, export-oriented sector and the poor, Kanak, rural, subsistence sector. Although migration for work in the urban and mining sectors was increasing, the majority of Kanaks continued to live on the reserves, and the white population in urban centres, especially in Noumea, the capital, continued to grow.

NOUMEA THE WHITE

Noumea is the third largest city in the Pacific island region (after Port Moresby and Suva), and because of mining, it is the most industrialised city in the South Pacific region. It is many times larger than any other town in New Caledonia and nearly monopolises most of the territory's activities.

It is the only city in the Pacific islands where most inhabitants are Europeans.[13] Noumea and its suburbs contain 60 per cent of the total population in New Caledonia. The capital contains 80 per cent of the Europeans, 90 per cent of the Polynesians, and 85 per cent of the Asians living in the territory (see Wacquant 1985). In this way, Noumea remains the bastion of the nonindigenous ethnic groups.

Noumea contains most of the colony's industries, commerces, and public services. It consumes 43 per cent of the territory's imports and produces more than two-thirds of the exports, including 89 per cent of the mineral exports. In 1983, nickel accounted for 90 per cent of all exports, according to Kircher (1986: 14).[14]

In 1980–81, a Noumean had an average annual earning of 438,000 CFP (South Pacific francs); a European Noumean earned an average of 787,000 CFP.[15] At that time, the average annual earnings of a rural Kanak were 105,000

Table 1. The current ethnic configuration

	1956	1969	%	1976	%
Europeans	25,160	41,268	41	50,757	38
Indonesians	2,889	1,809	2	5,111	4
Kanaks	34,969	46,000	46	55,598	42
Vietnamese	3,445	109		1,943	2
Ni-Vanuatu				1,050	1
together with					
Wallisians	1,227	6,219	6	9,571	7
French Polynesians	790	3,367	3	6,391	5
Other	n.d.	1,607	3	2,812	3

Source: Connell et al. 1985: 15.

CFP (Wacquant 1985). Disparities in income are reflected in disparities in health. From 1963 to 1968, Kanak age-specific death rates consistently were double those of Europeans, and the infant mortality rate was more than twice as high (Connell et al. 1985: 14).

In terms of employment, still in the early 1980s, the statistics show that 91 per cent of the top supervisory and professional positions and 73 per cent of the intermediate professional positions were held by Europeans, compared with 4 per cent and 18 per cent for the Kanaks. Similarly, Europeans comprised 91 per cent of the engineers and managers in the private sector, and the Kanaks 1.6 per cent. In the public sector, Europeans occupied 87 per cent of the administrative positions and the Kanaks 8 per cent (Wacquant 1985).

The employment disparity is paralleled by disparities in the French educational system. Kanak children were first allowed to attend French public secondary schools in 1952, and, although twice as many Kanak children as European children are in public schools, Kanak children represent only 6 per cent of the high-school graduates, compared with 80 per cent for European children. The first Kanak graduated from high school in 1962, and the first diploma in higher education was awarded to a Kanak in 1972. At the end of the 1970s, there were no Kanak doctors, lawyers, economists, or engineers and there were only seven Kanak university graduates and one secondary-school teacher. Kanaks represent 2 per cent of New Caledonians with a higher education [16] (AISDPK 1985: 6; Connell et al. 1985: 8; Kircher 1986: 15).

New Caledonia has the largest European population, both in absolute numbers and in proportion to the total population, of any country in the South Pacific region (except the Pitcairn Islands), and, with Guam and Fiji, it is one of the few countries where the indigenous population is a minority.

The French settlers born in New Caledonia (*caldoches*) are descendants of colonists and convicts. Among them are approximately 1,000 poor rural fami-

Table 2. Population born in New Caledonia, by ethnic group, 1976 (%)

Kanak	99.8
Indonesian	78.0
Vietnamese	60.1
European	60.1
Wallisian	49.8
French Polynesian	34.0
Ni-Vanuatu	20.4
Other	40.3
Total population	74.6

Source: Connell et al. 1985: 17.

lies (about 4,000 people) involved in small business and farming. Most have small farms of less than 25 hectares each. Similarly, there is a white proletariat in the urban centres – primarily Noumea – dominated by a small bourgeois minority that controls the economy and politics. Yet, despite the class differences, the white *caldoche* population is united in its fear and racism. This paranoia is perpetuated and fuelled by the white bourgeoisie.

In the postwar era, migration to New Caledonia has changed its character from a "movement, typified earlier by Asian immigrants to one typified by migrants from France itself and from other French territories in the South Pacific" (Connell et al. 1985: 16). This has served to perpetuate the French character of migration, with countries outside the French colonial system playing little part:

Indeed leaders from Tonga, the Gilbert and Ellis (*sic*) Islands (Kiribati and Tuvalu), and Fiji all requested the opportunity for their countries to receive New Caledonian work permits, at the time of the boom, but all were rejected (Crocombe 1975, cited in Connell et al. 1985: 17).

Another important feature of postwar migration has been its predominantly urban orientation. This has resulted in massive ethnic differences between Noumea and the rest of New Caledonia. According to Connell et al. (1985: 17), this has emphasised the numerical differences between a highly concentrated European and migrant population and the dispersed Kanak population.

The metropolitan French have mainly a narrow economic relation with the territory. They came because of high salaries and tax breaks (there was no income tax in New Caledonia before 1982). They are concentrated in Noumea in the secondary and tertiary sectors, and the group contains some moderates, but it also has the *pieds noirs* from Algeria and about 800 "refugees" from

Vanuatu. These people are especially staunch supporters of France and are totally opposed to independence.

After World War II, the Asian population, which, since the war, had consisted almost entirely of Javanese Indonesians and Vietnamese, fell sizably. "A more rural Asian population distribution has given way to a principally urban (Noumea) population as Asians have increasingly taken up commercial and administrative employment, to the extent that, in 1976, 61 per cent of Asians in New Caledonia lived in Noumea and a further 17 per cent in the peri-urban areas of Dumbea, Paita and Mone Dore" (Connell et al. 1985: 18).

Migration from Wallis and Futuna has increased, until there are now more Wallisians and Futunans in New Caledonia than in Wallis and Futuna (Connell et al. 1985: 19). Most are from Wallis and live in urban areas. "In 1976 45 per cent of Wallisians and Futunans were in Noumea and a substantial proportion of the others were in the peri-urban areas of Mont Dore (24 %), Paita (8.7 %), Dumbea (8.5 %) . . . and Thio (5.2 %)" (Connell et al. 1985: 19).

The Wallisian and Futunan population has grown (mainly because it has the highest birth rate of any ethnic community in New Caledonia) so that now the Wallisians constitute the third largest ethnic group in the colony. For the first time, in recent municipal elections in Noumea, the Wallisians presented their own list of candidates separate from the RPCR. This indicates that the Wallisians may be beginning to see themselves as an autonomous political force (AISDPK 1985: 8).

Migration from French Polynesia came with the postwar expansion in the public works programme, especially the construction of the Yate dam in 1955–56. Since then, there has been a steady out-migration, as Polynesians preferred to return home because of increased job opportunities (e.g., the construction of the French Nuclear Testing Centre in 1963). The increase in the French Polynesian community in New Caledonia is due to natural increase.

THE DEMAND FOR INDEPENDENCE

Post World War II development was accompanied by advancements in the field of education, and in 1976, the first group of Kanak students was sent to French universities. This was a very significant time in the development of the Kanak Independence Movement, because the French student revolution of 1968 influenced the development of Kanak political consciousness. The Kanak students, especially the high chief Nidoish Naisseline, returned to New Caledonia and rejected the assimilationist policies of the UC in favour of an assertion of Kanak culture and affirmation of Kanak identity. The *Foulards Rouges* (red scarves) was formed in 1969. This group of young, educated Kanaks began to raise questions concerning land rights, the place of Kanak language and culture in the educational system, and the right to publish Kanak-language newspapers (forbidden as "subversive" by the administration).[17]

It is at this time that we see the appearance of the word "Kanak." Until this time, "canaque" had been used to refer to the native people of New Caledonia. "Canaque" has Polynesian origins and was first used by Tongan and Tahitian crewmen of European ships in reference to the indigenous people of the territory. Up until the late 1960s, "canaque" was a pejorative word similar to "nigger." The young activists changed its spelling to Kanak, and the word began to take on a militant meaning.

In 1970, a new Kanak-led political party, the Union Multiraciale de Nouvelle-Caledonie/New Caledonia Multiracial Union (UMNC) was formed, and in the early 1970s, both the UC and UMNC pressed for *autonomie interne* – responsible self-government.

The early 1970s was a boom period for New Caledonia. There was increased immigration to the territory and the demographic balance there began to work against the Kanaks. Between 1969 and 1974, 25,000 immigrants – a quarter of the population then – entered the territory (Kircher 1986: 7).

From 1965 to 1971, a total of 15,000 French people arrived from the Metropole (Saussol 1986: 18). New immigration of 2,000 *pieds-noirs* from Algeria, ex-servicemen, and small businessmen also came with the nickel boom of 1969–74. Immigrants from Wallis Island and French Polynesia formed large minorities and saw themselves as dependent on the French for jobs and land and who therefore supported them. From 1969 to 1976, a total of 25,000 immigrants arrived in the territory (Colombani 1985).

This massive immigration was not only a result of the nickel boom, but also part of a conscious policy on the part of the French government to dilute the Kanak population and reduce the power of the independence movement. In a revealing letter, the French prime minister, Mr. Messmer, wrote to Mr. Deniau, secretary of state:

We must seize this opportunity to create a francophone country. The French presence in New Caledonia can only be threatened . . . by a nationalist movement on the part of the native people. . . . In the short term, a massive immigration of French citizens from the Metropole and Overseas Departments (eg. Reunion), should allow us to avoid this danger by maintaining and improving the demographic ratio amongst the ethnic communities. . . . In the long term, the indigenous peoples' nationalist demands can be avoided if the non-Pacific ethnic groups represent a massive majority. It is evident that we will obtain no long term demographic results without systematic immigration. . . . (Messmer 1985).

By 1974, the Kanaks accounted for only 42 per cent of the population, and they had not benefited very much from the prosperity of the boom. Few were employed in the private sector. Among wage earners, they remained the least numerous group and were predominantly unskilled labourers (see Fages 1972: 78). By 1976, they formed less than one per cent of the employer class (Ward 1982: 18). Roux (1974: 304) estimates that their economic power was 10 per cent that of other ethnic groups.

The global resources (monetary and other) of Melanesian households are on the average, two times less than those of European households and inferior to that of all other ethnic groups. . . . A veritable economic, education and cultural under-development affects the majority of Melanesians compared to other ethnic communities (Roux 1972: 301).

In the 1970s, independence was won in Fiji (1970), Papua New Guinea (1975), the Solomon Islands (1978), and most other colonial territories in the South Pacific. Concurrently, the UMNC and other new radical Kanak-led parties began to demand full independence – an independence recognising the primacy of the Kanaks as the legitimate people of New Caledonia. In 1976, PALIKA (Parti de Libération Kanak/Kanak Liberation Party) was formed out of the *Foulards Rouges* and another youth group (*Group 1878*). The PALIKA leaders had been exposed to Marxist ideology in France, and according to Kircher (1986: 8), "PALIKA's programme was the most radical expression of the polit- ical, economic and cultural ideals of independence." PALIKA supported Kanak independence, the return of all Kanak lands, the promotion of solidarity with the working class, the nationalisation of the nickel industry, and the estab- lishment of rural and urban co-operatives. PALIKA emphasised the establish- ment of grass-roots support by forming local committees. The French state reacted as follows:

Having embarked on an anti-autonomist course the French state was then obliged to intensify control of the Territory's democratic institutions against mounting Melanesian radicalism. . . . A revision of the basic Territorial status in 1976 indicated the limits of local responsibility: France ("the State") still appoints the high commissioner and the senior officials of the administrative services. It retains formal responsibility for foreign affairs, defense, external communications, finance and credit, justice, local government, secondary and tertiary education, and radio and television. Other matters – primary education, health, transport, agriculture, and land are formally Territory matters, but the Territory lacks the finance, the staff and the detailed legal authority to do much more than routine administration of these matters. Any major new departure – the recent land reform proposals, for example – requires elaborate coordination with Paris, visits each way by officials and politicians, months of planning, and dependence on metropolitan finance (Ward 1982: 20).

At the same time, the white settlers were also reacting. Vigilante committees and paramilitary groups were formed. The largest was the Comité d'Action

Contre l'Indépendance/The Anti-Independence Action Committee, with approximately 12,000 members concentrated primarily in Noumea (Kircher 1986: 9).

In the 1977 elections, the territory was presented with several policies, from a permanent connection with France and limited local autonomy to *Indépendance Kanak*. In the elections, the right and centrist parties formed a coalition that won control of the Territorial Assembly and the Governimg Council. This coalition served as the foundation for the RPCR (Rassemblement pour la Calédonie dans la République/Assembly for Caledonia in the Republic), formed in 1978.[18] From the election results it was clear that Kanaks were supporting the independence parties. As a result of the shift of Kanak support away from the UC to the independence parties, the UC shifted its policy from *autonomie interne* to full independence. According to Ward, this move was of great significance.

Although it had already lost some European and Melanesian support, the Union Caledonienne still encompassed both communities. And it was still one of the biggest parties. Its support for independence meant that such a goal was no longer the preserve only of radical Melanesian parties, but a serious option confronting New Caledonia and France (Ward 1982: 23).

In 1979, Paul Dijoud, secretary of state for overseas departments and territories, developed a new land policy and comprehensive plan for long-term social and economic development in New Caledonia. The collapse of the nickel boom in 1974–75 had produced serious unemployment and economic stagnation. Dijoud tried to resolve the intensifying divisions in New Caledonia with an integrated programme designed to repair the sagging economy and outbid the *indépendantistes* (see Ward 1982: 35–38)

Dijoud coupled the plan with a renewed assertion of French authority. There was no suggestion of new powers for the territory's political institutions. On the contrary, Dijoud stated that as long as New Caledonia remained French, "it is the Government of France who will command" (quoted in Ward 1982: 37).

The first consequence of the adoption of the Dijoud plan was the downfall of the UC Governing Council. The various factions supporting independence quickly came together to form a *Front Indépendantiste* (FI). Its campaign statements were anticapitalist and antiimperialist, for an independence both Kanak and socialist, and included the goal of immediate and unconditional return of traditional lands to the clans and the "territorialisation" of the mines. In a tense election, the conservatives emerged with 15 seats and the FI with 14. In percentages, 65 per cent of those who voted supported the conservative coalition and 35 per cent the FI[19] (Ward 1982: 45). Eighty per cent of the Kanak vote went to the FI, and support for the conservatives came mainly from the urban areas, where the white and migrant workers were concentrated.

In 1980, conditions continued to deteriorate and protests were organised by the whites and Kanaks alike (see Kircher 1986: 9). Meanwhile, support for independence was mounting. The Synod of the Eglise Evangélique made a unanimous declaration in favour of independence.[20]

THE POLITICS OF THE SOCIALISTS

The French presidential elections in 1981 increased the tension in New Caledonia. At the beginning of the campaign, the conservatives supported Chirac and the *indépendantistes* were divided between boycott, Mitterand, and the Communist candidate Marchais. The conservatives switched their support to Fiscard, and he won the majority of votes in the territory, except on the east coast of La Grande Terre and in the Loyalty Islands, where the Kanaks constitute most of the population (see Clark 1983).

When Mitterand was elected, the FI hoped that its request for an early transition to independence would be granted. The French Socialist party had previously met with FI representatives and, in 1979, had expressed "its full solidarity with the struggle of the FI" and affirmed "its intention to support and guarantee the right of the Kanak people to freely decide their future" (quoted in Kircher 1986: 9). However, Mitterand's victory offered no hope to the cause of the *indépendantistes*. On the contrary, the new prime minister underlined his intention to reinforce the "solidarity" between France and her overseas departments and territories.

In the 1982 territorial elections, the *indépendantistes* won a majority in the Governing Council and supported co-operation with the French socialist government. Mitterand, on his part, declared himself in favour of *autonomie interne* and the Governing Council began to assume more responsibility in the administration of the colony.

Violence and radicalism also increased in 1982–83. The secretary-general of the UC, Pierre Declerq, was gunned down by a white man, and the culprit was somehow never found. Demonstrations about the killing broke out everywhere in the territory.

Attempting to defuse the situation, the French Socialist government held roundtable talks at Nainville les Roches in July 1983. At this meeting, the government recognised "the innate and active right of the Kanak people – as the first inhabitants of the Territory – to Independence" (quoted in Kircher 1986: 10). Following this meeting, Lemoine, the secretary for overseas departments and territories, proposed another statute for New Caledonia, with provisions for a transitional period of *autonomie interne* followed by a referendum in 1989.

The FI opposed the Lemoine statute for several reasons: 1989 was too late for the referendum, since the upcoming 1986 elections for the French National Assembly were very likely to bring in a conservative majority that would oppose any move to independence; more important was that the statute proposed no

electoral reform. The electoral laws gave any French citizen resident in the
territory for six months the right to vote. Moreover, French military and government officials were allowed to vote the minute they arrived. Protests were
staged throughout the colony, but they went unheeded by the French government. The statute was unanimously opposed by the New Caledonian Territorial Assembly, but the government continued to turn a deaf ear and the statute
was adopted in May 1984. As usual, the fate of New Caledonia was decided in
the Metropole, with little consideration being given to local opinion.

According to Kircher (1986: 10), the FI felt betrayed by the Socialist government. The Socialists had been in power three years and little progress had been
made. "Even the more moderate FI leaders began advocating a change in tactics from negotiations to confrontation" (Kircher 1986: 10).

The FLNKS (Front de Libération Nationale Kanaks et Socialiste/Kanak
National Socialist Liberation Front) was founded at the end of September 1984.
It comprised seven pressure groups – five political parties, a trade union, and a
women's group (see Gabriel and Kermel 1985). Emphasis was placed on grass-
roots support, especially on the local action committees. Other ethnic groups
were invited to join the FLNKS in its struggle for national liberation "because
only solidarity with the liberation struggle will legitimate their citizenship in
tomorrow's socialist Kanak independence" (FLNKS, quoted in Gabriel and
Kermel 1985: 135). For the most part, the organisation formulated its ideas in
terms of the Kanak experience, with Kanak Socialist independence as its final
goal. In its founding charter, the FLNKS stated that:

1. The French government is an accomplice to colonialism and intends to maintain and
   support it.
2. Francois Mitterand, who became President of the Republic on May 10, 1981, did not
   fulfil his commitments.
3. The declaration of Nainville les Roches, concerning our right to independence, has
   not been respected nor put into practice.
4. The French government has refused all attempts on the part of the Independence
   Front to prepare for an accession to a Kanak Socialist Independence by imposing on
   us the Lemoine statute . . . (and) by directly menacing the Kanak people with cultural
   genocide by making us a minority in our own country.
5. Capitalist and imperialist exploitation by foreign interests continues to profit colonialist France and her allies.
6. The French government follows a policy of immigration which is aimed at preventing
   the Kanak people from: managing their own economy; realising their right to employment; achieving and maintaining their social, cultural and political integrity (1984,
   quoted in Gabriel and Kermel 1985: 233–35).

The FLNKS refused to participate in any elections that were not leading to
independence, and in November 1984, they boycotted the territorial elections.

Less than 50 per cent of the registered voters participated in the elections. On 1 December the Kanaks established a provisional government, and the French government sent in Edgar Pisani as a trouble-shooter. The following months proved to be a very stormy period in New Caledonia. There were many violent clashes (see Kircher 1986); several Kanaks lost their lives, and others were sent to prison.

In May 1985, the Socialist government proposed the Fabius/Pisani Plan. A referendum was to be held no later than December 1986 on the question of independence-association; i.e., and independence in association with France. The plan also proposed extensive regional development with large sums of money going to the rural areas "to remedy the economic and social inequalities of the Territory." The plan also proposed the reinforcement of a French military presence in New Caledonia (there was, and still is, a police and military force of at least 5,000 men in New Caledonia).

In August, the plan was passed and four regions were created; their councils, which constituted the Territorial Assembly (now called Territorial Congress), were to be elected by universal suffrage. However, the power still lay in the hands of France:

The Congress . . . has a purely consultative function. The real power rests firstly with the French High Commissioner, then with the Regional Councils and finally with the Executive Council, made up of the High Commissioner, the four Regional Presidents and the President of the Congress. The Executive Council, in which the FLNKS holds three of the five seats, is to assist the colonial power in making its decisions (Kircher 1986: 12).

The FLNKS was not totally satisfied with the Fabius/Pisani Plan. It was criticised for its colonialist aspects; yet, because it was perceived as being a step in the direction of independence, the FLNKS decided to accept the plan and participate in the territorial elections that were held in September 1985.

The elections clearly showed the polarisation in New Caledonian politics. The centrist parties, which Pisani had hoped would constitute a third force, received little support, and the population divided itself between the FLNKS and the RPCR. The FLNKS took more than 80 per cent of the Kanak vote (see Rollat 1985) and won three out of the four regions, thereby acquiring a majority in the Governing Council. The white-dominated RPCR received its support from the urban areas – particularly Noumea – and acquired a majority in the Congress.

The Fabius/Pisani Plan had set up a delicately balanced system where the two extremes could block each other or choose to co-operate if they wanted the colony to run. Meanwhile, the Kanak-controlled rural regions were offered the opportunity to learn more about self-government and rural development by administering the regional development projects.

THE POLITICS OF THE RIGHT

After the September 1985 elections, the RPCR opted for a blocking, or at least a holding, pattern until the legislative elections in spring 1986. They hoped that their French ally, the RPR, would win the elections and implement reforms that would repeal the Fabius/Pisani Plan. Jacques Lafleur, leader to the RPCR, said, "If the opposition wins (the National Assembly elections) we are saved. . . . We are determined to resist until March 1986" (quoted in Kircher 1986: 12).

Meanwhile, the extreme right launched a campaign of violence and intimidation. More than a dozen bomb attacks took place against pro-independence groups. In November and March 1985, two arms shipments destined for anti-independence groups were confiscated in Australia and New Zealand. Vigilante and paramilitary groups continue to be formed by the Europeans (see Kircher 1986: 12).

Chirac's RPR won the National Assembly elections in France in March 1986, and true to its word, the RPR began to dismantle the previous Socialist government's reforms in New Caledonia. The Fabius/Pisani Plan was canned, and in July 1986, yet another statute for New Caledonia was passed.

The new Pons statute, named after the new minister for overseas departments and territories, eliminated the land claims office and refused to recongnise the powers of the regional councils. Although the funds for regional development remained in place, the power to distribute them was taken out of the hands of the regions and transferred to the French High Commissioner. According to Pons:

The statute which I am proposing leaves the regions jurisdiction over the areas they are best adapted to handling, that is: reflection on regional development; realisation of local development projects; realisation of local infrastructure development; promotion of vernacular languages and cultural animation (quoted in *Le Monde*, 16 May 1985).

Moreover, the terms of the referendum was changed. The date was postponed until mid-1987. The vote was no longer to take place on the question of independence-association; the options are now total independence or remaining in the French Republic. One possible consequence of this choice is that the centrist groups and potential FLNKS sympathisers would be scared off by the thought of immediate and total French withdrawal. Pons did not calm their fears when he said, "If they want, they can choose Independence with all the serious consequences that comes with it" (quoted in *Libération*, 2 May 1986).

Under the Pons statute, the definition of the elector remains an issue. The six-month residency requirement still applies. The situation has polarised between two extremes. The French government proposes "one person, one vote," and the Kanaks maintain that they are the only ones with a legitimate right to vote. As Jean Marie Tjibaou, head of the FLNKS, has said, "It is unreasonable to ask a Frenchman if he wants to remain French. It is the Kanaks who have had French citizenship imposed upon them and therefore the Kanaks should be the ones to decide whether to be French or not" (personal communication, 4 October 1986).

The above stance on the part of the FLNKS has served to alienate members of the other ethnic minorities in New Caledonia, who fear that there would not be much place for them in an independent Kanaky. The FLNKS has sought to counter such alienation by calling on the non-Kanak groups to join them in the construction of an independent Kanaky:

For us, cohabitation is not a problem. We want to work with the Europeans. We have to make the Europeans understand that independence is not exclusive (Joredie 1985, quoted in Kircher 1986: 13).

And there is evidence that there is some move on the part of other ethnic groups to support the Kanaks. For example, in the 1985 territorial election, 11 per cent of Noumeans voted for the FLNKS, and the Kanak votes in Noumea number only 5 per cent (see Filloux 1985). But is it too little too late? Although constituting 42 per cent of the population, 52 per cent of the Kanaks are less than 20 years old and are ineligible to vote. Even with some sort of electoral reform (e.g., three years of residency), the Kanaks would not constitute a majority. Their only hope of winning a referendum on independence lies with their ability to solicit support from the other ethnic communities in New Caledonia.

NOTES

1. For a history of expropriations and property relations in New Caledonia, see Saussol (1979).
2. These political deportees came from Algeria, Tunisia, and Morocco (see Collinet 1978) and from the Paris Commune.
3. For details on the revolt, see Douglas (1980), Dousset-Leenhardt (1970, 1976), and Latham (1978).
4. In New Caledonia there is a judicial separation in which French and other non-Kanak minorities live under the *droit commun* and the Kanaks live under the *statut particulier*.
5. The head tax came into effect in 1900 (the decree was passed in 1895) and applied to all males. To pay off the tax, the Kanaks had little choice but to work for the settlers. According to Doumenge (1982: 113–14), the tax was equivalent to 10 days of labour for a settler.
6. The first 768 Vietnamese coolies arrived in New Caledonia in 1891. However, they

had been recruited from among the prisoners held on Poulo Condore, off the coast of Cochin China. They proved to be very unsatisfactory labourers (Thompson and Adloff 1971: 449).

7. Including the obligation to work for the settlers and in public works, this forced labour system kept the average Kanak outside his reserve at least six weeks a year (Doumenge 1982: 115).

8. Two religious groups were formed: U.I.C.A.L.O. (l'Union des indigènes calédoniens amis de la liberté en order/Union of Native Caledonians, Friends of Liberty and Order) founded by the Catholic church in 1946, and A.I.C.L.F. (l'Association des indigènes calédoniens et loyaltiens francais/Association of Native Caledonians and French Loyalists).

9. The population densities on reserves had sometimes reached 50 persons per km² of cultivable land – inadequate for the traditional subsistence cycle. Also, the more fertile soils were being turned over to commercial production (coffee), diminishing the areas available for food production.

10. It should be noted that the settler supporters of the UC gave their support for many different reasons, e.g., the advancement of New Caledonian businessmen and civil servants against the interests of metropolitan French. Not all of them were liberal and progressive, and almost all would have assumed that there would be continued white dominance.

11. Fifteen per cent of New Caledonia's budget is revenue from mining and metallurgy. In contrast, coffee accounts for less than one per cent of the territory's export value, and nickel accounts for 97 per cent (McTaggart 1976).

12. According to Saussol (1986: 17), nickel production increased 15 times from 1953 to 1970.

13. From 1956 to 1983, the population of Noumea and its suburbs went from 25,000 to 85,000. In 1983, the major ethnic groups were 11,000 Wallisians, 5,000 Tahitians, 4,000 Indonesians, and 2,200 Vietnamese. In 1983, the Kanaks in Noumea and its suburbs numbered 16,600, and the Europeans 43,000 (Saussol 1986: 18; Wacquant 1985).

14. Sixty per cent of New Caledonia's exports go to France, and 35 per cent of the territory's imports come from France (Connell et al. 1985: 7).

15. 100 South Pacific francs = about US $1.00.

16. In February 1985, the FLNKS boycotted the "colonial school system" for one month and 60 per cent to 70 per cent of the Kanak students were absent from classes (Kircher 1986: 15). This action stimulated the founding of a Kanak alternative school system known as "école populaire kanake" – a grass-roots organisation involving more than 1,500 primary school students and 260 volunteer teachers.

The objective of the école populaire kanake is to educate Kanak children into the social, political, economic, and cultural realities of Kanak life. Instruction emphasises Kanak traditions and language, with an emphasis on French as a second language. Special attention is also paid to practical skills, such as agriculture and fishing (Kircher 1986: 15).

Other iniatives on the part of the FLNKS include the founding in July 1985 of the weekly newspaper *Bwedando*, which has a circulation of about 5,000, and the setting up of the Kanak radio station *Dijdo*, which began broadcasting in September 1985.

17. In September 1969, Naisseline was arrested and jailed for "inciting" racial hatred by distributing pamphlets in a vernacular language (Kircher 1986: 8).

18. Many whites left the UC and joined the RPCR when the UC pronounced itself in favour of Kanak independence (Saussol 1986: 19).

19. At this time, the population of New Caledonia totaled about 65,000 Kanaks, 49,700 whites, 17,600 Wallisians, and 11,800 other immigrants.

20. The Eglise Evangélique stands in sharp contrast to the Catholic church in New Caledonia. The Catholic church is the largest denomination, with 65 per cent of the population and 90 per cent of the French settlers in its flock. Both its membership and clergy are predominantly white. Twenty-six per cent of the population of New Caledonia are members of the Eglise Evangélique. All its clergy and 90 per cent of its membership are Kanak (Kircher 1986: 15). The Eglise Evangélique has had a strong history of promoting Kanak interests.

REFERENCES

AISDPK (Association d'information et soutien aux droits du peuple Kanak).1985. *Kanaky: Bulletin d'Information et Soutien aux Droits de Peuple Kanak.* 2: 3

Benza, A., and J. C. Riviere. 1982. *Les chemins de l'alliance: L'organisation sociale et ses representations en Nouvelle-Calédonie.* Paris: S. E. L. A. F.

Clark, D. 1983. Anatomy, integration, development, elections in New Caledonia. *Political Science* 35: 16–37.

Collinet, M. 1979. Les Arabs en Nouvelle-Calédonie. *Bulletin de la Société d'Etudes Historiques de la Nouvelle-Calédonie* 36: 1–34.

Colombani, J. M. 1985. Nouvelle-Calédonie: Les racines de la crise. *Le Monde/Dossiers et Documents* March 1985.

Connell, J. et al. 1985. *Migration, employment and development in the South Pacific.* Noumea: South Pacific Commission.

Dornoy, M. 1984. *Politics in New Caledonia.* Australia: Sydney University Press.

Douglas, B. 1980. Conflict and alliance in a colonial context. *Journal of Pacific History* 25: 21–51.

Doumenge, J. P. 1975. *Paysans Mélanésiens en pays Canala.* Bordeaux: Centre d'Etudes de Geographie Tropicale, Travaux et Documents de Geographie Tropicale No. 17.

———. 1982. *Du terroir a la ville: Mélanésiens et leurs espaces en Nouvelle-Calédonie.* Bordeaux: Centre d'Etudes de Geographie Tropicale, Travaux et Documents de Geographie Tropicale No. 46

Dousset-Leenhardt, R. 1970. *Colonialisme et contradictions: Etude sur les causes socio-historiques de l'insurrection de 1878 en Nouvelle-Calédonie.* Paris: Mouton.

———. 1976. *Terre natale, terre d'exil.* Paris: G. P. Maisonneuve et Larose.

Fages, J. 1972. La communauté tahitienne de Nouvelle Calédonie. *Cahiers O.R.S.T.O.M.* 9: 75–86.

Filloux, F. 1985. Même Nouméa la blanche. *Le Monde* 3 October 1985.

Gabriel, C., and V. Kermel. 1985. *Nouvelle-Calédonie: La révolte kanake.* Paris: Labreche.

Gasher, P. 1975. Les problèmes de la main-d'œuvre en Nouvelle-Calédonie. *Cahiers d'Histoire de Pacifique* 1: 6–27.

Guiart, J. 1954. Naissance et avortement d'un messianisme. *Archives de Sociologie des Religions* 4: 3–44.

Howe, K. R. 1978. Tourists, sailors and labourers. *Journal of Pacific History* 13: 22–35.

Kermel, V. 1986. Le mouvement nationalist de l'après guerre au FLNKS. *Kanaky: Bulletin d'Information et Soutien aux Droits de Peuple Kanak* 3/4: 24–26.

Kircher, L. 1986. *The Kanaks of New Caledonia.* London: Minority Rights Group Report No. 71.

Kobayashi, M. 1980. Les Japonais en Nouvelle-Calédonie. *Bulletin de la Société d'Etudes Historiques de la Nouvelle-Calédonie* 43: 57–72.

Latham, L. 1975. Revolt re-examined: The 1878 insurrection in New Caledonia. *Journal of Pacific History* 10: 48–64.

Leenhardt, M. 1930. *Notes d'ethnologie néo-calédoniennes.* Paris: Institut d'Ethnologie.

———. 1932. *Documents néo-calédoniennes.* Paris: Institut d'Ethnologie.

———. 1937. *Gens de la Grande Terre.* Paris: Gallimard.

———. 1947. *Do Kamo.* Paris: Gallimard.

———. 1978. Notes sur le régime de l'engagement des indigènes en Nouvelle-Calédonie. *Journal de la Société des Océanistes* 61: 9–18.

Lenormand, M. 1953. Evolution politique des autochtones de la Nouvelle-Calédonie. *Journal de la Société des Océanistes* 9: 245–99.

McTaggart, W. 1976. New Caledonia and the French connection. In *Oceania and beyond,* edited by F. P. King, 179–99. London: Greenwood Press.

Messmer, P. 1985. Messmer to Deniau, 18 July 1972. In *Kanaky: Bulletin d'Information et Soutien aux Droits de Peuple Kanak* 2: 3.

Rollat, A. 1985. Le vote canaque apparaît indépendantiste à 80 %. *Le Monde* 3 October 1985.

Roux, J. C. 1974. Crise de la réserve autochtone et passage des Mélanésiens dans l'économie de la Nouvelle-Calédonie. *Cahiers O.R.S.T.O.M* 3.

Saussol, A. 1979. *L'héritage: Essai sur le problème foncier mélanésien en Nouvelle-Calédonie.* Paris: Société des Océanistes.

———.1986. Les grands ruptures économiques et sociales de la Calédonie coloniale (1843–1984). *Kanaky: Bulletin d'Information et Soutien aux Droits de Peuple Kanak* 3/4: 15–19.

Shineberg, D. 1967. *They came for sandalwood.* Melbourne: Melbourne University Press.

Thompson, V., and R. Adloff. 1971. *The French Pacific islands.* Berkeley: University of California Press.

Wacquant, L. 1985. Nouméa: Une place forte et son désert. *Le Monde Diplomatique* October 1985.

Ward, A. 1982. *Land and politics in New Caledonia.* Political and Social Change Monograph No. 2. Canberra: Australia National University, Department of Political and Social Change.

Winslow, D. 1986. Labour relations in New Caledonia to 1945. *South Pacific Forum* 3: 97–112.

13

Pohnpei Ethnicity and Micronesian Nation-building

GLENN PETERSEN

Most of the world's states are multiethnic, and in a great many of them, no one ethnic group or nationality constitutes a majority of the population. This is without a doubt the situation among the new states in the islands of the western Pacific Ocean. Nowhere is the complexity of cross-cutting cultural, geographic, linguistic, and political ties more evident than in the Federated States of Micronesia (FSM), which stretch across nearly 2,000 miles of the equator.

In this chapter, I intend to explore some of the problems that arise from this complexity. In particular, I will focus on the staunch opposition of the people of Pohnpei (formerly Ponape), one of the larger Micronesian islands, to the free association agreement negotiated with the United States and on their incipient alienation from both the FSM national government and the other ethnic groups with whom they share Pohnpei State.

The causes of this tension are to be found in the intersecting realms of ethnicity and development and in the paradoxical truth that, in Pohnpei's case, nation-building may in fact be – as Walker Connor (1972) phrases it – "nation-destroying." The Pohnpei assert their ethnic identity as a means of preserving rights to specific political, economic, and social forms; in making deliberate arguments about the character these forms must take, they incidentally differentiate themselves from other Micronesians. Their actions are not only responses to the exigencies of colonial and postcolonial life, but they are also equally products of consistent reflection on the constitution of Pohnpei culture and traditions.

Though it may strike some as ill-natured to say so, the Federated States of Micronesia is, in a sense, the product of an incomplete decolonisation process: the trimmings of an empire. American military demands facilitated the carving apart of the US Trust Territory of the Pacific Islands into four separate entities. Separate arrangements have been negotiated in the Northern Marianas, Belau (Palau), the Marshalls, and FSM (which embraces the islands known to geog-

285

raphers as the Eastern Carolines and Central Carolines). The United States has large-scale military interests in the Marianas, the Marshalls, and Belau; FSM comprises the remainder – the islands for which the United States has no *specific* plans. It could be argued that the logical basis of the federation is convenience: the convenience of American military, foreign relations, and budgetary establishments.

Struggles for national liberation ordinarily place a high value on unity; attempts by individual groups to achieve autonomy are perceived and dealt with as threats to the entire independence movement. Former colonial borders are treated as sacrosanct, sometimes even expanded. In the Micronesian case, however, ethnic divisions were heeded, or at least given lip-service, where they coincided with American interests and ignored where they did not. The Micronesians learned that, while some ethnic, regional, and cultural differences have political validity, others do not.

The FSM is by far the most ethnically and regionally heterogeneous of the new Micronesian political entities, and its national government thus faces greater contradictions than the others. As it is constituted, it exists as a product of precisely those forces and strategies that it must defend itself against to survive.

Furthermore, the very autonomy of the national government is in question. The FSM, like Belau and the Marshalls, has agreed to a relationship with the United States that falls short – some say considerably short – of independence. The compacts of "free association," as these new relationships are called, include treaties that give the US military control over the islands in perpetuity *and* concede to the United States the right to decide the issues that are to be defined as military.[1] This means the FSM cannot freely establish relations with other states. The national government is tied inexorably to its financial agreements with the United States and must, therefore, govern in a manner that convinces the United States that the FSM is making proper use of the monies it receives. It follows, then, that the FSM is compelled to give its obligations to the United States higher priority than to those of its four constituent states, despite constitutional provisions delegating to the states much autonomy and financial equality with the national government.

The several FSM states are not free, the national government's claims to the contrary notwithstanding, to devise their own development strategies. Were this right granted in fact as well as in theory, some of their decisions might well threaten the continued flow of US funding. (This is not a hypothetical issue; it is a major dilemma in current policy-making with the FSM.)

To a degree, these problems mirror those experienced by most other countries. The demands of the World Bank and the exigencies of decentralisation policies mean that few governments are free to make their own decisions or to grant full autonomy to provincial or local polities. Nevertheless, these governments are ultimately free, if they so desire, to negotiate bilateral agreements and to do without multilateral funding, and they are thus able to exercise greater control over the development strategies they pursue. This is not the case in Micronesia. The Micronesians have foreclosed their options in return for a 15-year agreement, though it must be acknowledged they did not have much choice in this.[2]

At least one group of Micronesians, the people of the island of Pohnpei, recognize the full range of implications I have sketched out here (indeed, they taught them to me), and, despite the lack of choice presented by the United States, voted in the 1983 FSM plebiscite to reject free association in favour of independence. Because the three other FSM states approved the compact, Pohnpei has acceded – for the present, at least – to the new relationship with the United States. Nevertheless, most Pohnpei do not wish to follow development strategies laid out by the United States and the FSM national government. The Pohnpei, however, are not the only people who live in Pohnpei State; the range of ethnopolitical complexities that characterize the so-called Micronesian nation-state are equally present within Pohnpei State. There are micropolities within microdivisions within microstates within Micronesia, and decisions made at one level – in this case, Pohnpei State – may well contradict decisions made at more inclusive *and* more particular levels.

As it now stands, when the Pohnpei attempt to make their own decisions about development, they must take into account both the pressures placed on them by the United States through the FSM national government and the wishes of the non-Pohnpei people from smaller, nearby islands (within Pohnpei State) concerning the proper nature of development. In general, the people of the smaller islands share the perspective of the national government, and the Pohnpei frequently find themselves opposing nearly everyone with whom they must deal. It is not surprising that their rejection of free association was widely – nearly universally – misunderstood.

In this chapter, I try to elucidate some of the questions, issues, and problems generated by this set of cross-cutting ties and requirements. I begin by describing the current Micronesian scene. I then discuss the Pohnpei's keen appreciation for the life they now live and their desire to preserve it. Next, I outline the existing and potential oppositions between the Pohnpei people themselves and the people of the surrounding coral atolls, many of whom live on Pohnpei Island proper. Finally, I examine the possibility that nation-building in Micronesia is in fact nation-destroying.

CONTEMPORARY MICRONESIA

For the purposes of this chapter, I am using progressively narrowing notions of Micronesia. Although the general culture area includes Kiribati, Nauru, and Guam, I use the term here to refer to the US Trust Territory of the Pacific Islands. The Trust Territory itself includes the Marshall Islands, the Caroline

Islands, and the Mariana Islands. Though the Marshalls and the Marianas
form relatively distinctive cultural entities, the Carolines do not. The Carolines
stretch across some 5,000 km of the western Pacific and are grouped under a
single rubric only because of an expansionist-minded 17th century Spanish car-
tographer. The leaders of Belau, in the extreme west of the Carolines, have
negotiated a separate agreement with the United States, as have those of the
Marshalls and the Northern Marianas. The rest of the Carolines are grouped
into "states" named after the largest island or group of islands within each,
Yap, Truk, Pohnpei, and Kosrae, and together form the FSM.

Each of the four FSM states has its capital on the large island after which it is
named. Although Kosrae is the sole island within its state, the others include
many small atolls. Before the arrival of the imperial powers into the area, the
people of most of the atolls engaged regularly in prodigious seafaring activities;
some still do. Complex social, economic and political ties linked the populations
of many of the smaller islands to Yap and Truk. These ties were of special
importance because of the occasional destruction wrought by typhoons, and
many remain viable, albeit attenuated.

The Marianas were occupied in the 1660s by the Spanish, who used Guam as
a port for galleons making the Manila-to-Acapulco run. The Chamorros of the
northern islands were moved to Guam and allowed to return only two centuries
later. The Western Carolines experienced Spanish missionary activities in the
early 18th century and gradually became part of commercial trade networks in
the late 18th and 19th centuries. New England whalers and Protestant missions
opened the Central and Eastern Carolines to the outer would in the mid-19th
century. German traders set up shop in the Marshalls in the mid- to late-19th
century in the company of American missionaries.

Arguments over a range of colonial boundaries and spheres of influence, including Borneo and the Philippines, led to a series of agreements between
Spain, Britain, and Germany, recognizing Spanish hegemony in the Marianas
and the Carolines and German rule in the Marshalls. The Spanish-German
arrangement, concluded in 1885, was short-lived. Following the Spanish-
American War of 1898, the United States took over Guam, and Germany
purchased the remaining Marianas and the Carolines. The Germans continued
their policy of expanding copra trade and instituted a land reform to that end.
They attempted to put an end to communal land tenure and met with quite
different degrees of success in the different parts of Micronesia.

Following the outbreak of World War I, the Japanese declared war on Germany and annexed the islands, where they had already begun pursuing commercial interests of their own. The League of Nations awarded Japan a mandate over the islands, and in the 1920s, Japan began large-scale development of
plantation agriculture, employing labour primarily imported from Japan.

Small cities grew up in the administrative centres as populations and commercial exports increased. Micronesians from the larger islands were educated

in Japan, and many were employed in semiskilled positions. Regular and apparently reliable transportation was provided to the outer islands. The Japanese also fortified the islands, and many of the most violent and destructive battles of World War II were fought in Micronesia, destroying the commercial infrastructure.

After the war, the United States repatriated the Japanese colonists; took control of the islands through a United Nations trusteeship agreement with special strategic provisions that effectively precluded UN oversight; and, for all practical purposes, ignored most of the area until the early 1960s. The Kennedy administration, recognizing that decolonisation had become the international norm, developed plans to bind the islands permanently to the United States through a plebiscite. Although originally planned for the mid-1960s, the plebiscite was not held until 1983, a sign of the Micronesians' intense efforts to alter the course of American schemes in the islands.

The United States had initially claimed the right, established by force of arms, to hold onto the area in perpetuity. The 1960s' policies included financial strategies meant to induce the Micronesians to willingly accept closer ties with the United States. Enormous increases in the Trust Territory budget transformed the Micronesian economy. By the mid-1970s, much more than US$100 million was being spent each year. The resulting economy has been aptly described as "the dependency of the dope addict."

Negotiations to end trusteeship took place within the vortex created by this crushing dependency and the continued demand by the United States that Micronesians – in an act of self-determination – cede to the United States perpetual military control of their islands, waters, and skies. The Northern Marianas voted in 1975 to become a commonwealth of the United States; these islands include Tinian, the island from which the atomic strikes on Japan were launched, and adjoin Guam, from where numerous B-52 strikes on Vietnam originated. Commonwealth is the same thoroughly ambiguous status accorded Puerto Rico.

In the Marshall Islands, US payments for the lease of the missile range at Kwajalein Atoll provide a subsidy essential to the new government. In Belau, the United States has plans for a guerilla warfare training base and a port facility for nuclear submarines. Although both the Marshalls and Belau voted in favour of free association, the Belau constitution prohibits the presence of nuclear materials in the islands without a 75 per cent vote of approval. Since the pro-compact vote in Belau has repeatedly fallen below this figure in the series of plebiscites demanded by the United States, its status is unclear.

FSM leaders long resisted demands for permanent US military control of their islands, but they finally acquiesced to American intransigence in 1982. In the 1983 plebiscite, FSM voted to approve free association. The sole exception was Pohnpei State, where the vote was 4,414 opposed and 4,116 in favour of the compact.[3]

This narrow margin is deceptive, however. Pohnpei State can be broken down for heuristic purposes into several blocs: the outer islands of Pingelap, Mokil, Ngatik, Nukuoro, and Kapingmarangi; the municipalities of Sokehs and Kolonia Town, which have large immigrant populations from the outer islands and other parts of Micronesia; and the rural, ethnic Pohnpei municipalities that are coterminous with the paramount chiefdoms of Madolenihmw, U, Kiti, and Net. When looked at in terms of these blocs, the difference in votes becomes significant. The ethnic Pohnpei of Pohnpei Island proper voted overwhelmingly against free association; the others approved it by nearly the same margin.

The ethnic Pohnpei were deliberate in their approach to the plebiscite, and their opposition to free association was clearly the product of their measured conclusion that associated status is inferior to independence.[4] They framed their desire for independence in a manner that grew both from a consciousness of themselves as a people with unique traditions and from the conclusion that anything less than independence threatens their continuity as a people sharing these traditions.

Taken in isolation, the Pohnpei vote is a fascinating episode, but there is more. The Pohnpei people share their island, their state, and their national state with other peoples. To the degree that the Pohnpei oppose free association, they also oppose the decisions of these other peoples. In the following two sections, I explore first Pohnpei's consciousness of and appreciation for a way of life they see threatened, and then the discord between the ethnic Pohnpei and the other peoples with whom they share Pohnpei State.

POHNPEI AND POHNPEI STATE

Fundamental to Pohnpei oral traditions are accounts of visits to the island by outsiders. Indeed, Pohnpei origin myths tell of the island's creation by voyagers from the south-east. According to these same accounts, the basic elements of Pohnpei cultural life – fire, food crops, and housing, for example – were brought to the island by foreigners. The modern political system, a series of autonomous paramount chiefdoms, traces its origins to an invasion by foreigners that resulted in the defeat of a dynasty of tyrants (the Sau Deleurs). There is, then, nothing insular about Pohnpei historical consciousness, and the colonial era has presented the Pohnpei with no radical break in their perceptions about the world around them. At the same time, I have also heard people speak of "*Pohnpei sarawi*," that is, a sacred or perhaps enchanted Pohnpei hidden by clouds and thereby protected from outside interference. All this suggests some ambivalence about the outside world.[5]

David Hanlon (1984) has pointed to another thread in Pohnpei historical consciousness, summed up in the phrase, "*Pohnpei sohte ehu*": "Pohnpei is not one" ("Pohnpei is not a unity" or "Pohnpei is not all the same" are other possible glosses). This is usually meant to express the Pohnpei recognition of marked differences among the various communities of the island. Although all Pohnpei speak a common language and share a common set of cultural traditions (*tiahk en Pohnpei*), they also share the perception that they are a heterogeneous lot. As Hanlon puts it, within their own world they see all the world's possibilities.

Pohnpei is by Micronesian standards a very large island, with an area of approximately 725 km². Its topography is rugged, and, until Europeans initiated construction of roads, most travel was on water. The population has been reckoned at 20,000 to 30,000 circa 1828, when Europeans first began writing about the island. Smallpox and other diseases introduced by whalers, traders, and missionaries reduced the population to about 3,000 in 1900, when the Germans conducted the first comprehensive census.

The wide dispersal of Pohnpei's matrilineal clans, along with what seem to have been extremely flexible land tenure practices, suggest that, in the past, kinship connections were as widespread as they are today: Pohnpei say that all Pohnpei are connected by bonds of kinship, and patterns of attendance at funerals bear this out. On the other hand, Pohnpei do place a high value on marrying within their own communities, and actual marriage patterns bear *this* out (Petersen 1982a).

We find, then, contradictory, complimentary, and cross-cutting patterns of behaviour and values in Pohnpei. People stress both local differences and the essential similarity of the whole. They perceive themselves as connected to the outer world and as separate from it. They welcome the foreign even as they accentuate the domestic. Pohnpei's relations with the surrounding coral atolls must be set within this context. Furthermore, Pohnpei's colonial history must also be taken into consideration if we are to understand Pohnpei's current attitudes toward outsiders.

Although the American missionaries who began work on Pohnpei in the 1850s possessed little overt authority, they did wield sizable influence through their schools. They staunchly opposed the Pohnpei socio-polity, perceiving it, in one missionary's phrase, as a "form of socialism." Their influence, though limited, was still significant; it can be seen, for instance, in Pohnpei's relatively minor opposition to the German land reform instituted in 1910. When the Sokehs chiefdom did rebel against a whole series of German practices, the people were exiled to Belau and their land given to a group from the Mortlock Islands, whose homes and crops had been destroyed by typhoons. The Germans helped transform a system in which chiefs had nominal title (and kin groups exercised rights) over land into a system of patrilineal primogeniture. Plots of land were deeded to individuals, and eldest sons were supposed to inherit these intact. Unoccupied lands, known as the *luhwen wehi*, were to be controlled jointly by the chiefs and the German governor.

Among their other objectives, the Germans hoped to engender a concept of private property in land to enhance coconut production and thereby create a peasantry and to get younger sons to reclaim lands that had been abandoned as a result of 19th century depopulation. Although today's Pohnpei hardly fits the model of a Central European peasantry, they do continue to produce copra and manifest strong support for a modified version of the German-introduced land tenure system.

Japanese plans for Pohnpei ran thoroughly counter to those of the Germans. Thousands of immigrants were brought in to work on plantations established in areas with relatively tractable terrain. Though some of this land was expropriated from Pohnpei families, much of it was *luhwen wehi*, control over which the Japanese claimed as solely their own. Today, Pohnpei speak with ambivalence about some aspects of the Japanese occupation, but they retain strong sentiments about Japanese use of and plans for their land. A widespread belief persists that the Japanese had plans to exile all Pohnpei men and require the women to marry Japanese; thus they would gain "legal" control of all Pohnpei land.

Following the war, the United States affirmed Japan's policy of denying inherent Pohnpei control over the *luhwen wehi* lands and instituted a homesteading programme. Both Pohnpei and outer islanders were able to take possession of empty lands and begin farming. They were supposed to receive quit-claim titles to this land, but few did, and the American failure to provide deeds served to exacerbate Pohnpei suspicions about the intentions of the latest colonial power occupying their island.

American development policy in the 1960s and 1970s consisted primarily in hiring Micronesians to work at government jobs in the various administrative centres. This brought large numbers of people from the coral atolls into the rapidly growing towns on each of Micronesia's larger islands. By the end of the '70s, most of the smaller islands in the Pohnpei District had more of their people living on Pohnpei than on the home islands.

To summarize: In a half-century, Pohnpei went through a series of sharp changes in both land tenure and population composition. Control over Pohnpei land was gradually eroded by the actions of four colonial administrations. The Sokehs rebels were not merely defeated and exiled; they were replaced by outer islanders. The Japanese brought in thousands of immigrants and led the Pohnpei to believe they would eventually be replaced on their own island by a Japanese population. The United States assigned land to outer islanders and promoted a policy of bringing large numbers of them to Pohnpei.

The Pohnpei people's presence on their own island was transformed.

At the same time, the United States engaged in what has been termed "political development," establishing Micronesian and Pohnpei governmental bodies that provided a series of new political venues (Hughes and Lingenfelter 1974). Each of the outer islands, Kolonia Town, and the autonomous Pohnpei chiefdoms became a municipality with an elected magistrate and council. The Pohnpei Legislature includes a representative from each of the outer islands and

Kolonia Town and from the Pohnpei municipalities/chiefdoms. In 1965, the first representative body to fully cover the Trust Territory, the Congress of Micronesia, was inaugurated. One of its first acts was to initiate political status negotiations with the United States, and, following the sequential departures of the Marianas, Marshalls, and Belau, it evolved into the Congress of the Federated States of Micronesia.

The people of Ponhpei are now conjoined with several other Micronesian and Polynesian peoples in governing Pohnpei State and, with even more culturally and geographically distinct ethnic groups, in constituting the FSM. The shifting ethnic make-up of the polities to which the Pohnpei are tied intersects with changes in Pohnpei authority over the island's lands: the resulting issues are the theme of this chapter.

It is difficult to provide any accurate figures for Pohnpei State populations. The 1980 census was notoriously inaccurate, and I have not yet seen the results of a recently-conducted interim census. If, however, the inaccuracies of the 1980 census are assumed to be relatively consistent, we can use those figures as an approximation.

The figures in table 1 are gross numbers. Sokehs does in fact have a large rural ethnic Pohnpei population, perhaps more than 1,000 persons. Part of Net

Table 1. 1980 Pohnpei state census

The four rural, ethnic Pohnpei municipalities:	
Madolenihmw	3,380
U	1,869
Kiti	3,558
Net	2,249
Total:	11,056
Others:	
Sokehs municipality:	3,663
Kolonia Town:	5,580
Outer islands:	
Kapingamarangi	510
Mokil	289
Ngatik	564
Nukuoro	308
Oroluk	10
Pingelap	369
Outer islands total	2,050
Total others:	11,293
Summary: Rural, ethnic Pohnpei	10,856
Others	11,293

is a suburb of Kolonia Town, and its population is not entirely rural ethnic Pohnpei. Many of the people counted in the Kolonia Town figures are people who identify themselves strongly with, and spend much of their time living in, the rural chiefdoms/municipalities.[6] Thus, rural ethnic Pohnpei do make up most of Pohnpei State's population, but they are not a large majority.

Membership in the Pohnpei State Legislature is proportional, with each municipality guaranteed at least one seat. Because of the complex character of the Sokehs and Kolonia Town jurisdictions, it is impossible to point to any clear, natural majority in the legislature, and at present it does not appear to operate on ethnic or geographic lines.

The governor of Pohnpei State achieves office through popular elections, first begun in 1979. Both men who have held the office since that time have been Pohnpei from U, one of the rural Pohnpei municipalities/chiefdoms.

Several of Pohnpei State's representatives to the FSM Congress are from the outer islands and outer-island communities on Pohnpei. This includes the two senior members of the Pohnpei delegation, one of whom is currently FSM vice-president and may well be the next FSM president. The FSM Congress itself, which elects the president from among its membership, is elected proportionately from the FSM states.

With the exception of Kosrae, the other states also have combinations of big islands and small, with outer islanders in varying measure dependent on the cash that flows through the big islands.[7] Many of the representatives to the FSM Congress are outer islanders, and the current (and thus far only) FSM president, Tosiwo Nakayama, is an outer islander from Truk State.

Both the Pohnpei Legislature and the FSM Congress are designed to ensure a maximum of minority ethnic participation in government. Within FSM there is nothing like a majority ethnic group, and it would be difficult to argue that any population has a significant plurality. Pohnpei State at present has no *clearly dominant* majority, but ethnic Pohnpei probably do constitute most of the population.

Finally, it should be noted that the FSM capital is on Pohnpei, occupying several buildings in the centre of Kolonia Town, many of them abutting Pohnpei State offices. There are plans to move the capital to an infertile and sparsely populated area of Sokehs. At this time, however, FSM is an extraordinarily visible part of the Pohnpei scene, and many Micronesian leaders and expatriates blame Pohnpei opposition to free association on a generalized Pohnpei feeling of being displaced on their own island by the national government. There is perhaps a grain of truth in this, but the issue is far more complex than so simple an argument acknowledges (Petersen 1986a).

This, then, is the context in which the 1983 plebiscite on free association took place. The outer islanders – those on the coral atolls and those living in Kolonia Town and Sokehs – found the guarantees that free association offered them acceptable: continued cash flow from the United States and a national government that would, in effect, ensure that all Micronesians are minorities and thereby guarantee minority rights. The Pohnpei, on the other hand, found themselves confronting both the reality of being governed by a non-Pohnpei national polity and the possibility of becoming a minority within their own local polity. The combination free association and federation represented diametrically opposed alternatives to the two parts of Pohnpei State.

POHNPEI CHOICES

It might be said that the outer islanders chose the continued benefits of colonialism while the Pohnpei sought to end external control over their lives and land. Many Pohnpei are convinced that if they do not achieve independence along with the end of trusteeship, they will never reclaim sovereignty on their own island. Their vote in the plebiscite, numerous misinterpretations of it notwithstanding, was no knee-jerk reaction against FSM and the federation. It was a demand for the only political status they deem likely to preserve their way of life.

Asked to make a crucial choice, the Pohnpei expressed deep concern about the quality of their culture and its future; they then responded with historical reflection, cultural analysis, and political courage. In what follows, I consider their own commentary on Pohnpei culture, as it exists in the present, and the ways in which that commentary represents the vision of the future they saw themselves charting with their votes.

The people of Pohnpei consistently identify generosity as a – perhaps as *the* – central element in their "*tiahk*," their culture or custom. They speak also of the role this deep-seated generosity plays in creating a sense of trust within communities. Another element they emphasise is the resiliency of Pohnpei culture – its depth and strength and the qualities of endurance it has shown. Pohnpei contrast these aspects of their lives with what they know of the ways of Americans, and their vote in the plebiscite was at least in part meant as a reaffirmation of Pohnpei over American culture.

Crucial to every aspect of Pohnpei life and culture are ceaseless rounds of feasting. Politics and economics, ritual and entertainment: all the strands are knotted together at the feast. Kava (Pohnpei *sakau*), pigs, dogs, fish, and, depending on the season, colossal yams or prodigious quantities of breadfruit are brought to a feast house, given to the chief or honoured guest, and then redistributed to those in attendance. Although diverse imported goods and even cash are sometimes added to the bounty, they can in no way replace the Pohnpei-produced items fundamental to feasting, and while the character of feasting has evolved during the past century, its importance and frequency have, if anything, grown (Petersen 1982a).

As a result, the Pohnpei remain deeply committed to farming, despite the influence American development strategies have had on their economy. Their active involvement in cultivating the land not only reinforces cultural values, it also provides them with the economic base from which flows their argument that they are quite capable of supporting themselves should the United States insist on cutting off all assistance to an independent Pohnpei or Micronesia.

During the weeks surrounding the plebiscite, I heard several people speak of the land as the Pohnpei equivalent of Americans' "*mwohni kohl*" – "gold money" or "hard currency." One man observed that the American paper currency in circulation, on which people have come to place so much reliance, is supported by gold that is not on Pohnpei or in Micronesia, but in the United States. Even under free association, the bullion symbolized by the currency will remain there. But, he said, "*My* gold is (in) my land. The money here is American and the gold that it stands for is in America. Pohnpei's gold is here: it is our land."

The Pohnpei term for land, in this context, is "*sahpw*," and as a cultural concept it has connotations that differ from "land" as an English-language term. Pohnpei plant much, and in many parts of the island all, of their land in permanent tree crops. The Pohnpei staple, breadfruit, grows on enormous trees that bear for scores of years.

Though *sahpw* is the general term for land in opposition to the sea or the sky and is also used to speak of a specific piece of land or farmstead, it also means cultivated land – land that feeds people – in opposition to "*wehl*" or "*nanwel*," the jungle. The Pohnpei word for land connotes the place where people live, whence they derive their livelihood, and the crops that surround their homes. To have land is to have crops, to have food, to be able to feast, and therefore to be a member of a community.

The phrase "*lopkupwu*" – "to cut down the food basket" – has been a recurring image in recent years. Pohnpei frequently store food in baskets hung from roof beams, and when a guest arives, the order is given to *lopkupwu*, cut down the baskets and feed the guest. *Lopkupwu* connotes more than merely cutting down the basket and offering the food, however. The phrase refers, in a broad sense, to the fundamental Pohnpei concepts of hospitality and generosity, and even more broadly to the whole notion of Pohnpei *tiahk*. This culture thrives. As a friend explained to me:

Pohnpei culture cannot be destroyed (*ohla*). Some of the apparent aspects of it – the formalities – will change, of course. These may become less dramatic than they are now and perhaps lose some of their importance. But the Pohnpei way of being doesn't change very much. We still take care of each other.

This is what we learn when we are children, as we become Pohnpei. We may take on new things, like money, and on the surface it will appear that we have changed. But it's still Pohnpei who are using the money and the way that we use it is still Pohnpei. Pohnpei culture can't be destroyed.

At the heart of this resilient culture are generosity, hospitality, "taking care of each other," "cutting down the food basket." And Pohnpei employ this deep-seated expectation of generalized benevolence in explaining other aspects of their culture. In the early 1970s, a Pohnpei legislator told me, tongue-in-cheek, that the only way to foster economic development on the island would be to chop down all the breadfruit trees, thus forcing people to work for a living. He repeated it to me in 1983, but this time it was in a different context:

Pohnpei resist changes. We try to keep foreign things at a distance. We work to preserve our *tiahk*, and I mean the feasts and ritual formalities. I don't mean that we preserve our traditional ways of treating each other and taking care of each other. In fact, one of the reasons that so little seems to get accomplished here is that it's so easy for us to go off on a visit. We can go anywhere and know that we'll get fed, without any worries about whether we've gotten much work done. We can always depend upon *lopkupwu* – someone will cut down a basket for us. *This* is the nature of Pohnpei culture; *this* is what we are trying to preserve.

There is in all of this the dramatic sense that Pohnpei culture is distinct from the ways of other peoples, particularly Americans. Pohnpei have a degree of admiration for Western technology and the efficiencies of its social organisation, but they have no more desire to be ruled by them than by any other foreign power.

The internal organisation of the Pohnpei community, despite its apparent hierarchy, emphasizes egalitarianism and generosity, the spirit of *lopkupwu*. Pohnpei perceive this habit of taking care of each other as fundamental to their culture, so much so that at times they say it actually seems counterproductive; so thoroughgoing is this sense of being well taken care of that it is sometimes blamed for fostering irresponsibility. But this apparent irresponsibility is for Pohnpei the stuff of freedom. Generosity has two faces: that which is sometimes constricting, when demands must be met, is at other times liberating, when someone else has shouldered the burden.

The Pohnpei's emphasis on the communal nature of their economy is matched by their concerns about preserving the communal character of their polity. The Pohnpei body politic – the community – is inherently small; as a community grows in size, it is apt to split apart, enabling its members to continue directly overseeing the activities of their leaders (Petersen 1982b, 1984).

In trying to comprehend the modern role of Pohnpei chiefs in all this, one encounters contradiction piled on contradiction. Chiefs serve as the ritual focus of any activity at which they are present, and demands for their presence are unceasing. Yet the organisation of labour at these activities is egalitarian; leaders use the humiliative language form when speaking of themselves, and high-ranking people are subject to much teasing and joking. Although the redistribution of feast goods has the largest portions going to those with the highest titles, those with the highest titles are quite likely to contribute more than they come away with – indeed, that is how most gain their titles.[8]

The Pohnpei readily assert the great authority of their chiefs, and complain about how much they must give to them, but the ethnographer who tries to observe this authority in action or record the economic inequities of feast redistributions immediately encounters the wide gap between that which Pohnpei say about their polity and that which may actually be seen. Though the sanctity and ritual status of the paramount chief are very real, their province is extremely limited.

A Pohnpei paramount chief is an essentially ritual figure. His secular authority runs up from – not down through – local chiefs. It is the local chiefdom, with its face-to-face interactions, that is the pre-eminent political unit of Pohnpei. This is *not* how it appears to most foreigners, be they missionaries, traders, colonial administrators, or anthropologists, but this is just as the Pohnpei wish it. The apparent strength of the chiefs is meant to protect local polities from external threats, be they neighbouring communities or colonial powers.[9]

The Pohnpei consistently interpret their current relations with the United States and the Micronesian national government in their own political terms. Many argue, for instance, that there is no mana (Pohnpei *manaman*) in free association – that it does not acknowledge their sovereignty.[10] In a brief remark delivered on Pohnpei radio the evening before the 1983 plebiscite, the speaker of the Pohnpei Legislature expressed doubts about the quality of the leadership that had negotiated free association and suggested that those who foresaw good in the new relationship were "false prophets." The Micronesian "slogan of unity is and ought to be," he said, "United we fall, and like our forefathers who displaced no other men on this sacred altar *Pohn pehi*, divided or separated we stand."[11] I can offer no more concise summation of Pohnpei views on the proper character of government.

The Pohnpei abhor centralisation. Proper government is for them small-scale and egalitarian. It is located in the face-to-face community where, as we are reminded by such *émigrés* from European tyrannies as Alfred Schutz and Hannah Arendt, a member of the *polis* can know more about the leader and the character of this person's leadership than the member knows about himself or herself. The ritual structure of the Pohnpei polity provides for apparently strong chiefs who ensure that the centre cannot hold. Pohnpei's experience with foreigners has drawn the paramount chiefs to the fore; these chiefs draw attention to themselves and away from the autonomous local communities.

In rejecting free association, the Pohnpei voted in 1983 to continue a complex of social, economic, and politial relations they have managed to preserve through a century of colonial domination. Their intense commitment to preserving these relationships keeps them in the relatively secure economic position that permits them to say "No" to the United States to free association. To understand why they found themselves in opposition not only to the FSM national government but to the other ethnic groups within Pohnpei State, we must look at relations between the people of Pohnpei and the people of the outer islands.

RELATIONS BETWEEN POHNPEI AND THE OUTER ISLANDS

The inhabited outer islands of Pohnpei State are all coral atolls with lagoons of varying size. The closest to Pohnpei Island proper is Ngatik, some 150 km south-west; the most distant, Kapingamarangi, is about 800 km away. Their 1980 populations ranged from 289 to 564. The outer islands are in many ways as similar to each other as they are different from Pohnpei.

The inhabitants of the two eastern islands, Mokil and Pingelap, speak what are variously described as dialects of Pohnpei or closely related but distinct languages. They had occasional contact with Pohnpei in the precontact era, but apparently had nothing like the integrated socioeconomic relations that characterize high island-low island interactions in the Central Carolines. Ngatik's population was wiped out by European sailors in an 1840 massacre; the island was repopulated by a variety of people, most of them from Pohnpei. Kapingamarangi and Nukuoro, both Polynesian outliers, had no relations with Pohnpei before the contact era; indeed, they seem to have been entirely isolated.

Increased contact among the islands began with the appearance of European ships engaged in whaling and trade. The Germans brought settlements of islanders to Pohnpei from all these islands and from Ta, Satawan, and Lukunor in the Mortlock group, Losap in the Truk area, Truk Lagoon, and Yap (Fischer 1970: 8). Most were established in Sokehs, whose people had been sent into exile following their abortive rebellion. The Japanese also moved groups of outer islanders to Pohnpei.

Even before the United States began its homesteading programme in the early 1950s, the paramount chief of Madolenihmw invited a group of people from Pis/Losap atoll to begin farming land in his domain. The US administration acquiesced to this plan and followed up by bringing in groups from Pingelap and Kapingamarangi also to occupy lands in Madolenihmw. All these settlements were on lands the United States referred to as "public domain" but that were known to the Pohnpei as *luhwen wehi*, unoccupied lands the chiefs had agreed to administer jointly with the administration.

The trials and tribulations of these settlers over the past several decades have been chronicled in Emerick (1960), Lieber (n.d.), and Severance (1975). In summary, the immigrants have experienced a mix of hospitality and antagonism from the Pohnpei. The Pis/Losap and Pingelap groups have become well-integrated on Madolenihmw, while the Kapinga people have moved back and forth between their farmsteads and the semiurban Kapinga community of Porakied on the outskirts of Kolonia Town.

Michael Lieber (n.d.: 59–60) points to several critical factors in the Kapinga migration, many of which are shared by the other outer islander settlements on Pohnpei. It has been US policy to promote assimilation of outer islanders on the assumption that "the various ethnic groups on Pohnpei would adopt the Pohnpei life-style and [traditional political] titles and blend together into a Pohnpei citizenry." Yet the administration also established the outer islanders in nucleated, ethnic villages that stand in strong contrast to the highly dispersed Pohnpei settlement pattern. This policy "constituted a visible denial of the possibility of realizing" assimilation.

Given the essential impossibility of interpreting interethnic relations on Pohnpei in terms of the US administration's ethnic policies, Lieber has instead pointed to US economic development policies. In the 1950s, when the United States essentially ignored Micronesia, small-scale subsistence farming and minor cash-cropping projects were emphasized. Homesteading on Pohnpei was the only real development programme created for outer islanders.

When the United States shifted strategies and began increasing Trust Territory budgets – US expenditures in Micronesia increased more than 20 times in less than two decades – outer islanders turned to government employment as their primary subsistence source (Lieber n.d.: 60–61). These latter conditions are those under which decolonisation is taking place in Micronesia: free association is usually described by wire service reports as a trade of permanent American "security" (read military) rights for a guaranteed US$1.4 billion in payments to FSM over 15 years.

Pohnpei had contact with outer islanders; indeed, relations with them have an important part in Pohnpei mythology and oral tradition. But with the new colonial policy – begun by the Germans in the early 20th century and continued by the Japanese and Americans – of settling outer islanders on Pohnpei, these relations have been significantly altered. Alienation of land for *communities* of outer islanders emphasized a policy of differentiating them from the Pohnpei. Furthermore, Lieber (n.d.: 55) notes:

The colonial administration intended to mediate the relations between Pohnpei and non-Pohnpei, protecting outislanders from encroachment of any sort by Pohnpei (including chiefs). This policy served to freeze ethnic boundaries, as colonial policy has done throughout Oceania.

This mediation of relations between Pohnpei and non-Pohnpei has been perpetuated. Development policy in the 1960s and 1970s, which encouraged staggering economic expansion in the absence of any increase in domestic production, created the dependency that now characterizes nearly all of Micronesia. Many outer islanders who had been farming on Pohnpei and who were integrating themselves into its political economy, turned toward wage-labour, government employment alternatives.

Kapinga, along with other outislanders and at least some Pohnpei, see their interests as clearly aligned with the continued, if not increasing dependence on American largesse. Kapinga universally express disbelief that Micronesia could "stand by itself, alone." They would prefer the Trust Territory to continue as before (Lieber n.d.: 33).[12]

Free association is indeed perceived by many Micronesians and by the US Congress as continued trusteeship.[13] From the Pohnpei perspective, the US and FSM national governments continue to mediate relations between the Pohnpei and the outer islanders by channelling nearly all of this $1.4 billion through government employment.

The outer islands are small and densely populated. The outer-island communities on Pohnpei are crowded. For the most part, those in Sokehs and Madolenihmw have enough land for current subsistence purposes, but they have space neither to accommodate their own population increases nor to accept immigrants from their home atolls. The communities in Kolonia Town and on its borders are effectively urban. Many individuals have homesteaded plots in rural areas, but most are not cultivating them at present. Malnutrition is a problem for some of the children in these groups (Demory 1976).

Although much uncultivated land remains on Pohnpei, little of it is unclaimed. Access to land is currently problematic and promises to remain so for quite some time to come. The new Pohnpei State Constitution, completed in 1984, includes among its 15 articles one devoted solely to land. It specifies that only native-born citizens (*pwilidak*) of Pohnpei State may acquire (or possess) land within the state.[14] It also states that "no land shall be sold, except as authorised by statute." It is going to take a great deal of work to achieve any acceptable legislation concerning land sales, and there is currently a moratorium on them. Furthermore, the municipal constitution of Madolenihmw, the only area with any open lands, specifies that anyone homesteading land there must become a Madolenihmw resident.

Though the Pohnpei experienced depopulation of about 80 per cent in the 19th century, their recent history has been one of repopulating their communities and reclaiming abandoned lands; any recognition they have of impending population pressures is tempered by a sense of unlimited resources. Some Pohnpei are highly articulate about the problems of population increase the island faces, and sterilization procedures have become popular among families with five or more children, but current annual population growth on Pohnpei remains high.

By and large, Pohnpei do not wish to return to a purely precontact economy, but their views about the island's future are based on expectations of continuing a way of life that is at its core agrarian. Land and farming remain central to all the Pohnpei wish to preserve. This is not so with outer islanders. To the extent they wish to be integrated into life on Pohnpei – as the Pohnpei experience it – they participate in this agrarian-based social life. But they recognize that their opportunities to do so are limited by the Pohnpei's own claims to the land. Their future, as Lieber says, is problematic.

American-instituted development policies have engendered deep dependency relations. The Pohnpei dilute this dependency – if they do not free themselves from it – by celebrating their agrarian traditions. In doing so, they create a situation that directs the outer islanders toward even greater dependence on the United States and FSM. The more strongly the Pohnpei push for independence, both political and economic, the more acutely the outer islanders feel themselves to be in danger of disenfranchisement. They have in part opted for and in part been forced into seeking a nonagrarian future. They are thus aligned with the rest of Micronesia in supporting free association and a high level of American subsidies instead of with the Pohnpei people with whom they share a common local government.

The Pohnpei now find themselves at odds not only with the national government and the other Micronesians, but with nearly half the population of their state. Theirs is a tenuous position, an anomaly. To develop and pursue a development policy that preserves their own ethnicity, they place themselves in opposition to neighbouring ethnic groups intent on pursuing utterly different strategies.

CONCLUSION

We have seen that the "traditional" Pohnpei political economy remains vital. In turn, it spurs the agricultural production that enables the Pohnpei to see both their culture and their economy as providing them with a foundation for independence. The Pohnpei clearly perceive the dependency that pervades modern Micronesian life. Most believe the United States instituted it purposefully to preserve its control over the islands. Most, I think, want to see it brought to an end for moral, philosophical, and practical reasons. The new free association relationship with the United States will not – cannot, they argue – do this. They believe, to the contrary, that free association will only increase dependency and result in the eventual integration of Micronesia into the United States.

Under free association, as the Pohnpei see it, the FSM national government represents the simultaneous and reciprocal continuation of dependency and American dominance; it also runs squarely counter to Pohnpei beliefs about what constitutes a proper political economy. Given the Pohnpei's success in preserving their own traditional political economy, these beliefs are not to be sneered at or dismissed as being merely "ideology" or "cultural superstructure"; they reflect, rather, a thoughtful and observant approach to the problems encountered by a small island trying to deal with a colonial power. Pohnpei insistence on community autonomy reflects their experience that it is the community's involvement in the process of governing itself that engenders its ability to support itself. To shift permanently the locus of authority or decision-making to a central government is to acknowledge the triumph of dependency and the impossibility of independence.

In terms both of traditional life and the practicalities of modern politics, then, the sensible course for the Pohnpei is freedom from the awkward free association agreement that ties them to the United States. This also means a lesser role for the FSM national government, i.e., a restructuring of the Micronesian federation into something that resembles more the form of government described by the FSM constitution.

But what makes sense from the Pohnpei perspective does not appeal to the peoples of the smaller islands. They want the economic, political, and social opportunities provided by both the US funding and oversight guaranteed by free association and a national government that is inherently constituted by minorities. The people of Pohnpei itself oppose such formalised political integration, preferring to see it evolve out of co-operative relations built over time. The outer islanders want the connections to be mandated by law; what they see best serving them is precisely the converse of what the Pohnpei believe to be in their best interests.

Given this contradictory situation, it is quite remarkable that no stalemate has developed in Pohnpei State. This is, I believe, in part a result of the enormous commitment of all concerned to achieving consensus. But it may also stem in part from the very vulnerability of the outer islanders. Whether the Pohnpei are inclined to help them or not, they live in a world that is framed by Pohnpei.

What will come of these strains? My own belief is that the Pohnpei will continue to be dissatisfied with free association and the increasing strength of the FSM national government. I do not think it impossible – in fact, I think it quite possible – that there will be a new movement calling for secession from FSM and genuine independence from the United States.[15] Neither the United States nor the FSM will be inclined to tolerate such a move, and perhaps violence will ensue. Political arson and murder have already occurred in Belau and the Marianas, and the FSM capital *is* on Pohnpei.

The opposition between the peoples of Pohnpei and the outer islands is not solely a product of either pre-existing cultural differences or the exigencies of colonial history. Pohnpei dissatisfaction with free association and a strong central government originates in the character of Pohnpei culture, as does the course the Pohnpei chart for their future. The outer islanders pursue a course that has been much more thoroughly influenced by the effect of American policies in Micronesia.

What is distinctive about this facet of ethnic relations in Micronesia, I believe, is that, even though disagreements between the various peoples focus on familiar questions of access to economic, political, and social values, these groups are not competing for control over access to the same resources. The

Pohnpei are aiming for local self-government and autonomy; the outer islanders for an integrated national system with a steady cash flow. While the two options are in some sense mutually exclusive, this is not a situation in which each side seeks to rule the other or to maintain a tight grasp on local hegemony.

If the Micronesians are to reclaim self-government, given their present political status they must accept American standards and prescriptions for the nature of that government. They must keep the FSM national state in place – and there's the rub, because states, as social institutions, require a high level of uniformity. Either all the regions exercise autonomy or none do; either all benefit or suffer (as the case may be) from dependency on the United States or none do. It is the state as a form of government that the people of Pohnpei oppose, and that obstructs the course they have struck toward reclaiming a genuinely Pohnpei polity.

The FSM constitution was drafted with an explicit intention of limiting the power of the central government (Meller 1985; Petersen 1986b). The FSM national government has proven to be, however, much more centralized than was intended (Hanlon and Eperiam 1983; Petersen 1986a). The pattern is not unusual, as Anthony Smith points out in *The Ethnic Revival* (1981). Ethnic self-determination movements recurringly encounter the same dilemma.

To safeguard their unique cultures and pre-modern histories, they [ethnic movements] must create a protective shell, their own scientific state, modelled on those of the units they fear and detest. But, by creating just such another state, they lay the basis for the inner erosion of that very culture and history they so wanted to safeguard and cultivate. For, of its nature, a scientific-technical state run by an army of professionals and technocrats is oriented to specialist concerns and universalist rational procedures and concepts, for whom the historicist vision and romantic imagination for past cultures is at best an irrelevance and at worst an obstacle to a computerised, future-oriented, scientific society. The whole power of the scientific state is then poised to drain away the last vestiges of that cultural uniqueness which it was created to serve (1981: 192).

Walker Connor has described this dilemma in great detail, focusing especially on the concept of "nation" and on world-political attitudes toward national self-determination. A nation, as Connor uses the term, is "a self-conscious ethnic group" and "*must* be self-defined" (1973: 3).

Paradoxical though it may appear, when they speak of self-determination of nations, statesmen, heavily influenced by popular, slipshod terminology in which the terms *nation* and *state* are regularly interutilized despite their vitally different connotations, usually do not have in mind self-determination for self-differentiating groups of people but rather are referring to self-determination for states or for colonial territories (1973: 13).

For the sake of convenience, I have been referring to the FSM federal government as the national government. As Smith and Connor indicate, however, this is something of a misnomer. In their terms, the FSM central government is clearly not a national government; it is a state. Furthermore, the notion of nation-building is itself a misnomer

since most of the less developed states contain a number of nations, and since the transfer of primary allegiance from these nations to the state is generally considered the *sine qua non* of successful integration, the true goal is not "nation-building" but "nation-destroying" (Connor 1972: 336).

The people of Pohnpei have a sophisticated understanding of this point, born of reflection and intense philosophical speculation. They see their own society imperiled by the ascent of the FSM state. Pohnpei nationality stems in part from the affirmation of local autonomy; outer-island nationality appears to do much the opposite.

The state policies of the FSM enforce an outer-island world-view that nests quite neatly with the *staatsrecht* of the United States and the free association. The atolls of Pohnpei State are, unfortunately, in an anomalous position. Their hopes lie in the direction of the federation, and they will continue to vote in that direction. Pohnpei's interests lie elsewhere. The two divisions share a single political entity, Pohnpei State. For one, state-building might indeed serve as nation-building. For the other, it may prove to be nation-destroying.

For the Pohnpei, whose ethnicity abhors the state, the answer to Smith's question, "Can the quest for a genuine congruence between ethnic community and scientific state ever really succeed?" (1981: 195), shall perhaps be "No." Like the ethnically heterogenous Melanesian states, FSM has a real potential for continuing separatist tendencies. As long as American interests support the hegemony of a strong central state – and there seems to be little prospect of a change in this – Pohnpei's ethnic imperatives will place it in opposition to that state.

NOTES

1. As the US Senate, which granted approval of the Compact of Free Association, understands the compact, the United States retains full control over the islands. The following excerpts from the transcript of the Senate hearing (1984) on the compact amply demonstrate this.

   Senator Johnston: Ambassador Zeder [head of the US Office of Micronesian Status Negotiations], with respect to denial, the provisions say that if the Government of the United States determines that any third country seeks access to or use of the Marshall Islands [these provisions hold for FSM and Belau as well] by military purposes, et cetera, then we can deny. [He then hypothesizes about Soviet fisheries.]

Could we determine that these ostensibly civilian personnel and ostensibly trade missions have a military usefulness and, therefore, a military purpose?

Mr. Zeder: Yes, sir, Senator, that's very clear and precise in the compact . . . .

Sen. Johnston: In other words, is it understood that we have full plenary power to say that any activity is military even though we may be wrong?

Mr. Zeder: Yes, we do, sir, and we intend to exercise it.

Sen. Johnston: Any activity whatsoever, we could determine to be military and prevent it?

Mr. Zeder: Yes, sir.

Sen. Johnston: I just want to be absolutely clear.

Mr. Zeder: Yes, sir.

Sen. Johnston: All right. I think that's clear.

2. The Micronesians long resisted American demands for perpetual denial rights and agreed only when it became clear that they would never achieve self-government (i.e., end US trusteeship) until they signed them away (Hanlon and Eperiam 1983: 96–97).

3. FSM's official report on the plebiscite provides slightly different figures: 4,437 No; 4,284 Yes (Plebiscite Commission 1983: 44). My figures are from the original tally sheet used in Pohnpei State; I do not know the source of the difference.

4. The plebiscite ballot was in two parts. The first called for simple approval or disapproval of the compact. The second asked the voter's preferred goal for future negotiations in the event of the compact's defeat. By putting "independence" on the ballot, it was expected that any claims that this was not a genuine act of self-determination would be thwarted. In Pohnpei State, more than 4,800 voters chose independence. Detailed accounts of the plebiscite can be found in Schwalbenberg (1984) and Petersen (1985a, 1986a).

5. The Pohnpei are not the only Micronesians who have a tradition of a disappearing island. In the Central Carolines there are stories of an island known as Kaafiror. When its people "heard about the doings of the Spanish and their cruelties to the Chamorros they decided to disappear, together with their island, rather than face the possibility of a similar fate" (Riesenberg 1975: 25).

6. It was recently decided that, for revenue purposes, Pohnpei censuses will record *de jure* rather than *de facto* residence. Many of the voters who have been registering in Kolonia Town may decide to register in their home municipalities/chiefdoms, and this may have some effect on ethnic geography in Pohnpei State.

7. Kosrae State is conterminous with Kosrae Island. It is the only single-island state in FSM, and for this reason, and because of particularly severe depopulation and successful mission activities, it has a distinctively different history than the rest of Micronesia.

8. Succession of chieftainship on Pohnpei depends both on genealogies and competitive giving.

9. I develop this notion at length in Petersen (1985b).

10. The Pohnpei's analysis of sovereignty in terms of mana is described in Peteresen (1985a).

11. Some of the language here is drawn from the preamble to the FSM Constitution, which reads in part, "Our ancestors, who made their homes on these islands, displaced no other people." The name Pohnpei refers to a traditional account about

ancestors who first built the island "upon an altar" – "*pohn pehi*" – that had been raised atop a bit of reef found jutting out of the sea.

12. Many, probably most, Micronesians resent the term largesse. Whether they agree with the policy or not, they know that US dollars come to Micronesia as a *quid pro quo* for American control of its strategic position in the Pacific.

    Lieber's reference to "stand by itself, alone" here is a literal translation of the Pohnpei term for independence, *utohr*.

13. Nowhere are these perceptions expressed more clearly than in a letter from Pohnpei governor Resio Moses and Speaker of the Pohnpei Legislature to FSM president Tosiwo Nakayama, written in August 1985 in response to the US Congress's post-plebiscite amendments to the compact. I quote a few passages:

    The multitude of amendments offered by the House of Representatives of the U.S. Congress represent something much different than a recognition of our inherent sovereignty and our dignity as a self-governing people. The amendments are patronizing in language, condescending in spirit, and meddlesone in fact.

    One must wonder whether the Congress really wants a self-reliant and progressive Pacific.

    The problem lies much deeper than the language of the amendments offered by either the House or the Senate. The problem lies in a basic misunderstanding within Congress of the true nature of the Compact, of the true sense of our people as a nation, and of the true responsibilities of the U.S. in these closing years of the Trusteeship. Cosmetic or even substantive concessions attained in the next few weeks over amendments made by the House or Senate will not rectify the fundamental misconceptions which lie at the root of these amendments.

    Changes in attitude cannot be made overnight, but we firmly believe that a very difinite and visible foothold, which truly and effectively mandates respect for ourselves as an independent, self-governing people, must be attained within the U.S. Congress before we accept implementation of the Compact, in any form.

    Pohnpei counsels "the need for patience and for a re-evaluation of our entire approach toward our continuing relationship with the U.S.

    As an emerging nation we must earn the respect of our neighbours. In our new partnership with the U.S., we must insist upon a recognition of the goals and aspirations of our people, and of the proper role of the U.S. in supporting our efforts towards economic, social, and political self-reliance. That requires more than a mere bargaining and redrafting of Congressional amendments. We must reach into the hearts and minds of the Congressmen themselves. It is time we stood up and let the world take notice.

14. The English-language version of the Pohnpei constitution says "acquire," but the Pohnpei-language version (in which it was drafted) says "*kak sapwasapw*," which can mean "acquire," "inherit," "possess," or "cultivate," among other English-language concepts. The ambiguity of the Pohnpei text is characteristic of Pohnpei political discourse.

15. In 1982, members of the Pohnpei legislature introduced a bill calling for a referendum on Pohnpei's continued participation in FSM. The matter never came to a vote (Hanlon and Eperiam 1983: 93–94). Similar legislation was introduced recently in the wake of the American amendments to the Compact of Free Association.

REFERENCES

Connor, W. 1972. Nation-building or nation-destroying? *World Politics* 24: 319–55.

———. 1973. The politics of ethnonationalism. *Journal of International Affairs* 27: 1–21.

Demory, B. 1976. *The illusion of surplus.* Ph.D. diss. Department of Anthropology, University of California.

Emerick, R. 1960. *Homesteading on Ponape.* Ph.D. diss. Department of Anthropology, University of Pennsylvania.

Fischer, J. L. 1970. *The Eastern Carolines.* New Haven: HRAF Press.

Hanlon, D. 1984. *Upon a stone altar.* Ph.D. diss. Department of History, University of Hawaii.

Hanlon, D., and W. Eperiam. 1983. The Federated States of Micronesia. In *Politics in Micronesia,* edited by R. Crocombe and A. Ali, 81–89. Suva: Institute of Pacific Studies, University of the South Pacific.

Hughes, D., and S. Lingenfelter. 1974. *Political development in Micronesia.* Columbus: Ohio State University Press.

Lieber, M. D. n.d. *Constitutionalism in Micronesia.* Laie, Hawaii: Institute for Polynesian Studies, Brigham Young University.

Meller, N. 1985. *Constitutionalism in Micronesia.* Laie, Hawaii: Institute for Polynesian Studies.

Petersen, G. 1982a. Ponapean matriliny. *American Ethnologist* 9: 129–44.

———. 1982b. *One man cannot rule a thousand.* Ann Arbor: University of Michigan Press.

———. 1984. Ponape's body politic: Island and nation. *Pacific Studies* 8: 112–36.

———. 1985a. A cultural analysis of the Ponapean independence vote in the 1983 plebiscite. *Pacific Studies* 9: 13–52.

———. 1985b. *Egalitarian strategies and hierarchical tactics.* Paper presented at the annual meeting of the American Anthropological Association, Washington, D.C.

———. 1986a. *Decentralisation and Micronesian federalism.* South Pacific Forum Working Paper No. 5. Suva: USP Sociological Society.

———. 1986b. Sympathy for the devil theory. Reviews of *Constitutionalism in Micronesia,* by Norman Meller, and *Decentralisation and political change in Melanesia,* by R. Premdas and J. Steeves. *Pacific Studies* 10: 107–24.

Plebiscite Commission. 1983. *Final report of the Plebiscite Commission,* Vol. 1. Pohnpei: Federated States of Micronesia.

Riesenberg, S. 1975. The Ghost Islands of the Carolines. *Micronesia* 11: 7–33.

Schwalbenberg, H. 1984. The plebiscite on the future political status of the Federated States of Micronesia. *Journal of Pacific History* 19: 172–84.

Severance, C. 1975. *Becoming Ponapean: The accommodation of the Pis-Losap homesteaders.* Paper presented at the annual meeting of the Association for Social Anthropology in Oceania, Stuart, Florida.

Smith, A. D. 1981. *The ethnic revival.* Cambridge: Cambridge University Press.

US Senate. 1984. *Hearing to approve the Compact of Free Association.* Committee on Energy and Natural Resources, May 24, 1984. Washington, D.C.: Government Printing Office.

14

Indonesia: Nation-building, Ethnicity, and Regional Conflicts

ERNST UTRECHT

The territory of the Republic of Indonesia (excluding East Timor) harbours about 150 million people. According to regulations inherited from the Dutch colonial government, the country's population includes three major "law groups" (in the still existing legislation referred to as *"rechtsgroepen"*): Indonesian ("the people living according to their own traditional, or *adat*, laws"); people of European origin ("who are subjected to Dutch private law"); and people of other, non-Indonesian, Asian origin (in the legislation referred to as *"Vreemde Osterlingen,"* foreign orientals).[1] The group of people of European descent consists of people of Dutch and other European descent, of other Western descent (white Americans, white Australians, etc.), and of Japanese origin. The non-Indonesian Asians include mainly Chinese (the biggest group) and a much smaller number of Arabs and Indians.

The group of autochthonous Indonesians (referred to as *Indonesia asli* or *pribumi* in postwar Indonesian laws) has been subdivided into so-called *rechtskringen* (law areas). There are minor and more significant differences in culture, especially in *adat* law, between the various *rechskringen*, but basically all *rechskringen* are *Indonesia asli, pribumi*.[2] According to C. van Vollenhoven, there are 19 *rechtskringen*, including the Moluccas and Irian Jaya (West Papua), both belonging to the Melanesian part of the Indonesian archipelago.[3]

Based on cultural-anthropological differences, the archipelago's population can be divided into Indonesians, Melanesians, and people of non-South-East Asian or non-Melanesian origin. The third major ethnic group consists of people of Chinese, Arab, other Asian, or European descent.[4]

The Indonesian group can be subdivided in some 16 groups; the biggest of them, the Javanese group, forms 70 per cent of the population of the archipelago. The Javanese live predominantly on the heavily populated island of Java. But more than 10 million Javanese have settled in the outer islands, for example, South Sumatra, several places in the coastal areas of Kalimantan (Borneo), and South and South-East Sulawesi (Celebes), and, recent transmigration pro-jects have sent Javanese to Irian Jaya and East Timor. The country's army and police are controlled by the Javanese, and it can be argued that in many ways Indonesia is a Javanese-dominated country.

In the precolonial era, several of the Indonesian subgroups had their own independent kingdoms; for instance, the Makasarese in South Sulawesi estab-lished the powerful sultanate of Goa and the Acehnese founded the sultanate of Aceh. In the Melanesian law area of Ternate in the northern part of the Moluc-cas, the Portuguese and later the Dutch were confronted with two powerful kingdoms, Ternate and Tidore. The latter controlled the western part of the most powerful empire of the archipelago, the Javanese empire of Matram.[5] The Indonesian archipelago in those days was divided among fully independent In-donesian kingdoms according to, in the words of G. J. Resink, "*buiten-Europees volkenrecht*" (law of nations outside Europe).[6]

There were many armed conflicts between the indigenous kingdoms, such as the fighting between Goa and the neighbouring Bugis state of Bone, between Mataram and the much smaller kingdom of Banten in the western corner of Java, between Mataram and Goa, among the small Hindu-Balinese kingdoms, and the conquest of Lombok (which before the conquest was ruled by the Mus-lim Sasak realm of Selaparang) by the Hindu kingdom of Karangasam.[7] Most of these conflicts, however, had their roots not in cultural differences but in eco-nomic differences in the widest sense. Thus, although 90 per cent of the In-donesians are Muslims, Islam did not function as a serious uniting force, even in the struggle against the Dutch. The Dutch, as non-Muslims and often even as enemies of Islam, were able to exploit successfully the conflicts among the Indonesian Islamic states in the archipelago. For instance, they enjoyed the full support of the Bugis in their war against Goa. One by one the Indonesian kingdoms lost their independence in the 18th and 19th centuries as a handful of Dutchmen played one Indonesian ruler off against another.

During the last four decades of Dutch colonial rule (before World War II), the Indonesian nationalists became very much aware that only a united In-donesian people would be able to achieve national independence and that only independence based on national unity would enable the Indonesians to con-solidate and maintain their state's newly-won independence. In 1928, an all-Indonesian nationalist youth conference put the struggle for national inde-pendence in the well-known *Sumpah Pemuda* (youth pledge): one fatherland, Indonesia; one nation, Indonesia; and one language, *Bahasa Indonesia*.[8]

Sumpah Pemuda was a very significant achievement because it was a political break-out from feudal and colonial containment, performed by a new genera-tion of Indonesians. Java was the centre of Dutch political and economic de-velopment in the archipelago, and the tertiary educational centres were located there. Indonesian youths from all parts of the archipelago who were seeking secondary or tertiary education, sometimes both, temporarily moved to Java, where, as most belonged to the Indonesian gentry, the aristocracy, and the rising middle class, they were placed in a more egalitarian milieu, outside the feudal and bourgeois upbringing they had received before leaving their homes in the outer islands or other parts of Java.[9] In places such as Batavia (now Jakarta), Bandung, Semarang, Surabaya, and Malang they got the opportunity to learn about modern ideologies, such as nationalism, communism, Islamic modernism, and others. Many became radicalised and gained a better under-standing of other, local cultures as solidarity among fellow Indonesians from other ethnic groups developed. Ethnic cultural differences were no longer bar-riers to establishing a common front against Dutch colonialism. This generation of Indonesians is referred to as the generation of the '30s.

The Dutch colonial rulers countered the platform of national unity by con-tinuing their traditional divide-and-rule policies of trying to exploit the existing differences in ethnic origin and religious beliefs – Muslims, Hindus (mainly in Bali), Christians, and adherents to pre-Muslim or pre-Hindu traditional beliefs. After World War II, the Dutch sought to undermine the young Indonesian republic, proclaimed on 17 August 1945, by establishing a federation of In-donesian states, and created local ethnic states such as the West Kava (Sun-danese) state of Pasundan, several states in Kalimantan, the state of East Sumatra, and the state of East Indonesia, encompassing also the Melanesian part of the archipelago.[10] Finally, Netherlands New Guinea (Irian Jaya), cul-turally the largest Melanesian law area, was excluded from the so-called trans-fer of sovereignty of 27 December 1949.[11]

Although the 1945 unitary Indonesian republic was restored on 17 August 1950, some separatist movements exist even today, especially in the outer is-lands, such as Aceh and East Indonesia (since 1963 including Irian Jaya), which tried to break away from the present unitary state. These movements are now not only based on economic grounds, but also on strong cultural and, especially in Aceh, religious sentiments. The separatist movement in Aceh wants to establish an independent Islamic state.

SUKARNO'S NATION-BUILDING

It is understandable that, as soon as the Dutch had left Indonesia (except Netherlands New Guinea), the Republicans (among them not only Javanese, but also Sumatrans, Sulawesians, and others) lost no time in demolishing the federal structure left behind by the Dutch and which they correctly considered to be a dangerous base for neocolonial manœuvrings.

In 1950, the republic was successful in defeating the time bomb left by the Dutch, that is, the secessionist movements, generally based on ethnic and reli-gious sentiments. In the outer islands – such as the so-called Republic of the South Moluccas (RMS) – and in restoring the unitary state of 1945.[12]

However, federalist rebellions started anew in 1956, and the PRRI-Permesta revolt in Sumatra and Sulawesi in 1958 (supported by the American CIA) was a serious challenge to the republic. The federalist movements, like their secessionist predecessors generally based on ethnic and religious sentiments (in fact, anti-Javanese and anti-Communist feelings), constituted a major manifestation confronting the young Indonesian republic.[13]

Less dangerous than the federalist movements but longer in duration were the Darul Islam movement in West Java and Kahar Muzakkar's Islamic-state movement in South Sulawesi. The scale of warfare was great. The Darul Islam leader, Kartosuwirjo, persisted in rejecting the authority of the republic and continued his guerrilla war until he was captured and the Darul Islam annihilated in 1962.[14] Kahar Muzakkar supported the PRRI-Permesta revolt, but after it was suppressed, Kahar's power and influence gradually crumbled. He lost his territory and was killed early on the morning of 3 February 1965.[15]

Despite such challenges as the Darul Islam revolt and Kahar Muzakkar's attempt to establish a state based on fundamental Islamic principles, the supporters of the concept of an Islamic state or of Muslim fundamentalism have never formed a majority. Even though, as mentioned earlier, 90 per cent of the Indonesians embrace the Muslim faith, in religio-political terms, the Muslims have always formed a minority. In Indonesia, the distinction has been made between the *santri* and the *abangan*, the first being devout and the second only nominal Muslims; the Indonesian *santri* constitute only about 30 per cent of Indonesia's total Muslim population. Concentrations of *santri* Muslims are to be found in Aceh, Minangkabau, West Java, Jombang, Bangil, and Pasuruan and Madura in East Java, Banjarmasin in Kalimantan, and in South Sulawesi. Because most of Indonesia's population is *abangan*, only "Muslim according to registration" and adherents of a syncretism of old Indonesian, Hindu, and Islamic beliefs (in which the Islamic element takes no more than 20 per cent), Indonesia culturally cannot be qualified as a Muslim country.[16]

Although Islam is seriously embraced by only 30 per cent of the Muslims, it has played a significant role as a weapon against *foreign* domination. Fighting against the Dutch, Indonesian rulers in the 17th and 18th centuries succeeded in using Islam as an instrument to rally militant mass support among the *abangan* population. Throughout the centuries after the arrival of Islam, the religion has been expressed as "we are Muslims, thus Indonesian." However, as mentioned earlier, Islam has never functioned as a serious uniting force. Apparently, economic and cultural differences were sufficiently strong so that Islam could not unite Indonesians living in different ethnic subgroups. In the post–World War II period, Islam has become a claim of identity for some sub-groups in the chief ethnic groups of Indonesia. For instance, some Acehnese see themselves as "true Muslims" in comparison with the Javanese *abangan* (seen by fundamentalist Acehnese as a *kafir*, "unbeliever," or a *murtad*, "apostate," a "traitor to Islam"). Similar feelings were to be found among the Bugis in South

Sulawesi and the Minangkabau in West Sumatra during the PRRI-Permesta revolt. In such feelings, anti-Javanese sentiments were strengthened by a "true Muslim" identity. During the days of Permesta in North Sulawesi, one could observe a combination of anti-Javanese and anti-Muslim sentiment among the Christians in Minahasa.

In 1945, during the last half-year preceding the end of the Japanese occupation of the archipelago, and when the creation of a national, independent Indonesian state was being prepared by Sukarno and his associates, the advocates of an Islamic state also embarked on activities to prepare for the establishment of an Indonesian Islamic republic, stubbornly neglecting the almost certain rejection by the *abangan* majority of the existence of such a republic. A so-called *Jakarta Charter* was formulated in which it was laid down that Muslims should live according to Islamic laws. But the *Jakarta Charter* never became part of Indonesian constitutional law. Instead, a secular state ideology was accepted, *Pancasila*, which prevented the founding of an Indonesian theocratic state.[17]

But the failure to get the *Jakarta Charter* of 1945 accepted as part of Indonesia's constitutional law did not deter the advocates of a Muslim Indonesian state from continuing their opposition to a national Indonesian government after 1945. In 1947–48, when the newly proclaimed republic was almost overrun by the Dutch colonial military forces that tried to reoccupy the former colony, a small group of fanatic advocates of an Islamic state – in close co-operation with a group of Muslim leaders who had rejected the Renville Agreement between the Indonesian and Dutch governments (which terminated the first Dutch colonial war in 1947) because it did not terminate Dutch control over the Indonesian economy – proclaimed the establishment of Darul Islam (Muslim area) State. Three other Muslim revolts, which broke out after the Darul Islam rebellion, were the Kahar Muzakkar Islamic-state movement, the revolt of Daud Beureuch in Aceh in 1953, and a struggle for an independent Aceh, with headquarters in neighbouring Malaysia and financial support from Muslims in the United States. The three revolts occurred in areas – West Java, South Sulawesi, and Aceh – where most of the population are *santri*; the revolts did not expand into the neighbouring areas, which are inhabited predominantly by non-*santris*: West Java area neighbouring *abangan* Central Java, Christian Central and North Sulawesi (except Muslim Bolaang Mongondow), and Christian Batak land.

The advocates of an Indonesian Islamic state also made use of constitutional avenues. A serious effort made by the Muslim political parties in the 1950s, especially the major organisations (Masjumi, Nahdatul Ulama, PSII, and Perti), failed to get the concept of a Muslim state accepted by the Konstituante (Constituent Assembly, 1956–59). During the ensuing period of Guided Democracy (1959–66), the Muslim parties lost much of their influence. The Masjumi, who refused to operate within the framework of Guided Democracy, was banned in 1960 (and has never returned to the political arena).

The 1950s were marked by Sukarno's "nation-building," the formation of a homogeneous, national Indonesian state in which there would be no contradictions or conflicts between ethnic, religious, and political groups. All citizens of the Indonesian state would feel that they belong to the same national entity and that they should serve the common interests of that entity, the nation.

Sukarno's political ideas on ethnic unity were influenced by the Dutch colonial practice of playing off the ethnic groups against each other. The concept of "uniting all the anticolonial and revolutionary potentials in the society" was his guiding principle since the prewar days. Sukarno never espoused the Marxist concept of class struggle. He developed his own nationalistic doctrine, Marhaenism, a kind of Indonesian populism. Except for the leaders of the Communist party of Indonesia (PKI), some militants among the modernist Islamic Masjumi cadres, and extremely orthodox Muslim leaders assembled in the conservative Nahdatul Ulama, all of Indonesia's political leaders supported Sukarno's populism. As members of the Indonesian bourgeoisie, the populists rejected Marxist class struggle and held to the concept of "pure" nationalism. According to Sukarno, the only enemy of the people is imperialism. By unifying the people and defeating imperialism, Sukarno assumed, economic conditions would improve and consequently class differences would diminish automatically. Hence, according to the Indonesian populists, there was no need to foster class struggle, as the Communists did. They also argued that social conflicts could only hamper the development of society and its progress to the stage where all would benefit.[18]

During the nation-building process, two myths were developed to strengthen the need for national unity: (1) inspired by Ernest Renan's nation concept, Sukarno presented the realm of Majapahit in the 14th century as the glorious Indonesian unitarian state of the past that the present Indonesian political leaders should view as the best example of unitarian nation-state building; (2) Sukarno also adopted the views of the Dutch colonial historians N. J. Krom and F. W. Stapel that the whole Indonesian archipelago had been directly ruled by the Dutch for 350 years. Sukarno's two views were not accepted by all. The first was supported by, among others, the lawyers, by the cabinet minister, M. Yamin, and by the historian Sutjipto. It was not accepted by the Dutch professor C. C. Berg, the Indonesian historian G. J. Resink, and the head of the National Archives, the historian M. Ali. Resink and Ali also rejected the second view, being joined in their criticism by myself, then professor of international law and member of the Supreme Advisory Council (DPA) and the Provisional People's Congress (MPRS).

The story of Majapahit has been described in Prapanca's historical epic, *Nagarakrtagama*. Being an extremely loyal court narrator, Prapanca glorified the reign of Majapahit king Hayam Wuruk, who ruled over an immense territory stretching from what is now Kampuchea to and including what is now Papua New Guinea and the Solomon Islands. The local rulers paid *upeti* to King

Hayam Wuruk. Yamin pointed out that paying *upeti* meant the paying of a tax by a vassal to his king. Hence, the local rulers were subjects of King Hayam Wuruk. In other words, they were some sort of governors ruling Majapahit's dependencies. Berg, however, arrived at the conclusion that Majapahit consisted only of Java and Bali, and the existence of "Great Majapahit," the mighty unitarian state that existed in the Indonesian archipelago during the 14th century, should be regarded as a myth. *Upeti* should be seen as a token of respect for King Hayam Wuruk and not as a tax paid by a vassal. For Resink and Ali, the then-insoluble problem of effective implementation of direct political and administrative control over the archipelago makes it impossible to accept the existence of a unitary state in those days. Such control needs developed interisland communication and corresponding military logistics, and even in the 1950s and 1960s such communication and logistics were not functioning well.

Like the Great Majapahit concept, the concept of the 350-year Dutch colonial rule over the entire Indonesian archipelago, or 350 years of "Netherlands Indies" was, too, for Sukarno an instrument to unify the Indonesian people in the nation-building process. After having enjoyed together prosperity during the glorious age of Majapahit, for 350 years the Indonesian people in all parts of the archipelago suffered and survived the tremendous hardships of colonial rule. Finally, united and in solidarity, together they liberated themselves from the colonial yoke. In particular, Resink pointed out that the "Netherlands Indies," the colonial state, was established only in the 19th century, and even in the 20th century, some parts of the archipelago were not yet placed under direct Dutch administrative rule, for instance, some areas in Aceh and Gajoland and in Netherlands New Guinea (now Irian Jaya). Until the 19th century, Indonesia was, as Resink has put it, an "internationally divided world" consisting of independent Indonesian states. Until then, the Dutch had direct control in only a few places, such as Amboina, Banda, Batavia (now Jakarta), and some towns on Java's north coast, which were military posts and trading centres. Only with reference to these few places can one speak about "350 years of Dutch colonial rule in the archipelago." The 19th century scramble for colonies, especially the efforts of the Germans and the Italians to acquire overseas possessions, forced the Dutch to put the whole Indonesian archipelago under their direct control and to create the "Netherlands Indies."

These two controversies in Indonesian historiography remained largely among academics and had no effect on Sukarno's public nation-building policies.[19] Moreover, Sukarno's authority was too strong to be undermined by the controversial views of Berg, Resink, Ali, and those who accepted their views.

The events following the attempted military coup of 1 October 1965 showed that Sukarno's populism contributed a great deal to successful nation-building, to the formation of one Indonesian nation embracing the entire Indonesian archipelago.[20] Indeed, it became the very basis of nation-building. On the other hand, it did little to solve social problems and impeded a solution to the most acute problem: the just distribution of land. Nor did it prevent the rapid rise in the 1960s of a military élite under Sukarno's successor, General Suharto. Populism also did not support the economic decolonisations of 1958 and 1963 (the nationalisation of Dutch and British enterprises and other property), the people's struggle against the encroaching power of their own military leaders, and the impoverishment of the vast majority of the people as a consequence of despoliation of the country's raw materials by other foreign enterprises and multinational corporations in co-operation with military and civilian compradors of foreign interests.

To eliminate ethnic contradistinctions, which had been used by the Dutch to stir up conflicting federal sentiments and to prevent the incorporation of Netherlands New Guinea into Indonesian territory, Sukarno consistently and systematically implemented the unitary doctrine in the appointment of functionaries. In all Sukarno cabinets, all ethnic groups were represented. However, during the PRRI-Permesta rebellion, when many military leaders originating from Sumatra and North Sulawesi joined the revolt, the Indonesian army and the state police became heavily Javanese-dominated.

In May 1963, after an open, internationalised armed conflict with the Dutch and intervention by the United Nations, West Irian was incorporated into Indonesian territory in conformity with the Indonesian Constitution of 1945 (which declares that West Irian, now Irian Jaya, is part of the territory of the former Netherlands Indies and that the territory, according to the principles of a total transfer of sovereignty, should be included in the territory of the Indonesian republic).[21] It has turned out, unfortunately, that the West Papuans just missed Sukarno's nation-building and became, instead, the victims of the military dictatorship that was to follow.

DISINTEGRATION UNDER SUHARTO'S MILITARY DICTATORSHIP

After the abortive military coup of 1 October 1965, the *santri* Muslims eagerly supported the army's operations to destory the Communist organisations (about a half-million Communists and persons regarded as Communists, most of them peasants, workers, and teachers, were killed) and reduce the numbers of the nationalists, finally to remove Sukarno from the presidency. Many Muslim leaders believed that, after having established the "New Order," the military would gradually return to the barracks. Instead of permitting the Muslims more room for participation in government, however, the army continued its harsh political line of eliminating the influence of political parties. his pitted the *santri* Muslims, who had hoped to establish an Islamic state after the fall of Sukarno, against the army.

To counterbalance any sizable opposition from the political parties, the military dictatorship took several political measures. To reduce, or even eliminate, the influence of the political parties in the Indonesian Parliament, the army placed the Golongan Karya (GOLKAR, functional groups) under military control.[22] Now the GOLKAR functions as a military-controlled political party.

In 1968, the military successfully carried out a policy of divide and rule among the Muslim groupings. To curb the influence of the Nahdatul Ulama, the military helped former Masjumi supporters, members, and sympathisers, whose leaders were far more militant than the Nahdatul Ulama leadership, establish a new Muslim political party, the Partai Muslimin Indonesia (Parmusi), in fact, the "new Masjumi," to counterweigh the Nadatul Ulama. Later in the same year, the army successfully meddled in the internal affairs of Parmusi by supporting an ambitious promilitary group within Parmusi that rejected the nomination of some new members in the party's leadership who were not liked by the Jakarta generals.

On 3 July 1971, the army-sponsored GOLKAR won the second Indonesian election (the first was held in 1955). Using intimidation and threats, arresting opponents regarded as dangerous, misusing government facilities, and using fraudulent election-campaign techniques, the GOLKAR obtained 227 seats in the Indonesian Parliament, leaving the Muslim parties far behind. A frustrated Nahdatul Ulama had to be content with only 58 seats, and Parmusi managed to garner 24.

Immediately after having the new Parliament installed, the military forced the representatives of the political parties to form only two political factions. The representatives of the four Muslim parties (Nahdatul Ulama, Parmusi, PSII, and Perti) had to join the Persatuan Pembangunan (Reconstruction Based on Unity) parliamentary faction, and the representatives of the five non-Muslim parties (PNI, IPKI, Partai Murba, Partai Katolik, and Parkindo) had to join the Demokrasi Pembangunan (Reconstruction Based on Democracy) parliamentary faction.[23] By reducing the number of factions, the military was able to exert more effective control over the activities of the political parties inside and outside of Parliament.

In January 1973 came the final attack on the existence of the political parties. After several months of pressure from the military dictatorship, the four Muslim parties were forced to merge into one political unit called Partai Persatuan Pembangunan (PPP), and the five non-Muslim parties merged into Partai Pembangunan Demokrasi (PDI).

Although the election of 1977 was also won by GOLKAR – in the same way it had gained success in the 1971 election – the PPP could claim an important election victory in Jakarta. GOLKAR leaders blamed the governor of Jakarta, Marine General Ali Sadikin, for having neglected GOLKAR's interests in the capital city. The fact was, however, that GOLKAR was not popular among many government officials in Jakarta.

For the election of 1982, the government introduced a new, fraudulent voting system, a so-called floating-mass system. All political organisations, including GOLKAR, were forbidden to campaign in the villages. The village chief, who was made a government official and ordered to join GOLKAR, was given the task to use traditional authority to make sure that the villagers would vote for GOLKAR. In this way, GOLKAR was able to beat PPP not only in Jakarta, but also in all areas regarded as Muslim or PPP bulwarks, except Aceh. The 1982 election defeat of the Muslim parties caused a serious split in the ranks of the PPP, leading to the Nahdatul Ulama's breaking away from the PPP in December 1984.

It has turned out that depoliticisation has not brought the results the army wished. Unexpected by the military, which had believed that militant Muslim leaders and fanatic Muslim youths would stop their activities soon after the emasculation of their political organisations, the Muslim opposition stepped up its attacks on the Suharto regime. Since the formal political avenues, such as the Nahdatul Ulama, Parmusi, PSII, and Perti, were put in a very tight strait-jacket and could not function as free political organisations, many of the militant Muslim leaders and youths sought other, more or less informal, avenues, often declared as illegal by the military, such as "study clubs," "institutes," and all sorts of other organisations that were kept relatively secret from the authorities. Young Muslim academics, teachers, and university and college students set up study groups or held seminars to discuss the role Islam should play in the country's economic and political development. Unattended by the security officials, they sharply criticised the unchecked corruption of the military élite and their civilian associates in their dealings with foreign investors and their handling of so-called development aid. In a later stage, plans were made, and often carried out, to confront the nation's corrupt leaders with the continuing impoverishment of the vast majority of the population. For instance, the Muslim action groups played an important role in the vehement mass protests against Japanese investors during the state visit of Prime Minister Tanaka of Japan to Indonesia in January 1974 (the so-called Malari protests), the vehement mass protests in February and March 1978 against the reappointment of General Suharto as head of state, and the bloody mass demonstrations during the 1982 election campaign.

Gradually, such Muslim groups also accommodated former members of banned leftist organisations, such as former students who had been members of the banned Consentrasi Gerakan Mahasiswa Indonesia (CGMI, Concentration of Indonesian Student Movements, an independent student movement that, on many occasions, supported the policies of the PKI), former members of the now illegal Pemuda Rakjat (People's Youth, the youth organisation of the PKI), former members of the leftist faction of the nationalist Partai Nasional Indonesia (PNI, National Party of Indonesia, established by Sukarno in the 1920s), and others. It was through the influence of these leftist elements that, in a later stage, several Muslim study groups and seminars adopted a so-called Marxist-

Muslim political approach or outlook. Since 1975, radicalised Muslim youths have regularly visited the Central and East Java countryside to assist the peasants in their resistance against the continuing harsh exploitation by local military commanders and landlords (now many of them are military too). They also carry out programmes "preparing the population for the founding of a *socialist* Muslim state after the removal of the corrupt and anti-people Suharto regime." According to reliable information, over the past seven or eight years, the "Marxist-Muslim" views are even being taught in several *peasantrens* (Islamic religious boarding schools).

Since the Muslim opposition to the Suharto regime has channelled its activities through informal or even illegal avenues, it has become extremely difficult for the army to keep control over the activities of the militant Muslim leaders and youth. And the controversy between the military on the one side and the Muslim commercial bourgeoisie on the other adds to the confusion. To find a new ally, the military élite saw themselves forced to allow the nationalists (and many former Communists) to revive Sukarnoism. Unfortunately for the military, Sukarnoism has now gained a large following also among the Muslims.

In the mean time, growing opposition to the ruling military élite, that is, the group around Suharto, within the army (the army has been seriously divided since 1978) has gradually put this group behind the walls of some of a beleaguered bulwark at the top of the army hierarchy. To set up an armed system that should effectively defend the bulwark, since 1982, at the initiative of the present commander of the armed forces, General Murdani, the army has been deploying small killing squads called *penembak misterius* (PETRUS, mysterious gunmen). More than 10,000 people have been murdered by PETRUS without any form of trial, in the streets, public buildings, shops, restaurants, coffee shops, the garden of their own house, and many other places. In April 1983, the regional military commander of Java and Madura admitted that his troops were responsible for 500 PETRUS killings around Jogjakarta in Central Java. The aim of the operations was to put a definite end to criminality. But, in fact, the PETRUS killings were directed at the elimination of people who, according to the military, might become a potential threat to the position of Suharto and his groups. The PETRUS killings are political murders, and many Muslim youths, branded by the army as being a "threat to the government," have become victims of the PETRUS killings.

Since the early 1980s, a small group of Muslim intellectuals, mainly students and young academics, have turned to Muslim fundamentalism, in the sense of a complete return to the Koran and the Islamic tradition as established by the Prophet Muhammed. Huge unemployment and military dominance and repression in almost every sector of the society have convinced these young Muslims that only Islam can bring an adequate solution to the present economic and political crisis.

So far, there is no indication that the new Muslim fundamentalist movement will develop into a mass movement and become strong enough to form a real threat to the military dictatorship. But the ruling military élite is not prepared to take risks. It is determined to eliminate the movement before it can claim a mass following, even only a very limited one. Some small groups of these fundamentalists appear unable to refrain from violence, and they have resorted to activities that include bomb attacks on government-owned buildings (the Sarinah department store in Jakarta, several banks in several cities, the Borobudur stupa in Central Java, and others). These activities prompted General Murdani to take other, more provocative, measures against the fundamentalists besides the dreadful PETRUS killings. On 12 September 1985, Murdani succeeded in provoking a Muslim upheaval in Jakarta's harbour district of Tanjung Priok, regarded by the army as a "bulwark of Muslim fundamentalists." Army and police units killed 63 persons and injured more than 100, all participants in a peaceful demonstration.[24]

After the Tanjung Priok shooting, General Murdani ordered the arrest of several retired armed forces and police generals led by a former "New Order" hawk, General H. R. Dharsono. The retired generals are accused of having made an attempt to push Muslims to overthrow the Suharto government. General Dharsono was put on trial at the Central Jakarta Court. In January 1986, the court sentenced him to a 10-year term of imprisonment for "subversion," that is, for having given support to Islamic fundamentalists. Dharsono appealed the conviction, even though never in the history of the New Order had a "political trial like this resulted in an acquittal."[25] The Court of Appeal reduced the sentence to 7 years of imprisonment.

The attacks against the Suharto regime by the Muslim opposition *outside* the PPP and other formal political avenues are usually financed by both the emerging Muslim commercial bourgeoisie and the traditional (Muslim) landlords, most of the latter being *kiyayis* and *hajis*.[26] The Muslim business world feels its interests severely threatened, and even damaged, by the military managers and many military commanders who hold firm control not only over the country's external trade (exports and imports), domestic investments, and national industry, but also over the local retail trade, such as the purchase of food (especially rice), fertiliser, insecticides and pesticides, and the country's infrastructure. The ever-sharpening conflicts between the Muslim businessmen, most of them genuine national (nationalist) traders and (small and middle-sized) industrialists, and the military managers, most of them compradors of foreign interests (and often seriously damaging national interests), are a manifestation of intraclass struggle in Indonesia.

THE OUTER ISLANDS IN THE "NEW ORDER"

The same facts – growing ineffectiveness of military rule and popular resistance against being ruled at gunpoint – have led to the army's losing its grip also in matters of control over several parts of the outer islands. Also in those parts, both militant Muslim radicals and militant Islamic fundamentalists have increased political and social unrest.

Not only in Java but also in the outer islands resistance is still felt from Communist groups, and the Communist resistance in the outer islands is stronger than the one in Java. The oldest guerrilla movement in the outer islands, the Communist groups in Kalimantan, has placed the army's security units in West and in East Kalimantan in a difficult position. In Kalimantan, there are two armed Communist movements: in West Kalimantan and the border area between Indonesia and Malaysian Kalimantan, Sarawak, we find the Pasukan Gerilya Rakyat Sarawak (PGRS, People's Guerrilla Army of Sarawak), in existence since 1966; and the border area between Sabah (Malaysian North Kalimantan) and Central and East Kalimantan accommodates the Pasukan Rakyat Kalimantan Utara (PARAKU, North Kalimantan People's Army). The nucleus of both guerrilla movements is formed by Indonesian-trained volunteers from the Sukarno government's *konfrontasi* (confrontation) with Malaysia (1963–66).[27] The main reason both PGRS and PARAKU have survived for two decades is that they enjoy the sizable support of the local Dayak communities that oppose Javanese (Jakarta) dominance in West Kalimantan and Malay rule in Sarawak and Sabah. The exploitation of Kalimantan by timber-hungry foreign companies and the deportation of many Dayak people from timber-rich areas to more remote and uninhabitable parts of Kalimantan have only worsened the relationship between the Jakarta government and the Dayak tribes of Kalimantan. Nowadays, the West and North Kalimantan guerrilla movements have become an ethnic, political, and economic problem.

The underground PKI in West Kalimantan gives full support to the PGRS. PKI activists are also working among the local Chinese population. In 1967, the West Kalimantan Chinese were forcibly evacuated from the northern part of West Kalimantan (Sambas-Sanggau area). The PKI now claims a strong following among the Iban Dayaks, and in 1974, the military authorities in Kalimantan admitted that, for the moment, they were unable to defeat the guerrillas. Once there was a rumour that the Indonesian marines, who, during the days of *konfrontasi*, had been the military instructors of the volunteers sent to the border area with Malaysia, were reluctant to fight against the PGRS. The other disadvantages of the army are the impossibility of *perang wilayah* (territorial warfare) in the sparsely populated wilderness of Kalimantan and the guerrillas being supplied with modern weapons left behind by the Americans and their South Vietnamese and Cambodian allies in Indochina.[28] Since the end of the 1970s, it has been difficult to get enough information to assess the political developments in Kalimantan. But from information that is available, it is clear that the guerrillas in Kalimantan still present a problem for the Indonesian military. The army has closed the area to in-depth news coverage.[29]

Some years ago, Communist activities were reported in South Sumatra, Central Sulawesi, and the island of Seran in the Central Moluccas. The movements in Central Sulawesi and Seran apparently also harboured anti-Javanese sentiments. The movement in Seran was led by "RMS supporters"; there is in remote parts of the Moluccas still some support for what is now called the RMS idea. But all these Communist and anti-Javanese activities were too weak to form an immediate threat to the Suharto regime.

Also, the activities *within* Aceh of the separatist National Liberation Front of Aceh Sumatra do not constitute a serious problem for the New Order of the Jakarta generals. The activities of the separatist Acehnese group are much more manifest outside Indonesia, especially in Malaysia, the United States, Iran, and, according to some reports, also in Libya. They receive financial support from Muslim groups in the United States and, according to the same reports, also from the Libyan government and groups in Iran. However, so far there is not sufficient information to give a clear picture of the activities of the separatist Acehnese inside and outside Aceh.[30]

But the separatist movement led by the Organisasi Papua Merdeka (OPM, Organisation for a Free Papua) in Irian Jaya (West Papua) has gradually become a matter of serious concern for the Jakarta generals, because the struggle for a free Papua has drawn unfavourable international attention to the Suharto dictatorship. One could say that the process of decolonisation of West Papua has resulted in a recolonisation by the Indonesian government. The military dictatorship is undoubtedly responsible for this unfortunate development.

The Sukarno government, in its effort to carry out nation-building after the incorporation of West Irian into Indonesian territory in 1963, had given to the new Indonesian province a special position to facilitate that nation-building process. Special regulations were introduced to give the West Papuans the feeling that they had joined the large Indonesian family and were given the same rights to be enjoyed by all Indonesian citizens from Sabang to Merauke. But it turned out differently in practice. The Indonesian military and civilian functionaries, most of them Javanese sent by the central government to West Irian, looked down on the "primitive" Papuan population and treated them as second-class citizens. All moveable goods left behind by the Dutch, such as cars, refrigerators, furniture, and transistors, were shipped to Java, and the population was placed under an arbitrary and corrupt local, more or less Javanese and more military than civilian, government. Soon, several local Papuan resistance groups, of which the OPM became the biggest and most important, were formed, leading to bloody skirmishes between West Papuans and units of the army.

The first armed conflicts were those led by the West Papuan leader Awom in 1965 in Manokwari and the Merauke revolt in October 1965, druing which the army killed approximately 3,000 local Papuans. In October 1966, the army, after hearing a rumour that a revolt had taken place in the village of Bunggiak in the Baliem Valley, killed 19 villagers. A couple of months later, 80 Papuans were killed in the village of Gulunu. The Arfak revolt was organised by the OPM in Manokwari, Ajamaru, and Teminabuan during January–April 1967, and in response, more than 1,000 Papuans were killed in the vicinity of Mano-kwari in bombing raids by the air force, tens of Papuan villages were levelled, and Papuan leader Johan Ariks was tortured to death by the military. General Sarwo Edhie Wiboho (who earlier had led the killings of approximately 500,000 Indonesian Communists in the immediate aftermath of the attempted military coup of 1 October 1965) carried out military operations in 1968 against the Arfak tribal people, killing about 3,500 Arfak and other Papuans. Sarwo Edhie also led operations against the guerrillas led by Awom and the brothers Man-datjan. The Mandatjan brothers surrendered, and two years later were shot in a prison in Jakarta. There were also many atrocities committed by the army dur-ing the so-called Act of Free Choice campaign and in the course of operations against Awom's third revolt.[31] Awom surrendered after the army had promised amnesty, but later the army reneged on its promise and Awom was executed.

Resistance against Indonesian rule continued. The OPM proclaimed an in-dependent Papua state, "West Papua New Guinea," with its own government, the "Provisional Government of West Papua New Guinea." The Indonesian army launched a heavy attack on the new "state" on 8 January 1976. Four bat-talions of élite paratroops and a battalion of marines (KKO), a total of 5,000 men, attacked villages and strongholds of the OPM guerrillas in the area be-tween the capital town of Jayapura and the border with Papua New Guinea (PNG). One week later, on 15 January, the army launched a second attack, even heavier, involving 15,000 troops. Violent clashes occurred between the Indonesians and West Irian guerrillas, especially around the small town of Genjem. Shooting also occurred around Lake Sentani not far from Jayapura, at Skopro, and around the junction of the Arso and Bewani rivers.

Also, the West Papuans have lost a great amount of land to the growing influx of migrants from other parts of Indonesia. As noted in TAPOL's *West Papua*:

The loss suffered by the original inhabitants is used to enhance the living conditions of the new arrivals; there is little or no compensation for the loss of land. Furthermore, such loss puts at peril the ability of the original inhabitants to maintain a social structure in which land occupies fundamental importance. As a result of the mounting opposition by the Papuans to the complete disregard of their human rights, stricter military control has been deemed necessary. In such a situation, the areas of transmigration have acquired significance in the continuing military strategy of complete dominance of the Papuan people.[32]

Foreign companies (Petromer Trend, Conoco, Kennecot, Freeport, Alcoa, to mention a few) are active in West Papua exploiting its natural resources, petro-leum, minerals such as copper, cobalt, gold, molybdenum, nickel, silver, and timber and copra, and the Indonesian authorities have guaranteed a favourable investment climate by providing land rights, a docile labour force (many Papuan workers have been replaced by Indonesians from other parts of the country), and security. TAPOL's *West Papua* comments: "In what way does the oil industry in West Papua benefit the West Papuans? The number of Papuans in the industry has been reduced steadily and by all accounts is now down to almost nothing."[33] It goes on to point out that

dislocation and suppression of the local inhabitants have resulted in the most powerful uprisings by the Papuans and reprisals by the Indonesian military: the continued suppression of Papuan interests in landownership, education, employment and housing have involved the abrogation of agreements in which both the military and the mining companies are implicated; the destruction of the culture of the Papuan people is indeed to *their* mutual benefit; the role of the military ensures that sovereignty over the natural resources remains out of the hands of the Papuans, thus, dispensing with the need to attend to the demands of one million inhabitants and, more significantly, eliminating the possibility of the "development policy" being disturbed in any way by Papuan interests.[34]

THE AGGRESSION AGAINST EAST TIMOR[35]

On 7 December 1975 the Indonesian army, supported by units of the navy and air force, began the brutal invasion in East Timor, a Portuguese colony that was in the process of political decolonisation. Radio FRETILIN in Dili reported "The Indonesian forces are killing indiscriminately. Women and children are being shot in the streets. We are all going to be killed. I repeat, we are all going to be killed. . . . This is an appeal for international help. Please, do something to stop this invasion." The operation, with an estimated 10,000 troops and an unknown number of naval craft, helicopter gunships, artillery, and quantities of napalm and fragmentation antipersonnel bombs, which had proved their effectiveness against civilians in Vietnam, was under the military command of Major-General Benny Murdani, with planning assistance from Lieutenant-General Ali Murtopo. Most of the Indonesian equipment was of American origin, in violation of the specific terms of their sale to Indonesia, which prohibited their use for such a purpose. Murtopo had been in obscurity for more than a year as a result of his part in the riots of January 1974 in Jakarta (riots following the Malawai protests). The situation in East Timor offered him an opportunity for a comeback; moreover, as did others in the military, Murtopo saw the East Timor liberation movement FRETILIN as a social and political threat to the security of the outer islands of the archipelago. At first, Murtopo had seemed to favour a nonmilitary solution, but later, evidently sensing the possibility of reestablishing his former position (as top security functionary and main adviser to Suharto), he came around in support of outright aggression.

On Christmas Day 1975, the army landed a further 15,000 to 20,000 troops in Dili.

Before the invasion, three local political forces were involved in a struggle for state power in East Timor, which then was still a Portuguese colony. The three local forces were Frente Revolucionare do Timor Leste Independente (FRETILIN), seeking a nonaligned nation based on populist and moderate socialist ideas; União Democrática Timorense (UDT), comprising mainly junior officials, small-business men, and town dwellers who favoured retention of links with Portugal; and a tiny group called Associação Popular Democrática Timorense (APODETI), who favoured a union with Indonesia. Most of FRETILIN's governing council were Catholics, and several of them regular church-goers. Some of the students and younger people in the movement were to the left of the main persuasion. In August 1975, after fruitless negotiations, the UDT attempted a coup. FRETILIN was quickly victorious, and it took control over the whole territory of East Timor. APODETI and a few UDT leaders who favoured integration with Indonesia then beseeched the Indonesian authorities to intervene, providing the pretext for the 7 December 1975 invasion.

Expecting an Indonesian invasion, the FRETILIN leadership proclaimed East Timorese independence on 28 November 1975. Hence, the Indonesian invasion in East Timor should be seen as an act of aggression against a sovereign state.

On 17 July 1976, President Suharto signed the Bill of Integration (to incorporate East Timor as "27th province" into Indonesian territory), passed by the Indonesian Parliament into law.

In resolutions passed in the General Assembly and the Security Council of the United Nations in December 1975, the top world organisation deplored the Indonesian invasion and called on all states to respect the right of the East Timorese people to self-determination. Since the fraudulent "integration" in July 1976, the Suharto regime has rejected the United Nations' right to discuss the question of East Timor. However, the United Nations General Assembly continued to pass resolutions each year from 1976 until 1982. The 1976 United Nations resolution rejected the act of "integration." From 1979, the resolutions stressed especially the need for international humanitarian aid in response to the evidence of severe food and medical problems. In 1983, 1984, 1985, and 1986, discussions on East Timor were deferred at the request of the UN Secretary-General, who had been asked by the General Assembly in its 1982 resolution to "initiate consultations with all parties directly concerned with a view to achieving a comprehensive settlement."

Unfortunately, East Timor's position in the United Nations is on the decline. The size of the majority in favour of the General Assembly's resolutions declined from that in 1975, when the vote was 72 for and 10 against, with 43 abstentions, to the 1982 proportion, when the vote was 54 for and 46 against, with 50 abstentions. Those voting consistently in favour of the resolutions have been Portugal and its former colonies, most African countries, and most social-ist countries, including the Soviet Union and the People's Republic of China. The initially small group of nations voting against the resolutions included three of Indonesia's four partners in ASEAN – Thailand, Malaysia, and the Philippines (Singapore abstained) – and Saudi Arabia, Qatar, Iran, India, and Japan.[36] The group of countries voting later with Indonesia against the resolu-tions included the United States, Australia, New Zealand and several Latin American and Middle East nations. The countries of West Europe since 1976 have generally abstained, with only the Republic of Ireland and Portugal voting for the resolutions.

In the mean time, towards the end of 1982 and in the beginning of 1983, the FRETILIN guerrillas, under the leadership of FRETILIN's new military com-mander, Gusmao Xanana, experienced a strong revival, which forced the com-mander of the East Timor units of the Indonesian Army, Colonel Purwanto, to hold talks with the guerrillas. It turned out, however, that the negotiations produced only an Indonesian plan to trap and destroy FRETILIN. The guerril-las responded by returning to conflict: in August 1983, 15 Indonesian soldiers were killed by FRETILIN guerrillas near the village of Viqueque. It is clear at present that the Indonesian Army cannot defeat the guerrillas (despite the army's man-power of 280,000 soldiers), and they form a serious threat to the position of East Timor's comprador government under Mario Carrascalao.

At the moment, Indonesia is trying to get United Nations approval of the 1976 East Timor "incorporation" (into Indonesian territory). The July 1986 decision of the Australian Labour party that the Australian government should recognise East Timor as Indonesia's 27th province was encouraging for the Indonesians. Portugal has vehemently protested against the Australian Labour party's "betrayal of the people of East Timor."[37]

NOTES

1. For the *rechtsgroepen* (Indonesian: *golongan hukum*), see Ernst Utrecht, *Pengantar dalam Hukum Indonesia* (10th edition by Moh. Saleh Djindang) (Jakarta, 1983), chap. 3 in particular.

2. For the *rechtskringen*, see B. ter Haar *Adat Law in Indonesia* (translated and edited by E. Adamson Hoebel and A. Arthur Schiller) (Jarkata, 1962), pp. 1–46 (Introduction by Hoebel and Schiller), pp. 6–10 in particular. The law area is a special block (on the ethnic map). The boundaries are drawn to include culturally homogeneous societies that, although sharing many traits in common with all Indonesian peoples, possess enough distinctive features of social organisation, especially in the field of law, to be set off as different from the societies of all other areas. The law-area concept of the Dutch *adat* law scholars is similar in character to the culture-area concept so familiar to American ethnologists. See, among others, Franz Boas, "Anthropology," in *Encyclopedia of the Social Sciences*, Vol. 2 (1930), p. 150b.

3. Van Vollenhoven's division in *rechtskringen*: 1. Aceh 2. Gayo, Alas, and Batak lands 3. Minangkabau 4. South Sumatra 5. Malay Territory 6. Bangka and Belitung 7. Borneo (Kalimantan) 8. Minahasa 9. Gorontalo 10. Toraja Territory 11. South Celebes (Sulawesi) 12. Ternate Archipelago 13. Ambon Moluccas 14. New Guinea (Irian) 15. Timor Archipelago 16. Bali and Lombok 17. Central and East Java, including Madura 18. Principalities of Yogjakarta and Surakarta 19. West Java. *Rechtskringen* nos. 1–11 and 16–19 are Indonesian, and nos. 12–15 are Melanesian, accordingly a cultural-anthropological division. Van Vollenhoven, *Het adatrecht van Nederlandsch-Indie*, Vol. 1 (Leiden, 1916–18, reprinted 1925).

4. Literature on the population of the Indonesian republic (and the former Netherlands Indies): Raymond Kennedy, *Selected Bibliography of Indonesian Peoples*, Yale Anthropological Studies, Vol. 4 (New Haven, 1945); W. F. Wertheim, *Indonesian Society in Transition: A Study of Social Change* (The Hague, 1959, second edition); C. A. Fisher's standard geography, *Southwest Asia* (London, 1964) (and subsequent editions); Joan Hardjono, *Indonesia, Land and People* (Jakarta, 1971).

5. M. C. Ricklefs, *A History of Modern Indonesia* (London and Basingstoke, 1981).

6. G. J. Resink, *Indonesia's History between the Myths* (The Hague, 1968) (most chapters were earlier published in Dutch); Ernst Utrecht, *Sedjarah hukum internasional di Bali dan Lombok (Pertjobaan sebuah studi hukum internasional regional di Indonesia* [Bandung, 1962]). It was Professor F. M. baron van Asbeck who introduced the concept of "buiten-Europees volkenrecht" in the study of modern law of nations. Van Asbeck clearly pointed out that general international law is mostly the law of Western, particularly European, interstate relations as put into operation since the days of Grotius (16th century). Before the colonial empires were established, the nations outside Europe, in Latin America, Africa, and Asia, had their own system of international law. Gradually, that international law outside Europe was converted into colonial (public) law. See van Asbeck, *Onderzoek naar den juridischen wereldbouw* (Leiden, 1916).

7. Studies on some of the wars within the archipelago: Java – Soekanto, *Sekitar Jogjakarta, 1755–1825 (Perjandjian Gianti – perang Dipanegara)* (Jakarta, 1952); Sagimun, *Pahlawan Dipanegara berduang (Bara api kemerdekaan nan tak kundjung padam)* (Jakarta, 1965); Ricklefs, *Jogjakarta under Sultan Mangkubumi, 1749–1792: A History of the Division of Java* (London, 1974); Bali and Lombok – Utrecht, *Sedjarah hukum internasional di Bali dan Lombok*; South Sulawesi – F. W. Stapel, *Het Banggaais verdrag* (The Hague, 1922); Resink, "The Law of Nations in Early Macassar," in Resink, *Indonesia's History between the Myths* (The Hague, 1968), pp. 39–58; Aceh – Anthony Reid, *The Contest for North Sumatra: Atjeh, the Netherlands and Britain, 1858–1898* (London, 1969); Paul van 't Veer, *Deer Atjeh-oorlog* (Amsterdam, 1969).

8. Literature on Indonesia's struggle for independence before World War II: among others, J. M. Pluvier, *Overzicht van de ontwikkeling der nationalistische beweging in Indonesie in de jaren 1930 tot 1942* (The Hague/Bandung, 1953); B. Dahm *Sukarno and the Struggle for Indonesian Independence* (translated from the German by M. F. Somers Heidhues) (Ithaca, New York, 1969); Sukarno (with introduction by Ruth McVey), *Nationalism, Islam and Marxism* (Ithaca, New York, 1970); B. B. Hering, *From Soekamiskin to Endeh: An Analysis and Documentary Collection Surrounding Soekarno's Early Political Activities* (Townsville, 1979).

9. Java is socially strongly stratified: the vast majority of common people, the *wong cilik*, are ruled by two higher social classes, the Javanese gentry, or *priyayi* (there are *priyayis*, most of them lower-ranking civil servants, appointed by the Dutch colonial

administration), and the Javanese aristocracy, or "court nobility," the *ningrat*, the higher-ranking indigenous authorities under Dutch rule. Titles are: *mas, mas ngabehi, raden,* and *raden panji* (usually Kediri area) for the gentry and *raden mas, pangeran,* and *pangeran hario* for the aristocracy. But there are *wong cilik*, often rich peasants, who assume the title of *raden* and gentry people who introduce themselves as *raden mas*.

10. Among others, see G. McT. Kahin, *Nationalism and Revolution in Indonesia* (Ithaca, New York, 1952); A. Arthur Schiller, *The Formation of Federal Indonesia 1945–1949* (The Hague/Bandung, 1955).

11. Holland was to retain West New Guinea (West Irian, Irian Jaya) for the time being; this was to prove, in due course, to be the last nail in the coffin of Dutch colonialism in Asia and Melanesia. For the Indonesian republic, the Round Table Conference (RTC) Agreements of 1949 only formed an interim political settlement. The Indonesian leaders had considered their participation in the RTC as a means of escape from the destruction of a terrible colonial war, not as an ultimate end in itself. And they were determined that a process of consolidation and of further decolonisation (nationalisation of Dutch property and the liberation of West Irian) should be taken firmly in hand at the earliest opportunity.

12. Ernst Utrecht, *Ambon. Kolonisatie, dekolonisatie en neo-kolonisatie* (Amsterdam, 1972); R. Z. Leirissa, *Maluku dalam perdjuangan nasional Indonesia* (Jakarta, 1975); B. van Kaam, *The South Moluccans*. Background to the train hijackings, London, 1980.

13. PRRI-Permesta: PRRI = Pemerintah "Revolusioner" Republik Indonesia ("Revolutionary" Government of the Republic of Indonesia), and Permesta = Perdjuangan Semesta (Overall [including all sectors of society] Struggle).

The PRRI-Permesta revolt did not originate in ethnic contradictions. It started as a manifestation of discontent with the central government's neglect of the interests of the outer islands and the fear among the religious leaders of a Communist take-over after the success of the Partai Komunis Indonesia (PKI, Communist Party of Indonesia) in the elections of 1955 and 1957. Only in the last phase of the revolt were there some elements of ethnic controversy, such as the outer islands being exploited by the Javanese. Literature: among others, see Rudy Pirngadie, *Peristiwa PRRI ditindjau dari sedjarah TNL* (Jakarta, no date); James Mosman, *Rebels in Paradise: Indonesia's Civil War* (London, 1961). For the role of the CIA, see: David Wise and Thomas B. Rose, *The Invisible Government* (New York, 1964), particularly pp. 136–46, and, for the extent of other American and British involvement, see William Stevenson, *Birds' Nests in Their Beards* (Boston, 1964).

14. In the Darul Islam movement, too, there were elements aiming at the establishment of an Islamic state. For literature on the Darul Islam, see, among others: C. van Dijk, *Rebellion under the Banner of Islam: The Darul Islam in Indonesia* (The Hague, 1981); S. Soebardi, "Kartosuwirjo and the Darul Islam Rebellion in Indonesia," *Journal of Southeast Asian Studies*, vol. 14, no. 1 (March 1983), pp. 109–33.

15. See, among others, Barbara S. Harvey, *Tradition, Islam and Rebellion in South Sulawesi 1905–1965* (Ithaca, New York, 1974); Mattulada, "Kahar Mazakkar: Profil patriot pemberontak," in *Manusia dalam kelmut sejarah*, ed. Taufik Abdullah, Aswab Mahasin, and Daniel Dhakidae (1978).

16. For a treatise on the dichotomy of *santri-abangan*, see C. Geertz, *The Religion of Java* (Glencoe, Illionis, 1960). Geertz incorrectly refers to a third "religious" group, the *priyayi* Javanese; the vast majority of them adopted a *halua* (refined) *abangan* culture.

However, the *priyayi* do not form a separate "religious" group since their *abangan* views do not differ basically from the views of the other *abangans*. As said above, the *priyayi* form a separate social class comparable with the gentry in England. For criticism of Geertz's incorrect *santri-abangan-priyayi* division, see, for instance, Koentjaraningrat's review of Geertz's *Religion of Java* in *Madjalah Ilmu-ilmu Sastra Indonesia*, 1963, no. 1, pp. 188–91; also Sartono Kartodirdjo, *The Peasants' Revolt in Banten in 1888: Its Conditions, Course and Sequel. A Case Study of Social Movements in Indonesia* (The Hague, 1966), p. 50, note. Long before Geertz, the Dutch had already observed the dichotomy of *santri-abangan*. But for the Dutch colonial administration, the dichotomy was irrelevant, because usually *santris* and *abangans* live in peace. It was during the preparations for the 1955 elections especially that Java was rife with vehement conflicts between *santris* and *abangans*. See Ernst Utrecht, *De onderbroken revolutie in het Indonesische dorp* (Amsterdam, 1974).

17. The *Pancasila*, "Five Foundations," or five basic principles of the Indonesian state, formulated by Indonesia's first president, Sukarno, are: *kebangsaan* (nationalism), *prikemanusiaan* (internationalism or humanitarianism), *kerakyatan* (democracy or representation), *keadilan sosial* (social justice), and *ke-Tuhanan yang Maha-Esa* (belief in One God) – in this order; see 1 June 1945 speech by Sukarno, *The Birth of Pantja Sila*, Ministry of Information, Jakarta (reprinted several times). The original formulation of *Pancasila* by Sukarno in 1945 has been manipulated: *ke-Tuhanan* has been made the first and dominant foundation. Sukarno himself accepted the manipulation to satisfy the anti-Communist groups and Muslim fanatics. Literature: Marcel Boneff et al., *Pantjasila, trents années de debats politiques en Indonesie* (Paris, 1980).

18. *Pancasila* became the most powerful instrument for implementing populism. In Sukarno's *The Birth of Pantja Sila* speech, he refers to the populist views of Ernest Renan as expounded in Renan's answer to the question, What is a nation? Also, during the days of "guided democracy," 1959–66, Sukarno implemented populism. For discussion of "guided democracy," see Oey Hong Lee, *Indonesian Government and Press during Guided Democracy* (Zug, Switzerland, 1971). See also Herbert Feith, "Dynamics of Guided Democracy," in *Indonesia*, ed. Ruth McVey (New Haven, 1963), pp. 304–409.

For Sukarno's populism as manifested in his Marhaenism, or "Indonesian socialism," see, among others, J. S. Mintz, *Mohammed, Marx and Marhaen: The roots of Indonesian Socialism* (London, 1965); Donald E. Weatherbee, *Ideology in Indonesia* (New Haven, 1966).

19. For the debates on the "Great Majapahit" and the notion of 350 years of Dutch colonial rule over the entire archipelago, see Resink, *Indonesia's History between the Myths*, and Utrecht, *Sedjarah hukum internasional di Bali dan Lombok*.

20. There is a huge amount of literature on the attempted military coup of 1 October 1965. Most recent are W. F. Wertheim, "Whose Plot? New Light on the 1965 Events," *Journal of Contemporary Asia*, vol. 9, no. 2 (June 1979); Coen Holtzappel, "The 30th September Movement: A Political Movement of the Armed Forces or an Intelligence Operation?" same issue of *Journal of Contemporary Asia*; Olle Tornquist, *Dilemmas of Third World Communism: The Destruction of the PKI in Indonesia* (London, 1984); Ernst Utrecht, "Sukarno's Populism Contributed Considerably to the Destruction of the Communist Party of Indonesia (PKI)," *Kabar Seberang* (Townsville, James Cook University), no. 16 (December 1985), pp. 93–99.

21. Robert C. Bone, *The Dynamics of the Western New Guinea (Irian Barat) Problem* (Ithaca, New York, 1958); J. M. van der Kroef, *The West New Guinea Dispute* (New York, 1958); C. Smit, *Deliquidatie van een imperium* (Amsterdam, 1962); Ernst Utrecht, *Papoeas in opstand* (Rotterdam, 1978).

22. Sukarno created the GOLKAR as an organisation of groups who fulfil certain functions in Indonesian society – peasants, workers, women, youth, teachers, religious leaders, national entrepreneurs, veterans (of the guerrilla war against the Dutch), the generation of 1945, members of Angkatan Bersenjata Republik Indonesia (ABRI, Armed Forces of the Republic of Indonesia), and the Kepolisian Negara Republik Indonesia (POLRI, State Police of the Republic of Indonesia), intellectuals – without having the opportunity of finding, by virtue of their functions, expression in the state administration. Originally, the functional groups consisted of popole who had no links with the political parties. But soon the political parties set up their so-called *organisasi massa* (ORMAS, mass organisations), groups of peasants, workers, women, and others who gradually were accepted by Sukarno as representatives of the functional groups and who had become members of, or built ties with, the political parties. And during the years of "guided democracy," 1959–66, the political parties, whose activities were much contained by both the government and the army, still could exert some political influence on the state administration through these ORMAS, *their* functional groups.

23. Nahdatul Ulama (NU) = orthodox Muslims, scholars and teachers, and most landlords, but also part of some from the emerging group of businessmen.
Partai Muslimin Indonesia (Parmusi) = Muslim modernists.
Partai Sarekat Islam Indonesia (PSII) = Muslim modernists.
Persatuan Tarekat Islam (Perti) = Muslim political organisation with main support in West Sumatra and West Java.
Partai Nasional Indonesia (PNI) = main national party.
Ikatan Pembela Kemerdekaan Indonesia (IPKI) = small nationalist party formed and supported by several army officers (among others, generals Nasution and Azis Saleh).
Partai Murba = Indonesian Trotskyist (Fourth International) movement.
Partai Katolik = Indonesian Catholics.
Partai Keristen Indonesia (Parkindo) = Indonesian Protestants.

24. Max Lane, "The Tanjong Priok Incident," *Inside Indonesia*, no. 4 (March 1985).

25. *Far Eastern Economic Review*, 23 January 1986. See also Yayasan lembaga Bantuan Hukum, *Eksepsi seorang prajurit. Let Jen (Purn) H. R. Dharsono didepan Pengadilan Jakarta Pusat, Tanggal: 29 Augustus 1985* (Jakarta, 1985).

26. *Kiyayi:* Muslim scholar or teacher (*ulama* in some regions of the Indonesian archipelago); *haji:* Muslim who has made the pilgrimage to the holy city of Mecca. *Hajis* enjoy great prestige in their villages, but not seldom they misuse that prestige to amass personal wealth.

27. The Sukarno government attempted to block the formation of the new British client-state of Malaysia (Malaya, Sarawak, Sabah, and Singapore), also referred to as a "British neocolonial project." Singapore did not directly involve the armed forces in *konfrontasi*, but sent volunteers to the border with Sarawak and Sabah.

28. In territorial warfare, the *entire population* of the territory concerned is mobilised and involved in military operations.

29. For the roots of the guerrilla movement in Kalimantan, see "Het verzet op Kaliman-tan," *Indonesia, Feiten en Meningen*, vol. 2, no. 5 (October 1975).

30. See the recent contribution by Geoffrey G. Gunn, "Radical Islam in Southeast Asia: Rhetoric and Reality in the Middle Eastern Connection," *Journal of Contemporary Asia*, vol. 16, no. 1 (March 1986) pp. 30–54.

31. During the negotiations on the transfer of sovereignty over West Irian to Indonesia in New York, agreement was reached on the inclusion in the New York Agreement of 1962 of a provision that the Papuans would be given a final choice between indepen-dence under Indonesia or not by the end of 1969; this provision is what the Act of Free Choice is referring to. In June 1969, the Papuans voted at gunpoint for West Irian's continuing incorporation into the territory of the Republic of Indonesia.

32. TAPOL [Tahanan Politik (Political Prisoner), British organisation concerned with the abuses of human rights in Indonesia and East Timor and the release of political prisoners], *West Papua: The Obliteration of a People* (London, 1983), pp. 52–53.

    Other literature: among others, see Nonie Sharp, *The Rule of the Sword: The Story of West Irian* (Malmsbury, Australia, 1977); Ernst Utrecht, *Papoeas in opstand*; R. J. May, ed., *The Indonesia-Papua New Guinea Border: Irianese Nationalism and Small State Diplomacy* (Canberra, 1979); Ralph R. Premdas, "The Organisasi Papua Merdeka (OPM): Continuity and Change in Papua New Guinea Relations with Indonesia," *Kabar Seberang*, no. 15 (July 1985), pp. 59–82 (also in *The Journal of Pacific Studies*, vol. 11 [1985], pp. 63–90).

33. p. 35.

34. p. 37.

35. Most recent literature: James Dunn, *East Timor: A People Betrayed* (Milton, Queens-land, 1983); Carmel Budiardjo and Liem Soei Liong, *The War Against East Timor* (London, 1984); Torben Retboll, ed., *East Timor: The Struggle Continues* (Copenhagen, 1984); William Sutherland, "Self-Determination and the Political Economy of Inter-national Law: Denial of a Right in East Timor," *The Journal of Pacific Studies*, vol. 11, pp. 45–62; Amnesty International, *East Timor: Violations of Human Rights* (London, 1985); Alexander George, *East Timor and the Shaming of the West* (London, 1985).

36. At that time, Brunei had not yet joined ASEAN. It was still a British protectorate.

37. *Townsville Bulletin*, 5 July 1986; *The Telegraph* (Sydney), 11 July 1986; *The Sydney Morning Herald*, 12, 19, and 24 July 1986; *The Australian Financial Review* (Sydney), 21 July 1986.

Contributors

Jeremy Beckett, Department of Anthropology, University of Sydney, Sydney, NSW 2006, Australia

Hans Dagmar, Department of Research Methodology and Statistics, University of Nijmegen, Postbus 9108, 6500 HK Nijmegen, The Netherlands

Susana B. C. Devalle, C. E. A. A., El Colegio de México, Camino al Ajusco No. 20, C.P. 01000, México, D.F., Mexico

Michael C. Howard, Centre for International Studies, Simon Fraser University, Burnaby, B.C., Canada V5A 1S6

Noel J. Kent, Ethnic Studies Program, University of Hawaii at Manoa, East-West Road 4, Room 4-D, Honolulu, HI 96822, USA

Jacqueline Leckie, Department of Anthropology, University of Otago, Box 56, Dunedin, New Zealand

Davianna Pomaika McGregor, Ethnic Studies Program, University of Hawaii at Manoa, East-West Road 4, Room 4-D, Honolulu, HI 96822, USA

Glenn Petersen, Department of Sociology and Anthropology, Baruch College, City University of New York, 17 Lexington Avenue, New York, NY 10010, USA

Ralph R. Premdas, Department of Government, University of the West Indies, St. Augustine, Trinidad

Paul Shankman, Department of Anthropology, University of Colorado, Campus Box 233, Boulder, CO 80309, USA

Robert Tonkinson, Department of Anthropology, University of Western Australia, Nedlands, WA 6009, Australia

Ernst Utrecht*, Transnational Corporations Research Project, University of Sydney, Sydney, NSW 2006, Australia

---

* Ernst Utrecht passed away in 1987.

Rangiuni J. Walker, Department of Anthropology, University of Auckland, Private Bag, Auckland, New Zealand

Donna Winslow, Département d'Anthropologie, Université de Montréal, C.P. 6128, Succ. A., Montréal, PQ, Canada H3C 4J7

DATE DUE

MAR 1 4 1995			
MAR 1 3 1995			
JUN 0 2 1997			
JUN 1 3 1997			
APR 1 0 2000			
APR 1 0 2000			
SEP 0 9 2000			
SEP 0 9 2000			
DEC 0 3 2000			
NOV 1 3 2000			

DEMCO 38-297